EU SANCTIONS: LAW AND POLICY ISSUES CONCERNING RESTRICTIVE MEASURES

Series Supranational Criminal Law: Capita Selecta, Volume 15

Published in the series:

1. *Supranational Criminal Law: a System Sui Generis*, Roelof Haveman, Olga Kavran and Julian Nichols (eds.)
2. *Double Jeopardy Without Parameters: Re-characterization in International Criminal Law*, Olaoluwa Olusanya
3. *Harmonization of Criminal Law in Europe*, Erling Johannes Husabø and Asbjørn Strandbakken (eds.)
4. *Sentencing and Sanctioning in Supranational Criminal Law*, Roelof Haveman and Olaoluwa Olusanya (eds.)
5. *Application of International Humanitarian and Human Rights Law to the Armed Conflicts of the Sudan: Complementary or Mutually Exclusive Regimes?*, Mohamed Abdelsalam Babiker
6. *Supranational Criminology: Towards a Criminology of International Crimes*, Alette Smeulers and Roelof Haveman (eds.)
7. *Individual Criminal Liability for the International Crime of Aggression*, Gerhard Kemp
8. *Collective Violence and International Criminal Justice - An Interdisciplinary Approach*, Alette Smeulers (ed.)
9. *International Criminal Law from a Swedish Perspective*, Iain Cameron, Malin Thunberg Schunke, Karin Påle Bartes, Christoffer Wong and Petter Asp
10. *The Implementation of the European Arrest Warrant in the European Union: Law, Policy and Practice*, Massimo Fichera
11. *The Principle of Mutual Recognition in Cooperation in Criminal Matters*, Annika Suominen
12. *The European Public Prosecutor's Office*, Martijn Willem Zwiers
13. *Victimological Approaches to International Crimes: Africa*, Rianne Letschert, Roelof Haveman, Anne-Marie de Brouwer, Antony Pemberton (eds.)
14. *The United States and International Criminal Tribunals*, Harry M. Rhea
15. *EU Sanctions: Law and Policy Issues Concerning Restrictive Measures*, Iain Cameron (ed.)

EU SANCTIONS: LAW AND POLICY ISSUES CONCERNING RESTRICTIVE MEASURES

Edited by

Iain CAMERON

intersentia
Cambridge – Antwerp – Portland

Intersentia Publishing Ltd.
Trinity House | Cambridge Business Park | Cowley Road
Cambridge | CB4 0WZ | United Kingdom
Tel.: +44 1223 393 753 | Email: mail@intersentia.co.uk

Distribution for the UK:
NBN International
Airport Business Centre, 10 Thornbury Road
Plymouth, PL6 7PP
United Kingdom
Tel.: +44 1752 202 301 | Fax: +44 1752 202 331
Email: orders@nbninternational.com

Distribution for the USA and Canada:
International Specialized Book Services
920 NE 58th Ave. Suite 300
Portland, OR 97213
USA
Tel.: +1 800 944 6190 (toll free)
Email: info@isbs.com

Distribution for Austria:
Neuer Wissenschaftlicher Verlag
Argentinierstraße 42/6
1040 Wien
Austria
Tel.: +43 1 535 61 03 24
Email: office@nwv.at

Distribution for other countries:
Intersentia Publishing nv
Groenstraat 31
2640 Mortsel
Belgium
Tel.: +32 3 680 15 50
Email: mail@intersentia.be

EU Sanctions: Law and Policy Issues Concerning Restrictive Measures
Iain Cameron (ed.)

Cover illustration: Francisco de Goya (1746-1828), Etching, Plate 44 from 'Los desastres de la guerra'

ISBN 978-1-78068-141-2
D/2013/7849/29
NUR 828

British Library Cataloguing in Publication Data. A catalogue record for this book is available from the British Library.

PREFACE

The present book grew out of a conference I organized in September 2011 at the Faculty of Law of Uppsala University. In addition to the authors, I would like to thank all the participants in this conference for helpful comments, particularly Martin Björklund, Therese Hydén, Nils Jareborg, Agneta Hilding-Quarnström, Per Saland, Magnus Ulväng, Jørn Vestergaard and Andreas von Hirsch. I am grateful to the Faculty of Law for funding the conference.

The Emil Heijnes Foundation generously provided the necessary publication funding. Lastly, I should say that the authors submitted their chapters at different times during the late spring of 2012. In general, they have tried to state the law and practice as it is on 30 June 2012. In a number of cases they have been able to take account of subsequent changes.

Iain Cameron

CONTENTS

ABOUT THE AUTHORS

Torbjörn Andersson

Torbjörn Andersson is Dean of the Law Faculty at Uppsala University. He is Professor of civil and criminal procedural law and formerly Jean Monnet professor of EC law. His research areas are primarily Procedural Law, EU Law and Competition Law, in particular issues relating to the parallel and conflicting enforcement of law.

Petter Asp

Petter Asp is professor of criminal law at Stockholm university, Sweden, and holder of Ragnar and Torsten Söderberg Chair of Legal Science. His research has focused on international aspects of criminal law (EU criminal law, criminal jurisdiction, cooperation in criminal matters etc.) as well as on national criminal law (especially the general part of the criminal law and sentencing). He is a member of the European Criminal Policy Initiative which in late 2009 published a Manifesto on European Criminal Policy and is currently the head of a legislative committee with the task of reforming (parts of) the Swedish legislation on money laundering.

Maria Bergström

Maria Bergström is Associate Professor in European Law at Uppsala University. She was previously research fellow at Stockholm University. She defended her thesis at the European University Institute (EUI) in Florence in 2003. Her particular research interests are concerned with competence issues, changing boundaries and the interactive development of national and EU law, particularly within the fields of constitutional, administrative, penal and procedural law. She is currently conducting research on public-private cooperation and the EU functional notion of the state, the related accountability dilemma and anti-money laundering regulation. Her recent publications include "EU Anti-Money Laundering Regulation: Multilevel Cooperation of Public and Private Actors", in Eckes, C., and Konstadinides, T. (eds.) *Crime within the Area of Freedom, Security and Justice: A European Public Order*, CUP, 2011 and Bergström, M., Svedberg Helgesson, K, Mörth, U., "A New Role for For-profit Actors? The Case of Anti-Money Laundering and Risk Management", 49 Journal of Common Market Studies 1043–1064 (2011).

Thomas Bull

Thomas Bull is a judge in the Supreme Administrative Court. Prior to this he was Professor of constitutional law at Uppsala University. Amongst his publications are *Regeringsformen – en kommentar* (with Fredrik Sterzel) [the Instrument of Government – a commentary] 2010 and Mötes- och demonstrationsfriheten. *En statsrättslig studie av mötes- och demonstrationsfrihetens innehåll och gränser i Sverige, Tyskland och USA: Freedom of Assembly*, a public law study of the content and limits in the freedoms of assembly and demonstration in Sweden, Germany and the USA] 1997.

Iain Cameron

Iain Cameron is Professor in Public International Law at the University of Uppsala. His research interests lie in human rights, international criminal law and civil liberties. He holds an LLD and an LLM in International Law. He has published extensively in the fields of international law and constitutional law, particularly on international criminal law and human rights issues. He has investigated the issue of legal safeguards and targeted sanctions for the Swedish government (2002), the Council of Europe (2006) and the European Parliament (2008). Since 2006 he has been a member of the European Commission on Democracy through Law (Venice Commission).

Christina Eckes

Christina Eckes is associate professor in EU law at the University of Amsterdam and senior researcher at the Amsterdam Centre for European Law and Governance (ACELG). In 2012/2013, she is Emile Noël Fellow-in-Residence at New York University. Her current research project Outside-In: Tracing the Imprint of the European Union's External Actions on Its Constitutional Landscape is funded by the Netherlands Organisation for Scientific Research (NWO). She has widely published on EU external relations and EU counter-terrorist sanctions, including a monograph entitled EU Counter-Terrorist Policies and Fundamental Rights – The Case of Individual Sanctions (Oxford University Press, 2009).

Thomas Elholm

Thomas Elholm is Professor of Criminal Law, University of Southern Denmark, Department of Law. He holds an LLM and a PhD in law from the University of Copenhagen. Since 2011 he is Chief Editor of the Scandinavian Journal of Criminal Law and Criminology.

Mikael Eriksson

Dr. Mikael Eriksson is a researcher at the Swedish Defence Research Agency. Before joining the agency he obtained his PhD at the European University Institute, Florence, Italy. He has also been involved in different research project at the Department of Peace and Conflict Research, Uppsala University to which he is an affiliated researcher. Eriksson's main research interests include critical security studies, targeted sanctions, and problems of liberal peace. He is particularly interested in the security dynamics of the Middle East and Africa. A book based on his doctoral dissertation, *Targeting Peace: Understanding UN and EU targeted sanctions* was published by Ashgate in 2011.

Suus Hopman

Suus Hopman is currently working as a LLD candidate at Uppsala University. Until recently she was a member of both the Dutch and Swedish bar associations. She worked as an attorney at Böhler Advocaten in Amsterdam; in that capacity she participated in EU-level and national criminal law procedures concerning blacklisting.

Sofia Marques da Silva

Sofia Marques da Silva is a doctoral researcher at King's College London. She graduated from the University of Durham LL.B and holds LL.M Degrees from Universidade Católica Portuguesa de Lisboa and King's College London. She has worked as a research assistant and is now a research fellow at the Centre of European Law at King's College London. Sofia's research interests are EU Security and Defence, Counter-Terrorism and EU Constitutional and Criminal law.

Cian Murphy

Dr Cian Murphy is Lecturer in Law at King's College London. Dr Murphy's first monograph, EU Counter-Terrorism Law: Pre-emption & the Rule of Law was published in 2012 by Hart Publishing. He is also the co-editor of the forthcoming EU Security & Justice Law: After Lisbon & Stockholm (2013 Hart Publishing). Dr Murphy's current research examines the effect of transnationalisation in counter-terrorism on constitutional principles across the world. In Spring 2013 he will be a Fulbright-Schumann Research Scholar at the Center on National Security & the Law at Georgetown University, Washington DC.

Kimmo Nuotio

Kimmo Nuotio is Professor of Criminal Law at the University of Helsinki and dean of the Faculty of Law. He is also the vice-director of the Centre of Excellence in Foundations of European Law and Polity funded by the Academy of Finland (2008–2013) and the director of the national doctoral programme in law "Law in a Changing World" coordinated by the University of Helsinki. He has broad research interests including the Theoretical Foundations of Penal Liability, Modernization of Criminal Law, Nordic, European, and International Criminal Law, Transnational law, the Risk Society / Welfare State, Political Philosophy and Law, Legal Integration in Europe and Researcher Skills and

Research Ethics. His latest publications include "European criminal law under the developing constitutional setting of the European Union", in *Europe's constitutional mosaic*, N. Walker, J. Shaw, S. Tierney (eds), Hart 2011, and "Theories of Criminalisation and the Limits of Criminal Law: a Legal Cultural Approach" in *Boundaries of Criminal Law*, R.A. Duff, Lindsey Farmer, S.E. Marshall, V. Tadros, M. Renzo (eds) OUP 2010.

Malin Thunberg Schunke

Malin Thunberg Schunke is an Associate Professor in Criminal Law at the University of Uppsala. She holds an LLD in Criminal Law (Uppsala University) and an LLM in Criminology and Criminal Justice (King`s College, London). Her research interests lie in national and international criminal law particularly EU judicial cooperation in criminal matters and human rights. She has been an Apprentice Judge at Stockholm City Court and has been working several years as an Assistant Prosecutor at the Prosecuting Office Stockholm. Her more recent publications include, "En kodifiering av tillräckliga rättssäkerhetsgarantier för misstänkta och tilltalade – Krav för ett fortsatt samarbete i brottmål inom EU?" in *Festskrift till Suzanne Wennberg*, Norstedts 2009, and *International Criminal Law from a Swedish Perspective*, Intersentia 2011 (joint author).

Michel Uiterwaal

Michel Uiterwaal is Advisor on Extractives, Human Rights and Conflict at IKV Pax Christi, Utrecht, The Netherlands. Until recently, he was an attorney at Böhler Advocaten in Amsterdam; in that capacity he has participated in several national and EU-level procedures concerning blacklisting.

ABBREVIATIONS

AC	Appeal Cases (United Kingdom)
AML	Anti-Money Laundering
BCBS	Basel Committee on Banking Supervision
CDD	Customer Due Diligence
CFI	Court of First Instance
CFSP	Common Foreign and Security Policy
CFT	Combating Financing of Terrorism
CJEU	Court of Justice of the European Union
COPRI	Conflict and Peace Research Institute
CUP	Cambridge University Press
EAW	European Arrest Warrant
EC	European Community
ECHR	European Convention for the Protection of Human Rights
ECJ	European Court of Justice
ECR	European Court Reports
ECtHR	European Court of Human Rights
ed.	Editor
EU	European Union
FATF	Financial Action Task Force on Money Laundering
FIUs	Financial Intelligence Units
ICC	International Criminal Court
ICJ	International Court of Justice
ICLQ	International and Comparative Law Quarterly
IS	International Studies
ML	Money Laundering
MLR	Modern Law Review
NGO	Non-Governmental Organisation
NJIL	Nordic Journal of International Law
No.	Number
OFAC	Office of Foreign Assets Control
OJ	Official Journal of the European Union
OUP	Oxford University Press
p.	Page
para.	Paragraph
PEPs	Politically Exposed Persons

PMOI	People's Mujahedeen of Iran
TEU	Treaty on European Union
TFEU	Treaty on the Functioning of the European Union
TFTP	Terrorism Finance Tracking Programme
UK	United Kingdom
UN	United Nations
UNSC	UN Security Council
UNTS	United Nations Treaty Series
v.	Versus
Vol.	Volume

TABLE OF CASES

EU COURTS

COURT OF FIRST INSTANCE/TRIBUNAL

Case T-315/01 Kadi v Council and Commission [2005] ECR II-3649.
Case T-228/02 People's Mojahedin Organization of Iran v Council (OMPI/PMOI I) [2006] ECR II-4665.
Case T-47/03 Jose Maria Sison v Council and Commission [2007] ECR II-73.
Case T-256/07 People's Mojahedin Organization of Iran v Council (OMPI/PMOI II) [2008] ECR II-3019.
Case T-284/08 People's Mojahedin Organization of Iran v Council (OMPI/PMOI III) [2008] ECR II-3487.
Case T-341/07 Jose Maria Sison v Council [2009] ECR II-3625.
Case T-318/01, Omar Mohammed Othman v Council of the European Union and Commission [2009] ECR II-00000.
Joined Cases T-37/07 and T-323/07 Mohamed El Morabit v Council [2009] ECR II-131.
Case T-49/07 Sofiane Fahas v Council [2010] ECR II-5555.
Case T-348/07 Al Aqsa v. Council [2010] ECR II-4575.
Case T-85/09, Yassin Abdullah Kadi v European Commission [2010] ECR II-5177.
Case T-181/08 Pye Phyo Tay Za v Council, [2010] ECR II-1965.
Case T-362/08 IFAW Internationaler Tierschutz-Fonds v Commission [2011] ECR II-11.
Case T-341/07, Sison v Council of the European Union, 23 November 2011, nyr.
T-562/10 HTTS Hanseatic Trade Trust & Shipping GmbH v Council of the European Union, 11 December 2011 nyr.
Joined Cases T-439/10 and T-440/10, Fulmen and Fereydoun Mahmoudian v Council, 21 March 2012 nyr.
T-509/10, Manufacturing Support & Procurement Kala Naft Co., Tehran Teheran (Iran) v Council and Commission, 25 April 2012, nyr.

ECJ/CJEU

Case C 68/88, Commission v Greece [1989] ECR 2965.
Case C-377/02 Van Parys [2005] ECR I-1465.
Cases C-189/02 P, C-202/02 P, C-205/02 P to C-208/02 P and C-213/02 P, Dansk Rørindustri and others v Commission [2005] ECR I-5425.
Case C-176/03 Commission v Council, [2005] ECR I-7879.
Case C-266/05 P Sison v Council [2007] ECR I-1233.

Case C-229/05 P PKK and KNK v Council [2007] ECR I-439.
Case C-355/04 P Segi and Others v Council [2007] ECR I-1657.
Case C-117/06, Gerda Möllendorf and Christiane Möllendorf-Niehuus [2007] ECR I-8361.
Case C-64/05 P Sweden v Commission [2007] ECR I-11389.
Joined Cases C-354/04 P and C-355/04 P Gestoras Pro Amnistía and others and Segi and others v Council [2007] ECR I-1579.
Joined Cases C-402/05 P and 415/05 P Kadi & Al Barakaat International Foundation v Council and Commission [2008] ECR I-6351.
Joined Cases C-120/06 P and C-121/06 P Fabbrica italiana accumulatori motocarri Montecchio SpA (FIAMM), and Fabbrica italiana accumulatori motocarri Montecchio Technologies LLC v Council and Commission [2008] ECR I-6513.
Case C-550/09 Generalbundesanwalt beim Bundesgerichtshof v E and F [2010] ECR I-6213.
Case C-340/08, M and others v HM Treasury [2010] ECR I-03913.
Joined Cases C-57/09 and C-101/09 Bundesrepublik Deutschland v B and D [2010] ECR I-10979.
Case C-548/9P Bank Melli Iran v Council, 16 November 2011, Grand Chamber, nyr.
Case C-27/09 French Republic v People's Mojahedin Organization of Iran (PMOI), Council and Commission, 21 December 2011, Grand Chamber, nyr.
Case C-360/10 SABAM v Netlog, 16 February 2012 (nyr).
Case C-380/09 Melli Bank plc v Council, French Republic, UK and Commission, 13 March 2012, Grand Chamber nyr.
Case C-376/10 Pye Phyo Tay Za v Council, 13 March 2012, Grand Chamber, nyr.
Case C-130/10 European Parliament v Council, 19 July 2012, Grand Chamber, nyr.
Joined Cases C 539/10 P and C 550/10 P, Stichting Al-Aqsa v Council, 15 November 2012, nyr.

ECtHR

Zana v Turkey, No. 69/1996/688/880, 25 November 1997.
Comingersoll S.A. v Portugal, No. 35382/97, 6 April 2000.
Segi and Others and Gestoras Pro-Amnistia and Others v 15 States of the EU, Nos 6422/02 and 9916/02, 23 May 2002.
Sürmeli v Germany, No. 75529/01, 31 October 2005.
Segerstedt-Wiberg and Others v Sweden, No. 62332/00, 6 June 2006.
Burden and Burden v UK, No. 13378/05, 12 December 2006.
Leroy v France No. 36109/03, 2 October 2008.
A and Others v UK, No. 3455/05, 19 February 2009.
Gül and Others v Turkey, No. 4870/02, 8 June 2010.
Sanoma Uitgevers v Netherlands, No. 38224/03, 14 September 2010.
Kiliç and Eren v Turkey, No. 43807/07, 29 November 2011.
Vejdeland and Others v Sweden, No. 1813/07, 9 February 2012.
Nada v Switzerland, No. 10593/08, 12 September 2012.

UN HUMAN RIGHTS COMMITTEE

Nabil Sayadi and Patricia Vinck v Belgium (Communication No. 1472/2006), final views, 22 October 2008.

NATIONAL COURTS

DENMARK

U 2007.1831 H
Copenhagen City Court, judgment of 27 March 2007, unpublished.
High Court, judgment of 6 February 2008, unpublished.
U 2009.1453 H
Copenhagen City Court, judgment of 15 March 2010, unpublished.

THE NETHERLANDS

Rechtbank 's-Gravenhage 13-5-2003, KG 03/514, LJN AF8506.
Rechtbank 's-Gravenhage 3-6-2003, KG 03/514, LJN AF9389.
Rechtbank Amsterdam 31-3-2005, HA RK 04-948, JOR 2005/118.
Gerechtshof Amsterdam 5-1-2006, 987/05, JOR 2006/200.
Gerechtshof 's-Gravenhage 8-11-2010, 200.076.673/01, LJN BO3682.
Rechtbank Amsterdam 21-7-2011, AWB 11/3132 BESLU, LJN BR2619.
Rechtbank 's-Gravenhage 21-10-2011, 09/748802-09, LJN BU9716.
Rechtbank 's-Gravenhage 21-10-2011, 09/748801-09, LJN BU7200.
Hoge Raad 28-10-2011, nr. 10/05147, LJN BQ9880.
Rechtbank Amsterdam 15-11-2011, AWB 11/5163 WET, unpublished.

SWEDEN

Hovrätten över Skåne och Blekinge (Court of Appeal), case no. B 685-09, decided 9 November 2009, unpublished.
Stockholm District Court, judgment 2011-04-13 in case no. T 9176-08 unpublished.

UK

Secretary of State for the Home Department v Rehman [2001] UKHL 47.
Kurdistan Workers' Party & Ors, R (on the application of) v Secretary of State for the Home Department [2002] EWHC 644 (Admin).

A (FC) and others (FC) (Appellants) v Secretary of State for the Home Department (Respondent), [2004] UKHL 56.
Lord Alton of Liverpool & Others v Secretary of State for the Home Department Appeal PC/02/2007 Open Determination 30 November 2007.
Secretary of State for the Home Department v Lord Alton of Liverpool & Others [2008] EWCA Civ 443.
Her Majesty's Treasury v Mohammed Jabar Ahmed & Others [2010] UKSC 1.
Al Rawi v the Security Service [2011] UKSC 34.
Tariq v Home Office [2011] UKSC 3.
Lord Carlile of Berriew CBE QC and Others and Maryam Rajavi v Secretary of State for the Home Department [2012] EWHC 617 (Admin).

USA

Whitney v California, 274 U.S. 357 (1927).
Dennis v U.S., 341 U.S. 494 (1951).
Brandenburg v Ohio 395 U.S. 444 (1969).
Bethel School District No. 403 v Fraser, 478 U.S. 675 (1986).
Texas v Johnson, 491 U.S. 397, 412 (1991).
City of Ladue v Gilleo, 512 U.S. 43, 59 (1994).
Holder v Humanitarian Law Project, 561 U. S. ____ (2010).

INTRODUCTION

Iain Cameron

1. OVERVIEW

The term "EU sanctions" covers a variety of quite different phenomena. The EU legislature has for a long time adopted legislation backed by administrative sanctions. More recently, it has obtained a competence to prescribe criminal penalties.[1] EU organs, such as the Commission, impose sanctions in individual cases, such as in the area of competition law. Under Article 7 of the Treaty on the European Union (TEU), the Member States of the EU can take disciplinary measures against an EU member state for violation of the human rights/democracy conditions of membership set out in Article 6 TEU.

This book consists of essays looking at what in common parlance are called "EU sanctions" but which are referred to in the Treaty on the Functioning of the EU (TFEU) as "restrictive measures". This chapter provides an introduction to this subject as well as to the other essays in the present volume. Study of the legal aspects of EU restrictive measures involves looking at different branches of law, procedural law, constitutional law/human rights and criminal law. It also involves overlapping, and at times colliding, legal orders: the EU legal order, the legal order of the European Convention on Human Rights (ECHR), binding on all EU member states, national legal orders and public international law. To obtain a picture of the subject as a whole, it is necessary to bring together experts having these different perspectives.

The EU implements United Nations Security Council (UNSC) sanctions as well as having its own, "autonomous", sanctions, which are the main focus of this book. The EU's use of autonomous sanctions has developed gradually, as its role as a world economic power has expanded.[2] However, these two types of sanctions are intimately linked in a variety of different ways. In particular, the development of EU sanctions goals and methods has followed the practice of the UNSC. Thus, in providing an introduction to the subject it is useful to begin by sketching out what is a sanction under international law, to describe the UNSC's

---

1 Case C-176/03, *Commission of the European Communities v Council of the European Union* [2005] ECR I-7879. See now Articles 82 and 83 TEU.

2 Kreutz 2005.

shift to "targeted sanctions" and say something about the purposes of sanctions. The scope, limits and the safeguards surrounding EU sanctions, are being constantly refined, something which adds to the complexity of the subject. I therefore give a brief overview of the pre- and post-Lisbon treaty legal bases for EU sanctions, saying something about the still developing case law on sanctions. I also take up a number of problems which are so far unanswered in the case law, inter alia the interplay between EU sanctions and national law. I close with a brief description of the internal procedures for adoption of sanctions, and the problem of coherence in EU foreign policy. In the course of these discussions, I will also introduce each of the essays in the present volume.

2. SANCTIONS UNDER INTERNATIONAL LAW

There is no authoritative definition in international law of *sanction*. One commonly used definition in international relations is the "deliberate, government-inspired withdrawal or threat of withdrawal of customary trade or financial relations".[3]

Where a state, a group of states, or an international organization (other than the UN) impose such punitive trade or financial measures on a third state, then under international law these either fall to be judged under the legal regime appropriate to counter-measures or are to be seen as acts of retorsion.[4] A counter-measure occurs when an entity governed by international law commits a wrongful act *vis-à-vis* another entity and the victim breaches its own obligations *vis-à-vis* the former in order to put pressure on the perpetrator to resume law-abiding behaviour. In addition to a prior unlawful act, a counter-measure must fulfil certain criteria (in particular, proportionality) to be lawful.[5] Sanctions are imposed because the target is doing something the sanctioning state, or organization, does not like – which may or may not be in breach of international law. A sanction will thus often be an act of retorsion, i.e. a coercive act not in breach of international law. However, due to the vagueness of some international law rules, and the absence of binding third party settlement of disputes, doubts can arise in practice as to whether an act should be categorized as a counter-measure or an act of retorsion. The suspension of a unilateral undertaking extending a benefit (e.g. aid) will usually be an act of retorsion. The suspension of a reciprocal undertaking will usually be a counter-measure – unless a treaty provides for suspension in such circumstances.

---

3 Hufbauer et al. 2007, p. 3. This definition excludes punitive diplomatic and political measures on the one hand – which, however, both the EU and the UNSC use – and military measures on the other. See, however, Section 4 below. It also excludes private consumer-led measures of boycott and other such actions.

4 Crawford 2002.

5 See Articles 50–52 International Law Commission Articles on State Responsibility (A/Res/56/83). Having said this, the extent to which this particular article reflects existing customary international law is a matter of controversy.

3. SANCTIONS UNDER THE UN CHARTER AND THE DEVELOPMENT OF TARGETED SANCTIONS

The first use of sanctions coordinated through an international organization predates the UN. The League of Nations imposed sanctions to punish Japanese and Italian expansionism during the 1930s.[6] The experience of these – totally ineffective – sanctions influenced the formulation of the sanctions power in the UN Charter (UNC) The basis for imposing Security Council sanctions is a determination under Article 39 that something constitutes a "threat against international peace and security".[7] All UN members have undertaken to carry out Security Council resolutions, and these have priority over other obligations in international law (Articles 25 and 103 UNC).[8] Thus UNSC sanctions are a special case under international law. The General Agreement on Trade and Tariffs (GATT), 1994, Article XXI(c) provides for an express exception for UN sanctions.

The end of the Cold War meant that the Security Council was no longer paralyzed by strategic factors, and it embraced sanctions with such enthusiasm that the 1990s have been called the "sanctions decade."[9] General trade sanctions were imposed against Iraq, following the defeat of Iraq in the second Gulf War of 1990 and in an effort to remove the regime of Saddam Hussein. The embargo included technology and goods necessary for public health and welfare infrastructure (damaged during the war), hospitals, medical products, etc. Estimates vary about the extent of the loss of life caused, or exacerbated, by this embargo but it was clearly a humanitarian disaster.[10]

This was the main reason for the UNSC's shift to "targeted sanctions", i.e. sanctions aimed at putting pressure on individuals and entities while minimizing unintended economic and social consequences for vulnerable populations and innocent bystanders.[11] Directing sanctions toward individuals is also in line with other developments in individual responsibility in international law, in particular the creation of the International Criminal Court. A targeted sanction usually works by identifying targets, which are then placed on a "blacklist." The Security Council establishes a sanctions committee for each set of sanctions it orders. Names for the blacklist can come from a variety of sources, including the UN secretariat. However, while different aspects of the implementation and evaluation of sanctions may be delegated to the UN Secretary General, the actual blacklisting, and the "penalties" applicable, is kept

---

6 For a historical account, see Doxey 1996.

7 See e.g. Wood 2011, de Wet 2004.

8 Article 103 is not as such *lex superior*, but is rather a "conflicts" rule. See the discussion in Simma 2011.

9 Cortright and Lopez, 2002.

10 Weiss, et al. 1997.

11 Cortright and Lopez 2002, p. 2.

firmly within the control of the Security Council. Thus, the main sources for names for UN blacklists are usually the members of the UNSC themselves.

In developing its targeted sanctions, a process which is still ongoing, the UNSC was influenced by the practice of the United States (US). The US, building upon its extensive experience of Cold War trade sanctions, began moving in the early 1980s towards targeted sanctions. The US maintains its own extensive unilateral sanctions lists, as well as being (usually) the main mover behind UNSC sanctions.[12]

The UNSC has developed its targeted sanctions in primarily three areas: freezing of targets' financial assets, travel bans and bans on the sale of military equipment and services. However, the UNSC has also used sanctions against an industry, such as the arms or internal security industry, an activity (e.g., research in the production of nuclear power), or a commodity (e.g., trade in high-value goods such as diamonds, oil, or timber).

The boundary line between a targeted sanction and a more traditional trade embargo is not hard and fast. In particular, a "targeted" sanction directed against a state's central bank affects all the bank's customers and makes trade with the state nearly impossible.

The value of targeted sanctions has been repeatedly endorsed at the UN level. However, the effective imposition of targeted sanctions involves having efficient administrative systems at the national level, police, customs and immigrations officials, as well as finance inspectorates monitoring banks, and so on. This can be problematic for many underdeveloped states. Moreover, it is usually essential to have the cooperation of neighbouring states to the target – often the states with the most interest in maintaining trade and friendly relations with the target. Thus, there are considerable capacity and competence problems at the national level connected to implementing targeted sanctions, and implementation by states in good faith cannot be taken for granted – meaning that supervision at the UN level is necessary. UN sanction committees thus tend to be supported by a monitoring team of experts, but the UNSC has limited possibilities in practice for penalizing non-cooperative states, short of adding them to a "secondary" sanctions list.

The growth and innovation of sanctions is an important part of the problems the subject has experienced. Three "processes" – in Interlaken, Bonn-Berlin and

---

12 It also has a number of different security-oriented "watch-lists", e.g. requiring heightened security concerning, or even denial of, air transport. These watch lists have resulted in problems for a large number of people who have either been wrongly placed on the list, or have names similar to people who are on the list. While all security and police agencies have, and must have, names of suspects in their files, the emergence of semi-public lists gives rise to a large number of human rights and other legal problems. These overlap to some extent with the problems caused by sanctions lists, but I will not go further into this issue in the present book.

Stockholm – have so far been initiated in which diplomats and experts have discussed targeted sanctions issues, focusing largely on efficiency.[13]

Targeted sanctions were originally directed against government representatives. However, the rise of non-state actors in international relations has led to targeted sanctions being used against rebels in international conflicts and then against suspected terrorists and their financers. This trend began in the United States, but the UNSC, and the EU, quickly followed suit. However, in doing so, a number of serious practical problems arose. It is one thing to direct a sanction against government ministers. It is another to direct a sanction towards a person or entity suspected of belonging to, or supporting, a terrorist group. Certain senior members of the group may be well known, but the rank and file, still less those associating with it, will not be known. And where it is a terrorist network, the "nodes" may be operating in almost complete isolation from one another. There might not even be a "core". One needs to use different types of intelligence, and this runs into problems of fair trial and effective remedies. Such problems are multiplied when one tries to provide for supranational remedies for supranational listing processes. The particular legal problems caused by anti-terrorist sanctions are the focus of several of the chapters in the present book.[14]

4. PURPOSES OF SANCTIONS AND EVALUATING THEIR EFFECTS

Generally speaking, the overriding purpose of a sanction is to pressurize the target to comply with the sanctioner's demands. Much of the international relations and economic theory doctrine on sanctions focuses on issues of efficiency: in other words, have sanctions accomplished, or contributed towards, the sanctioner achieving its goals? The first use of sanctions coordinated through the UN was in the 1960s, against the white settler regime in Rhodesia (now Zimbabwe). Galtung criticized the assumption that the economic disruption caused by these trade sanctions would translate into political pressure that will either overthrow the leadership of the targeted state or cause it to change its policies. He argued that there is no *necessary* link between the effectiveness in the infliction of economic pain and compelling the target to make policy

---

13 Biersteker et al. 2001, Brzoska 2001, Wallensteen 2003.

14 One problem which has arisen is that branding one party to a conflict as "terrorist" and imposing sanctions against it creates a difficulty for mediating in conflicts and so assisting towards bringing the conflict to an end. See Griffiths and Barnes 2008. The present book focuses on legal problems and so will not take up this issue in detail. See, however, the discussions of the "spillover" effect of sanctions on freedom of expression and association in Thomas Bull's chapter and the impact the UK sanctions have had on diplomacy in Sofia Marques da Silva and Cian Murphy's chapter.

changes.[15] However, an analysis in 1985 by a group of economists led by Hufbauer of a dataset of 116 cases of trade sanctions was much more positive, finding that sanctions were had in 34 per cent of cases contributed to the success of the overall policies.[16] As Mikael Eriksson explains in more detail in his chapter in the present volume, subsequent doctrinal analyses have broadly followed in two different tracks. The first track has critically analysed and attempted to justify, elaborate on, and improve the methodology of the Hufbauer study.[17] The second track questions the statistical evidence and scoring/ weighting system in the Hufbauer, and subsequent studies.[18]

Some very general conditions for "success" can be identified. One of these is the presence of an internal opposition that can be, and is, strengthened by sanctions. (The opposite, however, can also be the case: Galtung wrote already in 1967 of a counter-productive "rally round the flag" effect.) So too are the facts that the target is already going through economic difficulties, that the sanction causes significant losses for the target, and that the sanction can be imposed quickly by a small number of like-minded states. It also seems clear that threatened sanctions can be more effective than imposed sanctions, and that where the target has an expectation of continuing conflict in the future, i.e. the relationship between the target and the sanctioner is, and will continue to be, unfriendly, then it makes less sense to give way to the pressure exerted by the sanctioner now.[19] Tactically speaking, two quite different methods can be discerned: a sudden "sharp shock" and a "ratcheting" method, in which pressure is gradually increased if the target does not comply.

Beyond these, I would join the critics who consider that there are so many variables involved that it is not possible to devise a reliable "scientific" prescriptive or predictive model.

It is important to emphasize that the purpose(s) the sanctioner has, also determine whether or not the sanctions are a "success". At least eight different purposes can be identified. These are:

1) Deterrence. Sanctions are threatened in order to deter conduct, usually a norm violation;
2) Compliance. The sanctioning party's intention is that the receiver ought to change some aspect of its foreign or domestic policy;
3) Punishment. When it is too late or too difficult to bring about change, the goal is punishment;

15 Galtung 1967.
16 Hafbauer et al. 1985. The dataset was later expanded to 200 cases, Hafbauer et al. 2007.
17 A valuable comparative analysis of EU sanctions, even if one can question the weighting system used, can be found in Portela 2010.
18 See e.g., Pape 1997, Pape 1998.
19 Drezner 1999 referred to this as the "sanctions paradox".

4) Destabilization of a regime or disruption of the activities of a non-state entity;
5) Limitation/stabilization of armed conflict;
6) Solidarity: showing support to the activities of friendly states;
7) Symbolism. Here the sanctions provide the domestic audience of the sender, international constituencies (such as NGOs) and the receiver itself with evidence of disapproval but without inflicting serious material damage;
8) Signalling. A version of (7) but where the intent is to signal strong resolve to actually inflict material damage.[20]

Much can be said about all of these, but I will content myself with noting a small number of points here. First, empirically, sanctions cannot always be easily separated from military force, as they can be part of a policy of containment or combined military/economic response or used as a prelude to military intervention to convince domestic and/or international public opinion that "everything has been tried." Second, when the purpose is "solidarity" or "symbolism" then the very adoption of the sanction means that it is a "success".

Third, trade sanctions are often controversial within a state, representing as they do a balancing between business and other political interests, sometimes with different domestic constituencies. Trade sanctions which hurt the target in the sense of depriving it of things which it really wants or needs, obviously hurt the sanctioner too, in that the sanctioner no longer receives the income from selling the goods and services in question (and, worse, that some competitor receives this income). Sanctions can moreover generate significant costs for implementation. In particular the co-existence of extensive, and only partially overlapping, unilateral and multilateral lists of targets for financial sanctions create major administrative costs for banks and other financial institutions. These are costs that are transferred to consumers.

Obviously, disagreements on strategy and tactics of sanctions are multiplied when different states, with, e.g. different levels of trade and investment in a potential target, have to agree on them. Even relatively like-minded states such as EU member states can have very different views of the effectiveness of sanctions generally in obtaining objectives, and the desirability of particular sanctions directed at a particular target at a particular point of time.

Fourthly and finally, the development of targeted sanctions in the late 1990s and early 2000s means that our understanding of "effectiveness" in sanctions must change. How should we go about measuring the impact(s) of targeted sanctions? The classical macro model of a rational state actor pursuing a cost-benefit calculation must be modified, or added to, with a new micro model of sanction effects on a plurality of interests, both inside and outside the targeted

20 See e.g. Strandow 2005.

entity. This is the subject of the chapter by Mikael Eriksson in the present volume.

5. DEVELOPMENT AND LEGAL BASES OF EU SANCTIONS PRIOR TO THE LISBON TREATY

While the 1990s might have been the "sanctions decade", there were several examples of sanctions being used earlier, e.g. the unilateral US trade sanctions introduced against the USSR following the declaration of martial law in Poland. The issue thus arose several times in the 1980s whether there was a European Community (EC) legal basis for adoption of sanctions. In Centro-Com,[21] the Court of Justice (ECJ) finally ruled that since trade in goods generally falls under exclusive Community competence (then Article 133 EC Treaty), restrictive trade measures must in general be taken by the Community. National measures are only permitted under limited conditions, set out in different regulations.[22] National measures must respect the Common Commercial Policy (CCP). Embargoes, licensing requirements and other non-commercial measures were all considered to be measures having "equivalent effect" to export quotas, and therefore prohibited by Article 1 of Regulation (EEC) No 2603/69[23] unless exempted.

When the Treaty on European Union (TEU) was adopted in 1992, a legal basis for the adoption of sanctions had been set out in TEU Articles 11 and 15. Article 11(1) TEU set out the objectives of the Common Foreign and Security Policy (CFSP), inter alia to promote democracy and human rights and "to preserve peace and strengthen international security, in accordance with the principles of the UNC …" Under Article 15 member states were to adopt Common Positions to define the approach of the Union to a matter of geographical or thematic nature. Common Positions were to be adopted unanimously. The role of the European Parliament was limited under the CFSP to being kept "regularly informed" and to holding an annual debate (Article 21 TEU). The legal basis was for the member states acting together in the *EU*; as mentioned, the issue whether the *EC* had competence over trade sanctions was decided in Centro-Com. However, a link was provided between the EU legal basis and the EC by means of Article 301 EC Treaty which enabled the Council when "it is provided, in a Common Position … for an action by the Community to interrupt or reduce … economic relations with one or more third countries"

21 Case C-124/95 *Centro-Com* [1997] ECR I-80.

22 These are set out, as concerns exports in Regulation 1061/09 OJ L [2009] 291 p. 1, for imports, in Regulation 260/2009 OJ L [2009] 84 p.1 (for WTO Members) and Regulation 519/94 OJ L [1994] 67 p. 89 (for a number of non-WTO Members).

23 OJ [1969] L 324, p. 25.

to "take the necessary urgent measures". This was used for trade measures. Under Article 60 of the EC Treaty, "in cases envisaged in Article 301... the Council [could] in accordance with the procedure provided for in Article 301, take the necessary urgent measures on the movement of capital and on payments as regards the third countries concerned". This was used for financial measures. Measures under Articles 60 and 301 were to be decided by the Council by a qualified majority on proposals from the Commission. There was no requirement to consult Parliament before adopting the regulation.

As sanctions were constantly being developed, and so changing, it was nonetheless not certain that these EC Treaty provisions were sufficient. In such cases, it was possible to fall back on the "general clause" of Article 308, which provided that the Council "shall take appropriate measures to attain one of the objectives of the Community, in situations where such an attainment should prove necessary in the course of the operation of the common market and where the Treaty has not provided the necessary powers." In employing Article 308, the Council was to act unanimously on a proposal from the Commission and after consulting the European Parliament.

While the Centro-Com case definitely established community competence over trade and financial sanctions, some other matters still fell, wholly or partially, within national competence. One of the most frequent type of sanction used by the EU was (and is) an arms embargo, Article 296 of the EC Treaty provided for this to be implemented by Member States using national measures. Having said that, the scope of the prohibited goods and services was itself laid down in the Common Military List of the EU.[24] Thus, arms embargoes were imposed by a Common Position and enforced on the basis of export control legislation of Member States. Prohibitions on providing related financial or technical assistance to arms sales tended to be implemented through an EC Regulation.

As mentioned, another frequent targeted sanction is restrictions on admission (visa or travel bans). Where these are provided for in Common Positions, they are enforced on the basis of Member States' legislation on admission of non-nationals.

The fast development of sanctions by the UNSC during the 1990s caused a number of problems for the EC/EU legal framework. The sanctions against Yugoslavia resulted in a case before the ECJ, regarding a Yugoslav-registered civil aircraft which had been leased to a Turkish company, Bosphorus Airlines. Ireland, acting in accordance with the sanctions, seized the aircraft. The ECJ indicated that it could scrutinize EU implementation of UN sanctions but found that, under the circumstances, the seizure was not disproportionate and so did

24 OJ C 65/1 19.3.2009. http://eur-lex.europa.eu/LexUriServ/LexUriServ.do?uri=OJ:C:2009:065:0001:0034:EN:PDF xx.

not violate the right to property.[25] Later, this was the subject of an application before the ECtHR. The ECtHR found that the Irish implementation of EC law did not violate the ECHR. However, it stressed that European states that are members of the EC are still bound by the ECHR when they legislate or act collectively. The importance of international cooperation means that small divergences from what the ECHR normally demands can be acceptable, but the EC legal system must provide a level of protection of human rights and sufficient remedies against alleged violations of rights that are broadly equivalent to those of the ECHR.[26] Thus, the ECtHR warned the EU member states, and the ECJ, that, in an extreme situation, it would intervene to uphold human rights.

As mentioned, the UNSC soon began using sanctions against rebel groups – such as UNITA in Angola. This could, as a matter of EC law, be seen as an interrupting "economic relations with one or more third countries" as the object of the sanction was, in theory, the territory controlled by the rebel group. The original UN resolution 1267 directed against the Taliban (then generally recognized, however unwillingly, as the government of Afghanistan) encompassed even people associated with the Taliban such as Osama Bin Laden.[27] However, Article 301 EC as a legal basis became much more dubious when the UN following the 11 September attacks adopted resolution 1390 adding Al-Qaeda, a network terrorist group not connected to territory, to the Taliban sanctions. From an EU perspective, it was even more awkward that people regarded as being "associated with Al-Qaeda" could easily be, and were, nationals of EU states.

UN resolutions 1267 and 1390 were implemented by means of a common position and an EC regulation. It was initially delegated to the Commission to respond to additions to the UN lists by adding additional names to the EU lists.

Following the September 11 attacks, the UNSC also adopted, with a minimum of debate, resolution 1373 providing that states were under an obligation to introduce legislation against people suspected of financing terrorism.[28] The position was taken in the Council that common action was

---

25 Case 84/95, *Bosphorus Hava Yollari ve Ticcaret AS v. Minister for Transport, Energy and Communications, Ireland and the Attorney General, European Court of Justice* [1996] ECR 3953.

26 *Bosphorus Hava Yollari Turizm ve Ticaret AS v. Ireland*, No. 45036/98, 13 September 2001.

27 The UN legal basis for sanctions against Osama Bin Laden was Resolution 1267, which predated the September 11 attacks. Al-Qaeda as such became the object of sanctions through resolution 1390 (2001).

28 The operative parts of this resolution require states to "Criminalize the wilful provision or collection, by any means, directly or indirectly, of funds by their nationals or in their territories with the intention that the funds should be used, or in the knowledge that they are to be used, in order to carry out terrorist acts... Freeze without delay funds and other financial assets or economic resources of persons who commit, or attempt to commit, terrorist acts or participate in or facilitate the commission of terrorist acts [and] Prohibit their nationals or any persons and entities within their territories from making any funds, financial assets or economic resources or financial or other related services available, directly or indirectly, for the benefit of [terrorists or terrorist financers]".

needed at EU level, and this resolution was therefore made the subject of two common positions, setting out respectively, a procedure for listing targets at EU level, and the actual list, together with a directly applicable EC regulation.

Thus, as far as terrorism is concerned, although the basis in the EU, and EC, treaties was the same, different regulations in EC law applied, depending upon whether the person or entity in question was taken up or not in the UN sanctions lists against Al-Qaeda. As there was no criminal law competence (at the time) under the EC Treaty, breach of either EU sanctions, or EU implemented UN sanctions, was made punishable under national criminal and/or administrative law.

The UN sanctions against terrorist financing, as is well known, originally created a Kafkaesque situation for listed people and entities: no reasons were given for listing, no information could be obtained from the Security Council and there was no procedure for getting off the list. Faced with intransigence from the EU legislator, safeguards instead had to be developed, on a case by case basis, by the Court of First Instance, and, on appeal, by the ECJ. This case law follows the above differentiated legal basis, with parallel challenges being made to EU's implementation of UN sanctions, in particular in the Kadi case, and its autonomous terrorist sanctions, in particular in the *PMOI* cases. There is a detailed analysis of these leading cases in Torbjörn Andersson's chapter in the present volume. I give my own, personal, picture of the *Kadi* case in the next section. The safeguards developed in the *Kadi* and *PMOI*, and subsequent, anti-terrorist cases have later been applied to sanctions directed against members of governments and related targets (hereinafter "regime sanctions").

Although the present section deals with the pre-Lisbon treaty legal basis for sanctions, mention should also be made of the three policy documents on sanctions adopted by the Council in 2003 and 2004. These were produced by the policy unit of the Council Secretariat, together with the Commission and consist of basic principles, sanctions guidelines and best practices. The basic principles are meant as a simple guide to the reasons that the EU might have for resorting to sanctions.[29] There are considerable differences in views among the EU member states on the potential and actual value of sanctions generally and on their advisability and feasibility in a particular case and the basic principles – set out in ten short paragraphs – are an attempt to reach a degree of common ground on the matter.[30]

The more extensive (37 pages) sanctions guidelines set out technical provisions for formulating and implementing sanctions and standard wording for legal provisions. These are primarily directed at EU institutions and Member States.[31]

---

29 Available at the useful site of the European Commission, Sanctions or restrictive measures http://eeas.europa.eu/cfsp/sanctions/docs/index_en.pdf#10.1.

30 Kreuz 2005 points out that while the document was supposedly future oriented, it has a definite air to it of explaining past behaviour.

31 EU Council, Guidelines on implementation and evaluation of restrictive measures (sanctions) in the framework of the EU CFSP Document 15579/03, last updated by doc. 15114/05.

The EU best practices for effective implementation was originally a document on financial sanctions targeting terrorist groups but now covers both the listing process and application of financial sanctions. It is directed at national authorities responsible for implementing financial sanctions as well as financial institutions. The latest update of this paper was 2008.[32]

6. PERSONAL REFLECTIONS ON THE *KADI/AL-BARAKAAT* CASE AND SUBSEQUENT DEVELOPMENTS

Several states in the EU were clearly unhappy about the Kafkaesque situation created by Resolutions 1267/1390. However, other EU states were indifferent or even hostile to making improvements in the system, beyond – at best – some form of humanitarian exemption, unfreezing assets for basic needs. Some EU states, such as Sweden, Denmark and Germany, attempted to secure changes at the UN level and sponsored initiatives in the General Assembly and the Security Council. The European Commission also considered the situation to be unsatisfactory. However, amending a UNSC resolution obviously requires consensus, and the five permanent members can block changes by use of the veto. With the government of George W. Bush in charge of the US, there was little prospect of any significant reforms at the UN level.

I can take this opportunity to say something about how I got involved in the sanctions question. Amongst the people put on the UN 1267/1390 lists in late 2001 were three Swedish citizens of Somalian origin. The three were involved in the "al-Barakaat" system of informal money transfer – the only way to get money to the "failed state" of Somalia. Sweden has granted asylum to a relatively large number of Somalis, and so the Swedish branch of al-Barakaat had a steady stream of transactions, even if the sums of money going through were small. Al-Barakaat was channelling some of this money through a bank in the middle east which the US Office of Assets Control (OFAC) believed was linked to al-Qaeda. The US proposed the listing of several branches of al-Barakaat, including the Swedish branch, as well as the individuals formally responsible for the branches in question. In the wave of pro-American feeling following the great loss of life in the 11 September attacks, the UNSC rubber-stamped the US proposal, asking for little or no details why the US thought this to be necessary.

The case became a *cause célèbre* in Sweden. The Swedish government requested information from the UNSC as to why the three were blacklisted. No or little information was given: the UNSC referred to the US, and OFAC was not

32 EU Council, Best Practices for the effective implementation of restrictive measures, Council Doc. 8666/1/08 REV 1, 24 April 2008; http://register.consilium.europa.eu/pdf/en/08/st08/st08666-re01.en08.pdf.

interested in replying. At the time, and coincidentally, Sweden had invested considerable time, money and prestige in the latest in the series of expert-diplomatic conferences designed to improve the efficiency of targeted sanctions, the "Stockholm process". I was brought in, in December 2001, to lead the discussions on introducing proper legal safeguards. When I made the initial report in early January 2001 on why the then situation was unacceptable, and made various tentative proposals as to what could be done about it, the US reaction was swift. The US government threatened to "reconsider its commitment to the Stockholm process" if this issue was even discussed. The UK government (and the Russian government) made a similar threat. Faced with this ultimatum, the Swedish government agreed not to put discussions of legal safeguards on the agenda of the Stockholm process, however, as it did not want to drop the issue totally, I was given the task of investigating it.[33] Inter alia the Swedish Foreign Ministry sponsored a conference in early 2002 with diplomats and experts from several European states, including the UK, to discuss options. My report was published in October 2002.[34] The fifty page report explains the legal problems involves in the colliding legal systems and sketches out a number of possible solutions.

I accepted that the extension of sanctions to suspected terrorists meant that states proposing people or entities for inclusion on the lists could have legitimate security concerns. In other words, there was an understandable reluctance to share with an international body the intelligence information which was the basis for determinations that someone, or some entity, was involved in terrorist financing. I also accepted that (at the time) there was little prospect of getting the permanent members of the UNSC to agree to create a standing body with a "veto power" over UNSC decisions, or even some sort of advisory group, part of, or attached to, the UN secretariat. I therefore tried to propose a practical solution at the UN level, namely an arbitral body, which could balance these legitimate concerns with due process requirements. However, I also proposed, as an option, dropping entirely the system of UNSC blacklisting in anti-terrorist matters. As states either had ratified, or were in the process of ratifying, the UN Convention on the Financing of Terrorism, financing was now, or soon would be, a criminal offence in every state. Thus, the "administrative" system of freezing could be replaced with a more criminal-law oriented system, where freezing is a prelude to a criminal prosecution. This could be, if desired, combined with some sort of mutual recognition of freezing decisions between the US and the EU states (and other interested, democratic states), combined with effective remedies on the national level (where due process and intelligence concerns could be more easily reconciled).

33 Although it should be said that – in a spirit of civil disobedience – the report from the Stockholm process (Wallensteen 2003) contains a reference to my report to the Swedish Foreign Ministry, the only footnote in the report.

34 Cameron 2002.

I questioned whether freezing measures against terrorists had any real (as opposed to symbolic) value. I noted that the methods used for antiterrorist sanctions have been adapted from money laundering and that the logic of using targeted sanctions against terrorist groups that are not in control of territory is not clear.[35] There is little or no reputational effect, and antiterrorist sanctions are not realistically aimed at behavioural modification (which is the supposed purpose of sanctions against regimes). While some terrorism is partially financed by "dirty" money, much of it is not. Some terrorism is very cheap. Nor is the motivation for terrorism the making of money. Thus, the adoption of the money-laundering technique for antiterrorist sanctions is flawed.

I think it fair to say, that nothing much happened in response to my, and others', very critical voices.

In November 2003, the European Commission and the governments of Germany and Sweden sponsored a conference in New York to which all Security Council members were invited. I and Professor Eckhart Klein held the keynote addresses. The main thing which became apparent to me from this conference was that we were not, as they say in the gangster films, talking to "the man". A junior official from OFAC was present, but he thought the whole problem was European. I told him that the US (in fact, OFAC) had created the problem, and (with a degree of bravado) that the day would come when we Europeans dumped the problem back on them. He was not in the least frightened.

Most of the members of the UNSC considered that the problem was that states did not listen enough to the UNSC. I told them that if the UNSC continued to require democratic rights-respecting states to go against their most basic values of due process, it would paint the courts in these states into a corner. I was informed that, according to Articles 25 and 103 UNC, the dictates of the UNSC were to be obeyed and that was an end to the matter. National, and regional, courts had no competence to place themselves above the UNSC. I told them that courts were there to protect individual rights. The US Supreme Court does not accept that Security Council resolutions agreed to in New York by governments can divest US citizens of their constitutional rights.[36] Why should the European Court of Justice not decide in the same way? The audience was unimpressed. It was clear they did not want lawyers coming in and telling them what they could and could not do. When they told me the question was political, not legal, I told them that that is what absolute rulers used to say when they ordered a person's lands (and life) to be forfeit. But these days – at least in democratic states – were over and we had something called "legal rights" now.[37]

---

35 See also Maria Bergströms chapter in the present volume.

36 *Reid v. Covert*, 354 US 1, 77 (1957), *Diggs v. Schultz*, 470 F. 2d 461, 466–67, (DC Cir. 1976).

37 I would add that not all the points made by (non Swedish, Swiss and German) government representatives were rubbish. One sensible – and humbling – point was made by a South African diplomat. The South African delegation was known for its scepticism against sanctions in general – not surprising bearing in mind the US sanctions against the "terrorist"

In 2006, the Council of Europe asked me to report on the issue from the perspective of the ECHR. At the same time, Professor Bardo Fassbender was asked by the UN to examine the perspective of UN law. (By this time, the lawyers for the three Swedish citizens, heavily supported by the Swedish government, had managed to convince OFAC to take them off the list. Kadi and the Swedish organization al-Baraakat remained on it.)

My report was heavily critical of the existing system. Only minor and/or cosmetic improvements had been made since 2001. My report was presented at a meeting of legal advisers of Council of Europe states (CAHDI) in Strasbourg. A number of the legal advisers present, including those from Sweden, Greece and Germany, spoke strongly in favour of at least most of its conclusions. The UK legal advisers – joined by the Russian legal advisers, funny the company you keep when you are a permanent member – repeated the mantra that the UNSC was there to be obeyed.

The UNSC anti-terrorist sanctions were then, and are now, hardly the most serious step taken in the war against terror. At its height, this "war" gave rise to torture and rendition, as well as tens of thousands of deaths caused directly by the invasions of Afghanistan and Iraq. And today, the remaining flaws in the UNSC system pale into insignificance compared to the "blacklist" now being applied by the US, namely the drone targeting list.[38] Still, the UNSC lists were an injustice which struck at the heart of an international lawyer's commitment to international law. One can argue that a requirement for being an international lawyer is a large degree of optimism (or naivety): the cup is usually half-full, not half-empty. Reform is possible with good will on all sides, the rules are important, reason will prevail eventually. But by this time, my scepticism as to the advisability of seeking changes at the UN had become conviction. I had come to the conclusion that the reform process would get nowhere until someone set hard against hard. If European governments were not prepared to disobey the UNSC, then it was up to the traditional defenders of individual rights from Executive power to do something about it. I told the Swedish Foreign Ministry that, if they wanted real improvements to the UN sanctions system, their only chance was that the Council (i.e. including the Swedish government) lost the *Kadi/al-Baraakat* case in the ECJ.

ANC leaders during the 1970s and 1980s. They asked whether the issue was not a minor issue compared to the HIV/AIDs epidemic ravaging the under-developed world at the time, especially the African continent. My answer, after a while, was yes. The injustice of the UN anti-terrorist sanctions regimes fades into insignificance faced with the mass deaths of this epidemic. But while it was a small injustice, it was of considerable symbolic importance. Moreover, unlike HIV/AIDs, it was an injustice created by the Security Council, and which could be, albeit with some effort, fixed by the Security Council.

38 Thanks to Martin Björklund for this point.

However, the long-awaited judgment of the CFI in the case[39] found that there was no competence for the CFI to review UNSC sanctions, except where these violated *jus cogens* norms. Not surprisingly, I considered this to be a great disappointment. At a stroke it would remove any possibility of there ever being any improvement at the UN level. It was difficult to respect a court which steadfastly promised to intervene if the Security Council ordered states to commit genocide, slavery or mass torture, but considered that it could do nothing if it ordered states to confiscate individual's assets, or refuse them entry or exit permission, without a trial or indeed any sort of remedy. I called the judgment a judicial abdication.[40]

Fortunately, there were more people than I who were aghast at the CFI judgment. An appeal was lodged with the ECJ. Advocate General Maduro produced a well-reasoned opinion expressing the view that the present system violated the general principles of EC law. One of his solutions was particularly appealing to me, namely that the whole issue be "handed back" to the member states, but that they must still act within the framework of EU, including its protection of fundamental rights, and that they were therefore bound to provide genuinely effective remedies.

The ECJ ruled in the *Kadi* case[41] that the wording of Article 301 in the EC treaty could extend even to the Al-Qaeda sanctions – so there was an EC legal basis. However, it followed Advocate General Maduro in finding that the system violated the general principles of EC law. Maduro's solution was, unfortunately, too bold for the majority of judges on the ECJ – understandable in the sense that the ECJ has (so far at least) not been in the business putting obstacles in the way of increased EU competence. But the ECJ judgment at last set a "constitutional" limit to UN sanctions. It stated that when any executive decision is taken which infringes EC rights, reasons must be given "to provide the person concerned with sufficient information to make it possible to ascertain whether the decision is well founded or whether it is vitiated by a defect which may permit its legality to be contested."[42] It ruled that an appeal must lie to an independent and effective remedy. In sum, the Council regulation breached Kadi's rights of defence, the rights of effective judicial review and the right to property.

According to constitutional law, and by analogy EU constitutional law, the binding force international law receives in the national legal order s by virtue of the constitution. Thus, while states should try to respect international law, if international law goes against the constitution and the conflict cannot be reconciled, the constitution must be preferred. The UNSC sanctions against

39 Case T-315/01 *Kadi v Council and Commission* [2005] ECR II-3649 (Kadi I).

40 Cameron 2005. See also my criticism in Cameron 2006.

41 Joined Cases C-402/05 P and 415/05 P *Kadi & Al Barakaat International Foundation v Council and Commission* [2008] ECR I-6351.

42 Referring to Cases C-189/02 P, C-202/02 P, C-205/02 P to C-208/02 P and C-213/02 P, *Dansk Rørindustri and others v. Commission* [2005] ECR I-5425, para. 462.

Al-Qaeda as they were at present formulated were binding on EU member states by virtue of their obligations under the UNC, but could not be applied in EC law.

In my view, this was the only sensible approach to the issue. When faced with a bare command to do something which was contrary to the most basis EU values, the only response left to the ECJ was to say "shant!" This response was no longer really possible for the courts in the member states. By incorporating UNSC resolutions without further thought in EC regulations with direct effect, the Council had taken away the constitutional "gate" which exists to prevent "inappropriate" international law from coming in to a national legal order. Worse, as regulations have supremacy over national law, the Council gave UNSC a *supra-constitutional* status. These could not be challenged in the national courts of any EU member state, without endangering the fundamental principle of the supremacy of, then, EC, now EU, law over national law. A very few academic lawyers saw this judgment as a retrograde step, largely on the basis that it was hostile to international law, or that it might make it more difficult for the EU to play its proper role on the international stage, or that it was Eurocentric, forcing European standards on the rest of the world. However, in my opinion such views confuse the legitimacy of international law with the legitimacy of EU law. Although complaints are often made about the democratic deficit in the EU, the legislator(s) there are subject to at least a degree of accountability and the preparation of EU legislation is relatively transparent and subject to quality control.

International law on the other hand is not "democratic". Generally speaking, it is made by the strong states, and made in their interest. And, as regards UNSC resolutions in particular, the realities of how the Security Council works is a long way from the careful preparations which should, and usually do, characterize the national legislative process in a democratic *Rechtsstaat* and the EU.[43] The diplomats representing states in the Security Council are under pressure from their governments and (at least, perceived) public opinion to "do something" about a problem. As mentioned, for diplomats, especially those belonging to the five permanent members, the problem is that states do not listen sufficiently to the Security Council. International law in general, and Security Council resolutions in particular, cannot be legitimized in terms of the democratic, inclusive, transparent etc. "input" process. Instead, the legitimizing process is whether or not the norms in question are necessary and are well-formulated according to some substantive criteria. Norms which go against basic human rights principles are not legitimate in democratic states.

I do not need to go into detail on what has happened since the *Kadi/al-Barakaat* case. The UNSC reacted by adopting Resolution 1904 (2009) creating the office of a "Delisting Ombudsperson" which, however, was only given an advisory competence. Resolution 1904 also set out a time frame for the

43 See further the discussion in Torbjörn Andersson's chapter on mutual trust.

(re)consideration of the listings. Al-Barakaat was removed from the UN blacklist. It had become, quite simply, too embarrassing to keep it on the list on such flimsy grounds. Kadi was kept on the UN list. The Commission "independently" reviewed the UNSC's basis for listing Kadi and adopted a new Regulation confirming the EC listing. A new application was therefore brought by Kadi before the CFI.

In *Kadi II*, the CFI, now called the General Court, formulated exactly what safeguards must exist at EU (and, by analogy, UN) level for the sanctions to be valid.[44] After some initial grumbling about how its solution had been much better, the General Court in *Kadi II* proceeded to specify in detail what form a remedy must take at the EU level. This meant that a genuinely independent remedy going beyond the existing Ombudsperson must be created at the UN level, if the EU was to be able to implement UNSC resolutions. Moreover, the General Court also explicitly mentioned the elephant in the room, namely that the "preventive" and interim nature of the sanction – the rationale for having it at all – is wearing a bit thin, when it has been in place for ten years.[45]

The UNSC response was to adopt Resolutions 1988 and 1989 (2011). These separated the Taliban and Al-Qaeda sanctions. The Ombudsperson was not given a role to play in the Taliban (resolution 1988) sanctions. The criteria for delisting (paragraph 18) are political. They cover "individuals that meet the reconciliation conditions agreed to by the Government of Afghanistan and the international community". However, under Resolution 1989, the Delisting Ombudsperson or the designating State can de facto exercise delisting powers by default, unless the 1267 Sanctions Committee by consensus decides to retain the listing. But this is qualified by the possibility any member of the Security Council has to refer a delisting recommendation by the Ombudsperson or by the designating State to the full Security Council, where its normal decision-making rules will apply, meaning that delisting will require the votes of nine out of the 15 members of the Security Council and can be blocked by the veto of any of the five permanent members.

Where are we now after all this time?[46] In 2012 Kadi was also taken off the list. So far, the Ombudsperson has secured the removal of two other

---

44 Case T-85/09, *Yassin Abdullah Kadi v. European Commission* [2010] ECR II-5177 (Kadi II).

45 Para. 150. See also the Human Rights Committee decision on similar lines in *Nabil Sayadi and Patricia Vinck v. Belgium* (Communication No. 1472/2006), 22 October 2008, discussed by Scheinin 2010.

46 I should note that the CJEU later removed a level of pettiness, and unnecessary suffering, by excluding social security benefits and social security assistance benefits, such as income support, child benefit and housing benefit, granted to the spouses of presumed terrorists, from the scope of Regulation (EC) No 881/2002 concerning the freeze of funds of presumed terrorists. C-340/08, *M and others v HM Treasury* [2010] ECR I-3913. The Court stated that the main objective of a listing decision is to stop the persons or entities concerned from having access to economic or financial sources which they could use to support terrorist activities. It considers that the social benefits in question were solely used by the spouses

complainants from the list. Is then the Ombudsperson an effective remedy in practice? This is the issue before the CJEU (as it is now called) which is hearing *Kadi II* on appeal. At the time of writing, it has heard oral argument in the case and is considering its judgment.

The former, and present, UN rapporteurs on human rights and terrorism do not think the Ombudsperson is an effective remedy, and I agree with them.[47] It is undoubtedly a big improvement with what was in place in 2001. But there are still problems with the procedure and the fact that a permanent member can block the remedy means that, even if it can be "effective" in some, or even most, cases it can be blocked in others. Structurally, then, it cannot really be seen as "effective".[48] However, the CJEU may well accept it. It is under great pressure to do so.

The pressure which might exist in the opposite direction – the risk of the ECtHR deciding differently – may conceivably have been lessened by the ECtHR's recent judgment in *Nada v. Switzerland*.[49] Nada, a dual Italian-Egyptian national was listed under the 1267 Resolution sanctions. He resided in a small Italian enclave, Campione d'Italia, surrounded by the Swiss canton of Ticino and separated from the rest of Italy by Lake Lugano. The travel ban had the effect of forcing him to remain in the enclave, meaning inter alia that he could not leave for the purposes of obtaining medical treatment. The ECtHR found that Switzerland had violated Article 8 ECHR by failing to implement the UNSC resolution in a way which alleviated the burdens on the applicant, taking into account "the unique geographical situation of Campione d'Italia, the considerable duration of the measures imposed or the applicant's nationality, age and health".[50] However, as Judge Malinverni pointed out in his concurring opinion, the discretion left to the Swiss authorities was, in practice, almost zero.

So, even where conflict between the ECHR and UNSC legal orders seemed inevitable, the ECtHR managed to avoid it. In one sense, this is understandable; as an international court the ECtHR operates within a framework of general international law. However, I still do not think that the ECtHR would be prepared to find that UNSC resolutions free a state from complying with its obligations under the ECHR, in its own territory. It cannot, as this would mean that there would be no obstacle under the Convention to the UNSC ordering European states to arrest, detain (or, why not?) summarily execute a person

concerned in this case to meet the essential needs of their households, without their being any evident danger that they could be diverted to support terrorist activities.

47 Emerson 2012, Ginsborg and Scheinin 2011.

48 One can add here that, according to ECtHR, a constitutional complaint which results only in a declaratory judgment (*Sürmeli v. Germany*, No. 75529/01, 31 October 2005) or a statement of non-compliance (*Burden and Burden v. UK*, No. 13378/05, 12 December 2006) is not an "effective remedy" and does not need to be exhausted.

49 *Nada v. Switzerland*, No. 10593/08, 12 September 2012.

50 *Ibid*, para. 195.

deemed to be a threat to international peace and security. So, even for the ECtHR, the "constitutional" approach must be the last line of defence. I think that the ECtHR realizes this. Support for this can be found in the ECtHR's reasoning for finding a violation of the effective remedies requirement in Article 13. It referred to the judgment of the ECJ in *Kadi I* and stated that "The Court is of the opinion that the same reasoning must be applied, *mutatis mutandis*, to the present case, more specifically to the review by the Swiss authorities of the conformity of the Taliban Ordinance with the Convention. It further finds that there was nothing in the Security Council resolutions to prevent the Swiss authorities from introducing mechanisms to verify the measures taken at national level pursuant to those resolutions".[51]

Maybe the CJEU will accept the UN system. But one thing is clear. The CJEU knows, or should know, that it is being asked if it wants to "buy a pig in a bag".[52] If it approves the present UNSC system, no further improvements can ever be expected in it. And if a permanent member later starts using its veto, and blocking determinations by the Ombudsperson, the possibility in practice of "reopening" the issue at the EU level is zero.

7. THE EU'S AUTONOMOUS ANTI-TERRORIST SANCTIONS AND THE PMOI STANDARDS OF REVIEW

While I was investigating the UN system, the argument was occasionally made by representatives of EU states that the UN should introduce something resembling the EU system for sanctions against the financing of terrorism. I therefore looked at the EU system in 2003.[53] I found it gravely deficient for a number of reasons. The process for listing at first sight seemed better. Some criteria have to be satisfied before the Council can take a decision, namely there must be "precise information" which indicates that a decision has been taken by a national "competent authority" regarding a person or entity suspected to be engaged in the financing of terrorism. However, when I looked at the EU system, it appeared to me that the "safeguards" against deficient evaluations of the "proof" of terrorist activity, and against disproportionate or arbitrary decisions

51 Ibid, para. 212. This is also the interpretation placed on this passage by Emerson 2012.

52 The *Burden and Burden* case, above, indicates that the ECtHR can accept that a declaratory remedy (the UK declaration of incompatibility) which requires further political action to be effective can, if a practice develops of always complying with the declaration, *become* an effective remedy. But to state that the remedy is effective today requires taking the good will of the UNSC, now, and in the future, on faith. One possible way out is to state that the remedy has been effective in the specific circumstances of Kadi's application, while reserving judgment as regards other possible future applicants. Thanks to Sarah Cleveland for this point.

53 Cameron 2003a.

to blacklist, consisted of the fact that unanimous agreement was needed in the Council for listing in a common position. In other words, the safeguard was political rather than legal; the need for a collective political will on the part of the member states of the Council.

Moreover, even if there could be said to be some basis for meaningful *legal* review of the Council's decision, it seemed to me that the EU system was anyway applying what was a legitimate standard of proof for a *temporary* measure pending a trial – the freezing of the assets of a person or entity suspected of a serious offence – to what was in effect a permanent "penalty" intended as an alternative to trial.

Has the case law since 2001 improved the system, so as to remove these, and other, defects? In this section, I introduce, and comment upon, certain aspects of this case law. The leading cases in this respect are the two *PMOI* judgments. The background to these cases and the court's judgments are examined in detail in Torbjörn Andersson's chapter in the present volume so I can keep my treatment brief.

In the first *PMOI* case, the CFI stated that the Council had broad discretion in its assessment of the facts and that "the review carried out by the Court of the lawfulness of decisions to freeze funds must be restricted to checking that the rules governing procedure and the statement of reasons have been complied with, that the facts are materially accurate, and that there has been no *manifest error of assessment* of the facts or *misuse of power*. That limited review applies, especially, to the Council's assessment of the factors as to *appropriateness* on which such decisions are based".[54] This very limited scope to the review seemed to more or less rule out ever questioning the substance of the Council's decision.

However, in *PMOI II* the CFI seemed to realize its mistake and set a tougher standard of review. The CFI stated that it "must not only establish whether the evidence relied on is factually accurate, reliable and consistent, but must also ascertain whether that evidence contains all the relevant information to be taken into account in order to assess the situation and whether it is capable of substantiating the conclusions drawn from it."[55] This test, the CFI found in *PMOI II*, was not satisfied. The national basis for listing of PMOI was now – ostensibly – a decision by a French magistrate to investigate persons connected to PMOI (the original, British, basis having been successfully challenged in proceedings in the UK).[56] But the alleged link between the persons being investigated in France and the PMOI was not made clear, nor substantiated, in the information given to the Council, which admitted to the CFI that evidence

54 *Organisation des Modjahedines du peuple d'Iran, v. Council of the European Union*, T-228/02, ECR II-4665 [2006] para. 159 (emphasis added). The French name of the organization was employed for the first application, however, for the sake of simplicity I refer to this case as "*PMOI I*".

55 *People's Mojahedin Organization of Iran v. Council.* T-284/08, ECR II-3487 [2008] para. 55.

56 See further Sofia Marques da Silva and Cian Murphy's chapter in the present volume.

had not been given to it on this point. The CFI did not consider either that there was sufficient basis to conclude that the assessment made by the French investigating magistrate was based on "serious or credible evidence or clues".

The result was the delisting of the PMOI.[57] However, bearing in mind the PMOI's long-term renunciation of terrorist methods in its struggle against the present regime in Iran, the arbitrariness of the listing of the PMOI was obvious. It was listed for foreign policy reasons, presumably to placate the Iranian government and facilitate EU negotiations with Iran on its nuclear energy programme. The judgment in *PMOI II* does not mean that other less obviously arbitrary listing decisions will be questioned.

This is shown by the recent judgment of the CJEU in *Al-Aqsa v Council* considered in the next section.

8. COMPOSITE DECISION-MAKING, SECRECY AND THE SCOPE OF REVIEW

Considerable problems are created by the hybrid nature of the Council decision: it is a mixture between the principle of mutual recognition, and a centralized EU assessment to issue a coercive measure which limits basic human rights. The decision being challenged is a "composite" of EU and national decision-making. The "sum" of the decision may be greater than its parts, and the remedies which exist may only (at best) be capable of challenging the parts. In the *Al-Aqsa* case[58] the General Court had ruled that once a national measure has ceased to apply which formed the basis of a Council Decision in accordance with Regulation 2580/2001 and Common Position 2001/931, the EU decision to list a person or entity can only be upheld if there are clear grounds for keeping the person or entity concerned on the list, supported by serious and credible evidence. The national decision to list Al-Aqsa was taken in 2003 by a political authority, the Minister of Foreign Affairs in agreement with the Minister of Finance. It was based upon an internal (i.e. secret) assessment made by the Dutch civil security agency, the AIVD, that Al-Aqsa, a charitable organization devoted to assisting Palestine, had made transfers of funds to an organization engaged in terrorism. Al-Aqsa applied to a Dutch court for an interim order seeking suspension of the

[57] Council Common Position 2009/67/CFSP of 26 January 2009 and Council Decision of 26 January 2009 27.1.2009 OJ L 23/25, 23/37. A challenge by France to this decision was dismissed, C-27/09 *French Republic v PMOI, Council of the European Union, European Commission* (21 December 2011, Grand Chamber). The Court ruled that a subsequent (renewed) decision to list a person or entity should be preceded by a notification of the basis beforehand and by allowing the person or entity concerned to be heard, as the effectiveness of the "surprise" effect of a freezing measure no longer applies to such cases.

[58] Joined Cases C 539/10 P and C 550/10 P, *Stichting Al-Aqsa v. Council of the European Union*, 15 November 2012, nyr.

Ministerial ordinance. The Dutch court was given the AIVD memorandum, which it studied in camera. The court refused the application for an interim order, ruling that the memorandum provided sufficient grounds for the Minister's conclusion that money collected was going (indirectly) to Hamas, enabling the perpetration of terrorist acts.

Al-Aqsa was later listed, on Dutch initiative, by the Council. As the listing was in a regulation with direct effect, the Dutch ministerial ordinance was therefore annulled.[59]

The CJEU, unlike the General Court, considered that the decision taken in the past need not "necessarily still be in force or produce legal effects at the time the Council decides to continue to include a person on the list at issue... The essential question is whether, since that person was included in that list or since the last review, the factual situation has changed in such a way that it is no longer possible to draw the same conclusion in relation to the involvement of the person at issue in terrorist activities" (paras 80–82). The applicant submitted that it had no longer had any means of obtaining a review by a Dutch court of the factual accuracy of the AIVD allegations made in 2003. However, the CJEU considered that earlier refusal of the Dutch court to issue the order to be sufficient factual basis that the applicant was involved in financing terrorism. As no evidence had been provided by the applicant that the situation had changed, the CJEU set aside the judgment of the General Court.

This case shows the problem very clearly. It may be permissible for the Council to make a "context dependent" assessment of what is the national "competent authority" and what is the national "decision". However, if national administrative law does not provide a full (i.e. not simply a formal legality check) of the "decision" of the "competent authority", including taking into account new facts or changed circumstances, then the listed entity or person is in a Catch-22 situation. How does a system of "composite" decision-making (when the measure is partly national and partly at the EU level) avoid the risk that gaps arise in systems of legal protection? This is one of the problems with which national courts, and the EU courts, must continue to work on.[60]

Another problem is how does one cope with the secrecy of the proceedings? In *PMOI II*, the Council had been given some material classified as secret by the French government. However, at the express request of the French government,

59 The Dutch system for anti-terrorist sanctions is examined in detail in the chapter by Suus Hopman and Michel Uiterwaal in the present volume.

60 There is a similar problem as regards entry to an EU state of a listed person, or a person who is regarded as associated to a listed entity. As noted above, member states retain control over entry, and the decision to admit is discretionary. As long as EU law (non-discrimination) is followed concerning EU nationals and residents, one cannot question such national decisions taken on public order/national security grounds before the EU courts. If there is some form of judicial review process available at the national level, the national administrative court may refer to the EU listing decision as a sufficient basis for not admitting the person. The issue arose inter alia in Case T-181/08 *Pye Phyo Tay Za v Council* [2010] ECR II-1965, at para. 134.

it refused to disclose this material to the CFI. The CFI concluded "the Council is not entitled to base its funds-freezing decision on information or material in the file communicated by a Member State, if the said Member State is not willing to authorise its communication to the Community judicature whose task is to review the lawfulness of that decision".[61]

While this is undoubtedly a step forward, it does not solve the whole problem. On the contrary, it brings new problems as some form of mechanism must be created at the EU level. Christine Eckes' chapter examines in detail the requirements of the *PMOI* case law in this respect, and analyses how to reconcile secrecy with due process requirements.

It may be that a remedy can be created but I am sceptical. Part of the problem lies at the accountability level. It would appear that the decision-making in the Council decision is not accompanied by more than a minimal sharing of intelligence on the specific terrorist threats posed by a given individual or entity. This is not surprising. All attempts to "pool" intelligence at the EU level run into the problem that states will be very reluctant to put in valuable intelligence to the pool, when there is no guarantee that they will get out intelligence of similar, or even any, value.[62]

So, the Council will not really receive very high grade intelligence as a basis for its decision-making, and, even if it did, it has little chance of evaluating it properly. It is unlikely, at least in the foreseeable future, that the big, intelligence producing, EU states will accept the creation of a strong independent evaluative capacity at the Council level.

Another part of the problem is the technique of blacklisting itself. According to ECtHR case law, an effective remedy means that an independent body should have jurisdiction to review the substance of an executive decision. But what is the "law" the Council is applying when it adopts a common position listing a given organization as "terrorist"? What norm has the entity being blacklisted breached? The decision to blacklist is not necessarily an accusation that a person belonging to a given organization has committed a criminal offence on behalf of the organization, or that the organization itself has done so (in those states where entities can commit offences). Whether a person or entity has committed a crime is an issue which national criminal courts – not the General Court or the CJEU – obviously have long experience of testing. An accusation is made, the evidence is submitted and the court gives judgment.

By contrast, the General Court considers that listing is an interim and precautionary measure. It is does not regard the listing as itself a criminal penalty, to which the presumption of innocence applies.[63] This particular point

61 *PMOI II*, at para. 73.

62 Wetzling 2006.

63 See e.g. Joined Cases T-37/07 and T-323/07 *Mohamed El Morabit v Council* [2009] ECR II-xx and T- 49/07 *Sofiane Fahas v Council of the European Union* [2010] ECR II-xx.

is confirmed by case law from the ECtHR, which also – more controversially – does not regard mere listing as damaging reputation and as such, not involving the determination of a civil right within the meaning of Article 6 ECHR.[64]

An additional cause for concern is the fact that the initiative to list the great majority of organizations in the autonomous EU anti-terror sanctions lists comes from foreign governments. Terrorism according to the EU definition need not be directed against a democratic government. This might seem correct, but EU states as a whole, or certain important EU states, may have reasons for extending understanding to foreign governments facing terrorism/insurgency problems even if these governments are authoritarian or even dictatorial. We know that dictatorial governments have a tendency to call any opposition "terrorist". As is shown by the PMOI listing there is a clear potential for abuse. But even where the group in question does engage in terrorism (often, at times, very occasionally?), do we want to extend to dictatorial governments this sort of legitimacy?

Bearing this in mind, what would a decision to blacklist a terrorist organization ideally encompass, applying the principle of proportionality? I would say it should involve determining inter alia the following issues: how many civil casualties are being caused by the "counter-terrorist" campaign, whether the terrorist acts for which the organization in question is accused are really attributable to the organization, whether these are isolated incidents, or whether these instead go to the policy of the organization itself, whether the organization is still engaged in terrorism and finally whether the "benefits", foreign policy or otherwise, of making fund-collecting for this organization outweigh the "costs" in terms of the inevitable "overspill" restrictions in freedom of association and expression of people resident in EU states pursuing the same political goal as the organization, but not advocating terrorist means.

The CJEU does not, and cannot, take these types of policy consideration into account, because it is not deciding whether to list an organization as terrorist. Instead it determines whether or not the Council had *sufficient basis* for deciding to list an organization as terrorist. If we accept that we should have blacklisting at all, the question is how far can and should the CJEU go in this review process? The CJEU court is the guardian of an autonomous legal order, and while there are examples of the CJEU engaging in "close scrutiny" of executive decisions in other areas, this is something new. The CJEU judges naturally approach new areas from their own national perspective. The extent of a court's power to engage in an administrative review of an executive decision naturally varies from state to state. The extent of the discretion permitted to the executive depends upon both constitutional limits and judicial culture. In this sort of area closely connected to foreign affairs, where courts tend to show deference to the

64 *Segi and Others and Gestoras Pro-Amnistia and Others v. 15 States of the EU*, Nos 6422/02 and 9916/02, 23 May 2002. This was declared inadmissible on the basis that the applicants were not 'victims' of the common position.

government, it is safe to assume that there are few, if any, EU states where the courts can engage in such a wide-ranging review of policy matters.

9. CRIMINAL LAW, CRIMINAL PROCEDURE AND THE AUTONOMOUS ANTI-TERRORIST SANCTIONS

What effect does the EU listing have at the national level? Contributing financial assets, directly or indirectly,[65] to the organization, holding assets or receiving assets from it, become criminal offences. All organizations need to bring in, and spend, money. Inter alia they need money to hire a place to operate from, to pay volunteers for their costs and to organize opinion-building and other activities. The effect of an EU listing on the national level is akin to a prohibition of an organization.

But what is problematic with this? Organizational prohibitions are admittedly a blunt instrument from the perspective of criminal policy in that they target all the individuals in a group for things that certain individuals in the group have done, or plan to do. But they are not a new thing, certainly not as regards offences against the state. Some EU states, such as Spain and Germany, have established constitutional procedures for the banning of political parties. Continued membership of, or activities in support of, a banned organization is a criminal offence. However, there is an established review process for this before the highest national court, and such prohibitions are used sparingly.

Many other EU states target organized criminality by criminalizing in different ways membership of, or participation in, criminal organizations. Some overt activity in support of the organization, and knowledge of its activities, is a requirement and, in line with the criminal standard of proof, this must be proved beyond a reasonable doubt.[66]

But can and should EU listing affect national criminal proceedings, and if so, how? The inter-relationship between the Danish and Dutch criminal cases penalizing terrorist financing and the EU listing are examined in the chapters by, respectively, Thomas Elholm and Suus Hopman and Michel Uiterwaal in the present volume. The CJEU has touched upon the temporal aspect of this issue in

65 See, by analogy, Case C-117/06, *Gerda Möllendorf and Christiane Möllendorf-Niehuus* [2007] ECR I-8361. The CJEU stated that inclusion in the list of persons whose funds have been frozen because of their links with the Al-Qaeda network precludes carrying out an already agreed contract transferring ownership. The Court also ruled that immovable property consisting in buildings is an economic resource for the purposes of Regulation No 881/2002.

66 As regards crimes of unlawful association generally, see Meliá, 2008. As regards the impact of the EU framework decision on the national anti-terrorism legislation, see the essays in Galli and Weyembergh, 2012.

its ruling on German request for a preliminary ruling in the E, F case.[67] E and F had collected money for the Turkish organisation Devrimci Halk Kurtulus Partisi-Cephesi (DHKP C), which was listed by the EU in 2002. DHKP C had not challenged its listing. However, as noted above, the PMOI, and other, challenges to the lists had been successful, on the basis, inter alia, of failure to state reasons. These successful challenges led the Council to reissue the list, stating reasons and giving the listed organizations the opportunity to comment, on 29 June 2007. The Grand Chamber of the CJEU considered that, bearing in mind the fact that DHKP's inclusion on the terrorism list would have been seen as unlawful prior to 29 June 2007, such inclusion could thus not form any part of a basis for a criminal conviction of two of its members, as concerns activity prior to this date.

But, welcome though this judgment is, it certainly does not solve all the issues. And, while in some states the discretionary nature of prosecution can give some scope to avoid prosecuting groups and individuals, this option is not available for states which apply the principle of legality (obligatory prosecution). For these states, properly formulating the objective and subjective requirements of the offence at national law is obviously even more important. The devil is thus in the details. These issues of criminal law which have arisen, and will continue to arise, regarding the autonomous EU anti-terrorist sanctions reflect deeper conceptual problems in making these two very different systems fit together. Underlying the criminal law is the constitutional law concept of the separation of powers: a general prohibitory norm is promulgated by the legislature, applied by the executive (a prosecutor) in a concrete case and the legality of the executive's action is ruled upon by an independent court. Requiring the legislature to decide on criminalization also corresponds with our deeply felt notions that the ultimate power of the state – to inflict harm – should be exercised by the representatives of the people, and only after careful consideration.[68] If we can (or must) continue to have sanctions in the area of terrorist financing, can they be made compatible with fundamental principles of national criminal law and criminal policy? Kimmo Nuotio and Petter Asp consider the problems in making this "fit" in their chapters. "Overbroad" quasi-criminal legislation directed at organizations, has a spillover effect on the constitutional/human rights of freedom of expression and association[69] and

---

67 Case C-550/09 *Generalbundesanwalt beim Bundesgerichtshof v E and F* [2010] ECR I-6213.

68 See by analogy, the judgment of the UK Supreme Court in *HM Treasury (Respondent) v Mohammed Jabar Ahmed and others* (FC) [2010] UKSC 2. Under the UK United Nations Act 1946, the government can issue ordinances (orders in council) implementing UN sanctions. However, the court considered that the Act was not designed for such measures such as the al-Qaeda freezing sanctions which had such serious effects on individuals. The court therefore struck down the orders in council on the basis that such limits in liberty should be authorized explicitly by statute. While this judgment is not a rejection of the validity of these UN sanctions, it is another indication that judges are not happy with the UN system.

69 Other human rights are also involved. This can be illustrated by a Swedish case concerning personal data transfer, Stockholm District Court, judgment 2011-04-13 in Case no. T 9176–

Thomas Bull examines this in his chapter, inter alia examining the US Supreme Court's judgment in the Holder case and comparing the US approach with a Swedish case concerning prosecution for terrorist financing.

I think different approaches to criminal procedure (which in turn, are partly due to different constitutional traditions) explain to some extent the greater acceptability which anti-terrorist sanctions have in the US and the UK compared to many civil law states. It is not by chance that the blacklisting method was adopted in a common law country, the US, and is enthusiastically supported by another common law country, the UK. All states tend to be reluctant to "burn" intelligence methods and sources by exposing them in criminal trials. But the US and UK, as well as being exposed to a larger threat of terrorism as compared to many other states (to a considerable extent a self-made threat because of the foreign policies they have chosen to follow) have also a quite different tradition of criminal procedure, and rules for evaluating evidence, from that of continental Europe. The difficulty the "hearsay" rule can create for obtaining convictions in cases of organized crime (and terrorism) results in a greater willingness to use quasi-criminal, quasi-administrative methods (seizure of assets etc.) instead of bringing formal criminal charges. The more flexible nature of the common law makes it easier to accept mechanisms which blend legislature with executive, and executive with judiciary.

Many EU states would probably today be inclined to drop these types of anti-terrorist sanctions altogether. All EU states have – now – ratified and implemented in national law the UN Convention on Financing of Terrorism.[70] This means that they criminalize financing of terrorism, and are to cooperate with each other in combating this. The offence under this convention requires a basic intent to aid the commission of acts of terrorism by providing financing, but even indifference as to whether the money will be used for terrorism or not will suffice. This type of offence is acceptable in my view. But even if this makes the anti-terrorist sanctions, objectively speaking, otiose, we seem to be stuck with them for political reasons.

Could the (alleged) preventive effect instead be achieved within the existing framework of EU cooperation in criminal procedure, instead of living a parallel existence to it? The principle of mutual recognition means that, in EU states, a national prosecutorial decision freezing property belonging to an individual or group in one EU state can be enforced against property belonging to the

08, unpublished. A money transfer by person with a name similar to a blacklisted name was stopped by Western Union. He was required to provide considerable personal data to show that he was not the blacklisted person in question. The problems caused Muslims here are obvious: there are a limited number of Muslim names, and anglicised spelling differs, meaning that false positives are common.

70 Compare the argument made by the former UN special rapporteur on terrorism for abandoning Resolution 1373, Statement by Martin Scheinin to UNGA 3rd Committee, 26 October 2010, www.ohchr.org/Documents/Issues/Terrorism/statement_GA26.10.10.pdf.

individual or group in another EU state. How coherent are these "administrative" measures of blacklisting with other existing and proposed EU measures in justice and home affairs promoting the criminal law model for dealing with the problem of terrorism (investigation, trial, conviction, punishment/confiscation of assets)? Malin Thunberg Schunke in her chapter examines the present system of recognition of freezing decisions, and compares it to freezing by means of anti-terrorist listing.

10. COMPENSATION

The legal challenges before the CJEU so far discussed have been annulment actions. In concluding this section, something should be said about compensation as a remedy for listing in violation of fundamental procedural or material safeguards.[71] Under Article 340(2) TFEU "the Union shall, in accordance with the general principles common to the laws of the Member States, make good any damage caused by its institutions or by its servants in the performance of their duties". Under Article 268 TFEU the CJEU has jurisdiction in disputes concerning damages.

However, obtaining damages for losses allegedly caused by *legislative* acts is not easy. The reason for this is that – reasonably enough – "the prospect of actions for damages is liable to hinder exercise of the powers of the legislative authority whenever it has occasion to adopt, in the public interest, legislative measure which may adversely affect the interests of individuals".[72] Moreover, the external policy of the EU is an area where the CJEU has previously accepted that there is a wide sphere of discretion.[73]

The question of damages for sanctions has arisen inter alia in the *Sison II* case. Sison was the (alleged) head of the Philippines Communist Party, living in exile in the Netherlands. The Philippines Communist Party was listed as a terrorist organization by the EU. Sison himself had been earlier subjected to a Dutch unilateral decision freezing his assets (see further the chapter by Suus

---

71 There is – arguably – a relationship between the two as regards standing. One, as yet, unresolved, issue concerns whether a person or entity who has been delisted still has standing to pursue an annulment action. The act in question, as far as the person or entity is concerned, no longer exists. However, as there appears to be little prospect of success in obtaining damages (see below), the interest a person or entity has in being vindicated – obtaining a judicial pronouncement that the Council acted wrongfully – appear to be only capable of being pursued in the context of annulment action. This suggests that a generous approach should be taken to the question of standing.

72 Joined Cases C-120/06 P and C-121/06 P *Fabbrica italiana accumulatori motocarri Montecchio SpA (FIAMM), and Fabbrica italiana accumulatori motocarri Montecchio Technologies LLC v Council and Commission* [2008] ECR I-6513, at para. 121.

73 Case C-377/02 *Van Parys* [2005] ECR I-1465 at paras 51 and 53. See further Wakefield 2012 for a brief discussion of this and other recent case law.

Hopman and Michel Uiterwaal). The Court in an interlocutory judgment ruled, as regards Sison, that both the reasons provided for an initial and a subsequent listing decision should include a proper justification as to whether the person or entity concerned should be made the subject of a freezing measure, rather than merely referring to legal conditions for the application of Regulation 2580/2001 (in this case, references to national decisions). In the subsequent damages claim the General Court considered that the task of the judicature was to first determine whether the institution concerned enjoyed any discretion, next to take into consideration the complexity of the situations to be regulated, any difficulties in applying or interpreting the legislation, the clarity and precision of the rule infringed, and finally whether the error made was inexcusable or intentional. It considered that the procedural rules in Regulation 2580/2001 do confer rights (para. 52) and that there is no margin of appreciation for the Council in determining whether the factual conditions for listing are fulfilled (para. 57). However, given the lack of well-established precedent in the case-law before judgment was delivered in its interlocutory judgment in *Sison II*, and the factual complexities of the case, the violation of the rules in question, although clearly established, cannot be regarded as a sufficiently serious breach of Community law (para. 74). The General Court considered that the applicant was not raising an objection of the illegality as such, having regard to fundamental rights, of the general fund-freezing regime (the legislative act). Sisons was only questioning the correct application of that regulation in the particular circumstances of the case. But it in any event considered, with only summary reasoning but hardly unexpectedly, that the general regime of anti-terrorist sanctions, and the restrictions these involve in fair hearings and the right to property, was justified because of the magnitude of the interests at stake.

Compensation is another area where the EU courts will have to do some proper thinking and modify the practice they have developed for the quite different context of a measure of general application taken after a reasoned attempt to balance competing public goods. Listing decisions are quite different. Moreover, I would say that the argument for compensation as a suitable remedy increases in strength the longer the measure persists. As noted above regarding *Kadi II*, the General Court accepted that a measure which had been in place for over 10 years could hardly be described as "temporary".[74]

---

74 Here one can note that the ECtHR considers that the logic of the Convention (see in particular Article 17) means that one can adjust compensation levels, even down to zero, when terrorists are concerned. *McCann and others v. UK* 27 September, 1995, A/324. However, this means that the reviewing court must take a position on the reasonableness of the Council position to target the person or entity, and to maintain the sanctions in force over a period of years. This in turn means examining whether the complainants in a given case *were* actually or at least, probably, financing terrorism. Outside of the very obvious cases of abuse of the listing such as Al-Barakaat, this brings us back to the intelligence problem.

11. APPLICATION OF THE SAFEGUARDS TO REGIME SANCTIONS

I have, above, been critical to the rationale behind using sanctions against persons or entities suspected of being involved in terrorist financing. However, targeted assets freezing and travel bans make more sense when applied against the members of a government which the EU wants to pressurize for some reason, and the political and business élite which keeps that government in power. As with anti-terrorist sanctions, the EU can be implementing UNSC sanctions, or its own, autonomous sanctions. As noted, the growth of power of the EU as an international actor, and the fact that the UNSC can be blocked for political reasons, means that the EU may want to go further than the UNSC in sanctioning regimes. Examples of more extensive EU sanctions are those imposed against Zimbabwe, Iran and Burma (Myanmar).

Obviously, where a government is a "bandit" government, ruthlessly exploiting the natural resources of a state, the best way to hit it is to cut down, or off, its profits. These profits are often moved or invested abroad, including to states in the EU, so there could be considerable assets within the EU to freeze. Moreover, politicians, perhaps particularly those who are up to no good, crave respectability. They want to be accepted as natural members of the fine European political circles. They want to send their children to Oxford or the Sorbonne, and their spouses want to go shopping in Brussels and Paris.

The businessmen who reap the profits of their close contacts with a despotic regime, or even share their profits with members of it, are an integral part of such an exploitive system. It can be artificial to draw distinctions between who in the controlling regime is formally a member of the government and who is not.

Unlike the situation for terrorist associates, the "core" of the target is clearly identified. And the "periphery", the business circles, will usually be acting openly, or relatively openly, because effective business usually demands that people know who is in charge of what. Even where ownership is concealed, where companies are exploiting primary resources (timber, diamonds, etc.) the chain of ownership can presumably be traced, beginning with the geographical location of the primary resource. This can also be done, although presumably with more difficulty, where the trade is in manufactured products, import-export licences, etc. In any event, the intelligence problem is not so much identifying the periphery, but identifying the influence it has on the core (and vice versa), and determining whether this is sufficient to justify including given individuals on the blacklist. In other words, it is reasonable to assume that, for regime sanctions, if intelligence is there at the root of a decision to target, the targeting decision can be motivated by information on controlling interests etc. in the public domain which *can* be invoked in review proceedings.

However, this is not to say that intelligence problems never arise as regards regime sanctions, nor that, if and when intelligence is used as part of the targeting decision, it can be revealed without difficulty in judicial review proceedings. Where intelligence relating to, e.g. degrees of influence, comes from covert human sources or strategic surveillance then it will naturally be sensitive, so that states can be reluctant to reveal it to each other, let alone the General Court or the CJEU. This is illustrated inter alia by the *Fulmen, and Fereydoun Mahmoudian* case concerning the alleged activities of the applicants, a electrical company and its managing director, in support of the Iranian nuclear programme.[75] The General Court repeated its formula finding that the review of lawfulness of a listing decision must include the question whether the grounds are valid, based on concrete evidence and information. It dismissed the Council's defence that it need not provide evidence of the applicants' alleged assistance to the nuclear programme, and also that this evidence coming from confidential sources, could not be disclosed to the General Court.[76]

While the intelligence problem is probably less insurmountable compared to anti-terrorist sanctions, regime sanctions give rise to other problems. Several of these relate to human rights. Although family members of terrorist suspects are indirectly affected by freezing and travel bans,[77] in regime sanctions, family members of the "primary" target can also be targeted directly.

Another problem concerns the more political nature of the listing decision, and consequent greater difficulties in providing meaningful judicial review.

A third problem is the extent to which state-owned entities can claim "human rights" at all. A fourth problem concerns the extent of control which a targeted entity must exercise over another entity before the latter can be subjected to sanctions. This is also a problem which can exist with anti-terrorist sanctions.[78]

A preliminary problem the General Court had to deal with in 2010 was the applicability of the anti-terrorist case law of the General Court and the CJEU to regime sanctions. The initial Council position was that the two types of sanctions were quite different, and the safeguards developed in the *PMOI* and *Kadi* cases were not applicable at all.

This was – predictably enough – rejected by the General Court in *Pye Phyo Tay Za v Council*,[79] which also raised the first two problems mentioned above. Pye Phyo Tay Za had been listed as a person benefitting from the economic policies of the government of Myanmar. His father was a leading businessman linked to the regime and he himself was the managing director of one of his

75 Joined Cases T-439/10 and T-440/10, *Fulmen, and Fereydoun Mahmoudian v Council and Commission*, 12 March 2012, nyr.

76 *Ibid.* at para. 100.

77 See *inter alia* the *M and others* case, above.

78 See the discussion in Thomas Bull's chapter of the Swedish appeal court judgment in case B 685–09, decided 9 November 2009.

79 Case T-181/08 *Pye Phyo Tay Za v Council* [2010] ECR II-1965.

father's construction companies. The applicant wanted clear and specific reasons why he was listed, otherwise he argued that judicial review was not meaningful. The General Court considered that, unlike in *PMOI*, the applicant was listed not for something he had done, but for who he was.[80] It accepted the Council's position that there was a presumption that family members of leading businessmen linked to the Myanmar government benefited from the economic policies of that government. It was possible for the applicant to show that he had dissociated himself from his father, and that he did not therefore benefit.[81] On appeal the CJEU noted that it was not easy to establish a link between family members and the lack of progress in Myanmar towards democracy and human rights – the basis for the sanctions. It held that precise, concrete information was necessary to show that a person was benefitting from the economic policies of the ruling regime.[82] The relevant regulations contained no presumption of benefit and the General Court had erred in law by accepting this.

It is unclear to what extent this judgment places sets real obstacles in the way of ever listing family members. It is an acceptable strategy, in my view, to target family members in order to prevent circumvention of the sanctions. In other words, the assets of family members who do not have their own sources of income (beyond those necessary for a moderate lifestyle) can presumably be frozen on the basis that these assets are, in fact, the assets of the primary target. However, going beyond that, and "punishing" the primary target by making his or her family members' lives more difficult is much more controversial. This is using individuals as a means to an end: punishing them for something someone else is doing. Thus, it seems correct for the CJEU to require that family sanctions must be justified on the basis that the individuals concerned benefit directly from the ill-gotten gains of the regime. As to how much evidence of this is necessary, and what form it can take, this is likely to arise (repeatedly) in the future.

As regards the aim of the sanction, the Council will naturally want to keep these relatively open. As Michael Eriksson argues in his chapter, an effective targeted sanctions policy requires a flexible application of carrots and sticks. The Council should be able to react speedily to changes on the ground in the targeted regime, adding and taking away from the list of the specific targets, to "reward" compliance and punish transgression and to be in a position to pronounce credible threats. But the more subjectively the aims of the sanctions are framed, the more difficult it will be for the EU courts to exercise meaningful review.

The third problem is illustrated by the *Manufacturing Support* case.[83] According to ECtHR case law, a company can enjoy certain rights under the

---

80 Ibid. at para. 122.

81 Ibid. at para. 167.

82 C-376/10 *Pye Phyo Tay Za v Council Judgment of the Grand Chamber*, 13 March 2012, nyr at paras 67, 69 and 70.

83 T-509/10, *Manufacturing Support & Procurement Kala Naft Co., Tehran Teheran (Iran) v. Council and Commission*, 25 April 2012, nyr.

Convention. It may even be entitled to non-pecuniary damages under ECHR Article 41.[84] However, the Council and Commission argued on a point of admissibility, that as a wholly owned company of the Iranian state, it had no "human rights". The General Court considered this issue went to the merits. As it later went on to find that the rights of defence and effective judicial protection had been infringed, it would appear that this was rejected. However, it is likely that this issue too will arise again.

The fourth problem is illustrated by the *Melli bank PLC* case.[85] The CJEU ruled that for a subsidiary to be listed under the regime sanctions against Iran it was sufficient to show that the latter was "owned or controlled" by the mother company (Bank Melli Iran) which itself had been listed because of its involvement in the financing of the Iranian nuclear programme.

While these cases have solved certain problems, more remain. The case law concerning regime sanctions is now much extensive than that concerning anti-terrorist sanctions and many more cases are in the pipe-line. These come in waves. With every new set of sanctions, such as those implemented recently against the Bashar al-Assad regime in Syria, a new set of applications are filed.

12. LEGAL BASES FOR, AND COHERENCE OF, EU SANCTIONS AFTER THE LISBON TREATY

The Lisbon Treaty codified certain changes which had come about as a result of case law and distinguished between two types of anti-terrorist sanctions.

The first basis for sanctions is now Article 215. This is now stated explicitly to cover natural or legal persons and groups or non-State entities. Moreover, it covers both financial and trade sanctions. The Council votes by qualified majority (although unanimity is retained for adoption of decisions (the common position as a legal instrument no longer exists) within the framework of the CFSP. The rights of the European Parliament are limited to being informed. A procedural right to appeal to the CJEU against the decision taken under the CFSP is given under Article 275. This exceptional judicial competence codifies the present legal position, as clarified in *Gestoras Pro Amnistía and others* and *Segi*,[86] where the court found that the principle of effective judicial remedies meant that a listed entity or person must have a right of appeal to the court.

---

84 See *Comingersoll S.A. v. Portugal*, No. 35382/97, 6 April 2000.

85 C-380/09 *Melli Bank plc v Council, France, UK and Commission*, Grand Chamber, 13 March 2012, nyr. See also T-562/10 *HTTS Hanseatic Trade Trust & Shipping GmbH vs Council*, 11 December 2011, nyr, where the General Court ruled that a clear and direct link needed to be established between an entity and the country subject to the sanction, the fact that the entity represented an Iranian partner firm being insufficient.

86 Joined Cases C-354/04 P and C-355/04 P *Gestoras Pro Amnistía and others and Segi and others v. Council of the European Union* [2007] ECR I-1579.

Two additional changes regarding sanctions should be mentioned as regards this first legal basis. Article 215(3) provides that acts adopted must contain the necessary legal safeguards. Moreover, the Lisbon treaty makes the Charter of Human Rights and fundamental freedoms legally binding. Having said this, the content of the rights affected by targeted sanctions is not so different from the situation before.

The second change concerns the Parliament's expanded power over the issue of regulation of terrorism. The amended treaty provides for a division between sanctions directed against "EU internal" (which fall under Article 75) and "EU external" suspected terrorists and terrorist groups (which fall under Article 215, above). Article 75 refers to Parliament's competence acting together with the Council "Where necessary to achieve the objectives set out in Article 67, as regards preventing and combating terrorism and related activities" to adopt a regulation to "define a framework for administrative measures with regard to capital movements and payments, such as the freezing of funds, financial assets or economic gains belonging to, or owned or held by, natural or legal persons, groups or non-State entities".

This article was the basis of a case brought by the Parliament against the Council following the Council's adoption of a regulation, 1286/2009 of 22 December 2009, amending the Al-Qaeda sanctions (Regulation (EC) No 881/2002), on the sole legal basis of Article 215.[87] The parliament had a number of arguments for its position, inter alia the need for strong legal safeguards in the area of freedom, justice and security, which militated in favour of improved democratic legitimation, i.e. involving the parliament, and the impossibility of drawing a conceptual distinction between "EU internal" and "EU external" terrorist suspects. An organization with "external" aims in a non-member state, e.g. secession or seizure of governmental power, could consist of residents or nationals of one or more EU states, physically present and acting within the EU. Similarly, an organization with internal aims, i.e. within an EU state, could consist of non-EU nationals or residents, acting either within and/or outside of the EU.

The CJEU rejected the Parliament's arguments. The CJEU had previously held that a dual legal basis is not possible where the procedures laid down for each are incompatible – as it found to be the case here.[88] The argument regarding lack of a conceptual distinction was dismissed with little reasoning: Article 215 provided a *sufficient* legal basis for the al-Qaeda regulation, even if the distinction could be argued to be illogical.[89] While the democratic anchoring of EU decisions is to be preferred, the continued exclusion of the Parliament from CFSP decisions was a deliberate choice of the framers of the Lisbon Treaty.[90]

[87] C-130/10 *European Parliament v. Council* (Grand Chamber) 19 July 2012 nyr.
[88] *Ibid.* para. 45.
[89] *Ibid.* para. 74.
[90] *Ibid.* paras 81–83.

Finally, it is not a choice between a legal ground providing for legal safeguards and a legal ground which does not: legal safeguards are a requirement also of Article 215.[91]

The Court's reasoning in the case is not strong. It was more sympathetic to the Parliament's rights/democratic legitimacy argument in the later "*Frontex*" case.[92] I think the Parliament is correct in arguing that there is no logical way of distinguishing between the "internal" and "external" threats posed by network terrorism – a conclusion that most security agencies in Europe drew a while ago. Of course, one can say that this division should not have been made at all: the Parliament should not be involved in either situation.[93] But once one accepts that the treaty specifies that the Parliament is to be involved in "internal" sanctions, then I would say that the only logical distinction which can be made is on the rights/legitimacy basis the Parliament advances, meaning that one should distinguish between sanctions directed against individuals and entities *physically located* respectively, within, and outside the "area of freedom, security and justice" i.e. in the territories of the member states.

Admittedly, this is difficult to do at the present time, because, as noted above, the UNSC Al-Qaeda list is seen as "external", even though it includes nationals and residents of EU states. However, there would be no need to maintain this situation for ever. The EU states who sit in the UNSC, including the permanent members France and the UK, can block new UNSC listings of EU nationals and residents in this list, and possible future sanctions lists.[94] These people and entities could instead be listed in an EU list. The same purpose is served. This is the approach followed by the US after all; US nationals tend not to be listed in UNSC lists.

Another argument for keeping the two issues separate concerns the fact that decisions to list organizations aimed at seizure of governmental power, or secession, in third states involve very delicate matters of foreign policy. The Council can justifiably be doubtful about letting Parliament in here. But this objection relates mainly to the operative decisions, not the framing of the system itself and its safeguards.

So, I would say that neither of these arguments against the Parliament's position is very convincing. But the language of politics is not (necessarily) logic. What probably weighed heavily with the Court are the political realities of

91 *Ibid.* paras 83–84.

92 Case C-355/10, 5 September 2012, nyr, "provisions on conferring powers of public authority on border guards ... mean that the fundamental rights of the persons concerned may be interfered with to such an extent that the involvement of the European Union legislature is required" (at para. 77). Thanks to Kieran Bradley for this point.

93 See also Eckes 2009, pp. 100–105.

94 Under Article 34 TEU, there is a duty on EU states that are permanent Security Council members to "ensure the defence of the positions and interests of the Union". The interests of the Union include the interests of the member states, which in turn include the interests of their citizens and residents.

sanctions decision-taking. Finding that Article 75 was the proper legal basis would mean accepting that the consensus requirement (in CFSP decisions) would be removed: sanctions could be adopted by qualified majority voting in the Council. The Court must have been aware of the unacceptability of such a result to the member states, bearing in mind the very different approaches to sanctions they can have, in principle and in concrete cases.

Where does this case leave us? The EU is committed to legislating on a system of sanctions for internal terrorists, even if this may not, objectively, be necessary any more (if it ever was). But there are considerable problems in creating a system satisfactory to all the member states because they look upon this issue differently. Some states, such as Sweden, have no national administrative system in place. Instead they regard the criminal law approach as being sufficient (which it is, under the UN Convention on Financing). The FATF does not think so and has criticized states with no national administrative listing system. The supposed legal duty at international law – UNSC resolution 1373 – to introduce an administrative listing system in national law, parallel to whatever criminal law methods exists for interim freezing of terrorist assets, is very thin indeed. Resolution 1373, apart from having been heavily criticized does not explicitly require an administrative freezing system at all.[95] This is only an interpretation given to it by the FATF, an American-dominated organization, pursuing an American agenda. Sweden and other EU states in the same situation have been putting off the FATF on the basis that the EU will legislate soon on the matter. As Maria Bergström shows in her chapter in the present volume, the influence the FATF has exerted over the EU as regards the regulation of money laundering has been extensive. It is – sadly – not very likely that the FATF will forget about its criticism, and it is difficult for the Commission to ignore the explicit wording of Article 67 TFEU, so EU legislation there will be. However, the sceptical EU states, or some of them at least, are likely to take a rights-oriented approach that whatever EU administrative freezing system is introduced for "internal" suspects, it can only be temporary pending criminal investigation (i.e. there should be a sunset clause), and/or that a high threshold of proof should be required before freezing can occur.

On the other hand, other EU states already have their own national anti-terrorist lists. Two such states are the Netherlands and the UK. How do EU sanctions fit into, and compare to these national systems for the proscription of terrorist organizations? The chapters by Suus Hopman and Michel Uiterwaal and Sofia Marques da Silva and Cian Murphy in the present volume analyse the working of these systems. An EU system would have to either be a complement to these existing national systems or replace them. If it is a complement to them, the administrative costs for financial institutions are increased. But an obligatory, and exhaustive, EU list – replacing the national lists – will not be

95 See the operative parts of the resolution, quoted in footnote 28 above.

acceptable to states such as the UK which has its own foreign and domestic policy reasons for having more extensive lists.

13. POST-LISBON INTERNAL PROCEDURES FOR THE ADOPTION OF EU SANCTIONS

What are the internal procedures for the adoption of EU sanctions? Texts for Council CFSP Decisions and Council Decisions are prepared by the European External Action Service (EEAS) Sanctions Team, in close co-operation with the Council Legal Service and relevant geographic or thematic counterparts.[96] Proposals for Regulations are prepared by the Foreign Policy Instruments Service in the European Commission, then submitted to inter-service consultation with all the other relevant parts of the Commission (always the Legal Service, and, as regards financial sanctions, DGs Internal Market (MARKT), Economic and Financial Affairs (ECFIN), EuropeAid (AIDCO), Humanitarian Aid (ECHO), Justice, Freedom and Security (JLS) (where terrorism is concerned), Taxation and Customs Union (TAXUD) and Trade (for trade restrictions) plus the geographical desk (in EEAS). The text is translated into the Union official languages and adopted by the College of Commissioners, generally by written procedure, then transmitted to the Council. Both types of proposals are discussed in the Council's Foreign Relations (RELEX) Counsellors working group, which normally meets twice a week, attended by Brussels-based diplomats, to prepare all legal and financial texts relating to CFSP. The diplomat representing the rotating Presidency chairs the meetings supported by the Council Secretariat and its Legal Service. The Commission and the EEAS also attend.

Simple texts – such as extending (roll-overs) may be agreed in one session; in other cases, where there are new texts or national sensitivities, it can take several meetings. Council CFSP decisions require unanimity while Regulations based on a Commission proposal can be adopted by qualified majority – though in practice, it is very rare for Regulations to progress if RELEX Counsellors cannot reach consensus, as a reluctant unhappy Member State can simply block the following CFSP decision.

Once agreed by RELEX Counsellors, CFSP related texts are tabled in the Political and Security Committee (PSC) – chaired by a representative of the HR whose role in Article 38 TEU is to ensure monitoring of the CFSP. It is not subordinate to COREPER in CFSP matters.

---

96 This section is an updated version of King 2008, 11–13. Most of what King writes is quoted verbatim, however, because of the updating I have not used quotation marks. I am grateful to Esa Paasivirta for updating.

Both Common Positions and Regulations must then be approved by COREPER (the Permanent Representatives or ambassadors of the Member States), which is tasked with preparing all of Council's work and ensuring overall coherence of EU policy as well as the observance of legality, subsidiarity and provision of reasons.

Legal acts are often adopted at the first available meeting of the Council (that is, Ministers) – which may be a Competitiveness or Agriculture formation of the Council – rather than the Foreign Affairs Council (FAC) although sometimes either the timetable or political considerations will make the FAC the most appropriate choice. Lengthy discussions at PSC or COREPER on sanctions texts are relatively rare, but both these Committees and the Council itself frequently discuss overall policy towards a third country, which may include sanctions.

The Commission is generally empowered in Council regulations, in line with Article 291(2) TFEU, to give effect to listing (or de-listing) decisions of the UNSC and Council by amending annexes to regulations. This is not the rule for "EU autonomous" restrictive measures, where the Council retains implementing powers.

14. COHERENCE IN SANCTIONS POLICY

In this final section, for the sake of completeness, I say something very briefly about another type of EU "sanction" namely EU decisions to withdraw trade/aid benefits.[97] These withdrawals of privileges are not restrictive measures, however, they can be linked to them, and they can obviously have a similar pressurizing effect. Indeed, the more the EU trades with another state, import or export, the more potential there is for such trade measures to have an effect.[98]

The EU legal basis for measures involving suspensions/restrictions in trade and aid is different from restrictive measures. The adoption of commercial, development and association agreements, and so the suspension of these, or parts of them, fall under the TFEU. Article 207 provides for agreements to be made concerning commercial policy with third states by the Council on proposals by the Commission. Article 218 provides that the European Parliament must give its assent to association agreements, as well as other significant agreements. In addition, the Parliament has the right to be consulted on all other agreements, except for trade agreements concluded on the basis of Article 207.

The EU builds in "democracy" and "human rights" clauses as "essential elements" of its aid and trade agreements, particularly the Cotonou agreement.

---

97 See e.g. Bartels 2005.

98 See for EU sanctions Portela 2010.

Nonetheless, sanctions applied to WTO members must still comply with GATT and other WTO treaty rules.[99]

The purpose of the "essential elements" clause is to establish a reciprocal undertaking to respect human rights. This gives either party the lawful basis for suspending the treaty in whole or in part if either party considers that human rights/democracy are being breached. The Council can vote by qualified majority to partially suspend such a treaty, but unanimity is required for full suspension. The scope for unilateral suspension of aid is typically even wider than for trade. Aid agreements usually include other grounds for suspension, such as diversion of funds intended for one sector (e.g. education) to another sector. Particularly in times of armed conflict, precautionary suspensions are intended to avoid the risk of diversion of aid funds.

Much could be said about these subjects, but it will suffice to say that sanctions obviously have to be properly fitted into the EU's foreign policy as a whole and that the different decision-making procedures which exist for different parts of this foreign policy add to the coherence problems in the area.[100]

99 See e.g. Bartels 2007.

100 See e.g. Elsuwege 2010.

ON ASSESSING TARGETED SANCTIONS BLACKLISTS

Mikael Eriksson

1. INTRODUCTION

Targeted sanctions, and in particular those measures adopted against individuals on so-called blacklists, have increasingly come to be endorsed by the United Nations (UN) and the European Union (EU) as a novel way of exercising power over government decision-makers and non-state actors in the international system. This growing trend in the pursuit of justice, or as part of a contemporary "justice cascade" as one researcher has termed it, has also been noted by a number of sanctions scholars.[1] There is, however, a problem with the scholarship tasked with analysing the use of sanctions in that, scholars have not yet been able to articulate a methodological assessment approach that addresses some of the ontological problems sanctions theory faces. After all, a policy that is popular in use and has dramatic implications for governments and citizens across the globe requires analytical tools that can give sharp judgments on the impact the tool has in achieving the goals it is intended to achieve. The quest for appropriate assessment tools has also characterized they way in which the field of sanctions studies has developed. Yet, despite what could be argued to be severe shortcomings in well thought of sanctions assessment frames, scholars and journalistic accounts have a tendency to grade sanctions regimes either as highly effective or as failures (especially in the light of implementation problems in recent years, e.g. the negative human rights implications for targets subject to sanctions).[2] On what basis such judgments and verdicts take place is unclear. Recently a broadly-based consortium of sanctions scholars tasked itself to carefully design an approach that would try to live up to a standard of appropriate sanctions assessment. Whatever the good intentions in such a programme, there will always be a number of unsolvable and enduring problems attached to sanctions assessment programmes. This chapter will discuss some of

1 Cortright and Lopez 2000, Wallensteen and Staibano 2005, Biersteker and Eckert 2008, Portela 2010, Eriksson 2011, Charron 2011, Giumelli 2011, Carish and Ricard-Martin 2011.
2 Hufbauer et al. 1985, 1999.

these. Consequently, this chapter reflects upon the scientific challenges in assessing targeted sanctions "blacklists". More specifically, it seeks to offer a critical approach to how to think of the evaluation of the effectiveness of sanctions.

1.1. WHY STUDY SANCTIONS ASSESSMENT?

An important development that warrants an alternative reading of contemporary sanctions is that the shift to *targeted* sanctions in the 1990s (from earlier comprehensive sanctions) has come to pose new theoretical challenges to the way we study sanctions. Essentially new rules have "changed the game" of sanctions practice and therefore also how we should think of this tool.[3] This shift, I argue, also has to be reflected in the way we think about sanctions assessment. After all, decision-makers dealing with issues like armed conflicts and international crisis and those who implement targeted sanctions need good tools to evaluate their effectiveness and the type of impact.[4] Sanctions, one should not forget, is part of a tradition on economic warfare. Thus it needs the planning, operation and enforcement like that of a military operation. Not only do strong indicators and assessments provide data to increase target accuracy, they also down the line give the sender – especially if the policy is efficacious and successful – further, and much needed, legitimacy. Legitimacy is an important factor for any sanctioning body, as it will shape the utility of the tool as the "audience" perceives it. Moreover, evaluations of sanctions that provide significant correlations could also be used as "proof" to mobilise public opinion and to protect the sanctions tool from being challenged in the courts (in particular by helping to satisfy proportionality, due process, due diligence and other legal requirements).[5]

Finally, the reason for thinking critically about sanctions evaluation practices still have a tendency to contain analytical foundations elements that seldom match the environment in which a sanctions policy operates. In fact it many times skews reality. In effect, several assessments of sanctions may at times create more havoc than they are intended to show in its attempt to give a verdict about policy effectiveness. By this I mean that there is a common tendency in the field of sanctions research to go about evaluating sanctions regimes (e.g. EU or UN sanctions) empirically without defining and sorting out the relation of each object and subject with the others within the complex chain of adopting,

3 See also Eriksson 2011.

4 As noted for instance by former UN Secretary-General Kofi Annan (UN Press Release SG/SM/7360, 2000–04–17).

5 Three international processes on targeted sanctions have previously tasked themselves with giving recommendations with regard to targeted sanctions (the Interlaken Process, the Bonn-Berlin Process and the Stockholm Process).

implementing and terminating a sanctions regime policy. Consequently, I would like to emphasise in this chapter that the sanctions ontology should be sorted out before any methodology is applied.[6] In the end deciding on sanctions and the carrying out of the policy fully is a daunting task and needs to be taken seriously.

The rest of this chapter will provide a general introduction to targeted sanctions. The understanding of sanctions will thereafter be informed in part by a social constructivist approach to help pose critical questions can be asked of the sanctions study field, in particular with regard to the notion of causality. In the third and concluding part with sanctions assessment research will be discussed.

2. TARGETED SANCTIONS: AN OVERVIEW

Scholars have labelled the 1990s, when UN sanctions regimes the proliferated, the "Sanctions Decade".[7] The turn to this new practice is well summarised in the academic literature.[8] Below follows a brief overview of what sanctions are, why they have come to be developed as a policy option, and what general assumptions exist in the literature dealing with this policy.

2.1. WHAT ARE TARGETED SANCTIONS?

Targeted sanctions involve measures such as travel bans, financial sanctions, assets freeze measures, arms embargoes, specific trade sanctions, flight bans, admissions restrictions, diplomatic sanctions, and boycotts, as well as a number of specific measures applied on rough diamonds, timber, luxury goods, etc. These measures are adopted and meant to be implemented to deal with domestic and international crises, as well as armed conflicts.[9] From traditionally having been state- and society-oriented (i.e. "conventional" or "comprehensive"), sanctions are now targeted by means of blacklisting individuals (i.e. "entities"); groups involved in armed conflict or terrorism; and other states and entities posing a threat to peace and security or associated with international crimes/political violence/human rights abuse. Sanctions are adopted by different actors, either on a unilateral or on a multilateral basis. The most usual players are the United Nations Security Council (UNSC), the European Union, the African Union, the United States and the United Kingdom. Recently (in 2011) the Arab

6 For an introduction to the relationship between ontology and methodology, see Hall 2003.

7 Cortright and Lopez 2000.

8 Cortright and Lopez 2000, 2002a, 2002b, Doxey 1999, Tostensen and Bull 2002, Hufbauer et al. 2007, International Journal of the Canadian International Council vol. LXV, no.1. 2009/10, Eriksson 2011, Charron 2011.

9 Cortright and Lopez 2002, pp. 1–22.

League has also played a key role with regard to supporting sanctions, both its own and the UN's (e.g. on Libya 2011 and Syria 2012).

As indicated, the primary goals of targeted sanctions are mostly to promote democracy, stop human rights violations and the suppression of internal opposition, enforce peace agreements and prevent spoilers, assist in the pursuit of individuals for prosecution before regional and international courts, and ensure compliance with treaty obligations.[10] Secondary goals would concern the promotion of the sender's reputation domestically and internationally; and the maintenance of international norms and structures.[11] To these observations one could also add other sanctions objectives such as preventing and containing armed conflict, achieving compliance with international law, reversing the conflicting parties' military aggression, building support for military action, as a tool in negotiations, preventing the export of sensitive technologies, restoring democratically elected governments, limiting the spread of weapons, constraining international spoilers, and bringing suspected terrorists to justice.[12] Most recently, UN (and EU) targeted sanctions have been applied to actors involved in sex crimes in conflict-ridden contexts (e.g. the Democratic Republic of Congo).

There have been different definitions of sanctions over the years, but the sanctions field has been greatly shaped by Hufbauer et al.'s (1985) accounts of their understanding of economic sanctions. In their view, sanctions "... mean the deliberate government-inspired withdrawal or threat of withdrawal, of 'customary' trade or financial relations".[13] Later, Cortright and Lopez, having worked extensively in the field, have offered perhaps the clearest account of what targeted sanctions are: "In our definition, a smart sanctions policy is one that imposes coercive pressures on specific individuals and entities and that restricts selective products or activities, while minimizing unintended economic and social consequences for vulnerable populations and innocent bystanders".[14] The definition suggests both an instrumental and an actor-specific approach with ethical undertones. It also implies an 'efficacy' in that smart sanctions can achieve better results in a shorter time since they are more apt in effectively reaching goals and undercutting specific group support for the target government.[15] These definitions focus on what targeted sanctions *are*. However,

10 This is not to say that all states are liberal democracies. There are also a number of states and regional actors imposing sanctions. For example, the Arab League and the African Union are two newcomers to the sanctions policy world.

11 See Cameron 2008.

12 As noted by Gottemoeller: "Nevertheless, 'sanctions' may feel better than nothing: they are less feeble than scolding an ambassador and less bloody than sending in the marines. They provide a frisson of moral satisfaction" (2007, 100).

13 Hufbauer et al. 1985, p. 2.

14 Cortright and Lopez 2002b, p. 2.

15 See the discussion on travel bans by Kaempfer and Lowenberg 2003 and by Cosgrove 2005.

they neglect the process of imposing and implementing targeted sanctions. This can be defined as:

> "… a flexible and multivariate process embedded in a larger strategic context involving a sender and a target, where the decision-making, perception and interactions between these actors, during well-defined episodes in a sanctions regime, shape a non-violent political outcome impact".[16]

What lies beneath the use of targeted sanctions is the rationale of avoiding hurting those actors that are not responsible for the policies which the sender intends to change. Thus, the policy of targeted sanctions is a non-violent and ethical instrument. By introducing targeted sanctions upon carefully selected individuals and commodities, instead of entire countries and societies, the sender anticipates changing, steering or controlling the political behaviour of the target. This is done by hitting the political heart of the decision-making power, thereby reducing the political and economic capabilities of those blacklisted.[17] Rather than inflicting collective punishment and suffering, which was embedded in the rationale of comprehensive sanctions, targeted entities could be held accountable.[18] The ethical aspect of sanctions should on the other hand not suggest that it is less forceful. As noted, sanctions remains a tool for economic warfare.

2.2. TWENTY YEARS OF TARGETED SANCTIONS PRACTICE

In the mid-1990s, following the end of the Cold War, a growing norm against comprehensive sanctions began to take shape public opinion and informed scholarship. The debate was referred to as the "humanitarianism" debate. The criticism it involved was based on the vast examples of negative and unintended side effects of sanctions, which had increasingly become socially visible in countries such as Iraq, Haiti and Cuba.[19] The UN sanctions imposed on Iraq (August 1990–May 2003) would perhaps account for the greater part of this criticism.[20] Following the widespread criticism of Iraqi sanctions by various actors both inside and outside the UN, member states consequently began to look more seriously into ways in which to improve the sanctions tool.[21] In all,

16 Definition based on Eriksson 2011, p. 41.

17 Cortright, Lopez and Conroy 2000, p. 4.

18 A problem here is whether targets are listed as free agents under state protection or in their public capacity. The separation is not entirely clear in international law.

19 See Hawkins and Lloyd 2003, pp. 443–45.

20 A collection of "critical" voices are presented in Arnove 2003.

21 For instance, in response to the humanitarian impact of the comprehensive Iraq sanctions, the ambassadors of China, France, the Russian Federation, the UK and the US wrote to the

the turn to more intelligent and "smart" sanctions reflected a changing attitude of the UNSC.[22]

2.3. THE CLASSICAL PRINCIPLE OF SANCTIONS

The "general theory of sanctions" was introduced by Galtung in 1967.[23] Based on a case study of the situation in Rhodesia (now Zimbabwe) following the UN-imposed sanctions in 1965–79, Galtung defined sanctions as actions initiated by one or more international actors (the "senders") against one or more others (the "receivers") with either or both of two purposes: to punish the receivers by depriving them of some value and/or to make receivers comply with certain norms the senders deem important.[24] Galtung thereafter criticised the "naïve" assumptions of sanctions practice existing at the time, which expected external economic disruption, and the consequent economic and social hardship, to convert into domestic political pressure that would induce the incumbent regime of the target country to alter or modify its policies.[25]

Rather than the population affected redirecting the pain on to the regime, early studies showed that the regime was more likely to garner political support since it would be in a position to use domestic propaganda against the sender. This would also cause a "rally round the flag" effect. The rally effect is still seen in many ongoing sanctions regimes, for example, in contemporary Zimbabwe where the EU has inter alia blacklisted incumbent President Robert Mugabe for not holding free and fair elections in line with international standards. Notwithstanding the criticism by Galtung and others, the "economic pain to political gain" still appears to have some influence among practitioners. The implicit or explicit motivations for sanctions continue to factor in such elements such as "financial cost–benefit" calculations, the "costs of casualties", "political gains and losses", "trade-offs between future human rights gains and immediate violations", etc. But, as pointed out by Tostensen and Bull (2002) and other writers, the pain–gain principle cannot be simply applied. This is because even where both the target of sanctions and the targeter accept that the same economic/political costs apply, the target of sanctions may treat these costs and their relative weights differently.[26]

UN Security Council that sanctions "... should be directed to minimize unintended adverse side effects of sanctions on the most vulnerable segments of targeted countries" (S/1995/300).

22 Craven 2002, 44, and Chesterman and Pouligny 2003, p. 504.

23 Galtung 1967, p. 379.

24 *Ibid.*

25 *Ibid.*, p. 388.

26 Tostensen and Bull 2002, p. 375.

2.4. HISTORIC TURNS IN THE SANCTIONS LITERATURE

As Wallensteen (2000) has identified in his examination of sanctions scholarship, different waves of debates have turned and succeeded each other in the sanctions field over the 20th century.[27] From where he ends one could now also argue for yet another sanctions wave. Scholarship herein is marked by an increasing number of studies which make detailed and well operationalized examinations of targeted sanctions regimes and how various restrictive measures are both being adopted and implemented by different senders. There is also a question in the literature on the more general institutional responses to dealing with problems of implementation of sanctions (Sutterlin 2003). Charron (2011) has recently contributed to sanctions research by linking UN targeted sanctions to different types of conflicts. Charron finds that UN sanctions tend to be clustered around concern of armed conflicts, international norm-breaking states, and terrorism. This suggests that UN sanctions are not only a tool for conflict prevention and conflict management during war, as generally understood.

Based on rich empirical data, Giumelli finds that sanctions are imposed to coerce, to constrain and to signal.[28] Signalling is particularly important in sanctions practice he argues, because it does not only aim to achieve a direct material effect, but also a psychological impact. Eriksson suggests that signalling is constantly taking place between the sender of sanctions and the target, which can be observed in behaviour and in counter-reactions. The initiation and changing of Security Council sanctions (e.g. new sanctions lists, added targets, new commodities being targeted, etc.) are new signals to the target.[29] Moreover, sanctions research is increasingly becoming situated in broader strategic contexts, for example, with regard to the impact of targeted sanctions on civil war.[30] A number of evaluations have also been made with regard to specific sanctions measures, such as arms embargoes.[31]

The literature is also witnessing increasing intersections of political science and law, especially where security and strategy questions intersect with case law, human rights concerns and institutional practice. Notably, a number of both national and EU court challenges dealing with blacklisting of entities have attracted scholarly attention. For instance, where sanctions procedures have been unclear, blacklisted individuals, groups and companies have expressed numerous complaints about unclear listing and de-listing procedures.[32] Here one can distinguish a rather expansive research domain dealing with legal,

27 See also Wallensteen 1968, 2000.

28 Giumelli 2011, p. 33.

29 Eriksson 2011, p. 250.

30 Strandow 2006.

31 Luck 1999, Rydell 1999, Brzoska 2002, Knight 2004, Vines 2007, and Fruchart et al. 2007.

32 See for instance the *Kadi* case and the judgment of the European Court of Justice on 3 September 2008.

institutional and human rights practices of targeted sanctions;[33] studies evaluating aspects of the UN Security Council's practices (e.g. institutional procedures of Sanctions Committees),[34] and the general applicability of international law in these circumstances;[35] the implementation of counter-terrorism measures (closely aligned with targeted sanctions);[36] and more general institutional responses to dealing with problems of implementation.[37] Finally, an increasing number of studies have also begun examining region-specific actors - other institutions such as the European Union, the African Union, etc. - or assessing particular sanctions regimes.[38]

In sum, then, the continued interest in *assessing* sanctions - i.e. factors determining the impact they are able to achieve once adopted and implemented under different sanctions regimes - is characteristic of recent studies on sanctions. Below follows a brief discussion on some of the notions on which this interest rests.

2.5. THE INTEREST IN SANCTIONS ASSESSMENT

As mentioned, much of contemporary sanctions literature has been greatly influenced by the work of Hufbauer et al. (1990). These scholars undertook one of the most serious efforts to evaluate existing sanctions regimes in the early 1990s (though their focus was not on targeted sanctions). Their methodology and approach have set high standards on thinking on sanctions efficacy. Their assessment approach and way of thinking about sanctions also pose a number of problems and challenges with regard to how to understand sanctions, and in particular with regard to the "measurement" of efficacy. These critiques have also been well covered in different studies (e.g. Pape 1998). The first problem is that sanctions assessment studies like the one presented by Hufbauer et al. (1990) are too static and their definition of sanctions too narrow. Jentleson (2000) summarised these problems by referring to the problem of defining what economic sanctions encompass, the different roles sanctions and sanctions

33 Eriksson 2009, Gowlland-Debbas 2001, Cameron 2003a, 2003b, 2008, Andersson and Cameron 2003, Geiss 2005, Biersteker and Eckert 2006, 2008, Dewulf and Pacuée 2006, Lavranos 2006, 2007, Fassbender 2006, Fitzgerald 2007, Foot 2007, Shagabutdinova and Berejikian 2007, Marty 2007, Almqvist 2008, Conte 2008, Porretto 2008, and Rosand, Millar and Ipe 2008.

34 Farral and Rubestein 2009, pp. 191–214.

35 Rosand 2004, Bianchi 2007, Eeckhout 2007, Farrall 2007, Flynn 2007, Franck, Chesterman and Malone 2007, ch. 7, Chesterman 2008 and Stenhammar 2008.

36 Jimeno-Bulnes 2004, Gregory 2005, Lopez et al. 2006, Millar and Rosand 2006, Bures 2006, Stiles and Thayne 2006, Biersteker and Eckert 2007, Cortright and Lopez 2007 and Rackow and Stegmiller 2007.

37 Sutterlind 2003, Hurd 2007 and Allen 2008.

38 Hazelzet 2001, Anthony 2002; de Vries 2002, Wallensteen, Eriksson and Staibano 2004, 2005, Rackow and Stegmiller 2007; and Portela 2010, Eriksson 2010.

objectives can have, the common problem of a selection bias, the reliability and validity problems that a policy outcome is confronted with, the problems of attributing causality, the standard for success rate, etc.[39] Today the sanctions scholarship have taken not of many of these challenges though some of them will continue to haunt sanctions evaluation attempts.[40]

The idea and tradition of assessing the efficacy of sanctions by means of ranking continues in studies on targeted sanctions as well. However, targeted sanctions have only been imposed for about two decades, and this relatively short period has not yet allowed for much systematic investigation. Today only a few scholarly attempts have yet been made to observe the efficacy of targeted sanctions more systematically. For instance, as Hufbauer et al. (2007) concluded, "... the evidence seems to suggest that sanctions targeted very narrowly against rogue regimes and their leaders can serve useful symbolic purposes but may not be adequate to achieve coercive goals, such as regime change".[41] A judgment like this is interwoven to a particular assessment logic that may not do justice to all aspects of a sanctions regime that shape a particular policy outcome.

It should be recognised that the search for assessing effectiveness has been, at least sometimes, bound up with a desire also to *promote* sanctions as a non-violent instrument of foreign policy. But a more objective motivation behind better methods of assessment is the old idea of "science speaking truth to power". Scientific assessment will give decision-makers the necessary tools for further refinement and implementation. Yet what seems more important – rather than seeking definite conclusions or explanations of the efficacy of sanctions in this realm – is to demonstrate *how* and *why* sanctions have worked as they have. To do this, we need to take a different and more critical reading of the theoretical assumptions on which sanctions work. Reference to social constructivist thinking may be helpful here.

Since the early 1990s social constructivism has been at the forefront of pointing out inconsistencies, flaws, and the biases of erroneously created models and theories seeking to explain the world through the lens of a single

39 Jentleson 2000, p. 126.

40 A main problem with arriving at patterns of success and failure, in the tradition of Hufbauer et al. 1990, is the use of numerical scoring systems that grade the efficacy of sanctions. One of the main methodological problems here is, the subjectivity of the individual coder when evaluating a sanctions regime or a sanctions "case", something which poses a challenge to assigning success and failure to sanctions regimes. This is not news in any sense for the social sciences, but it needs to be kept in mind when drawing policy conclusions. The point about the dangers of subjectivity is also pointed out by Pape in his response to Elliott's defence of the study by Hufbauer et al.: "Optimism and pessimism are relative concepts; whether one should be considered optimistic about a certain policy instrument depends in part on how one's views compare with the judgments of others" (Pape 1998 p. 67). Their assessment study is also problematic for many other reasons, not least because of selection bias, relational problems (i.e. effectiveness as compared to what?), and the lack of consideration of alternative goals other than those *officially* stated in the sanctions regime Hufbauer, Schott, and Elliott 1990, p. 41.

41 Hufbauer et al. 2007, p. 133.

paradigm.[42] Partly this has been done by revisiting many of the assumptions on which classical International Relations (IR) paradigms rest, e.g. by contextualising and re-conceptualising the assumptions in situations where they are misleading or problematic. Constructivism as an entry approach typically critically corrects norms and perceptions that are sometimes taken for granted (classically in IR paradigms). Rather than being a typical paradigm itself, the approach is typically considered a meta-theory more about the foundations of science and ontology than about methodological applications per se.

2.6. AN ALTERNATIVE READING ON THE PRACTICE OF TARGETED SANCTIONS

To demarcate social constructivism – which in its entirety encompasses a wide spectrum of understandings of, and approaches to dealing with, social reality – we will apply some of the ideas advanced by Kratochwil, who represents a more critical branch of this theory orientation.

Kratochwil's general approach to tackling social phenomena, including policies like liberal institutions' and politically organised entities' use of sanctions to project power, goes beyond typical framework paradigms. Instead his approach calls for a critical examination of the particular problem at hand, by addressing the normative and conceptual basis that "permits" the problem under study to occur. Thus, from a critical constructivist approach, studying a policy like targeted sanctions more broadly without a clear ontological vindication is problematic. This is too often the case in sanctions studies, where those studying sanctions rely on preconceived understandings, assumptions or traditions regarding reality without explaining how these constitutive elements hang together. Usually, the material studied is very empirically oriented without posing relevant theoretical questions.

A social constructivist understanding of sanctions is likely to deem a targeted sanctions policy to be an archetypical policy instrument typically enforced in a blunt and rudimentary way, much detached from the overarching goal it is meant to tackle. This in part is due to the fact that the social reality is simply too complex for one single policy to address it. In fact, the complexity of subjective and contextual factors simply does not allow for a mechanically prescribed solution to socially identified problems as several sanctions assessment studies seem to assume. Rather than understanding how sanctions work by simply assuming how they would fit a particular logic (e.g. on the basis of the structural conditions of an anarchic world), and then explaining how such a policy would work out in a larger number of cases, a social constructivist viewpoint would

42 Social constructivism has different theoretical frameworks to it. See e.g. Wendt 1999, Ruggie 1998 and Katzenstein 1996.

probably go about trying to understand sanctions by questioning and critically examining some of the assumptions on which the policy rests (especially regarding any claimed notions of causality between the adoption of the sanctions policy and its outcome). By doing so, one cannot but come to the conclusion that the social reality in which a sanctions policy operates is both too complex to draw inferences from and too difficult to engage with. This is particularly clear with regard to sanctions assessment efforts where there has been a tendency to accept the social reality without questioning the epistemological problems that exist when trying to grasp this in single policy assessment. For example, a number of studies, as noted above, attempt to prove average effects of the policy by assigning "success" and "failure" despite the fact that the object under study is seldom homogeneous or able to be held constant. After all, context time-periods, targets and issues are likely to change both within and in between sanctions regimes.[43] Thus, rather than simply accepting the policy of targeting and its current practical application, the scholar needs first to present the subordinate rules that shape the sanctions policy and how these "hang together" (e.g. perceptions of the instrument by the senders and targets involved, access to resources to maintain and evade sanctions, institutional decision-making complexity, the role of norms, culture, tradition and differences in sanctions regime contexts, etc.). Moreover, norms and rules are particularly important in this regard, because they explain social interaction ("the rule-governed character of human action").[44]

A good way to illustrate the argument above, and ways to address the ontology of targeted sanctions, is to refer to the analogy of the constitutive vs. the regulative rules in a game of chess.[45] The constitutive rules signify the rules of the game, while the regulative rules specify independent rules such as interpersonal conduct, thereby governing actions and behaviour.[46] Concretely, this could suggest that the instrument is constituted and defined by, on the one hand, legal texts, such as the UN Charter and the European Council/ Commission guidelines, but also regulative rules such as traditions of application and traditions of evocations (when to apply, how to apply, and for what and for whom, i.e. social rules). These then form the basis for the parameters of sanctions policy ontology. Typically, studies on sanctions stop at only examining the formal constitutive rules, which do not necessarily encapsulate aspects that are equally important. For that reason, before looking at particular forms of behaviour or structures, scholarly work examining the sanctions instrument needs also to identify what particular norms underlie those forms of behaviour and structures, and how context-specific norms shape such rules guiding human

43 Dashti-Gibson, Davis, Radcliff 1997.
44 Kratochwil 1989, pp. 10–12.
45 See e.g. Searle 1969.
46 Searle 1995.

action. There is a need to understand not only regulative rules along the lines traditional sanctions work, but also constitutive rules, i.e. the rules that decide the lines along which traditional sanctions work and that "make sense" of the conditions that enable a particular social action.[47]

In essence, enforcing sanctions is a complex task as it involves both constitutive and regulative principles when adopting and enforcing sanctions. In effect, sanctions assessment many times neglects factors such as causality or how political intentionality plays out among different elements to a sanctions regime. This problem gets apparent in reductionist assessment attempts where sanctions are abridged to static cases, where different formal and informal policy objectives are amalgamated with different levels of analysis, and where important contextual aspects including developments over time and space may change. We can add the implications of negative side effects, unintended consequences and random events.

3. ENDURING CHALLENGES TO SANCTIONS ASSESSMENTS EFFORTS

The field of targeted sanctions invites a multitude of methodological approaches to studying sanctions. Hence, an assessment of the role and impact of targeted sanctions can be done in many different ways. In fact, the diversity is reflected in the contemporary literature of targeted sanctions, which includes both quantitative and qualitative studies. Below I will discuss some of the recurrent and enduring challenges to any sanctions assessment: intentionality, collective action problems, unpredictability, the "thief and police pastime", learning, the technical and functionalist assumption, the role of symbolic and non-symbolic elements in targeting, the role of compartmentalisation and perceptions of sanctions, the before-and-after conundrum, and finally the problem that sanctions generally tend to pursue liberal goals by illiberal means.[48]

3.1. INTENTIONALITY

Intentionality, as is often assumed in sanctions assessment studies, presupposes that a particular policy action will lead to a particular outcome. It conventionally takes for granted that sanctions are imposed with the intention of achieving a particular outcome and the decision to impose them is taken on the assumption that there is a relational link between a particular policy action and a particular

47 Kratochwil and Ruggie 1986 have called these the inter-subjective aspects of action.

48 These factors cause problems not only for specific sanctions assessment efforts, but also for practitioners operating sanctions policies along some of these trajectories.

outcome. However, given that targets are moving subjects, and that perception constitutes an important element in the interaction between the sender and the target, the realisation of the intention, for example, a change of political behaviour of a target requires a behavioural change that is not likely to follow a straight, logical or coherent path.[49] Different actors along the policy and implementation chain have different agendas, preferences, interests and reasons for maintaining sanctions. Taken together these are not likely to generate a straightforward and linear achievement of the intention. Added to this there may be unintended consequences and negative side effects that may have unexpected implications. Although one should not go so far as to reject causality, one should be very sceptical about the way it is attributed in several sanctions assessments.

3.2. COLLECTIVE ACTION AND FREE-RIDER PROBLEMS

Sanctions entail a large-scale collective action problem, both for the sender and for the neighbours of a targeted state.[50] This problem is rarely treated as part of the complex sanctions assessment schemes. On the one hand, there is the problem of how to engage member states of a collective security institution, like the EU and the UN, in a joint strategy against a common target so that the impact of sanctions may be as great as possible. The reason for this is that, while an institution has to unite behind one policy agenda, each member state has its own interest based on its foreign policy trajectory. On the other hand, there is a problem for the governments neighbouring a state where blacklisted targets are located. Hence how can one engage these neighbours to implement sanctions in such a way that they do not place their own national interests first? A case where this dilemma played out occurred in South Africa, over a policy regarding Zimbabwe in a context of EU targeted sanctions on the Mugabe government. How should a sender act in order to convince a state that is a neighbour of a target entity that its national foreign policy interest should be placed second to, let us say, an EU institutional policy? The political interests of the neighbouring states may go against the will of the sender, and the challenges become even more profound if there are economic interests in violating or working against sanctions. Economic interests, such as timber, oil or diamond smuggling, encourage deviant behaviour and cheating both among senders and among targets, causing a free-rider problem (e.g. one state may benefit from maintaining

---

49 A major point demonstrated in Eriksson 2011.

50 This refer to a situation in which every actor in a given group has a choice between two alternatives and where, if everybody concerned chooses the alternative act that is individualistically, the outcome will be worse for everyone involved, in their own estimation, than it would be if they were all to choose the other alternative. Put differently, multiple actors would all benefit from a certain action, which has an associated cost making it unlikely that any one can or will undertake and solve it alone. See for example Sandler 1992.

an embargo, the other may benefit from smuggling).[51] Not only do these problems pose a considerable challenge to any sanctions practitioner, but they also pose a conundrum for any serious attempt to measure the efficacy of sanctions.

3.3. UNPREDICTABILITY

The sender has generally, either alone or in combination with other actors, to manage many different and unpredictable variables at the same time when implementing sanctions. Assessment studies will always have a hard time accounting for this unpredictable environment. For example, over time targets may come and go, the dynamics between a sender and the target may change, and new and old issues may arise that affect the goals of the sender. This suggests that sanctions are applied in a very unpredictable environment that is far from static and consequentially requires very flexible handling in order to stay tuned to the developments that triggered the policy in the first place. Yet there are signs indicating that the international community is using a static approach to employing sanctions.[52] By a static approach I mean that the sender typically responds mechanically, following a predetermined institutional decision-making framework, rather than pre-empting the actions of a target.[53] The formal goals and intentions behind sanctions resolutions tend to guide sanctions assessments, but changing goals and changes in the policy environment shaping the outcome of sanctions will create havoc for the assessment of sanctions. A number of sanctions assessment studies nonetheless also take a static approach.[54]

3.4. THE THIEF-AND-POLICE PASTIME

Sanctions regimes, including the implementation, function in effect like a *thief-and-police* game. The sender imposes a policy principle and expects a behavioural

---

51 This has been confirmed in various contexts, not least through the sanctions programme against Iraq, where oil smuggling undermined the efficacy of sanctions.

52 For example, little effort is usually invested in follow-up and counter-target behaviour over time.

53 For example, EU sanctions guidelines provide suggestions on how EU Common Positions should be worded. Such provisions provide for language harmony across various sanctions regimes. However, the drawback with this is that common definitions and language style do more to serve the design of a sanctions policy than to address the actual problem on the ground in the target country (which changes from day to day).

54 In Eriksson 2011 an idea was proposed to investigate sanctions regimes in a more dynamic way that would capture policy changes. Hence the role of episodes within a case was introduced. The use of episodes within a case had not been tried in the more classical assessment studies presented by Cortright and Lopez or Hufbauer etc.

change. The target usually responds by evading or simply ignoring the sender. Senders, however, have usually taken a static policy decision and therefore do not react to the target's behaviour, or do not react in a timely manner. Hence, this game runs contrary to what could be an effective policy practice given that the political environment changes from one day to another (e.g. parties, interests, resources, etc.). Sanctions assessments simply tend to ignore that blacklisted actors are, or are entities owned by, thinking and acting entities and not factors in a fixed sender–target relationship. The more things that are made subject to sanctions, the more things there are to cheat about, and the less use a static model will be. The question then is how to get away from the current assumption of a static situation and respond more actively to events on the ground. One way to do this is to examine and acknowledge the problems of institutional bureaucracy, as will be examined in the next section.

It seems necessary to clarify what kind of social processes really take place (i.e. between the sender and the target; amongst the targets; between the targets and their domestic opponents; between the sender and the target's neighbours; etc.).[55] To get a fairer and more realistic understanding of targeted sanctions, one must disentangle the dynamics of these crucial relationships, not least within well-defined and disaggregated periods of time, throughout the existence of sanctions regime, since the political dynamics in which a policy is set will change over time. Related to this, then, is the need to have the sanctions ontology sorted out before the methodology is applied.

3.5. ERUDITION

Once targeted sanctions have been imposed, the target is expected to learn and become aware of the amount of resources that the sender has vested in ensuring that the objectives of sanctions can be achieved. For example, the target will learn what resources and political will the sender has at its disposal to ensure that proper action is taken. The longer the time that passes after the adoption of targeted sanctions, the more likely it is that the target will be able to get this information and use, if it is able to do so, it against the sender (for instance, for evasion purposes). Thus, the target can easily learn whether or not the sender is really only "all talk" or actually "walking the walk" with its endorsed sanctions policy. For example, it could try to find out if the sender is tracking money in order to ensure a proper assets freeze, or seeking to stop entities or people at the borders in order to enforce a travel ban. Few assessment studies take this learning factor into account. What makes sanctions assessment study problematic in this regard is that both the target and the sender can be

55 By social processes I mean here different kinds of factors, actors, norms, narratives, contexts, issues, etc. that exist and interact with one another in a given sanctions regime.

"disaggregated" and that different parts of these disaggregations can learn in different ways, at different speeds. In particular, the different actors forming the sender (i.e. states and components of international organisations) learn and modify their perception of the target, leading to a vibrant, reciprocal dynamic that shapes a sanctions outcome in a non-linear way.

3.6. THE TECHNICAL AND FUNCTIONALIST APPROACH TO SOCIAL DILEMMAS

There is a tendency in the sanctions assessment literature to overstate the potential of the technical or functionalist element of sanctions practice to solve universal social problems facing peace and security.[56] Baldwin notes, for instance, that part of the sanctions literature is typically overwhelmed with conventional-wisdom statements of what traditional forms of sanctions can and cannot do.[57] Consider for instance claims or conclusions that economic measures are more likely to succeed in inducing policy changes than non-economic measures[58] or (as in the case of EU sanctions) that targets are more likely to respond positively when the EU's sanctions position is shared by other states.[59] The question is how one could reach such conclusions given the limited data that exist with regard to the many variables that are likely to play into the dynamics of a sanctions regime.[60] In fact there seems to be a general perception of *social* problems as being *technical* problems and that the way to solve these is by providing a "technical solution". For example, lists of targets for sanctions are currently being designed to provide accurate identifiers such as names and personal numbers so that these can be screened more precisely by financial institutions. This technical accuracy will make an assets freeze more effective. In this vein societal problems are tackled as problems of ignorance, implying that the more *technically* informed the policy, the better the solutions to the problems faced become. A policy like targeted sanctions is, within this paradigm, a technically engineered solution to a social deficiency (e.g. the potential for the outbreak of armed conflict). Yet, rather than starting at this end, one could instead consider the situation as a social problem; does the target pose a threat to the sender at all? If so, can the sender change or redefine its own interests or

---

56 Tostensen and Bull 2002 p. 385.

57 Baldwin 1985, pp. 55–58.

58 Portela 2008, p. 260.

59 Ibid., p. 263.

60 A similar question is also raised by Tostensen and Bull 2002: "Despite the formidable methodological challenges, some academics claim that having analyzed a large number of sanctions episodes ex post facto, fairly robust generalizations can be made about the circumstances under which sanctions are likely to be effective. In turn, it is argued, these insights can be used prescriptively when new sanctions regimes are to be launched. We doubt whether this optimism is well founded." 2002, p. 395.

values so that the threat is reduced or disappears? Much like the scientist speaking truth to power, this view reflects a naturalist understanding of reality, in which political decision-makers should rely on technical expertise and scientifically proven solutions. While technical solutions can sometimes solve these social problems, social solutions are usually better able to solve them.

As a general social constructivist position would suggest though that the problem with a naturalistic and technocratic approach to social problems is that it simply lose more touch with the underlying processes enabling the very problems, than what it seeks to address. A common deficiency in such an approach is a lack of knowledge of the local political dynamics in the target state, and the overuse of universal prescriptions while maintaining an over-confidence in western models as the best practices for problem solving. Putting it differently, it is as if the solutions were looking for the problems instead of being tailored to the difficulties they encounter. Or, as Kratochwil (2007) characterises it, technological responses are likely to draw our attention away from addressing real political issues. In fact, by applying organisational solutions to problems, one is likely to neglect local circumstances that had no relationship with the receiver's organisational arrangement.[61] While local circumstances (e.g. ethnic structures, historical power structures, cultural identities, which may well have considerable impact on target behaviour and sender perceptions, etc.) are sometimes well known, they are too refined and usually too complicated to be integrated into a sanctions strategy.

3.7. SYMBOLIC AND NON-SYMBOLIC REFERENCE OBJECTS

A general epistemological problem in the field of sanctions research is that we are dealing with social and not material phenomena. Although the policy of targeted sanctions generally refers to physical components, such as "infrastructure", "secure borders", "financial operators", "customs", "assets", "arms", "timber", "conflict diamonds", etc., these are merely material factors. After all, material objects targeted by sanctions, like rough diamonds, have per se no meaning without a relationship to other objects or material phenomena, or to their user (which gives the object meaning), at least if one defines "object" on the basis of a set of relationships. It is the subjects using the specific blacklisted objects (e.g. the diamond dealer, the customs official, the arms broker, etc.) and the interactions occurring here that give these objects a meaning. Hence, when sanctions are assessed it is often the social processes that gave the objects meaning that need careful consideration. If we accept this view, we could also admit that the crucial parts of a sanctions implementation chain are not

61 Kratochwil 2007, p. 42.

necessarily the material components themselves but the relationships between them. Consequently, it is not the number and type of sanctions instruments that matters, but how they are dealt with and by which norms (among both senders and targets, and in the relations between them). In effect, then, there is little material capabilities to "measure" when trying to understand or assess the role of these immaterial components. For example, the quantity of assets frozen can therefore not be an indicator of the efficacy of sanctions[62], any more than a quantity of detected illegal timber can indicate the extent of target evasion.[63] On the contrary it is perhaps better to try to focus on the kind of action and counteraction that take place between the sender and the target and to try to understand what impact this has in reference to the overall crisis. This relational understanding is seldom captured in conventional assessment studies.

3.8. COMPARTMENTALISATION AND PERCEPTIONS

There is a tendency in parts of the sanctions assessment literature to focus exclusively on the sanctions instrument per se when examining its efficacy without looking at some important background processes that may shape outcome. This is problematic because the nature of the targeted sanctions policy is compartmentalised in the sense that there are different links in the complex chain of deciding, implementing and sustaining a targeted sanctions policy. For example, complex interaction (i.e. the process) that takes place between the sender and the targets (decision structures, response structures, persecution, conceptualisations, etc.).[64] Also related to this is the issue of the perceptions of sanctions by sanctions practitioners.

Because assessment studies are mainly dealing with individuals and groups, one needs to analyse and account for the engaged actors' perceptions of the sanctions (i.e. the sender vis-à-vis the target and the perception of the target *vis-à-vis* the sender). Perception is important because it shapes the attitude and behaviour of the actors, underlying any explanation of the interaction that takes place within a sanctions regime. It is also important because it helps detach the analytical approach from an objective "outside" understanding from the target's point of view. Yet these cognitive aspects are mostly absent from much of the scholarly literature on sanctions, hence the problem of verifying an objective

62 For example, the question of sanctions efficacy was investigated by the House of Lords (UK) and the amount of assets frozen was interpreted as a measurement of success. See Impact of Economic Sanctions: Evidence, 2007.

63 The target's view, position, needs, and environment, etc. would also have to be taken into account.

64 It is often said about weapons that it is not the weapons that kill people but the humans using them. The same analogy can be made about sanctions: it is not sanctions that instigate coercion, but the decision-makers deciding to use them.

reality through measuring or scoring. Instead we need to apply socially constructed concepts and value assignments, and acknowledge that an "objective" reality can more easily be constructed through inter-subjective understanding; and, given that we are dealing with individuals, it becomes imperative to take into account the role of the subject's conceptualisation of his or her own situation and of sanctions. Seeking to understand targeted sanctions from the point of view of the subject will also help explain their impact and efficacy.

Moreover, by examining the role perception plays amongst the actors involved in decision-making, one can identify the particular narratives (i.e. constructed understanding of how targeted sanctions are expected to work) that exist throughout the sanctions decision and implementation chain (e.g. within and across sanctions instruments, actors, decision-makers and institutions, etc.). For example, if members at the UN Security Council (e.g. diplomats, Secretariat staff, etc.) have certain perceptions and expectations regarding targeted sanctions, and they are different from those of the practitioners (e.g. banking regulators, customs officials etc.) or the targets, how do these expectations meet, and how does this affect the possible impact of sanctions?

3.9. THE BEFORE AND AFTER CONUNDRUM

A swift response is often necessary to address a crisis before it unfolds further, and the adoption and implementation of targeted sanctions can address this need. It is rarely acknowledged in sanctions assessment studies that two distinct political dynamics are likely to shape the impact of the sanctions outcome in a substantial way. On the one hand, there are the underlying dynamics *prior* to the enforcement of the policy, and on the other the dynamic between the sender and the target *after* a sanctions policy has been imposed.

In the period prior to the adoption of a targeted sanction, there is a moment at which the sender (i.e. the actors making up the sender body) deliberates over the possibility of imposing sanctions measures. The potential sender is still undecided as to whether to move the crisis issue one step up the security ladder. This moment is usually characterised by uncertainty, both for the potential sender and for the target(s). Consider for instance the number of political questions which collective bodies like the UN and the EU have to decide upon (and later forge a coalition around) before being able to implement the policy: which states are sanctions-prone (or positive), and which states are sanctions-resistant (or sceptic)? Will the negotiated outcome regarding a joint sanctions position be easy or difficult to achieve amongst the policy coalition partners? Do particular interests drive some of the sanctions-participating states? What options and measures do the implementers have at their disposal, and who should bear their cost? How do the domestic constituencies of the sanctioning actors view this policy (e.g. lobby groups, corporate and public interests)? If sanctions were to be adopted, how would these measures best destroy the target's honour and credibility, and how would this affect the sender? These and many other uncertainties generate pressure on the sender as well as the target. Meanwhile, pressure is also generated because of the uncertainty surrounding the potential target's reactions; will it comply, act, ignore, stall, negotiate with the potential sender, or negotiate with the domestic opponent? Thus, for both the sender and the target, the situation before sanctions are put into place is an important object of study in its own right.

A related problem is that there is a dynamic that takes place once the sanctions have been enacted and implemented. Here, the sender and the target have formed their political standpoints, and have chosen what behaviour and positions to take vis-à-vis each other. For example, the sender may at this point have moved from passing a "judgment" to imposing its own "verdict" and "punishment" on the target. This verdict is also translated to a policy practice. However, once the decision has been taken to establish a sanctions regime and to implement this practice, maintenance of sanctions becomes a goal in and of itself. Yet, in this post-decision phase, the policy-goal is likely to become problematic for all parties concerned, since the formally stated objective of the sanctions regime typically refers to a situation already having taken place, and thereby implicitly ask a target to "undo" his or her previous behaviour (e.g. sanctions are imposed for a failure to comply or for not having demonstrated a particular behaviour). Hence, several sanctions regimes have stated goals that are unrealistic or unachievable before they are even implemented. For example, there are sanctions regimes imposed with references to government killing peaceful demonstrators. Sanctions are then imposed as a punishment for such acts, yet there is no way the sanctioned entity can undo this particular action, and so be delisted. De-listing can only take place by a political decision by the sender to forgive and forget, or accept something less, e.g. an undertaking to appoint a national or international inquiry.

What sanctions research often fails to address is the problem the practitioner faces once having adopted a sanctions policy against a target. The sender is the only one in a position to lift the sanctions measures at the same times as backing down from sanctions is going to be difficult to justify to public opinion. In conclusion on this point, it is difficult to see how these points relate back to the issue of what the sender is really likely to achieve by evoking and implementing sanctions.

3.10. LIBERAL GOALS BUT ILLIBERAL MEANS

As noted, the turn to targeted sanctions from comprehensive sanctions was an ethical move by members of the international community, notably the UN Security Council. It was ethical because it sought to minimise the negative side effects of comprehensive sanctions. Formally, assessment studies tend to assess to what degree a sender has achieved a particular stated sanctions goal. Since the UN Charter builds on a liberal idea, the goal of any UN practice needs to be assessed according to a liberal institutionalist element. However, as multilateral bodies tend to be dominated by veto power and by strong-state interests, sanctions are often a construct based on compromise or sometimes formed on the basis of illiberal standards. For example, sometimes the goal of the sanctions regime is to prevent or deter. Sanctions are therefore implemented without little or no regard to legal safeguards which may be applicable under international law in favour of the entities that are being subjected to coercion (as there is often an element of surprise attached to the policy). As dealt with in more detail in other chapters of this book, lack of evidence, lack of standards, and lack of transparency (e.g. non-disclosure of evidence with regard to blacklisted entities) is an illiberal way to carry out a policy. Moreover there is a lack of a democratic element, as decisions to adopt sanctions are generally transferred to governments and foreign ministries (diplomats) and not made by vote of the members of democratic parliaments. Sanctions also contain illiberal elements as de-listing so far has been legally unsafe (no due process, no review process, no disclosure, etc.). Hence sanctions assessment studies are plagued by the conflict that exists by virtue of the fact the standards against which formal sanctions goals are assessed are liberal but the means that are pursued to attain the particular goals may be illiberal. This internalised conflict is also likely to play into any sanctions outcome as it forms part of senders', targets' and audiences' views of the policy. For example, there are ample documented statements by blacklisted entities that illustrate a perceived unfairness of the targeted sanctions imposed on them.[65]

3.11. SUMMARY

Targeted sanctions could be said to be currently conceived and practised in the same way as most social policies which seek to solve social problems on the basis of scientific arguments. While it may seem natural to prove the usefulness of targeted sanctions by relying on statistical studies, to demonstrate effectiveness, successes and failures, this is mostly a misapprehension; such an understanding would call for objective truths – something that social science seldom can provide, especially if we accept that causality does not exist in social science in the same way as in natural science.[66] This point has given rise to one of the most frequent debates in the sanctions field.[67] Many times, statistical studies of sanctions miss the individual context and dynamics of each case not least with regard to complex

65 Eriksson 2011.

66 Provided that natural science is better able to prove objective "truths".

67 Note for example the exchange on the matter between Baldwin and Pape (Baldwin and Pape 1998) and Pape and Hufbauer (Pape 1997).

background variables, the dynamic between the sender and target, etc.[68] Those relying on a statistical approach risk falling down here. Rather than asking if sanctions are useful, or whether they can accomplish their projected goals, statistical correlations merely serve to illustrate aspects of a problem rather than evaluating them in any other sense. No case study is likely to base an assessment on what the decision-maker *hoped* to achieve at the outset because there exist multiple goals that change over time within a particular sanctions regime.

Segments of the social science community seem to legitimise their claims and findings as exact sciences through explanations and predictions. However, these explanations and predictions are problematic once they are transferred to politicians, who quite commonly use them as a way of legitimising their own policies. A positive development is that governments and international institutions are becoming more transparent and open to the scientific community when presenting their case. Nevertheless, studies so far seldom acknowledge the difficulties and problems these governments and international institutions encounter in this regard.

4. FINAL REFLECTIONS

Part of acquiring a better understanding of targeted sanctions and the impact they can achieve is to be clearer regarding ontology. This means an ontology that helps us better define the nature of the actors, their relationships, and their perceptions and what enables them. In this chapter, therefore, I have tried to illustrate what aspects such a rethinking would involve. The call for a reconsideration of ontology followed the shift in both practice and theoretical rationale when comprehensive sanctions were replaced with the use of targeted sanctions. The field of sanctions assessment would benefit from critical questioning of existing assumptions.

While traditional IR paradigms simply proved too weak in explaining how to go about understanding sanctions ontology, a turn to critical constructivism and its emphasis on ontology instead of methodology was suggested. This approach was then used to introduce a set of problem areas of contemporary thinking on sanctions.

Following this, a discussion was presented on the role of causality and the need for clarity and for the adoption of a dynamic and non-linear approach to the impact of sanctions. As concluded, we should remain sceptical about the oversimplification of sanctions assessment that is often found in sanctions assessment studies. It is simply not as easy to infer from a policy adoption/implementation process that targeted sanctions are linear. On the contrary, targeted sanctions – given the many actors, the fixed processes, and the norms

68 Hufbauer et al. 1990 and 3rd edition 2007.

and processes that take place – seems to be anything but non-linear. This chapter has also looked at a number of common assumptions made in the literature. Several of these assumptions seem neither to be rooted in a particular ontology or articulated in such a way that it better render how it works in reality.

In addition to noting the absence of reifications underlying assumptions when assessing targeted sanctions, a discussion was also presented on alternative ways of understanding why certain assumptions about, and practices concerning, targeted sanctions exist. This was done partly by discussing how targeted sanctions fit into a broader understanding of science and practice.

What does this examination then tell us? Predictions are ruled out as a methodological option, both since the scope and focus of this research are too complex and because the social reality does not lend itself for observations in such a traditional way. What is more important is perhaps not to seek definite conclusions about or explanations of the efficacy of sanctions but rather to *illustrate* how and why an alternative ontological reading could form a better way to study the complexities of targeting. This point of departure follows the suggestion of Kratochwil (2007): "The issue is not a test versus non-test but what 'can count' as a test or provide sufficient evidence to establish a proposition (or to justify a particular judgment) at least presumptively".[69] Instead a middle ground was provided here, suggesting that sanctions policies are far too complex measures to assess, and therefore offering only *illustrations* of this intricacy, for example, what implications this has for the general approach of assessing the impact on a target. These illustrations are also intended to make informed empirical comments that will contribute to a broader theoretical argument that emphasises the complexity of using targeted sanctions without abandoning their use.

69 Kratochwil 2007, 30.

DEVELOPING MULTIPLE EU PERSONALITIES: TEN YEARS OF BLACKLISTING AND MUTUAL TRUST

Torbjörn ANDERSSON*

1. EU AND MUTUAL TRUST

The principle of mutual trust became operative within EU procedural law about when the millennia shifted time. In 1999 the European Council concluded that mutual recognition should be the cornerstone of judicial cooperation in both civil and criminal matters. It asked the Council and the Commission to adopt a programme of measures to implement the principle of mutual recognition.

In respect of criminal matters, such a programme was decided by the Council in early 2001.[1] In the introduction of the programme it is submitted that mutual recognition is designed to strengthen cooperation between member states but also to enhance the protection of individual rights. Furthermore, it is considered to ease the process of rehabilitating offenders and to contribute to legal certainty, since it has the effect that a ruling delivered in one member state will not be contested in another.

As to mutual trust, it is held that the implementation of mutual recognition in criminal matters presupposes that member states have trust in each other's criminal justice systems, a trust that is supposed to be grounded, in particular, on their shared commitment to the principles of freedom, democracy and respect for human rights, fundamental freedoms and the rule of law.

All this was put in solid writing in the draft programme and has been repeated in a number of subsequent documents since.[2] It may be worth mentioning the connection between approximation and harmonisation on the one hand and recognition of judgments on the other. From the perspective of

---

* This is based on a paper presented at a colloquium in Uppsala on Targeted Sanctions organized by Professor Iain Cameron. I would like to thank the professor for yet another opportunity to submit new ideas on the subject, but also for affording it a decade of hard labour in legal science and international politics; I am certain it has made a difference.

1 2001/C 12/02; OJ C 12, 15.1 2001.

2 See e.g. EU Commission, 2011 and the European Council "The Stockholm Programme' in OJ C 115, 04/05/2010 P. 0001–0038.

European integration, judicial cooperation through mutual recognition is only the second best alternative. Yet even as such, it will not work without some sort of common minimum standards.[3] Thus, some approximation is needed in order to create the mutual trust necessary for the basic functioning of mutual recognition.[4]

Now, let me take a more general, panorama-like, approach to law and trust, to allow for a subsequent return to EU and mutual trust from a different direction. In my view, like other legal conceptions and the law itself, the notions of *the national state* and *the national legal order* are social constructions, carried by a collective of believers. As such, legal notions are dependant on an uncountable number of measures working for preserving belief. Such measures provide a wide range of characteristics; various threats of, and occasional usage of, public coercion and force, but also propaganda, rhetoric, languages, symbols and race and the cultivation of ideas like similarities, differences, minorities, majorities, identity, anthems, flags, sport teams etc. I would suggest that the notions of the national state and the national legal order need to be nurtured by these measures, because these notions are like fairies; when too few believe in them they cease to exist. And in the same respect as the EU concept of mutual trust, trust is a very important measure for the preservation of the ideas of the national state and the national legal order.

Trust could mean a lot of things. The trust that is the core of the EU concept and that preserving national legal orders is perhaps best illustrated by a comic strip from MAD, occurring sometime in the 1970s. It goes like this:

> The husband to the wife: – The car has broken down again. I'll take it to Bjorn at the garage tomorrow.
> The wife: – But last time you said that Bjorn always cheats you!
> The husband (indignantly): – If I'm to be cheated, let me be cheated by someone I know!

Basically, you can say that within states and national legal orders, the law is dependant on that kind of trust. There must be trust between citizens and the state, state organs, courts, legal system and the legal machinery, but also between individuals. The cost of transactions will be enormous in a context where distrust rules, as will be the difficulties to legislate, regulate and govern. Obviously, Europe and the world have seen examples of societies where there is a lack of trust, where the public order has to be enforced through sheer coercion and force and where the relations between individuals are solely based upon raw power, violence and individual resources.

---

3 Tampere Special European Council conclusion 37.

4 In the context of civil procedure, see Andersson 2005, p. 245 et seq.

Whereas a state and its legal order need internal trust to remain and to function, they benefit from cultivating distrust in respect of foreign individuals, foreign law and foreign judgments. It has repeatedly been observed that for a concept, or *something*, to preserve its identity it needs something different or other to be defined against.[5] Without foreign states and legal orders there would be no state and legal order; and if trust is a necessary element of the national state and legal order, there must be distrust in foreign states and legal orders.

Accordingly, states may recognise and enforce foreign civil and criminal judgments, but only where the state has accepted to enter an agreement with the other state and only after subjecting the judgments to extra national review. And generally, national rules on *ordre public* must be fulfilled. Thus, internal trust combined with external distrust preserve the state identity.

The EU principle of mutual trust may be seen as a bold attempt to dismantle the barriers between the state and the interstate. In fact, the making of the EU as a creation sui generis can be understood as a mix of the state and the interstate, just like the EU legal order may be seen as a mix of, or something in between, international and national law. Accordingly, early on EU advocates aspired that the new legal creature be characterized as supranational, not international, law, perhaps not only to establish a conceptual distinction between the two but also for the sake of establishing hierarchical relations. Furthermore, the principle may be seen as the start of a process of questioning something which may be characterized as our chauvinistic understanding of the nature of the state and law. Above I tried to illustrate that the trust which is at issue here is not trust in domestic law, legislation and courts in the sense that they are more fair, just, correct or flawless than their foreign cousins, but trust in that which is familiar and more easily understood. And that kind of trust deserves to be attributed at least a flavour of chauvinism.

Anyway, the principle of mutual trust is a quite heavy tool for the development of the EU, that is, economical and political integration via cross-border enforcement. And the principle is supposed to apply in most policy areas and legal fields of the EU, including criminal law and criminal procedure. But concepts and notions may be just as hard to change as natural facts. Mutual trust cannot be created by mere legislation. Perhaps you may regulate car repairs in a such a way that the husband has to bring the car to new mechanics each time, but you cannot order him to trust the stranger the way he trusts Bjorn (whom he knows cheats him) and eventually he will find a way to escape bringing the car to someone he does not want to bring it to. Similarly, you have to find ways to create and cultivate mutual trust, before you can have a system of mutual recognition working. And this means that judges, academic lawyers and, yes, people, have to switch from distrust to trust and adjust their conception of the state and the law and act accordingly. That is no small thing. In the field of criminal law and

5 See e.g. Foucault 1964.

criminal procedure such a mental shift must be encouraged by creating common minimum standards,[6] but also by stressing the underlying legal and constitutional values shared by the member states in the Union, particularly in respect of the legal certainty and integrity of individuals, including human rights.[7] And during a little more than a decade the EU and its member states have seen an accelerating development of secondary legislation on criminal procedure based on mutual recognition and also the beginning of mutual recognition in judicial action, although signs of reluctance and hesitation are evident. It remains to be seen whether the quest for mutual trust will succeed.

2. THE EU AND BLACKLISTING

Thus, in the first decade of this century the EU saw the emergence and early development of interstate integration via mutual trust in the fields of criminal and criminal procedural law. And this process started under due consideration of the delicacy of differences of procedural law between member states and under recognition of the sensitivity of member states, lawyers and citizens in respect of their versions of legal certainty and human rights. As has been implied, from the point of view of the traditional concept of a state and its legal order, this is remarkable. What is even more interesting though, is the simultaneous development of blacklisting which took place in more or less the same field of law and which contains a similar challenge to the concept of the state and the national legal order, except that this development was not founded on mutual trust and respect for legal certainty and individual integrity.

Generally, blacklisting is sorted in the category of international sanctions beside legal-political instruments like embargoes and wars. As such it is considered to be a comparatively nice kind of sanction, since it is directed at designated individual targets and is not intended to inflict suffering and hardship on collectives of individuals. In the modern world, the practice of blacklisting individuals and undertakings started out in the US after the Second World War in order to hinder the Nazis from exploiting their loot. Subsequently the practice grew and was employed in most political conflicts to which the US was a party. Now, blacklisting is an accepted legal-political tool for enforcing the foreign and security policies of the UN and EU.[8]

For the purpose of this paper, I will focus on the role of the EU in the blacklisting regime in view of the parallel emerging need for mutual trust within the Union in respect of criminal procedure and sanctions. There are a number of

---

6 *Cf.* in the field of civil procedure Andersson 2005, p. 250 et seq.

7 See the Tampere programme cited above.

8 On blacklisting in general and in an EU context see Fitzgerald 1999, Andersson, Cameron and Nordback 2003, Cameron 2008, Eckes 2010 and Cameron 2010.

blacklisting programmes in force under EU law; this paper is delimited to EU blacklisting measures concerning the freezing of assets of individuals and undertakings to prevent financing of terrorism. I distinguish between *external* and *internal* blacklisting measures, since some EU measures in this area are mere implementations of UN blacklists whilst the others contain blacklists created by EU institutions (often called "autonomous EU sanctions"), although they too can be (and are as concerns terrorism) based on resolutions of the UN Security Council. Under UN Security Council Resolution 1373, the EU Council creates blacklists which are to be enforced in its member states. Under UN Resolutions such as 1267/1390 the EU Council and the EU Commission implement blacklists created by the Security Council, the consequence of which is the direct effect of the blacklists in the member states.

The logics of international law and national law differ. Even though international law is increasingly about facilitating cooperation between states, a fundamental function of it is still about ensuring peaceful coexistence. In other words, roughly put, a large part of international law may be understood as a means to avoid armed conflicts and wars between sovereign states. Basically, only states are treated like subjects; although they are to be handled with care, individuals, undertakings and other organisations are but objects. When individuals hold rights under international law, it is because, in relation to other states (not individuals), states have undertaken the obligation to respect individual rights. And when human rights are infringed, only states may be held responsible under international law, not individuals.

Under national law as we know it, individuals are subjects, like states. Principles such as the rule of law, the *Rechtsstat* and division of powers, can be interpreted as means to create *trust* in the state with its citizens. Through enforcing and consequently upholding such principles, such means, citizens dare to entrust the state with holding and exercising exclusive powers for the benefit of the collective society. There is a necessary element of submission in the relation between a state and its citizens and that element requires trust to work.

Under international law, at least theoretically, all states are sovereign and equal and there is simply no place for peaceful submission. As to individuals, from the perspective of international law the trust of individuals may be important, but only indirectly, in so far as it is directed towards the national legal orders. If individuals are not subjects why should it matter that they trust in international law? The trust between states ought to be more important, but also that element must be considered quite weak; generally, it would seem like the inclination to set aside international law is hard to resist when it would cost to abide by it. Rather than drawing from principles like the rule of law when it really matters, it seems like the international legal order is glued together by things like strength, necessitated coexistence, ideas of humanitarian benevolence, fear, a desire to avoid loss of reputation, mutual political and economical interests and mutual distrust.

In order for the EU to achieve its aspirations of supranationality, it needs to be trusted by member states and by individuals. In my view it is perfectly possible to see doctrines like those of direct effect, EU law creating individual rights, the principle of judicial control and the whole EU Charter of rights, as means for the EU to prove trustworthy enough to interfere with the economic and political integrity of European individuals. As referred above on several occasions, the development of a system for mutual recognition in the field of criminal law requires that the features of the rule of law, the Rechtsstaat and the division of powers are upheld at all levels of the Union legal order.

Since the blacklisting regime emanates from the UN Security Council and the context of international law, it follows the logic of international law. Consequently, when the international security and power structure is challenged and where the ultimate power works in the context of a legal order which is not founded on the trust of individuals, it is not surprising that that power uses the system for sanctions rather than elaborating schemes for the creation of trust to overcome its own fear and to restore power and security. Thus, I would say that the blacklisting regimes are built on the opposite of trust, that is fear of and distrust in individuals. But it is only true on the one hand, that the system of blacklisting is based on fear, or lack of trust. On the other, blacklisting brings with it an unqualified claim for obedience, or trust if you like, addressed to organs responsible for *enforcing* the blacklists. In a way, the system of blacklisting is an expression of a totalitarian order: there is a lack of trust top-down, but a command for trust down-up. You may say that the blacklisting regime, as it was construed and applied, was one example of how the law went medieval in 2001.

In the following sections I will try to describe briefly how the system was supposed to be comprehended when designed, developed and refined for world wide use.

Just like criminal law rules, blacklisting acts are construed as imperatives – "thou shalt not!" The peculiar thing is that the targets themselves are not addressed by the acts, but the addressees are the general public. Accordingly, when blacklists are used to prevent the financing of terrorism, the general public is prohibited to transfer assets to those blacklisted. In respect of external blacklisting of terrorist suspects, the UN Security Council initially gave no reasons as to why the subjects listed were targeted.[9] Even now, the reasons given are often of a very summary nature. Although the Security Council has itself (through the controversial Resolution 1373) purported to forbid the financing of terrorism, states themselves still decide who are terrorists and who are not. Thus, targets are not listed as a consequence of the application of some

9 A requirement was introduced in Resolution 1735 (2006) that states proposing people or entities for inclusion on the Al-Qaeda list must give a "statement of case" explaining in what way the target is associated with Al-Qaeda or the Taliban. Even later, it was recognised in Resolution 1822 (2008) that parts of this could be made public.

clear legal rule; there is no legal rule prescribing blacklisting as the consequence of illicit behaviour. No, external blacklisting acts are unilateral commands, expressions of the will of high power in a manner which, as said, may be characterized as medieval. From the point of view of supporters of international law this may be undesirable, but the structure of that legal order makes it not only lawful but also logical. As long as it abides by its own rules the UN Security Council can decide pretty much what it wants to and rightfully claim that it is lawful. Consequently, the lack of explicit reasons and the lack of application of specific legal rules are supplemented by a lack of judicial review. Even after the Security Council accepted, with great reluctance, in Resolution 1989 (2011) that a sanctions decision can be reviewed by an Ombudsman, it retained ultimate control over the annulling of the decision. Thus, ultimately, you cannot prove a blacklisting wrong or have it altered by recourse to some other body but the Security Council itself. This is natural: since blacklisting acts are not acts of law or the judiciary, but political acts they cannot be subject to judicial review, particularly since there is no court or other body to which the Security Council has to answer. Furthermore, since the acts suffer from a lack of transparent motivations and application of law, there is not really anything to review but whether or not the names in the lists refer to the persons they are intended to refer to.

In the 1970s Kurt Vonnegut used the metaphor of a card game to describe the American society and its discourse. The American Constitution, he said, is a guarantee securing that card players use only kings and queens as top cards; because nothing beats the ace of spades.[10] Similarly, to me it seems like the regime of external blacklisting is dependant on the UN Security Council playing the ace of spades over and over. You cannot argue with the ace of spades, neither can you prove it wrong or escape it.

From the point of view of the UN Security Council, and accordingly from the permissive context of international law in which it dwells, it would seem apparent that "the principles of freedom, democracy and respect for human rights, fundamental freedoms and the rule of law" are attractive but dispensable, although considered vital by the EU for creating mutual trust. And this is, because it was quite clear from the start that as originally construed the system of external blacklisting comes in conflict with a number of general principles of law, recognised as such by the EU.

As to internal blacklisting, it is a light version of external blacklisting. An internal blacklisting decision requires that there has been taken a decision by a competent national authority to instigate investigations or prosecute for terrorist acts or attempts to perpetrate, participate in or facilitate terrorist acts. Or at least, the blacklisting decision must be based on precise information or material in the relevant file which indicates that such decision has been taken by a

10 Vonnegut 1981, pp. 11–12.

competent national authority. The decision is to be based on serious and credible evidence or clues or "condemnation" for such deeds. The blacklist has to be reviewed every six months by the Council to ensure that there are grounds for keeping the names in the list.

When the regime of internal blacklisting was introduced it was still an open question whether or not, and to what extent, it was subject to judicial review, but it is clear that already from the start a slightly higher degree of legal certainty was built into the system. Eventually it became clear how the Council, the Commission and the member states made use of the system.

Anyway, the original schemes of external and internal blacklisting preventing financing of terrorism looks like this from an EU perspective:

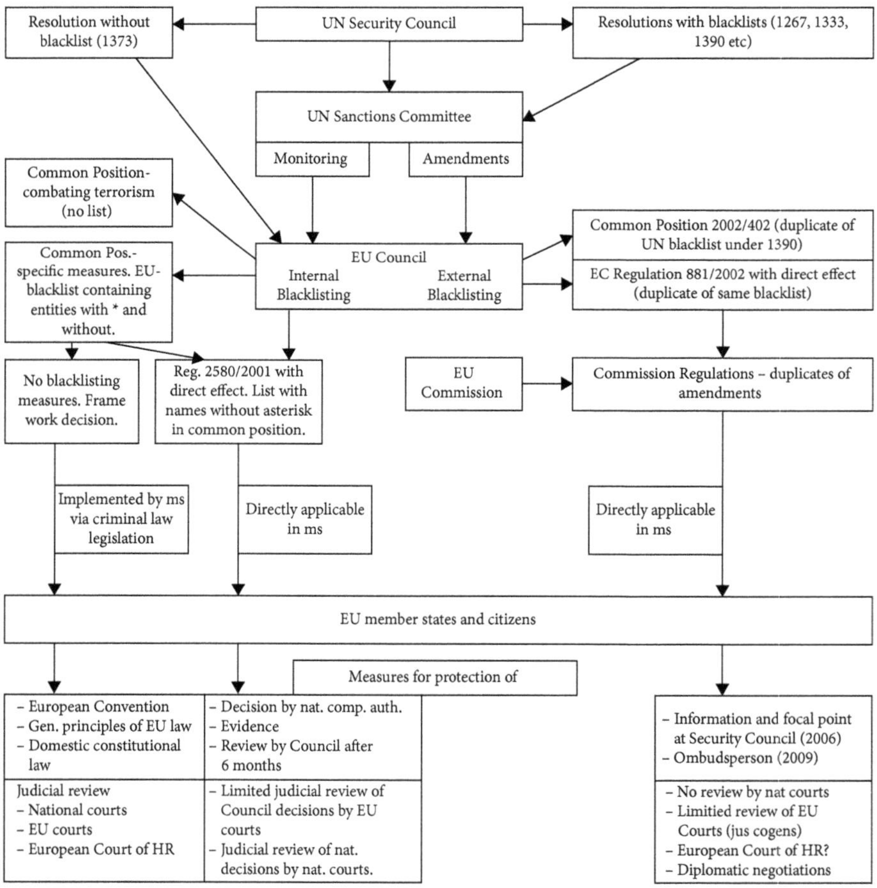

Thus, the EU and its legal order play important roles in the creation, enforcement and review of the blacklisting regimes emanating from the UN Security Council. Yet, this position seems difficult to reconcile with EU's aspirations for closer intra-European integration in the field of criminal law and its desire for an ever stronger supranational definition. On the one hand, the development of the blacklisting regimes can be seen as another sort of dismantling of barriers between the interstate and the state, but by applying international law measures directly to individuals, setting aside guarantees of legal protection for individuals provided by EU law, the European Convention on Human Rights (ECHR) as well as by the constitutions of the member states of the EU. On the other hand, as said before, the development of EU integration in the field of criminal law would require mutual trust between states and between states and EU and, most important, that foreign and EU criminal law be trusted by individuals, officials and courts.

These simultaneous developments of breaking the barriers between interstate and state seem to follow parallel lines, yet go in opposite directions. Enforcing the blacklisting regimes, it has been argued, would strengthen the EU identity as a player in the field of international law.[11] Upholding individual protection in spite of its obligation under international law would emphasise that EU is something else than basically just another form of international cooperation between states. Thus, during the first decade of this century the EU found itself in the centre of two opposing movements pressing the Union to determine its loyalty and identity and, accordingly, to define itself.

The developing use of blacklisting for freezing of assets as a means to fight terrorism gives rise to immediate legal difficulties. This is especially so, when the implementation is undertaken within the EU legislative and judicial system and thus confronted by human rights requirements, binding through the ECHR, the EU Charter of Rights and as general principles of law common to all EU member states. Very soon after EU domiciled entities began being blacklisted, targeted sanctions containing freezing requirements were being questioned before courts in the EU. Gradually, the blacklistings were reviewed by courts at domestic and EU level. The most common objections were that freezing of assets without a trial before a court violated the right to dispose of one's property under the ECHR and that blacklisting violated the right of accused individuals to have effective judicial control of the accusation. The counterarguments were, and are, basically three. First it is said that targeted sanctions are of a provisional nature and necessary to impair the financing of terrorism. Second, it is said that targeted sanctions are not penal in character, which is why normal individual protection should not apply. The third is simply an argument of law, not of reason: Under international law every state is under an obligation to honour its undertakings in agreements unconditionally. Thus, none of the UN member states can question decisions by the UN Security Council, not by using internal constitutional law, nor, in view of the primacy at international law of the UNC, by using the ECHR.

11 See e.g. de Burca 2010.

In the following sections I will try to shed some light on the choices made by the EU legal order by referring to the case law of the EU courts regarding internal and external blacklisting. For this purpose I have chosen to concentrate on a number of interrelated cases concerning internal and external blacklisting. As examples of the former I use three cases concerning People's Mujahedin Organisation of Iran. As examples of external blacklisting I have used cases connected to *Kadi*. Terminologically, the entry into force of the Lisbon Treaty has caused some confusion, as the Court of First Instance (CFI) changed its name on to the General Court. For judgments from this court before 30 November 2009 I refer to the CFI, and after this date to the "General Court". I also at times simply use the term "the Court". I have used the abbreviation ECJ, or the name Court of Justice, when the Court of Justice of the EU is concerned.

3. THE CASES

3.1. INTERNAL BLACKLISTING – CASE LAW

3.1.1. The first PMOI case[12]

On 28 March 2001, thus before the coming into force of UN Resolution 1373 (the basis of EU internal blacklisting), the Secretary of State of the Home Department of the UK decided to list People's Mojehedin Organization of Iran (PMOI) as a forbidden organization under the UK Terrorist Act, as from 2000. PMOI brought two separate actions against this decision in the UK; one before the Proscribed Organisations Appeal Commission (POAC) and one before the High Court.[13] In May 2002 the Council updated the list in Common Position 931(2001), thus including PMOI.[14] It also, by a Council Decision, updated the list attached to EC Regulation 2580, adding PMOI.[15] In a number of subsequent Common Positions and Council Decisions the PMOI was kept in the list.[16] In between these decisions by the Council, there was a decision by the POAC that there had

12 T-228/02, ECR 2006 II-4665.

13 The High Court dismissed the action, finding that POAC rather than itself was the right forum. For more details on the UK proscription procedures see the chapter by Sofia Marques da Silva and Cian Murphy in the present volume.

14 2002/340 CFSP.

15 By Council Decision 2002/334/EC of 2 May 2002 implementing Article 2(3) of Regulation (EC) No 2580/2001 and repealing Decision 2001/927, the Council adopted an updated list of the persons, groups and entities to which that regulation applies. The applicant's name was included in that list, in the same terms as those employed in the Annex to Common Position 2002/340.

16 Common Position 2002/462/CFSP; Council Decision 2002/460/EC; Common Position 2005/936/CFSP; Common Position 2005/847/CFSP; Council Decision 2005/848/EC; Council Decision 2005/930/EC.

been no need to hear PMOI before the UK Home Secretary took the decision to list the organisation.

In the first case before the CFI, the PMOI brought an action for annulment and a declaration of inapplicability (as against the organisation) of the relevant Common Positions and Council Decisions. The most relevant pleas supporting the claim, at least for the purpose of this article, contain allegations that the EU acts infringed the right to a fair hearing, essential procedural requirements (to state reasons), the right to effective judicial protection, the presumption of innocence and constituted manifest errors of assessment.

The CFI found that it was outside its competence to review acts like Common Positions. As to the disputed Council Decisions the CFI first ruled that the decisions, as regards sanctions for infringing the decision, possessed a legislative nature and were of general application, but still, in respect of those blacklisted, were of direct and individual concern. Therefore, the right to a fair hearing should apply.[17] In accordance with established case law, the safeguarding of the right to be heard comprises two parts. First, the party concerned must be informed of the evidence adduced against it to justify the proposed sanction ('notification of the evidence adduced'). Second, it must be afforded the opportunity effectively to make known its view on that evidence ('hearing'). Moreover, the obligation to state reasons and the right to effective judicial protection also applied. But the CFI made some submissions as to limitations and the purpose of those rights in cases concerning internal blacklisting.

Internal blacklisting leading to freezing of assets, requires procedures at two levels, one domestic and one EU, since the Council when the list is drawn up has to base it on a decision taken by a competent authority in respect of the persons concerned.[18] In the second phase the Council must decide to include the party concerned in the blacklist, on the basis of precise information or material in the relevant file which indicates that such a decision has been taken. Next, the Council must at regular intervals ensure that there are grounds for keeping the party in the list. The existence of a decision by a national authority is an essential precondition for the adoption, by the Council, of an initial decision to freeze funds, whereas verification of the consequences of that decision at the national

17 The court made a reference to its earlier decision in the *Yusuf* and *Kadi (I)* cases, which concerned external blacklisting; in those cases the CFI held that the principle of a fair trial should not apply, using the argument that since those persons were listed by decision of the Security Council, nothing they could say would make it possible to alter the decision to blacklist them. In this case, even if the EU internal blacklisting is undertaken due to an obligation under the UN, the names are put on the list after an assessment by the Council, an assessment which may be influenced by facts and arguments brought forward by blacklisted subjects.

18 That is irrespective of whether such a decision concerns the instigation of investigations or prosecution for a terrorist act, an attempt to perpetrate, participate in or facilitate such an act based on serious and credible evidence or clues, or condemnation for such deeds. If it is a decision to instigate investigations or to prosecute, it must be based on serious and credible evidence or clues.

level is necessary in the context of the adoption of a subsequent decision to freeze funds.

The CFI held that the general principle of observance of *the right to a fair hearing* requires, unless precluded by overriding considerations concerning the security, that the evidence adduced against the party, should be notified to it, in so far as possible, either concomitantly with or as soon as possible after the adoption of an initial decision to freeze funds. Subject to the same reservations, any subsequent decision to freeze funds must, in principle, be preceded by notification of any new evidence and by affording the blacklisted person or entity the possibility to let their views be known. However, observance of the right to a fair hearing does not require either that the evidence be notified to it before the adoption of an initial measure, or that that party automatically be heard after the event. The hearing of a party beforehand would risk depriving the decision of its effectiveness. Furthermore, since the internal blacklisting procedure requires a decision by a competent authority, the CFI considered that the protection of the party's right to a fair hearing should primarily be guaranteed before that domestic authority. Questions concerning the appropriateness of the decision or whether it is well-founded or whether the decision infringes individual rights, should exclusively be brought up before the national authority or before a domestic court. That should not apply though, when the Council uses new facts which have not been considered by the domestic authority – such facts should be notified to the individual or entity and they should be given an opportunity to express their views on these.

As to *the obligation to state reasons*, the CFI held the following. Unless precluded by the security, the statement of reasons for an initial decision to freeze funds must make actual and specific reference to "precise information or material in the relevant file which indicates that a decision has been taken by a competent authority. Like the right to a fair hearing, the obligation to state reasons at EU level does not cover the substance of the decision – whether the decision is correct or constitutes an infringement of individual (human) rights – except in respect of new facts which have not been considered by the competent national authority trigging the decision at EU level. Moreover, the statement of reasons for a subsequent decision to freeze funds must state the actual and specific reasons why the Council considers, following re-examination, that the freezing of the funds of the party remains justified.

In respect of *effective judicial protection*, the CFI found that the Council enjoys broad discretion in its assessment of the matters to be taken into consideration for the purpose of adopting economic and financial sanctions at EU level. Since the EU Courts may not substitute the Council's assessment of the evidence, facts and circumstances justifying the adoption of such measures for that of their own assessment, the review carried out by the CFI of the lawfulness of decisions to freeze funds must be restricted to checking that the rules governing procedure and the statement of reasons have been complied with, that the facts are materially accurate, and that there has been no manifest error of assessment of the facts or misuse of power. That limited review applies, especially, to the Council's assessment of the factors as to the appropriateness on which such decisions are based.

When applying these points of law to the specific case, the CFI first held that at no time before the action was brought was the evidence adduced notified to the PMOI. The initial decision to freeze its funds, and subsequent decisions, did not mention the 'specific information' or 'material in the file' showing that a decision justifying its inclusion in the list was taken by a competent national authority. The PMOI had not been appraised of the specific evidence adduced against it in order to justify the sanction envisaged and was not in a position effectively to make known its views on the matter.[19] Those considerations were applicable both to the right to a fair hearing and the obligation to state reasons. The CFI considered that none of the relevant Council decisions satisfied the requirement of a statement of reasons; they merely stated, in the second recital in their preamble, that it was 'desirable' to adopt an up-to-date list to which Regulation 2580 should apply.

Furthermore, the CFI held that the PMOI had been unable effectively to make known its views to the Council, and that PMOI, in the absence of any statement in the decision of the actual and specific grounds justifying that decision, had not been put in a position to avail itself of its right of action before the CFI. Moreover, the CFI assessed that neither the written pleadings of the different parties to the case, nor the file material produced before the CFI, enabled PMOI to conduct its judicial review, since the organisation was not even in a position to determine with certainty, after the close of the oral procedure, exactly which was the national decision on which the decision was based. The CFI observed that the UK and the Council had diverging views as to which was the relevant domestic decision justifying the blacklisting of PMOI and concluded that it itself, after the oral hearing, was not capable to review the legality of the decision.

The CFI held, in conclusion, that the decision was lacking a statement of reasons and had been adopted in a procedure depriving PMOI of its right to a fair hearing. It held that it, the CFI, could not review the legality of the decision. The CFI annulled the decision in so far as it concerned the PMOI.

3.1.2. *The second PMOI case*[20]

After the oral hearing in the first case, which was held on 7 February 2006, but before the judgment was delivered, the Council adopted Decision 2006/379 of

19 The Council's argument that it heard the applicant before proceeding with the freezing of funds was not accepted.

20 T-256/07, ECR 2008 II-3019.

29 May 2006 implementing Regulation 2580/2001 and repealing Decision 2005/930/EC. By that decision, the Council continued to include PMOI's name in the list. On 21 December 2006, the Council adopted Decision 2006/1008. By letter of 30 January 2007 the Council informed the applicant that, in its opinion, the reasons for including the applicant in the list were still valid and that it therefore intended to maintain it in the list. Enclosed with that letter was the Council's statement of reasons. PMOI was also informed that it could submit observations to the Council on the continued inclusion of it in the list and on the reasons stated in that regard, and any supporting documents.

In the statement of reasons enclosed, the Council pointed out, inter alia, that a decision had been taken with respect to the PMOI by a competent authority (the same decision by the Home Secretary) proscribing the applicant as an organisation concerned in terrorism, under the Terrorism Act 2000. After noting that that decision, which under the above-mentioned law was subject to review, was still in force, the Council held that the reasons for including the PMOI in the list still applied.

By decision of 14 December 2007, the POAC refused an application by the Home Secretary for permission to lodge an appeal before the Court of Appeal against the POAC's decision of 30 November 2007.[21] In an addendum to that decision dated 17 December 2007, the POAC gave as the reason for its refusal the fact that none of the arguments advanced by the Home Secretary had a reasonable chance of succeeding.

On 20 December 2007 the Council adopted Council Decision 2007/868. The PMOI was contained in the annex. On 28 December 2007 the Home Secretary made an application to the Court of Appeal for leave to appeal against the POAC's decision. Decision 2007/868 was notified to the PMOI. The Council took the view that the reasons for continuing to include it in the list still held good. With regard to the POAC's decision, the Council observed that the Home Secretary had sought to bring an appeal against it. The statement of reasons enclosed with the second letter of notification is identical to that accompanying the first letter of notification.

The CFI made the following findings.

---

21 In that decision, the POAC *inter alia* described as 'perverse' the Home Secretary's conclusion, in his decision of 1 September 2006 refusing to lift the applicant's proscription, that the applicant was, at that period, still an organisation 'concerned in terrorism' within the meaning of the Terrorism Act 2000. According to the POAC's assessment, the only belief that a reasonable decision maker could have honestly entertained, whether as at September 2006 or thereafter, was that the PMOI no longer satisfied any of the criteria necessary for the maintenance of their proscription. In other words, on the material before it, the POAC found that the PMOI was not at the time of its decision and had not been, as at September 2006, concerned in terrorism.

The CFI held that the contested decision did not meet the requirements for automatic nullity.[22]

As to the binding effect of the annulling judgment in respect of subsequent Council blacklisting decisions, it was submitted that on the one hand the annulling effects were explicitly concerned only with the contested decision, but on the other that the Council was also under an obligation to certify that subsequent decisions would not suffer from the same defects which caused the annulment of the previous decision. Having said that, the Council may enact an identical, fresh decision (even with retroactive effect) as compared to that annulled, if the annulment depended on a procedural defect which was corrected. The CFI held that maintaining the PMOI in the list but by a fresh decision did not infringe the former judgment.

Both *the statement of reasons* for an initial decision to freeze funds and the statement of reasons for subsequent decisions must refer to the legal conditions of application of Regulation 2580/2001, but also to the actual and specific reasons why the Council considered that the person concerned must be made the subject of a measure freezing funds. Furthermore, subsequent decisions must be preceded by 'review' of the situation of the person or entity concerned, both for the purpose of establishing whether he or it is still engaged in terrorist activity, and to check whether it 'remains justified'. When the grounds for a subsequent decision to freeze funds are the same as those relied on when a previous decision was adopted, a mere statement to that effect may suffice. Consequently, the CFI held that the fact that a fresh decision concerning PMOI was based on the same national decision and on the same evidence, did not affect the legality of the decision.

Neither Regulation 2580/2001 nor Common Position 2001/931 precludes the imposition of restrictive measures on persons or entities that have in the past committed acts of terrorism, despite the lack of evidence to show that they are at present committing or participating in such acts, if the circumstances warrant it. This means that if a person, or entity, is not suspected of having been involved in terrorist activities the preceding six months, he or it can still be kept in the list if the circumstances warrant it and it is motivated.[23] Accordingly, the CFI held that the lack of evidence of terrorism activity was not sufficient to nullify a decision to keep an organization in the list.

---

22 As a basic rule, the CFI found, acts decided by EU institutions must be considered to be valid until they are formally annulled. But measures tainted by a grave irregularity cannot be tolerated by the Community legal order but must be treated as legally non-existent. The purpose of this exception is to maintain a balance between stability of legal relations and respect for legality. The gravity of the consequences attaching to a finding that a measure of a Community institution is non-existent means that, for reasons of legal certainty, such a finding should be reserved for quite extreme situations.

23 *Cf.* the approach of the Danish courts, discussed in Thomas Elholm's chapter in this volume.

The Council has to prove that freezing of the funds of an entity is or remains legally justified, but the burden of proof has a relatively limited scope in respect of the EU procedure for freezing funds. In the case of an initial decision, the burden of proof essentially relates to the existence of precise information or material in the relevant file which indicates that a decision by a national authority has been taken with regard to the person concerned. Furthermore, in the case of a subsequent decision to freeze funds, after review, the burden of proof essentially relates to whether the freezing of funds is still justified, having regard to all the relevant circumstances of the case and to the action taken upon that decision of the competent national authority.

The Council has broad discretion as to what to take into consideration for the purpose of adopting economic and financial sanctions. That does not mean that the Court should not review the interpretation made by the Council of the relevant facts. The Court must not only establish whether the evidence relied on is factually accurate, reliable and consistent, but must also ascertain whether that evidence contains all the relevant information to be taken into account in order to assess the situation and whether it is capable of substantiating the conclusions drawn from it. Nevertheless, when conducting such a review, the Court must not substitute its own assessment of what is appropriate for that of the Council. In addition, where a Community institution enjoys broad discretion, the review of observance of certain procedural guarantees is of fundamental importance. Those guarantees include the obligation for the competent institution to examine all the relevant elements of the individual case and to give an adequate statement of the reasons for its decision.

As to *the obligation to state arguments*, the CFI nullified the Council decision taken, after the decision by POAC in the UK refusing appeal against its decision, submitting that the decision by the Home Secretary was perverse. The CFI submitted that the reasons communicated by the Council, as to why maintaining the blacklisting was justified, were simply that the original reasons held good. Furthermore, the CFI considered that the statement of reasons enclosed with the second letter of notification was strictly identical to that enclosed with the first letter of notification. With regard to the POAC's decision, the Council just noted, in the second letter of notification, that the Home Secretary had sought to bring an appeal. Considering the date when Decision 2007/868 was adopted and all information relevant at that time, and taking account of the particular circumstances of the case, the CFI submitted that that statement of reasons was obviously insufficient to provide legal justification for continuing to freeze the applicant's funds.

The CFI found that that statement of reasons did not make it possible to grasp how far the Council actually took into account the POAC's decision, as it was required to do. The statement did not explain the actual specific reasons why the Council took the view, in spite of the findings of fact made by the POAC and the legal conclusions which the Council drew from those findings, that the continued inclusion of the applicant in the list at issue remained justified in the light of the same body of facts and circumstances on which the POAC had had to rule.

The CFI seemed particularly struck by the lack of comments on the POAC decision, since its conclusion was that the only belief that a reasonable decision-maker could have honestly entertained, as from September 2006, was that the applicant no longer met any of the criteria necessary for the maintenance of its proscription as a terrorist organisation. In those circumstances, the Council ought to have re-evaluated its assessment of the existence of a decision taken by a competent national authority on the basis of 'serious and credible evidence' within the meaning of Common Position 2001/931.

The CFI observed that the Council strove to make good the clear inadequacy of its statement of reasons by maintaining that it was still reasonable to consider, when Decision 2007/868 was adopted, that the applicant was involved in acts of terrorism, as defined in Regulation 2580/2001, and that the freezing of its funds therefore remained justified. But the CFI reiterated earlier findings that the statement of reasons for a measure must in principle be notified to the person concerned at the same time as the act affecting him and that failure to state the reasons, or the obvious inadequacy of the reasons stated, cannot be remedied by the fact that the person concerned learns the reasons for the measure during the proceedings before the EU courts.[24] Furthermore, even if the CFI acknowledged that the Council could have regard to the existence of appeals against the POAC's decision and to the Home Secretary's actual recourse to them, it was not sufficient for the Council to state that the Home Secretary had sought to lodge an appeal in order to be relieved of the need to take into specific consideration the findings of fact made by the POAC against which no appeal lay and the legal conclusions which it drew from those findings.

The CFI found this point emphasized by the fact that, on the one hand, POAC, the judicial authority competent to review the lawfulness of acts of the Home Secretary, had described the refusal to lift the applicant's proscription as 'unreasonable' and 'perverse' and, on the other, when Decision 2007/868 was adopted, the Council had been informed of the POAC's refusal to grant the Home Secretary leave to introduce such an appeal and of the grounds of that refusal, namely, that, according to the POAC, none of the arguments put forward by the Home Secretary stood a reasonable chance of prospering before the Court of Appeal.

In short, the CFI found that proper and sufficient reasons had not been adduced for the continued freezing of the applicant's funds under Decision 2007/868, in conjunction with the list annexed to that decision.

---

24 See first case above.

3.1.3. *The third PMOI case*[25]

The Mojahedin saga before the CFI continued shortly afterwards.[26] By Council Decision 2008/583/EC of 15 July 2008 implementing of Regulation (EC) 2580/2001 and repealing Decision 2007/868/EC, the Council nonetheless maintained, with others, the applicant's name on the list. Recital 5 in the preamble to the decision that refers to the *PMOI*, states:

> 'In the case of one group, the Council has taken account of the fact that the decision by a competent authority on the basis of which the group was included on the list has not been in force since 24 June 2008. However, new information concerning the group has been brought to the Council's attention. The Council considers that this new information warrants the group's inclusion in the list.'

The decision was notified to the applicant on 15 July 2008. The Council stated:

> 'the Council has again decided to include [the PMOI] on the list ... The Council has taken note of the fact that the competent authority decision which served as a basis for including [the PMOI] on the list is no longer in force as of 24 June. However, the Council has been provided with new information relevant to this listing. Having considered this new information, the Council has decided that [the PMOI] should still be included on the above-mentioned list. Therefore, the Council has amended the statement of reasons accordingly.'

The new information was based on the fact that the anti-terrorist prosecutor's office at a Paris court, in April 2001, had opened judicial inquiries against PMOI and investigated several members of the organization under French law. This was supplemented by the fact that the same prosecutor's office in March and November 2007 had brought new charges of money laundering and fraud against alleged members of the PMOI. According to the Council this constituted a decision having been taken by a competent national authority, in the context of Common Position 931.

The PMOI made a claim before the CFI to have the Council Decision 2008/583 annulled. One of the grounds was that its right to defence had been infringed. The CFI submitted that it is common ground that the Council adopted

---

25 T-284/08, ECR 2008 II-3487.

26 The UK Home Secretary had tried to appeal against the POAC decision mentioned above. In its judgment, the Court of Appeal upheld the POAC's findings and moreover stated that the closed material adduced by the Home Secretary reinforced the Court of Appeal's conclusion that the Home Secretary could not reasonably have considered that the PMOI intended in future to revert to terrorism. By order of 23 June 2008, which entered into force on 24 June 2008, the Home Secretary therefore removed the PMOI's name from the list of organisations proscribed under the Terrorism Act 2000, and this was approved by both Houses of Parliament in the United Kingdom.

the contested decision without first informing the applicant of the new information or new material in the file which, in its view, justified maintaining it on the disputed list. A fortiori, the Council did not enable the applicant effectively to make known its view of the matter, prior to the adoption of the contested decision.

As regards the rights of the defence, it was therefore considered clear that the contested decision was adopted in disregard of the principles stated by the Court in the first *PMOI* judgment.[27]

Without having to, the CFI went on to examine other grounds of annulment. The CFI found that neither the information contained in the contested decision, its statement of reasons and the letter of notification,[28] complied with the requirements in respect of *proof*. In consequence, it had not been established to the required legal standard that the contested decision was adopted in accordance with the provisions laid down in Common Position 2001/931 and

27 The CFI rubbed it in. It found that the Council's arguments totally failed to substantiate its claim that it would have been impossible for it to adopt the decision under a procedure that would have respected the applicant's rights of the defence. Particularly, the alleged urgency was by no means established. Even assuming that the Council was not under an immediate duty to remove the applicant from the disputed list following the POAC decision of 30 November 2007, the possibility for the Council to continue to rely on the Home Secretary's decision which had served as a basis for the initial decision to freeze the applicant's funds came to an end as of 7 May 2008, when the Court of Appeal gave its judgment. Between that date and the date of adoption of the contested decision, more than two months lapsed. The Council had not explained why it was not possible for it to take steps immediately after 7 May 2008 with a view either to removing the applicant from the disputed list or to maintaining it in that list on the basis of new evidence. If the Council had received new material only in June 2008, it should have been communicated. The CFI observed that the Council refrained from communicating those new elements to the applicant, without alleging the existence of any material or legal obstacle to doing so, and even though, by the first *PMOI* judgment, the Court had annulled one of its earlier decisions, precisely on the ground that no such communication of the elements relied on had been made prior to its adoption. The CFI pointed out that, neither the judgment of the Court of Appeal nor the Home Secretary's order of 23 June 2008 had an automatic and immediate effect on Decision 2007/868 to freeze funds which was then in force. In accordance with the presumption of legality attaching to Community acts, that decision remained in force and continued to produce legal effects, even though its national 'substratum' had disappeared, as long as it was not withdrawn, declared void in an action for annulment or declared invalid following a reference for a preliminary ruling or a plea of illegality. Therefore, the CFI found it incorrect, both in law and in fact, to state that, following the entry into force of the Home Secretary's order and the communication, more or less simultaneously, of new material by the French authorities, a new decision to freeze funds had to be adopted as a matter of such urgency that it was not possible to comply with the applicant's rights of the defence. Furthermore, the CFI considered that the Council's omission to comply with a procedure clearly defined in the first *PMOI* judgment, made with full knowledge of the facts and without any reasonable justification, may be material to any consideration of the abuse or misuse of powers or procedures alleged by PMOI. In short, the CFI held that the continued freezing of the applicant's funds by the contested decision was the result of a procedure during which the applicant's rights of the defence were not respected and that the decision should be annulled, in so far as it concerned the applicant.

28 Nor even those contained in the Council's two answers to the Court order of 26 September 2008.

Regulation 2580/2001. The Council had not provided the Court with any precise information to indicate that the judicial inquiry opened by the anti-terrorist Prosecutor's office in Paris in 2001 and the supplementary charges brought in March and November 2007 constitute, in respect of the applicant, a decision meeting the definition in Common Position 2001/931. Thus, the Council made that allegation without adducing any evidence in support of its contention.

The refusal by the Council and the French authorities to communicate, even to the CFI, some allegedly relevant information, had had the consequence that the CFI found itself unable to review the lawfulness of the decision. The CFI considered that the production of only the information contained in the Council's answers to the CFI, did not enable either the applicant or the Court to verify that the contested decision was adopted in compliance with Common Position 2001/931 and Regulation No 2580/2001 and is not vitiated by a manifest error of assessment.

In conclusion, the CFI found that it had not been established that the decision was adopted in compliance with Common Position 2001/931 and Regulation 2580/2001 and that the very circumstances of its adoption infringe the applicant's *right to effective judicial protection.*

3.2. EXTERNAL BLACKLISTING

3.2.1. Kadi I – the Court of First Instance[29]

When Kadi and Al Barakaat Int Foundation came before the European Court of Justice in 2008 they had a long and troublesome road behind them and had no real reason for optimism. On 17 October and 9 November 2001 the UN 1267 Sanctions Committee published inter alia two additions to its summary blacklist, including the parties.[30] Accordingly, Kadi's name was added to the list attached to EC Regulation 467/2001.[31] On the 27 May 2002 the Council adopted Common Position 2002/402/CFSP and the Regulation 881/02. Annex I to the regulation contained the list of persons, groups and entities affected by the freezing of funds imposed by Article 2 of that regulation. That list included the parties.

Kadi and Al Barakaat both brought actions before the CFI seeking annulment of Regulation No 467/2001, the former seeking annulment also of

29 T-315/01, 2005 ECR II-3649; T-306/01, 2005 ECR II-3533.

30 The Al Barakaat Int Foundation was the last remaining name in the list out of four, domiciled in Sweden and involved in Havala banking between Sweden and Somalia. Three persons were taken away from the UN and EU blacklists at different stages during the proceedings. Mr Kadi, domiciled in the UK, appeared in the list named as alternative aliases.

31 This was done through Commission Regulation (EC) 2062/2001 of 19 October 2001 amending, for the third time, Regulation No 467/2001.

Regulation No 2062/2001 and the latter annulment also of Regulation 2199/2001, in so far as those measures concerned them. In support of his claims, Mr Kadi put forward three grounds of annulment alleging breaches of fundamental rights. The first alleged a breach of the right to be heard, the second, breach of the right to respect for property and of the principle of proportionality, and the third, breach of the right to effective judicial review. For its part, Al Barakaat based its claims on 1) that the Council was incompetent to adopt the contested regulation, 2) infringement of Article 249 EC and 3) breach of its fundamental rights.

One of the big issues in this case concerned the legality of the EC regulation(s) on blacklisting individuals, due to a lack of a proper legal basis in the EC Treaty. After the Lisbon Treaty it is clear that there is a legal basis for using directly effective regulations to blacklist individuals.

As to whether the blacklisting *infringed the Treaty* by being individually addressed and of no general scope, the CFI held that the regulation had general application, since it prohibited anyone to make available funds or economic resources to certain persons; the fact that those persons were expressly named did not affect the general nature of the prohibition.

According to the Court the obligation of the Member States to respect the principle of the primacy of obligations undertaken by virtue of the Charter of the United Nations (UNC) was not affected by the EC Treaty, for it is an obligation arising from an agreement concluded before the Treaty. Therefore, the Court concluded that resolutions adopted by the Security Council are binding on all the Member States of the Community which must therefore, in that capacity, take all measures necessary to ensure that those resolutions are put into effect and must set aside provisions of Community law that raise any impediments to their obligations under the Charter.

As to the scope of the review of legality, the Court found that the European Community is based on the rule of law, but that in the relevant area there existed structural limits on judicial review. Since the Security Council had the exclusive right to determine what constitutes a threat to international peace and security and the measures required to maintain them, the Security Council alone held the responsibility for this. Thus, the jurisdiction of national or Community authorities and courts does not cover the legality of such decisions and therefore the CFI declined jurisdiction to review indirectly the lawfulness of Security Council decisions.[32]

---

32 The Court held that: 1) jurisdiction to review would be incompatible with the undertakings of the Member States under the UNC, especially Articles 25, 48 and 103 thereof, and also with Article 27 of the Vienna Convention on the Law of Treaties; 2) it would be contrary to provisions both of the EC Treaty, and of the Treaty on European Union (TEU), in particular Article 5 EU, in accordance with which the Community judicature is to exercise its powers on the conditions and for the purposes provided for by the provisions of the EC Treaty and the TEU and it would be incompatible with the principle that the Community's powers and,

Still, the CFI found that it was empowered to check, indirectly, the lawfulness of the resolutions of the Security Council in question with regard to *jus cogens*, understood as a body of higher rules of public international law binding on all subjects of international law, including the bodies of the UN, and from which no derogation is possible. The result of the limited review undertaken by the Court was that, not surprisingly, the blacklisting effect of interfering with the parties' property did not infringe their fundamental rights, that (as a result of the exemption for humanitarian needs) the blacklisting did not make the parties subject to inhuman and degrading treatment, and that blacklisting was not an arbitrary, inappropriate or disproportionate interference with the right to private property of the persons concerned.[33]

With regard to *the right to be heard*, including the applicants' alleged right to be heard by the Community institutions before the regulation was adopted, the CFI held that the institutions had no jurisdiction to examine individual situations, since they were required to implement the resolutions. The Court found that the principle of Community law relating to the right to be heard cannot apply in such circumstances, where to hear the person concerned could not in any case lead the institution to review its position. The Court found that that the re-examination procedure conferred no right directly on the persons concerned to be heard by the Sanctions Committee, was not improper under the mandatory prescriptions of the public international order. Furthermore, the Court held that where a temporary precautionary measure restricts the availability of the applicants' property, observance of the fundamental rights of the persons concerned does not require the facts and evidence adduced against them to be communicated to them, once the Security Council considers that there are grounds concerning the international community's security that militate against.

As to *the right to effective judicial review*, the Court found that the parties had been able to bring actions for annulment before the CFI and that in dealing with that action, the Court carried out a complete, but limited, review of the lawfulness of the regulation. The Court concluded that there was no judicial

therefore, those of the CFI, must be exercised in compliance with international law; 3) with particular regard to Article 307 EC and to Article 103 UNC, reference to infringements either of fundamental rights as protected by the Community legal order or of the principles of that legal order cannot affect the validity of a Security Council measure or its effect in the territory of the Community.

33 Specifically the Court put forward the following arguments to support this finding: 1) the measures in question pursued an objective of fundamental public interest for the international community, the campaign against international terrorism, and the UN are entitled to undertake protective action against the activities of terrorist organisations; 2) freezing of funds is a temporary precautionary measure which, unlike confiscation, does not affect the very substance of the right of the persons concerned to property in their financial assets but only the use thereof; 3) the resolutions of the Security Council at issue provide for a means of reviewing, after certain periods, the overall system of sanctions; 4) those resolutions set up a procedure enabling the persons concerned to present their case at any time to the Sanctions Committee for review, through the Member State of their nationality or that of their residence.

remedy available to the parties, the Security Council not having thought it advisable to establish an independent international court responsible for ruling in actions brought against individual decisions taken by the Sanctions Committee, but any such lacuna in the judicial protection available to the applicant was not in itself contrary to *jus cogens*. The Court held that the limitation of the applicant's right of access to a court, was inherent in that right as it is guaranteed by *jus cogens* and that such a limitation is justified both by the nature of the decisions that the Security Council is led to take and by the legitimate objective pursued. The party's interest in having a court hear his case on its merits was not enough to outweigh the essential public interest in the maintenance of international peace and security in the face of a threat identified by the Security Council. The Court attributed special significance to the resolutions successively adopted by the Security Council provided a mechanism for re-examining whether it is appropriate to maintain those measures after 12 or 18 months.[34]

Consequently, the CFI on 21 September 2005 dismissed the pleas alleging breach of the right to effective judicial review and, as a result, the actions in their entirety.

3.2.2. *Kadi I – ECJ*[35]

The parties appealed the judgment to the European Court of Justice. As to the potential conflict between decisions by the Security Council implemented by the EU Council on the one hand, and the protection of individual rights within the EU system on the other, the ECJ quashed the findings of the CFI. The ECJ held that the EC must respect international law, including UN measures, as a starting-point, but that the UNC does not impose the choice of a particular model for the implementation of resolutions adopted by the Security Council since they are to be given effect in accordance with the procedure applicable in that respect in the domestic legal order of each member state. Thus the UNC leaves the Members of the UN a free choice among the various possible models for transposition of those resolutions into their domestic legal order. Furthermore, immunity from jurisdiction for a Community measure like the contested regulation cannot find a basis in the EC Treaty and the few derogations from the primacy of the treaties that exist, could never authorise any derogation from the principles of liberty,

34 Furthermore, the Court considered that, in the absence of an international court having jurisdiction to ascertain whether acts of the Security Council are lawful, the setting-up of a body such as the Sanctions Committee and the opportunity, provided for by the legislation, of applying at any time to that committee in order to have any individual case re-examined, by means of a procedure involving both the "petitioned government" and the "designating government" ..., constitute another reasonable method of affording adequate protection of the applicant's fundamental rights as recognised by *jus cogens*.

35 C-402/05P and C-415/05 P, 2008 ECR I-6351.

democracy and respect for human rights and fundamental freedoms enshrined in Article 6(1) EU as a foundation of the Union.

Therefore, judicial review should not be excluded and Article 307 EC could in no circumstances permit any challenge to the principles of the foundations of the Community legal order, one of which is the protection of fundamental rights, including the review by the Community judicature of the lawfulness of Community measures as regards their consistency with those fundamental rights; the review by the Court of the validity of any Community measure in the light of fundamental rights must be considered to be the expression, in a community based on the rule of law, of a constitutional guarantee stemming from the EC Treaty as an autonomous legal system which is not to be prejudiced by an international agreement.

In any event, the existence, within that UN system, of the re-examination procedure before the Sanctions Committee could not afford generalised immunity from jurisdiction within the legal order of the Community. According to ECJ, the procedure before the Committee still did not provide individuals with a real opportunity of asserting their rights and depended on each of its members not using their veto. There is no requirement that the Sanctions Committee has to communicate to the applicant the reasons and evidence justifying his appearance in the summary list or to give him access, even restricted, to that information. And if the Committee rejects the request for removal from the list, it is under no obligation to give reasons.

Therefore, the EU courts must ensure the full review of the lawfulness of all Community acts in the light of the fundamental rights forming an integral part of the general principles of Community law, including review of Community measures which, like the contested regulation, are designed to give effect to the resolutions adopted by the Security Council.

As to alleged infringements of fundamental rights, the ECJ held that neither the regulation nor the common position provided for a procedure for communicating the evidence justifying the inclusion of the names of the persons concerned in the list and for hearing those persons, either at the same time as that inclusion or later. Because the Council neither communicated to the appellants the evidence used against them nor afforded them the right to be informed of that evidence within a reasonable period after the measures were enacted, the parties were not in a position to make their point of view in that respect known to advantage. Therefore, the appellants' *rights of defence*, in particular the right to be heard, were not respected.

Given the failure to inform them of the evidence adduced against them, the parties were also unable to defend their rights with regard to that evidence in satisfactory conditions before the Community judicature, with the result that their right to an effective legal remedy had also been infringed. And that infringement had not been remedied later, in the course of proceedings. Thus, ECJ considered itself unable to undertake the review of the lawfulness of the regulation with the result that it held that the fundamental right to an effective legal remedy had not been observed. Accordingly, ECJ held that the pleas of breach of *right to defence and the principle of effective judicial protection*, were upheld.

As to whether the blacklisting constituted an infringement of *property rights*, the Court held that the regulation was adopted without offering Kadi review, in a situation in which the restriction of his property rights was significant, having regard to the general application and continuation of the freezing measures affecting him, constituted an unjustified restriction of his right to property.

Thus, the ECJ ruled that the regulation had to be annulled. However, it considered that annulment with immediate effect would be capable of seriously and irreversibly prejudicing the effectiveness of the restrictive measures imposed by the regulation and which the Community is required to implement, because in the interval preceding its replacement by a new regulation the parties could take steps seeking to prevent measures freezing funds from being applied to them again. Therefore, the ECJ decided that the effects of the contested regulation, in so far as it included the names of the appellants in the list, should be maintained for a brief period, so as to allow the Council to remedy the infringements found, but also with due consideration of the considerable impact of the restrictive measures concerned on the parties' rights. ECJ set the dead line to three months as from the date of delivery of the judgment.

3.2.3. *Kadi II*[36]

The Court of Justice delivered its judgment on 3 September 2008. By letter of 8 September 2008, the Permanent Representative of France to the UN, acting on behalf of the EU, requested the 1267 Sanctions Committee, as a matter of urgency, to make available on its website, in accordance with paragraph 13 of Resolution 1822 (2008), the summary of reasons for Kadi's inclusion in that committee's list. By letter of 21 October 2008, the Chairman of the Sanctions Committee communicated the summary of reasons to France's Permanent Representative to the UN and authorised its transmission to the applicant and/or his legal representatives. Subsequently, that summary of reasons was also published on the Sanctions Committee's website. By letter of 22 October 2008, France's Permanent Representative to the EU transmitted that summary of reasons to the Commission, in order to enable it to comply with the judgment of the Court of Justice in *Kadi I*. On 22 October 2008, the Commission sent Kadi a letter informing him that, for the reasons set out in the summary of reasons provided by the Sanctions Committee and attached to that letter, it envisaged adopting a legal act with a view to maintaining his listing in Annex I to Regulation No 881/2002 in accordance with the first indent of Article 7(1) of that

---

36 T-85/09, Judgment 30 September 2010.

regulation. The Commission further informed the applicant that the purpose of its letter was to give him the opportunity to comment on the grounds included in the summary of reasons and to provide any information to the Commission that he might consider relevant before it took its final decision. The deadline set for the applicant for that purpose was 10 November 2008. The summary of reasons attached to that letter was drafted in identical terms to the summary of reasons communicated by the Sanctions Committee.

By letter of 10 November 2008, the applicant submitted his comments in response to the Commission. Kadi requested the Commission to disclose the evidence supporting the assertions and allegations made in the summary of reasons and also the relevant documents in the Commission's file; requested a further opportunity to make representations on that evidence, once he had received it; and attempted to refute, providing evidence in support of his refutation, the allegations made in the summary of reasons, in so far as he was able to respond to general allegations.

On 28 November 2008, the Commission adopted Regulation 1190/2008 amending for the 101st time Regulation No 881/2002. The preamble contained information on the above-mentioned steps taken by the Commission in order to comply with the judgment by ECJ in the *Kadi* case and the assessment that it had carefully considered the comments received from Kadi and given the preventive nature of the freezing of funds and economic resources, the Commission considered that the listing of Mr Kadi was justified for reasons of his association with the Al-Qaeda network. The regulation entered into force on 3 December 2008 and applied from 30 May 2002.[37]

Mr Kadi sought to have regulation 1190/2008 annulled by the General Court (formerly the CFI). The Court, after reiterating the findings of the ECJ in the first *Kadi* case, made some observations as to the *temporality of targeted sanctions*. In view of the fact that then nearly 10 years had passed since the applicant's funds were originally frozen, it could be questioned that the freezing of funds is a temporary precautionary measure which does not affect the very substance of the right of the persons concerned to property in their financial assets but only the use thereof. The same, the Court went on, was true in respect of the statement of the Security Council, repeated e.g. in Resolution 1822 (2008), that the

37 After this, the Commission by letter of 8 December 2008 replied inter alia that after having carefully considered the comments received from Kadi in a letter dated 10 November 2008, the Commission considered the listing justified for reasons of association with the Al-Qaeda network. The narrative summary of reasons was attached to this letter. The Commission also enclosed the text of the contested regulation, drew the applicant's attention to the possibility of challenging the regulation before the Court and informed the applicant that individuals, groups and entities concerned might submit at any time a request to the Sanctions Committee to have their names removed from the list, and provided details of the relevant contacts and the address of a website where the applicant might obtain further information. The narrative summary of reasons enclosed with the Commission's letter of 8 December 2008 was identical to the summary of reasons.

measures in question 'are preventative in nature and are not reliant upon criminal standards set out under national law'. The Court found that in the scale of a human life, 10 years in fact represent a substantial period of time and the question of the classification of the measures in question as preventative or punitive, protective or confiscatory, civil or criminal seemed to be an open one.[38]

As to the infringements of *the rights of the defence and of the right to effective judicial protection*, the Court considered that the applicant's rights of defence had been 'observed' only in the most formal and superficial sense, as the Commission considered itself strictly bound by the Sanctions Committee's findings and therefore did not envisage to question them in the light of the applicant's observations; furthermore the Court found that the Commission failed to take due account of the applicant's comments and as a result he was not in a position to make his point of view known. The procedure followed by the Commission, in response to the applicant's request, did not grant him even the most minimal access to the evidence against him. In fact, the applicant was refused such access despite his express request, whilst no balance was struck between his interests and the need to protect the confidential nature of the information. The few pieces of information and the imprecise allegations in the summary of reasons appeared clearly insufficient to enable the applicant to launch an effective challenge to the allegations against him so far as his alleged participation in terrorist activities was concerned.[39]

The Court applied criteria identical to those used by the ECtHR to the facts of the case, and found it clear that the applicant was not in a position to mount an effective challenge to any of the allegations against him, given that all that was disclosed to him was the summary of reasons. And the Court found it telling that the Commission made no real effort to refute the exculpatory evidence advanced by the applicant in the few cases in which the allegations against him were sufficiently precise to permit him to know what was being raised against him. The Court found the regulation adopted in breach of the applicant's rights of defence.[40] Furthermore, given the lack of any proper access to the information

---

38 The General Court stated further: "Although a discussion of this question is outside the scope of these proceedings as it is defined by the pleas set out in the application, the General Court considers that, once there is acceptance of the premise, laid down by the judgment of the Court of Justice in Kadi, that freezing measures such as those at issue in this instance enjoy no immunity from jurisdiction merely because they are intended to give effect to resolutions adopted by the Security Council under Chapter VII of the UNC, the principle of a full and rigorous judicial review of such measures is all the more justified given that such measures have a marked and long-lasting effect on the fundamental rights of the persons concerned."

39 The Court used a particular piece of information to illustrate its point, commenting that the applicant was a shareholder in a Bosnian bank in which planning sessions for a terrorist act against a United States facility in Saudi Arabia 'may have' taken place, was a particularly telling, but in no way unique example, of allegations not otherwise substantiated and thus irrefutable.

40 The Court remarked that the fact that the applicant had an opportunity to be heard by the Sanctions Committee in the re-examination procedure with a view to him being removed from its list clearly does not remedy that breach of his rights of defence.

and evidence used against him, Kadi had had to defend his rights in unsatisfactory conditions before the Court, resulting in a breach of his right to effective judicial review.[41] Consequently, the General Court found itself unable to undertake a review of the lawfulness of the regulation, which in itself constituted that Kadi's fundamental right to effective judicial review had not been observed.

As regards the Council's argument that the additional procedural safeguards put in place by the Commission in response to the judgment of the Court of Justice in Kadi corresponded to those put in place by the Council in response to the first PMOI judgment, the General Court found that the Council had disregarded the procedural differences between the two Community regimes used for the freezing of funds. The Community fund-freezing regime at issue in the cases culminating in the PMOI judgments is characterized by a two-tier procedure, one national, the other Community. Under that regime, the rights of the defence are in the first place effectively safeguarded as part of the national procedure, in which the party concerned must be placed in a position in which he can effectively make known his view on the evidence against him, subject to review by the national courts, or, as the case may be, the ECtHR. Those safeguards of the rights of the defence which exist at national level relieve the Community institutions from the obligation to provide fresh safeguards at Community level. However, external blacklisting is characterised by an absence of any safeguards of the rights of the defence which could be the subject of effective judicial review at the level of the procedure before the Sanctions Committee. Therefore, the Community institutions had to ensure that safeguards are put in place and implemented at Community level.

Finally, after having found that the regulation constituted an unjustified and disproportionate restriction of Kadi's right to property, the Court annulled the regulation on this ground too. The General Court did not make the judgment subject to any qualifications or limitations. The decision was taken on the 30 September 2010.

4. DEVELOPING MULTIPLE PERSONALITIES?

During the recently passed decade the EU legal institutions have had the opportunity to make a choice between trust and no trust in respect of its view on

---

41 The Court held that that infringement had not been remedied in the course of the action. Indeed, given that, according to the fundamental position adopted by the Commission and supported by the Council and the intervening governments, no information or evidence of that kind could be the subject of investigation by the Community judicature, those institutions adduced no evidence to that end. Moreover the Court observed that, although the Commission had taken formal note of the guidance given in the judgment of the Court of Justice in *Kadi*, it had produced no information concerning the evidence against the applicant.

applying criminal and quasi-criminal sanctions, or to uphold both contradictory views and develop a troublesome schizophrenia, risking a sufficiently precise determination of its identity and definition.

The system of blacklisting persons and organizations as subjects for the freezing of their assets, with the purpose to fight terrorist activity, seems to have entered the EU to stay. That is despite the fact that it is in many ways contrary to individual fundamental rights and to the ideal of the *Rechtsstaat*, a common and basic feature of most civilized states and particularly so in the EU. Furthermore, it is quite clear that blacklisting has not proven effective in view of its purpose.[42] The positive aspects of blacklisting can only be described negatively: using blacklisting spares the civil population from being the subject of an embargo, or even, conceivably, an invasion.

In my view, the Lisbon Treaty does not change much as regards external blacklisting. Small changes have been introduced. Now, under Article 215 it is possible to make non-state entities targets of financial sanctions, something considered legal also before Lisbon by the judgment of the Court of Justice in the *Kadi I* case. Furthermore, under Article 215 there must be safeguards for individuals, the Charter of Human rights and fundamental freedoms is now binding and there is an explicit right for individuals directly affected to appeal against Common Positions. As is clear from above, this is a codification of a position taken by the Court of Justice pre-Lisbon.

As to the initial position of the EU judiciary, illustrated by the case law referred above, it would seem like it favoured the idea of blacklisting belonging to international law and that the standards of international law should apply. In the first Kadi case the CFI held that its possibility to review an act by the UN Security Council was limited to the question of whether or not *jus cogens* had been breached. In the first *Mojahedin* case the same Court held that in respect of internal blacklisting, although the right to a fair hearing should apply as well as the obligation to state reasons and the right to effective judicial protection, those rights were subject to severe limitations. Since internal blacklisting presupposes a decision by a competent national authority, questions concerning the appropriateness of the decision or whether it is well-founded or if it infringes individual rights, should exclusively be brought up before the domestic authority or court. Only in cases where the Council uses new facts, may the European judiciary review the substance of the matter. As to effective judicial protection the Court found that the Council enjoys broad discretion and that review must be restricted to checking whether the procedural rules and the statement of reasons have been complied with, that facts are substantively accurate and that there has been no manifest error of assessment of facts or misuse of powers.

Over time it seems like the positions of the ECJ and the General Court gradually have narrowed the scope and effect of the ace of spades being played by

42 See Cameron 2008.

the UN Security Council. Furthermore, the respect towards the EU Council and the member states governmental decisions in this field has suffered from the findings of the courts.

As the law stands today in respect of external blacklisting, it is clear that the EU judiciary now exercises full judicial review of all EU acts regarding the freezing of assets of individuals. As to internal blacklisting the review is more limited, but the limitations are qualified by the existence of a reviewable decision by a domestic authority based on all facts constituting the ground to put the individual or organization in the list.

It is now clear that, in respect of external blacklisting, the introduction at the Security Council of a possibility to apply to be taken off the list and the new procedure before the Commission, do not meet the requirements of the right to defence under EU law. An individual must have recourse to an effective right of defence, meaning a right to be informed of the reasons, underlying facts as well as a right to put forward counter-arguments and have them genuinely scrutinized. The EU judiciary will not accept formalistic, but ineffective, fulfilments of the requirements.[43]

As to internal blacklisting, the requirements are quite harsh in respect of the Council's decision to put and keep a person in the list. That goes for the Council's assessment of the motivation and content of the domestic decision, as well as for the Council's considerations as why to maintain a name in the list. Furthermore, internal blacklisting decisions are subject to requirements of prompt information to the listed persons and an effective and genuine evaluation of the response.

Finally, from the latest judgment by the General Court in the second *Kadi* case, it seems clear that blacklistings cannot be seen as provisional measures. As said, ten years must be considered to be a considerable period of time in terms of a human life.

Still, it must be remembered that both of the *Mojahedin* and *Kadi* cases were quite obvious examples of infringements of procedural rights. The cases reveal a number of grave errors and unfounded decisions and badly concealed attempts to maintain persons in the list in spite of poor reasons for it, all of which can be attributed to decisions by EU institutions and national authorities. It is still difficult to say whether the courts will reject a blacklisting where procedural requirements are met and where the evidence presented is only vague, but not obviously lacking in substance. Thus, it remains to be seen whether the EU courts will manage to re-establish the trust in the EU-project, a trust it needs to proceed, but which has become severely tainted after the involvement in the business of blacklisting individuals and organizations.

In my view, the findings of the General Court in the latest *Kadi* case in 2010 are very important. When the court held that blacklisting in that case could not

43 See further the discussion in the introductory chapter in this volume on safeguards for anti-terrorist and regime sanctions.

be seen as a temporary measure, it basically swept the ground of arguments supporting the acceptance of EU blacklisting. The ace of spades argument already rejected, the rejection of the provisionality argument would really lead to a complete disarmament of the blacklisting regimes and points at directing EU measures against terrorism along the only sensible path, that of harmonized and domestic criminal law legislation. This is what EU already has chosen when dealing with suspected terrorists with connection to EU states. Furthermore, the decision shows that a choice has been made, that the EU continues to aspire to be a legal order and that it did not give in to the temptation to follow commands without reason. Under those circumstances, the disgrace of allowing and enforcing a system of blacklisting can be overcome; under the requirements set up by the EU judiciary the system is bound to be ineffective and inconvenient to use, at least in the EU. Thus, the judgment shows that there are reasons to trust the EU; even if it takes a decade there is a fair chance that the law works and that the nice words in the EU Charter of Fundamental Rights have a real meaning.

In order to give something of an answer to the question on the future position of the EU in respect of blacklisting, I would say that it is clear that the judiciary seems to favour individual rights and safeguards, whereas the Council, the Commission and the member states' governments appear to take their obligations under international law seriously. Peculiar enough, this could mean that the former upholds a supranational identity and mutual trust within the EU, whilst the latter identifies the EU as a subject in the context of international law rather than something different. I guess that leaves the EU in a kind of schizophrenic state, with multiple personalities, which is not surprising considering the complexity of the Union legal order, but which does not make the future process of finding an identity easy.

THE PLACE OF SANCTIONS IN THE EU SYSTEM FOR COMBATING THE FINANCING OF TERRORISM

Maria BERGSTRÖM

1. INTRODUCTION

Combating terrorism is a global challenge, one of the main objectives of the European Union,[1] and 'one of the fastest developing policy regimes within the EU.'[2] Due to its historical context and focus, and although EU competence is widening, the European Union's fight against terrorism has so far mainly been targeted at *combating the financing of terrorism* (CFT). The aim of this policy is to stop the flow of money to terrorist groups and to use the intelligence gathered from financial surveillance to identify and prosecute terrorists. The methods used are mainly to tighten controls on money transfers and involve sensitive issues such as the misuse of non-profit organisations by terrorists, and the exchange of personal data.[3]

The introduction of measures against the financing of terrorism, were the first steps taken by the US in its "war on terror" following 11 September 2001.[4] Hence, terrorist financing as such, only came under the spotlight after the 9/11 attacks.[5] In Europe, and increasingly so following the attacks in Madrid and London in 2004 and 2005 respectively, CFT is a core component of the EU's strategy in the fight against terrorism.[6] Adopted in 2005, this strategy commits the Union to combating terrorism globally, while respecting human rights and

---

1 The extraordinary European Council of 21 September 2001 defined terrorism as one of the main challenges facing the world and identified the fight against terrorism as one of the European Union's priority objectives.

2 Eckes 2011, p. 127.

3 According to the Council of the European Union, The European Union Counter-Terrorism Strategy, 30 November 2005, tackling the misuse of the non-profit sector remains a priority. See also Allam and Gadzinowski 2009, p. 37.

4 Having said this, it is of course difficult to establish exactly 'when and how the view developed that attacking the money trail was a key element in the fight against terrorism.' Levi 2010, p. 666.

5 O'Neill 2012, p. 33.

6 The European Union Counter-Terrorism Strategy, above.

allowing its citizens to live in an area of freedom, security and justice. The Strategy, that follows the Action Plan on Combating Terrorism,[7] is built around the following four strands:

- **Prevent** people from turning to terrorism and stop future generations of terrorists from emerging;
- **Protect** citizens and critical infrastructure by reducing vulnerabilities against attacks;
- **Pursue** and investigate terrorists, impede planning, travel and communications, cut off access to funding and materials and bring terrorists to justice;
- **Respond** in a coordinated way by preparing for the management and minimisation of the consequences of a terrorist attack, improving capacities to deal with the aftermath and taking into account the needs of victims.

The EU Strategy in the fight against terrorism is being implemented through a number of different measures, many of which are derived from pre-existing anti-money laundering (AML) programmes.[8] The CFT initiatives can be divided into two different but complementary approaches both derived from international sources. The first aims at 'directly cutting off the funds and economic resources of terrorist suspects or terrorism supporters, the other at stopping the misuse of the financial system in order to channel money (criminal or not) to terrorist purposes.'[9] Firstly, targeted asset-freezing sanctions, i.e., provisions for freezing terrorists' assets and the financial freezing methods implementing the UN Security Council (UNSC) Resolutions 1267 (1999) and 1373 (2001), targeting individuals and groups suspected of providing assistance to terrorist organisations. Secondly, the AML measures implementing the Financial Action Task Force on Money Laundering (FATF) recommendations that focus on preventive action rather than the practice of listing suspects and freezing their assets. Accordingly, the EU Strategy from 2005 mentions both approaches, and notes that 'the EU has already put in place provisions for freezing terrorist assets. The next stage is to implement the EU-wide legislation concerning money laundering and cash transfers, and to agree steps to impede money (wire) transfers by terrorists.'[10] Otherwise, there is nothing at all about

7 The Council of the European Union, *EU Action Plan on Combating Terrorism*, last updated on 9 December 2011. For an analysis of these documents, see Murphy 2012, pp. 27 et seq., with further references.

8 According to the European Union Counter-Terrorism Strategy, above, it is necessary to ensure that financial investigation is an integral part of all terrorism investigations and that these measures and others which build on the Financial Action Task Force's recommendations, form part of the EU's comprehensive strategy for combating terrorist financing.

9 Gargantini 2011, p. 160.

10 The European Union Counter-Terrorism Strategy, above, para. 29. As noted in the introductory chapter of the present volume, the FATF does not consider that the EU legislative framework for freezing is complete.

anti-terrorist sanctions – which gives rise to the question as to how central these really are to counter-terrorist strategy.[11]

The next part of this chapter provides a brief overview of the EU System for combating the financing of terrorism thereby briefly outlining both approaches. Due to their greater effect on the EU legal framework, focus will be set on the AML measures. The third part of this chapter is then focusing more closely on some theoretical and practical challenges connected to the specific methods and measures discussed in the previous sections. The concepts of security and securitisation are used as an analytical tool in analysing the diverging but complementary approaches developed within this field. Finally, some conclusions are drawn discussing the coherence of applying AML tactics to terrorist sanctions.

2. THE EU SYSTEM FOR COMBATING THE FINANCING OF TERRORISM – AN OVERVIEW

2.1. BACKGROUND

US President George W. Bush (in)famously used the term "Global War on Terror" to cover the US response to the 9/11 attacks in New York and Washington in 2001. The term illustrates the securitisation of threats to the financial sector since finance was to be used as an explicit means in this global war on terror. Money trails of the hijackers 'revealed blueprints for the architecture of the terrorist organisation',[12] while at the same time they illustrated the vulnerabilities of the international banking system.

Certain European states have had long experience of fighting terrorism, for example, the UK, with paramilitary organisations in Northern Ireland, the left-wing Rote Armee Fraktion in Germany, the Brigate Rosse in Italy, and the terrorists of ETA in Spain.[13] Generally speaking, the European paradigm of anti-terrorism has been law enforcement and policing.[14] The EU in any event has tried to promote a criminal justice approach to the fight against terrorism,[15] where human rights law has to be respected in the criminal prosecution of

11 The same can be said as regards the European Security Strategy 2003, which simply mentions (on p. 7) that the EU "has responded after 11 September with measures that included the adoption of a European Arrest Warrant, steps to attack terrorist financing and an agreement on mutual legal assistance with the U.S.A. The EU continues to develop cooperation in this area and to improve its defences".

12 Allam and Gadzinowski 2009, p. 37.

13 See e.g. Levi 2010, p. 651.

14 Allam and Gadzinowski at p. 41. Although this is something of a simplification, as the anti-terrorist campaigns in Spain and Northern Ireland involved at times both military and para-military elements.

15 See, e.g. Murphy 2012.

terrorists.[16] This is at times difficult to reconcile with the military and military-type responses favoured by the US in certain situations. Given the global context of the struggle against terrorism, the EU member states must (or feel they must) collaborate with the US.

For example, there is an EU-US Agreement on Terrorism Finance Tracking Programme (TFTP)[17] that took effect on 1 August 2010.[18] This agreement allows the transfer to US Treasury of certain categories of data regarding bank operations stored in the EU. The initial interim agreement was rejected by the European Parliament since it did not sufficiently protect EU citizens' privacy. The new agreement introduces certain safeguards to accommodate legitimate concerns about security, privacy and respect of fundamental rights. Each US request has to be verified by Europol as to its necessity for fighting terrorism. The data transferred to the US Treasury can be accessed only for counter terrorist purposes and extraction from the TFTP database has to be justified by evidence on a case-by-case basis. According to the Council, EU citizens have access to administrative and judicial redress.[19] However, doubts still exist as to how strong these safeguards actually are in practice.

Although the world's first law directed at money laundering was the 1986 US Money Laundering Control Act, and terrorist financing as such came into focus after 9/11, the UN had been first to introduce international rules on the subject with the adoption of the 1999 International Convention for the Suppression of the Financing of Terrorism.[20] Before 9/11, this convention had only been acceded by four States (Botswana, Sri Lanka, UK, and one Central Asian state).[21] With the change in global priorities, the adoption of the eight FATF special recommendations that requested the Member States to take immediate steps to ratify and implement the 1999 convention, and the passing of UNSC Resolution 1373 (2001) on targeted asset-freezing sanctions, the UN convention was 'rapidly adopted at a global level'.[22] Illustrative for the time, the meeting at which UNSC Resolution 1373 was adopted lasted only three minutes.[23] This fact may underline the concern about possible lack of scrutiny and legitimacy of the actions, as well as lack of proportionality and effectiveness. As it has been summarised by

16 Council of the European Union, *EU Counter-Terrorism Strategy – Discussion Paper*, 23 May 2012, p. 11.

17 This Terrorist Finance Tracking Programme (TFTP) was set up by the U.S. Treasury Department shortly after 11 September 2001.

18 Agreement between the European Union and the United States of America on the processing and transfer of Financial Messaging Data from the European Union to the United States for the purposes of the Terrorist Finance Tracking Program, OJ 2010, L 195/5.

19 Council of the European Union, *EU Action Plan on Combating Terrorism*, 15 November 2010, p. 22. See also Archik 2011.

20 UN International Convention for the Suppression of the Financing of Terrorism adopted on 9 December 1999.

21 Levi 2010, p. 652.

22 O'Neill 2012, p. 34.

23 Murphy 2012, p. 120.

Murphy, Resolutions 1267 and 1373 that are a key source of EU counter-terrorism policy, demonstrate 'a worrying tendency towards the pre-emptive exercise of power: the empowerment of executives, the lack of clear rules and the absence of due process.'[24]

As the international regulatory framework of combating the financing of terrorism consists of two complementary approaches I will begin with saying something about the relevant UN resolutions. This can be kept brief, as this is the subject of other chapters in this volume.[25] I will then turn to the general AML measures.

2.2. FINANCIAL FREEZING MEASURES

The change to 'smart' or 'targeted' sanctions, i.e. regulations imposing anti-terrorist sanctions on individuals, companies and organisations rather than states, was revolutionary. As put by Vestergaard, with the adoption of sanctions 'targeted at private individuals and organisations as a result of resolutions that are binding on UN members, the Security Council has taken on a role as international legislator. However, it has not simultaneously developed satisfactory protection against arbitrariness, abuse and exaggerated interventions.'[26] There are a number of instruments that can be applied including financial sanctions such as freezing of funds and other financial assets, bans on transactions and investment restrictions. Economic sanctions as a tool to preserve international peace and security have a long history but applying them to the type of terrorism which was the subject of the 9/11 attacks is something new.[27] As is well known, in the context of counter-terrorism, and the 'war on terror', 'two strands of targeted sanctions operate at European and international level'.[28] The primary source of these sanctions are UNSC Resolution 1267 (1999) with further amending resolutions, and UNSC Resolution 1373 (2001).[29]

Unlike the 1267 sanctions list, the resolution 1373 sanctions leave it to the states themselves to draw up and implement the list.[30] Within the EU, the

---

24 E.g. *op.cit.*, p. 122.

25 See in particular the chapters by Iain Cameron and by Torbjörn Andersson.

26 Vestergaard 2011, p. 178.

27 Murphy 2012, pp. 115–116, with further reference to Eckes 2009.

28 *Op.cit.* at p. 116.

29 UN Security Council Resolution 1267 (15 October 1999) on the situation in Afghanistan, targeting individuals and entities because of their association with Osama bin Laden and Al-Qa'eda, and UN Security Council Resolution 1373 (28 September 2001) Threats to international peace and security caused by terrorist acts, which is a general list developed by the EU itself to implement the Member States' international obligations. See further Murphy 2012, pp. 116–121.

30 See further, Murphy 2012, pp. 120–121.

provisions of UNSC Resolutions 1267 (1999) and 1390 (2002) are reflected in Council Regulation (EC) 881/2002.[31] The non-Al-Qaeda/Taliban provision of the EU with regard to counter-terrorism financing can be found in Council Common Position 2001/931/CFSP (cf. UNSC Resolution 1373 (2001)).[32] In addition, Council Regulation 2580/2001 on 'EU external terrorists' in contrast to 'EU internal terrorists', targets any sort of financing of terrorist activities thus giving effect to UNSC Resolution 1373 (2001).[33] As noted in the introduction to this volume, before the Lisbon Treaty, there was no explicit basis in the constitutive treaties for the freezing of funds of "internal" terrorists suspects. Even now, "internal" terrorist suspects listed by the EU have to present an EU wide threat since the EU does not have competence to enforce measures against purely domestic terrorists of the Member States.[34]

As is well known, the basic problem with the UNSC sanctions regime with regard to both human rights and constitutional legitimacy is the lack of access to any form of independent judicial review of the Sanctions Committee's decisions.[35] While improvements have been made, the question is whether these are sufficient to satisfy the demands placed by the CJEU.

---

[31] Council Regulation 881/2002 of 27 May 2002 imposing certain specific restrictive measures directed against certain persons and entities associated with Osama bin Laden, the Al-Qaeda network and the Taliban, and repealing Council Regulation (EC) No 467/2001 prohibiting the export of certain goods and services to Afghanistan, strengthening the flight ban and extending the freeze of funds and other financial resources in respect of the Taliban of Afghanistan, OJ L 2002, 139/9. This regulation on freezing the funds of certain persons and entities associated with the Al-Qaeda network, is implementing UNSC Resolutions 1267 (1999) and 1390 (16 January 2002) The situation in Afghanistan.

[32] Council Common Position 2001/931/CFSP of 27 December 2001 on the application of specific measures to combat terrorism, OJ L 2001,344/93. The purpose of this common position is to apply further measures to combat terrorism, in addition to the United Nations Security Council Resolution 1373 (2001). Specifically, it establishes a list of individuals, groups and entities involved in terrorism whose funds and other financial assets are to be frozen as part of the fight against the financing of terrorism. See also Council Common Position 2009/67/ CFSP of 26 January 2009 updating Common Position 2001/931/CFSP on the application of specific measures to combat terrorism and repealing Common Position 2008/586/CFSP, OJ L 2009, 23/37.

[33] Council Regulation (EC) 2580/2001 of 27 December 2001 on specific restrictive measures directed against certain persons and entities with a view to combating terrorism, OJ L 2001,344/70. This regulation is an EU measure that builds on the administrative and judicial procedures relating to terrorist organisations in EU and non-EU countries. The regulation provides for the establishment, review and amending of a list of persons, groups and entities to which it applies. This list has been updated by successive regulations and decisions.

[34] Levi 2010, p. 653.

[35] Vestergaard 2011, p. 179. See further the chapters by Andersson, Cameron and Eckes in the present volume.

2.3. ANTI-MONEY LAUNDERING MEASURES

2.3.1. Money laundering: beginnings

Although money laundering is an international phenomenon and constitutes a major problem around the world, the phenomenon and the term has not been noticed for more than 25 years. The term 'money laundering' (ML), although in use earlier, seems only to have been introduced in legislation in 1986 in the US Money Laundering Control Act of 1986.[36] In the early days, ML was recognised mainly as a domestic problem. However, the dirty money that was laundered often came, and still comes today, from the trade in drugs, human trafficking and other transnational criminal activities.[37] ML is a crime that hinders the proper workings of financial systems,[38] something which is particularly threatening since a sound financial infrastructure is one of the fundamental features of a stable society.

Attention to ML as a global problem began with the prohibition of the laundering of drug proceeds in the United Nations Convention against Illicit Traffic in Narcotic Drugs and Psychotropic Substances (the Vienna Convention).[39] The Vienna Convention was still limited to drugs and did not specifically refer to the term 'money laundering'. In 1988 principles dealing with money laundering were also adopted by the Basel Committee on Banking Supervision (BCBS).[40] This body consists of banking supervisory authorities in a number of states and aims to produce common standards of supervision of banking and financial institutions. The Council of Europe Convention on Laundering, Search, Seizure and Confiscation of the Proceeds from Crime (Strasbourg Convention),[41] from 1990 is the first multilateral treaty which deals generally with 'laundering offences'.[42] The Strasbourg Convention also widened the so-called 'predicate offences' beyond drug-trafficking. The term 'proceeds' in the Strasbourg definition covers 'any economic advantage from criminal offences', whereas the term 'predicate offence' covers 'any criminal offence as a result of which proceeds were generated that may become the subject of an offence as defined in the 'laundering article'.[43]

36 Kersten 2002, p. 50.
37 Braithwaite and Drahos 2000, p. 105.
38 Combating Financial Crime and Money Laundering, 1997.
39 United Nations Convention against Illicit Traffic in Narcotic Drugs and Psychotropic Substances of 19 December 1988.
40 Prevention of criminal use of the banking system for the purpose of money-laundering, www.bis.org/publ/bcbsc137.htm.
41 Council of Europe Convention on Laundering, Search, Seizure and Confiscation of the Proceeds from Crime, 1990 (Strasbourg Convention).
42 This section is based on Kersten 2002, p. 50.
43 Article 1 of the Strasbourg Convention.

2.3.2. *Financial Action Task Force on Money Laundering*

The Financial Action Task Force on Money Laundering (FATF) has become a major player in AML regulation. The FATF is not created by treaty. It was established in July 1989 by decision of the Paris summit of the G-7, as a response to the G-7's recognition of the threat to banking and other financial institutions by drug ML.[44] The FATF is thus a part, albeit, autonomous, of the Organisation of Economic Cooperation and Development (OECD). It currently consists of 34 Member States and two regional organisations.

The FATF sets standards or model rules and then tests member states against these. It works by peer-review: panels composed of national experts in law and banking are established which periodically evaluate states' laws and practices. The FATF can apply, and has, applied, sanctions in the form of warning states which are considered to be failing to comply with the "non-binding" FATF standards. This results in significantly higher transaction costs for financial institutions in the blacklisted state, as financial institutions in other FATF states demand greater security when dealing with them. This type of "blacklisting" partially explains relatively high degree of compliance with the FATF standards. As far as EU states are concerned, the standards are, in fact, binding, as they have been incorporated into EU legislation (below). After 9/11 the FATF recommendations were subjected to extensive revisions, which among other things resulted in the adoption of 8+1 special recommendations thus widening the applicable area of the model rules. Yet, as was mentioned above, AML measures were in place in Europe two decades before the 9/11 attacks, where the rationale for their introduction had nothing to do with terrorist financing.

2.3.3. *Anti-money laundering and the European single market*

The emergence of the European single market required European rules on financial transactions. On 1 January 1993, a number of rules were adopted such as rules on free movement of capital, and the liberalisation of the banking, insurance and investment services.[45] Preventive measures to ensure that an open and liberal financial market was not abused by criminal elements, such as the first AML directive in 1991,[46] were also adopted. The elimination of national borders demanded compensatory measures to delimit financial cross border crimes. Hence, the rationale for adopting the first AML directive was clearly compensatory to the development of the internal market.

---

44 Winer 2002. See also O'Neill 2012.

45 Sideek 2002; Sideek 1999.

46 Council Directive 91/308/EEC of 10 June 1991 on prevention of the use of the financial system for the purpose of money laundering, OJ L 1991, 166/77.

The first AML directive was the first stage in combating ML at European level. It was strongly influenced by the existing international standards and from the beginning, it was emphasised that any Community action should take particular account of the recommendations adopted by FATF.

The first directive required Member States to prohibit ML and to oblige the financial sector, comprising credit institutions and a wide range of other financial institutions, to identify their customers, keep appropriate records, establish internal procedures to train staff and guard against ML and to report any indications of ML to the competent authorities.[47]

The preamble of the first directive states that ML must be combated mainly by penal means and within the framework of international cooperation among judicial and law enforcement authorities thereby referring to the Vienna and the Strasbourg conventions. Nevertheless, clearly lacking criminal law competence at the time,[48] the EU adopted the directive employing the legal bases of former Articles 57(2) and 100a of the EC Treaty on the right of establishment and the establishment and functioning of the internal market.[49]

The preamble further states that ML has an evident influence on the rise of organised crime in general and drug trafficking in particular and that there is more and more awareness that combating ML is one of the most effective means of opposing this form of criminal activity, which constitutes a particular threat to Member States' societies. Yet, the directive recognised that a penal approach should not be the only way to combat ML 'since the financial system can play a highly effective role'.[50]

2.3.4. *Revising the FAFT recommendations towards fighting organised crime*

At the first revisions in 1996, the forty FATF recommendations were widened in scope to reflect evolving ML typologies. For instance, the 4th recommendation was changed to 'each country should extend the offence of drug money laundering to one based on serious offences'. According to Kersten, this corresponded to a growing trend based on 'the dramatic increase in non-drugs based organised crime and on the realisation that having a wide range of predicate offences should improve suspicious transaction reporting and above all

47 Recital 4 of Directive 2005/60/EC of the European Parliament and of the Council of 26 October 2005 on the prevention of the use of the financial system for the purpose of money laundering and terrorist financing, OJ L 2005, 309/15.

48 See, however, the limited third pillar measure, Council Framework Decision 2001/500/JHA of 26 June 2001 on money laundering, the identification, tracing, freezing, seizing and confiscation of instrumentalities and the proceeds of crime, OJ L 2001 182/1.

49 After the Lisbon Treaty, these articles have been amended and renumbered to Articles 53 and 114 TFEU.

50 Directive 91/308/EEC above.

facilitate international co-operation between judicial and police authorities in different countries.'[51]

In 2000, the UN General Assembly adopted the United Nations Convention against Transnational Organised Crime. This Convention is a framework convention, designed to deal with a variety of illegal activities ranging from ML to trafficking in human beings. The focus was now clearly transnational organised crime of a certain severity. In the 2000 UN Convention, 'serious crime' is defined as 'conduct constituting an offence punishable by a maximum deprivation of liberty of at least four years or a more serious penalty'.[52]

On 4 December 2001, the second AML directive was adopted, amending the first AML directive.[53] The second AML directive specifically referred to the widened definition of ML, beyond that of drugs offences, as reflected in the 1996 revisions of the forty FATF recommendations.[54] The directive further stated that the suppression of organised crime was particularly closely linked to AML measures.[55]

The other main change was an extension of the obligation of the directive to certain non-fiscal activities and professions, i.e. auditors, external accountants, tax advisors, real estate agents, notaries, lawyers, dealers in high-values goods whenever payment is made in cash amounting to € 15,000 or more, and finally, casinos.[56]

2.3.5. *Revising the FATF recommendations towards combating the financing of terrorism*

The second AML directive was soon to be replaced when FATF after 9/11 explicitly extended its recommendations to include the financing of terrorism, adopting eight special recommendations for that purpose.[57] According to these, each country should take immediate steps to ratify and implement the 1999 UN International Convention for the Suppression of the Financing of Terrorism,[58] and implement the UN Resolutions on the Prevention and Suppression of the Financing of Terrorist Acts.[59] Each country should criminalise the financing of terrorism, terrorist acts and terrorist organisations, and ensure that such offences

---

51 Kersten 2002, p. 55.

52 Article 2b of the United Nations Convention against Transnational Organized Crime adopted on 15 November 2000.

53 Directive 2001/97/EC of the European Parliament and of the Council of 4 December 2001 amending Council Directive 91/308/EEC on prevention of the use of the financial system for the purpose of money laundering, OJ L 2001, 344/76.

54 Recital 7 in Directive 2001/97/EC.

55 Recital 10 in Directive 2001/97/EC.

56 By Directive 2001/97/EC newly inserted article 2a into Directive 91/308/EEC above.

57 Agreed upon at a special meeting after the 11 September attacks.

58 1999 UN International Convention for the Suppression of the Financing of Terrorism adopted on 9 December 1999.

59 FATF Special Recommendation I.

are designated as ML predicate offences.[60] FATF also agreed upon rules about freezing and confiscating terrorist assets,[61] rules about reporting suspicious transactions related to terrorism,[62] and rules concerning international co-operation, alternative remittance, wire transfers, and non-profit organisations.[63] On 22 October 2004, a ninth special recommendation on cash couriers was developed with the objective of ensuring that terrorists and other criminals cannot finance their activities or launder the proceeds of their crimes through the physical cross-border transportation of currency and bearer negotiable instruments.[64]

The third AML directive brought the regional EU rules into line with the global, revised and expanded, 2003 FATF recommendations,[65] i.e. the forty recommendations on ML and the nine special recommendations on terrorist financing. In the recitals of the directive,[66] it is specifically stated that the EU should continue to take particular account of the recommendations of the FATF as the foremost international body active in the fight against ML and terrorist financing. It is further emphasised that the directive should be in line with the new international standard brought about by the revised and expanded FATF recommendations.[67] As a result, the preventive measures of the directive now cover not only the manipulation of money derived from crime, but also the collection of money or property for terrorist purposes.[68]

In this respect, the solution to the problem of ML was to establish a standard for risk analysis 'the risk-based approach' which has a prominent position in the third AML directive as well as in the amended FATF recommendations that it builds upon.[69] Accordingly, the biggest change in the third AML directive is this introduction of a risk based approach.

The starting point is that the risks differ between countries, customers and business areas and over time. The operators themselves are the best analysts of where the risk areas are, or might arise, as they best know their business and their customers. The idea is that the resources should be used where the needs

---

60 FATF Special Recommendation II.

61 FATF Special Recommendation III.

62 FATF Special Recommendation IV.

63 FATF Special Recommendations V to VIII. Recommendation VI has been covered by Directive 2007/64/EC of the European Parliament and of the Council of 13 November 2007 on Payment Services (PSD) in the internal market, OJ L 2007, 319/1, and Recommendation VII was addressed by Regulation (EC) 1781/2006 of the European Parliament and of the Council of 15 November 2006 on information on the payer accompanying transfers of funds, OJ L 2006, 345/1.

64 FATF Special Recommendation IX is covered by Regulation (EC) 1889/2005 of the European Parliament and of the Council of 26 October 2005 on controls of cash entering or leaving the Community, OJ L 2005, 309/9.

65 FATF 40 Recommendations of 20 June 2003, incorporating the amendments of 22 October 2004.

66 Directive 2005/60/EC, above.

67 Recital 5 in Directive 2005/60/EC.

68 Recital 8 in Directive 2005/60/EC.

69 For a critical analysis of the risk-based approach, see Herlin-Karnell 2011.

arise and the framework is supposed to be more flexible and adjustable to the risk. Within a risk-based approach, businesses are expected to make risk assessments of their customers and divide them into low and high-risk. In order to enable operators to assess whether a situation involves a risk of ML and terrorism financing and to then act accordingly, the directive introduces more detailed provisions. For this purpose, the directive specifies a number of customer due diligence (CDD) measures that are more extensive and far-reaching for situations of higher risk, such as appropriate procedures to determine whether a person is a politically exposed person. The risk-based approach further emphasises that the evaluation of who is high or low risk is to be a continuous process. As a result, the concept of "know your customer" as used in the financial sector, is now in practice applicable to all covered by the directive.

Besides extending its provisions to any financial transaction which might be linked to terrorist activities, and the introduction of the risk-based approach, the main changes of the third AML directive were the widening of identity checks on customers opening accounts,[70] that checks apply to any transaction over € 15,000,[71] stricter checks on politically exposed persons (PEPs),[72] and the introduction of penalties for failure to report suspicious transactions to national financial intelligence units (FIUs).[73] Further, in comparison with the second AML directive, the third directive now explicitly covers also trust or company service providers and instead of 'dealers in high-value goods', 'natural or legal persons trading in goods', amounting to € 15,000 or more.[74]

2.3.6. *Reflections on the legal basis*

The first and second directives were introduced to protect the financial system and other vulnerable activities and service providers from being exploited for ML and terrorism financing purposes. The rules cover, in other words, not only the proceeds of crime but also the collection of funds that can be used for terrorism purposes. Against this background it is perhaps less surprising that the third EU AML directive is based on the legal bases for establishment and the internal market. Still, this choice of legal basis can be questioned.

---

70 Article 6 in Directive 2005/60/EC.

71 Article 7 in Directive 2005/60/EC.

72 Article 13(4) in Directive 2005/60/EC, According Article 3(8) 'Politically exposed persons' means natural persons who are or have been entrusted with prominent public functions and immediate family members, or persons known to be close associates, of such persons.

73 Article 39, Section 4 on penalties, in Directive 2005/60/EC. See also Council Decision 2000/642/JHA of 17 October 2000 concerning arrangements for cooperation between financial intelligence units of the Member States in respect of exchanging information, OJ L 2000, /271/4.

74 Article 2 in Directive 2005/60/EC compared with article 2a in Directive 91/308/EEC inserted by Directive 2001/97/EC.

The third AML directive, as well as its predecessor, outlines a long list of actions to be considered an offense when committed intentionally (Article 1). The directive applies to a large number of private actors whose participation is no longer voluntary. Recital 41 of the directive states that the importance of combating ML and terrorist financing should lead Member States to establish effective, proportionate and dissuasive sanctions in national law for failure to respect the national provisions adopted pursuant to the directive. Article 39.1 provides that Member States shall ensure that natural and legal persons covered by the directive can be held liable for infringements of the national provisions adopted pursuant to the directive. Again, the directive states that sanctions must be effective, proportionate and dissuasive, which resembles, among other the wordings of the environmental crime case.[75] The directive further provides that sanctions should be provided for natural and legal persons. Hence, there are rules on liability also for legal persons (Article 39(3) and 39(4)) and the directive states that sanctions should be tailored to the operations of legal persons when they are often involved in complex ML or terrorist financing operations.

The use of administrative sanctions is governed by Article 39(2), which states:

> Without prejudice to the right of Member States to impose criminal penalties, Member States shall ensure, in conformity with their national law, that the appropriate administrative measures can be taken or administrative sanctions can be imposed against credit and financial institutions for infringements of the national provisions adopted pursuant to this Directive. Member States shall ensure that these measures or sanctions are effective, proportionate and dissuasive.

In sum, the requirements imposed in the form of customer due diligence, reporting and record keeping of statistics are extensive and cover a wide range of private actors. The sanctions required, however, are largely of an administrative rather than criminal nature. A comparison between Article 39(1) and 39(2) does not preclude Article 39(1) from including criminal sanctions should this be required in order to be effective, proportionate and dissuasive. After Lisbon, this is no longer a problem, should the EU legislator decide to adopt minimum rules on criminal sanctions relying on the new legal basis for criminal law in Article 83(1) TFEU.

---

75 The third AML directive was published one and a half months after the ECJ's judgement in the environmental crimes case. Compare ground 48 of the European Court of Justice's judgment on 13 September 2005 in case C-176/03 *Commission v Council* [2005] ECR I-7879: "... the last-mentioned finding does not prevent the Community legislature, when the application of effective, proportionate and dissuasive criminal penalties by the competent national authorities is an essential measure for combating serious environmental offences, from taking measures which relate to the criminal law of the Member States which it considers necessary in order to ensure that the rules which it lays down on environmental protection are fully effective."

3. SECURITY, SECURITISATION AND RISK-MANAGEMENT

3.1. A CHAMELEON THREAT?

The EU legal basis is now clear, but it should be stressed that the policy underlying the field has undergone a transformation. The field of AML regulation illustrates the ongoing shift within the EU from embracing mainly internal market matters towards introducing compensatory measures, via criminalisation as a means to make EU law effective, and then a further shift towards the securitisation of certain issues. ML has been formulated as a chameleon threat that must be fought, since 'it is perceived to facilitate drug trafficking (in the 1980s), organised crime (in the 1990s) and, post September 11, terrorism'.[76] Hence, the fight against organised crime and later terrorism has put AML regulation high on the political agenda.

In the legal understanding of the term, national security is often invoked to justify the exercise of state power against individuals, but at the same time national security has implications for the division of power between the different branches of government. Securitisation is often seen as an attempt to shift policy making to a less accountable forum,[77] something which also has effects on human rights.[78] I would argue that securitisation has indeed been used to secure, or at least resulted in, increased competences for the EU. AML regulation has been the result of securitisation of transnational criminality, and more recently, securitisation of financing of terrorism including targeted asset-freezing sanctions.

Placed in the context of the securitisation of transnational criminality,[79] it has been argued that the EU AML framework constitutes a new paradigm of security governance.[80] The regulatory agenda is linked to the reconceptualisation of security towards making the fight against non-military threats such as drug trafficking, organised crime and terrorism a top political priority globally. The securitisation process has led to "the creation of money laundering counter-measures – which are deemed essential to counter these threats".[81] Arguably, the further shift within AML regulation towards the fight against terrorism and the risk-based approach provides rich empirical evidence. AML and targeted asset-freezing sanctions are thereby exemplifying the shift towards securitisation of threats to the financial sector in general.

---

76 Mitsilegas, *Money Laundering Counter-Measures in the European Union*, 2003, p. 186 with further reference to Mitsilegas, *Countering the Chameleon Threat of Dirty Money*, 2003.

77 Cameron 2011.

78 Vestergaard 2011.

79 See e.g. Giraldo and Trinkunas 2010.

80 Mitsilegas 2003.

81 Mitsilegas 2003, p. 3.

3.2. SECURITY, SECURITISATION AND RISK-MANAGEMENT

Without any theoretical ambition in relation to the fast evolving field of security studies, this chapter makes use of some of the key concepts developed in the international relations theory in order to analyse some empirical examples from the regulatory fields of AML and targeted asset-freezing sanctions. In doing so, I draw upon the concepts of security and securitisation used in Alan Collins' Contemporary Security Studies from 2010.[82]

When feeling secure, people are assured that they will continue to enjoy the things most important for their survival and wellbeing. In contrast, existential threats are the most serious threats individuals or states can face. Individuals threatened with death, or states threatened with external invasion and conquest, are seen to justify the most extensive measures to secure against them. Whereas the state and its defence from external military attacks is studied in traditional security studies, non-traditional security studies focuses on non-military challenges to security. Already in the 1980s, the traditional conception of security based solely on military threats at the state level was being questioned by academics.[83] Since then, the concept of security has been broadened beyond the state and military defence which has been commonly accepted. The answer to the question who or what should be secure, still includes the state, but extend also to other referent objects of security, such as individuals, economies or the environment.[84] It has been argued that security must refer to the security of people in general, not just for the inhabitants of particular states, hence formulating the concept of world security.[85] Similarly, societal security has been presented as an alternative to the state, as well as the individual, thereby introducing the notion of a collective of people being secured.[86]

In a broad sense, the answer to the question secure against what, i.e. the actual threats, embrace ethnic conflict, human rights, under-development, famine and environmental degradation.[87] Further, in the post-Cold War era, the fight against non-military threats such as drug trafficking, organised crime and terrorism has become a top political priority globally.[88]

In the international relations literature, securitisation refers to the classification of certain phenomena, persons or entities as existential threats requiring emergency measures. This process of securitisation was introduced by scholars working at the Conflict and Peace Research Institute (COPRI) in

82 Collins 2010.
83 Mitsilegas 2003, p. 3 with further references.
84 Collins 2010, pp. 490–498.
85 Walker 1993, p. 140.
86 Roe 2010.
87 Walker 1993, p. 140. See the analysis by Mitsilegas 2003, p. 5.
88 Mitsilegas 2003, p. xiii.

Copenhagen. These scholars, later known as the Copenhagen School, placed primary importance on determining how an issue becomes a security issue.[89] In brief, when an issue is being securitised, it is made critically important thereby requiring emergency actions beyond the state's normal course of action. Within the understanding of this literature, a specific speech act by a securitising actor elevates the issue to a matter of importance and security. Whereas securitising actors are usually policy makers or bureaucracies, transnational actors and individuals are not excluded.[90] Hence, we think of something as a security issue, because "the elite, such as political leaders, have convinced us that it represents a threat to our very survival".[91] As a result, the elite use such speech acts in order to legitimise the use of emergency power to counter the threat. Threats however do not simply exist, but have to be articulated as a threat in order to become a matter of security. We speak then of "securitization". I would argue that ML is a good illustration of securitization: money laundering was portrayed by the administration of George W. Bush, as a security threat, thus requiring (and legitimating) a security-oriented response.

Similarly to the process of securitisation in the international relations literature, the concept of risk and risk management signals that an issue is put high on the business as well as the political agenda. To call something a risk is to call for action, risk assessment and risk management.[92] Risk management is expanding in both range and scope across organisations in the public and the private sectors, and has become something of a contemporary standard for dealing with uncertainty in an organised manner.[93] As a result, risk management focusing on the risk-based approach is used not only by the business sector, but increasingly also by regulators.[94] Within this context, future, anticipated risks must be prevented, leading the focus of regulation towards prevention. In this respect, transnational criminality including ML and terrorism financing provide some illustrating examples in the regulation of security in a risk society.

---

89 The process of securitisation is explained by in Emmers 2010. This chapter also notes limitations with the concept.

90 Collins 2010, p. 498.

91 Collins 2010, p. 6.

92 Bergström, Svedberg Helgesson and Mörth 2011, pp. 1045–1046 with further references.

93 Power, 2004, and Power, 2007. For an integrated analysis of the concepts of risk and securitization, see Bergström, Svedberg Helgesson, Mörth 2011. In this article a linkage is shown between the concepts of risk and securitisation, both emphasising the structural threats and uncertainties in the case of AML. Compare Mitsilegas 2003, p. 3, on 'reconceptualising security in the risk society'.

94 Hood, Rothstein, and Baldwin 2001.

3.3. SOME REFLECTIONS ON MONEY LAUNDERING AND SECURITISATION

In the EU, the securitisation process of ML has successively increased EU regulatory competence. This has resulted in a rigorous regulatory regime, putting strong demands on both public and private actors throughout the union.

Clearly, this shift with the reframing of ML as an existential threat linked to organised crime and terrorism has consequences for the division of power between the different branches of government on different levels, but also between public and private actors in this field that complicate the accountability dilemma even further.[95] Hence, the shift towards securitisation of ML indeed implies a shift of policy making to a less accountable forum, thereby not only including state actors on the national level. Arguably, and as a result, we can talk about a new and mixed model of accountability, where a legal model of accountability is emerging for for-profit actors entrusted with public tasks.[96] Besides, the shift towards security governance challenges fundamental legal principles, such as principles of criminal law and human rights.[97]

4. THE COHERENCE OF APPLYING AML TACTICS IN TERRORIST SANCTIONS

AML measures and financial freezing measures are in line with the risk society that treats the future as predictable and calculable.[98] As de Goede argues, the war on terror recognises that 'the sheer uncertainty and randomness of terrorist attack renders conventional risk assessment techniques inadequate.'[99] Murphy develops this argument with a discussion of preventive and pre-emptive approaches:[100]

> Both preventive and pre-emptive approaches aim to avoid harm by incapacitating dangerous groups and individuals. However, since the al-Qaeda attacks, as the risk is considered incalculable, the potential damage catastrophic, and any harm intolerable, measured action based on prudential assessments is impossible. It is at this point that the approach shifts from prevention to pre-emption.

He then argues that pre-emption entails a greater intervention without concrete evidence of harm and that these tendencies can be observed in post 9/11 counter

95 See further Bergström, Svedberg Helgesson and Mörth 2011.
96 Bergström 2011.
97 See for a comprehensives analysis of AML in this respect, Mitsilegas 2003.
98 *Cf.* Murphy 2012, p. 10.
99 De Goede 2008 p. 164, cited in Murphy, pp. 10–11.
100 Murphy 2012, p. 11.

terrorism attacks. As a result, he argues that a pre-emptive approach to counter terrorism challenges and reshapes rule of law principles.[101] The use of the notion 'war on terror' thereby implying a shift beyond law enforcement mechanisms and the execution of civilian of soft power consequently need to be coupled with a strong emphasis on human rights, civil liberties and due process. Against the threat of terrorist action, it is necessary to strike an acceptable balance between liberty and security. Here it is of utmost importance that perceived terrorist threats are not overweighing restrictions on individual privacy and wrongful decision-making.[102] Thereby we must never accept that suspects are being deprived their right to defend themselves against financial sanctions. Nevertheless, despite the ruling in *Kadi* and *Al-Barakaat*,[103] Mr Kadi's assets in the EU remained frozen in the absence of due process at international level.[104] Hence, the procedural rights granted by the CJEU do not provide the necessary basis for challenging the freezing of assets and financial means.[105] Further, the reversed burden of proof where suspects must prove their innocence raises additional due process concerns.

While preventive and pre-emptive measures with far reaching consequences for civil liberties and due process are being shaped and implemented, it has been argued that AML measures are little effective in preventing the financing of terrorism, which in contrast requires comparably little money that need not be the proceeds of crime, but often come from entirely legitimate sources.[106] For example, the European Commission has calculated that the Madrid bombings in March 2004 were estimated to have cost € 8,000.[107] Similarly, FATF estimated the direct costs for the Madrid bombing to € 10,000 and for the London bombing in July 2005 to £8,000.[108] This can be contrasted with the € 10,000 threshold for money transfers set up by FATF special recommendation IX thus implemented

101 *Op.cit.* at p. 13.

102 Allam and Gadzinowski 2009, p. 42.

103 Joined Cases C-402/05 P & C-415/05 P *Kadi and Al Barakaat* [2008] ECR I-6351.

104 Murphy 2012, p. 145. On due process, see also Harlow and Rawlings 2010 with further reference to della Cananea 2009.

105 Vestergaard 2011, p. 199.

106 Y/Zen 2005, p. 14. This argument was supported by the written evidence given by Professor Iain Cameron to the House of Lords European Union Committee, *Money Laundering and the financing of terrorism: Volume II: Evidence*, 19th Report of Session 2008–09, (22 July 2009), HL Paper 132-II, p. 230; and in the presentation by Dr. Erik Wennerström, Swedish Foreign Ministry, at the Workshop on Accountability and Anti-Money Laundering, held at Hotel Kung Carl, Stockholm, on 25 April 2009.

107 Communication from the Commission to the Council and the European Parliament on the Prevention of and the fight against Terrorism financing through measures to improve the exchange of information, to strengthen transparency and enhance the traceability of financial transactions, COM (2004) 700 final, p. 3, cited by O'Neill 2012, p. 31.

108 Financial Action Task Force, *Terrorism Financing*, 2008, p. 7, cited by Allam and Gadzinowski 2009, p. 38.

through Regulation (EC) 1889/2005.[109] In contrast to terrorism financing, money laundering involves large amounts of money that can affect the financial sector's stability and reputation. As a result, AML measures aims both to prevent organised crime, but also to protect the stability of the financial system. In contrast, funding of terrorism may rely on both legitimate source and criminal activity.[110] In addition, the sources from which terrorism is financed 'have been (and remain) various and not mutually exclusive; and, in principle, they may be readily substituted for each other'.[111]

Hence, there is a fundamental difference between dirty money that aims to be inserted into the financial system and legitimate money attempting to fund illegal activities, which may require different counter methods. Thereby, the purposes behind ML and terrorism financing are completely different where criminal activity generally is driven by profit while terrorism is driven by political ends.[112] Accordingly, the EU definition of terrorism focuses on the aim of the act where it is not the action itself that labels it a terrorist act, but the motivation behind it.[113] Hence, terrorism financing focuses on the purpose for using the funds and not on the cleaning process.

In sum, ML starts with dirty illegal money but ends with clean legal money. It is driven by profit and involves large amounts of money. Methods used involve preventive action. Terrorism financing on the other hand may well start with clean money but the purpose for which the money is used is illegal. It is driven by political ends, and only relatively small means are necessary. In addition, terrorism financing often rely on small but numerous contributions. Here the methods used involve repressive practice of listing suspects and freezing their assets.[114] However, there is a risk that controls on legal sources of finance may 'displace terrorism finance from legal into illegal channels.'[115] In line with this, Levi further argues that it seems plausible that tighter financial and precursor controls ultimately 'reshape rather than resolve terrorism risks'.[116] In sum, however, AML measures and financial freezing measures although somewhat similar and complementary, are diverging both in aim, focus and counter methods.

As a result, 'financial intelligence efforts have had little externally discernible impact on reducing levels of terrorism or on criminal conviction.'[117] Thereby,

109 Regulation (EC) 1889/2005 of the European Parliament and of the Council of 26 October 2005 on controls of cash entering or leaving the Community, OJ L 2005, 309/9.

110 O'Neill 2012, p. 39.

111 Levi 2010, p. 653.

112 Allam and Gadzinowski 2009, p. 38.

113 Murphy 2012, p. 57. The EU definition of terrorism can be found in Council Framework Decision 2002/475/JHA of 13 June 2002 on Combating Terrorism, OJ L 2002, 164/3.

114 *Ibid.*

115 Levi 2010, p. 662.

116 *Ibid.*

117 Levi 2010, p. 650.

Levi argues that there are evaluation problems in knowing whether the lack of effects is due to measurement failure, i.e. to estimate how much harm terrorist attacks would have entailed in the lack of controls, but also theory failure and implementation failure.[118] In addition, there is a great risk that risk based analyses focus on what regulators are likely to punish them for, rather than on any real evidence on threat actions.[119] Nevertheless, AML was 'the best fit available',[120] and there was a policy making and global evaluation/enforcement mechanism already available.

What AML measures and financial freezing measures have in common, however, is the shift in intensity and transformation of the respective policy field following the 9/11 attacks. This chapter has therefore tried to provide a common ground by using the concepts of security and securitisation as an analytical tool for analysing the diverging but complementary approaches developed within these fields. As a result, the securitisation of both policy fields, have resulted in increased competencies for the EU. In order to develop the European tradition of law enforcement and policing, these increased competencies must be accompanied by enhanced safeguards regarding human rights, civil liberties and due process.

118 *Ibid.*
119 *Op.cit.* at p. 667.
120 Levi 2010, p. 653.

HOW, IF AT ALL, DO ANTI-TERRORIST BLACKLISTING SANCTIONS FIT INTO (EU) CRIMINAL LAW?

Kimmo Nuotio

1. CRIMINAL LAW BEYOND THE STATE: INTRODUCTION

During the last two decades criminal law has travelled significantly beyond the state.

International criminal law has emerged, the UN has sharpened its profile, and regionally transnational actors such as the EU and Council of Europe (CoE) have developed an impressive body of law to deal with the new issues.

Three leading topics and drivers have been international core crimes, cross-border organised crime and international terrorism. The criminal law profiles of these three regimes are somewhat different. The anti-terrorism activities have since late 1990s developed a higher security profile, both in comparison to how these have been dealt with in the past by the international community and in comparison to international core crimes and cross-border organised crime.

The erection of the UN anti-terrorism regime directly under the Security Council is the clearest example of the high-security reframing. The anti-terrorist blacklisting sanctions targeting individual natural and legal persons present an immense challenge to European criminal law which is about to strengthen its structures and principles as it matures towards increased legality. In my paper I will go more deeply into the question of what is the role of these sanctions in EU criminal law. As is evident, it not only touches European criminal law generally, but also very heavily the developing constitutional principles and guarantees and thus the entire normative framework of European law.

This is a field where there is considerable research interest today. Anti-terrorist blacklisting has become a topic of discussion of debate which attracts the attention of many fields of legal scholarship, including international and European law and human rights and constitutional law. Perhaps traditional criminal law scholarship has been more marginal because the criminal lawyers have been digesting the new legal frameworks concerning terrorist offences.

Criminal procedural lawyers have also been occupied by other matters relating to criminal law co-operation, such as the new mutual recognition instruments. A more ordinary legal framework has been produced, involving a European system of enforcement of freezing orders, for example, covering the area of terrorist offences.[1]

A pioneering work in European law is Christina Eckes' book on EU Counter-Terrorist Policies and Fundamental rights. The Case of Individual Sanctions. I wish myself to discuss some very basic issues concerning the difficult relationship of blacklisting sanctions and criminal law. In order to be able to do that, one has to take a detour through national legal orders. In order to keep the issues of principle in focus, I have chosen to make this tour on a rather abstract level, and so my discussion of case law is kept to a minimum.

As indicated by the above mentioned, the international law approach already reveals some basic characteristics of the profile of the efforts to address the substantive issues. Common to these fields of action is that the regulated and combated phenomena are perceived as particularly dangerous and thus requiring consistent criminal policy responses. The Palermo Convention from 2000 is a milestone in the field of combating international organised crime, but the two other fields are even more exceptional in that the UN Security Council has been involved in the development of them. The UN Security Council has decided on the establishment of the *ad hoc* international war crime tribunals, but in the case of measures against international terrorism, the UN Security Council has by its own action directly created the central legal framework and even the supervision mechanism in order to secure effective implementing by the state parties.

Anti-terrorist blacklisting sanctions are a novelty in several respects. As dealt with in more detail in Iain Cameron's introductory chapter in this volume, the employment of targeted sanctions by the UN Security Council is a relatively new thing. It continues the line of development that started with the launching of larger-scale sanctions targeting entire states in order to influence their behaviour. These blunt instruments were often criticised. At any rate, the sanctions targeted at states fit the classical understanding of international law better than the new sanctions targeted at individuals do. In the anti-terrorist regime the sanctions targeted at individuals concern especially terrorist financing. Criminalisation and prevention of terrorist financing present new ways to approach terrorist offences.

The emergence of individual sanctions regime is a product of a very complex phenomenon. It coincides with the efforts to define terrorism in international law, the Convention for the Suppression of Financing of Terrorism[2] being a path-opener in this respect. The UN Security Council introduced sanctions as regards

1 Council Framework Decision 2003/577/JHA of 22 July 2003 on the execution in the European Union of orders freezing property or evidence.

2 1999, UNTS 2178, p. 197.

Taliban and Osama Bin Laden in its Resolutions 1267 (1999) and 1333 (2000), already before 11 September 2011.[3]

The famous post-9/11 Security Council Resolution 1373 called upon the states to "become parties as soon as possible to the relevant international conventions and protocols relating to terrorism, including the Convention for the Suppression of the Financing of Terrorism".

Resolution 1373 (28 September 2001) is adopted under the powers of the SC under Chapter VII UNC. The first two paragraphs are binding on states, and they formulate duties concerning: prevention and suppression the financing of terrorist acts; criminalising the wilful provision or collection of funds by their nationals or in their territories with the intention that the funds should be used in order to carry out terrorist acts; freezing without delay funds and other financial assets or economic resources of persons who commit, or attempt to commit, terrorist acts or participate in or facilitate the commission of terrorist acts; prohibiting their nationals or any persons and entities within their territories from making any funds, financial assets or economic resources or financial or other related services available under certain circumstances.[4]

It was entirely exceptional that a SC Resolution set out duties for the states to criminalise action as the ordinary procedure would have been to negotiate an international treaty. The legal basis of the SC action was also entirely exceptional, as it denoted crime to be a threat to the peace and security of mankind, a label usually reserved for armed conflict.

Without a doubt the new high-security oriented paradigm brought about changes in how the phenomenon of terrorism was seen. A more indirect approach to dealing with terrorism has been taken, perhaps because the root causes of, particularly, "Caliphate" terrorism were seen as being too great a task to deal with, or because it was felt that there could be no rational basis for engaging with a loose network (or networks) with vague aims involving inter alia the creation (at least in the Islamic world) of some form of Caliphate.[5] The idea was to limit the capacity of relevant groupings to commit major terrorist attacks (at least in Western states) by targeting the people next to the terrorists themselves. As noted in the introductory chapter, the logic behind such an approach (at least as regards suppressing the financing of terrorism) is questionable. It means criminalising activities at a very early stage, no longer requiring completed offences or an attempt, but only preparatory stages.[6]

3 Www.un.org/Docs/sc/committees/1267/1267ResEng.htm.

4 See also the later Resolution 1540, 28 April 2004, concerning duties as regards ensuring that weapons of mass destruction do not come into the hands of terrorists.

5 See, e.g. Lehto 2008.

6 Having said this, criminalisation of preparatory stages is not a new phenomenon as regards crimes against the state.

Indirect liability is also based on the view that the sympathizers and promoters of terrorist activities, at least, are not unamenable to pressure (and so are not ideologically completely locked). And this is when blacklisting sanctioning mechanisms enter the field.

The European Council acted immediately after 9/11, but the agenda was not exactly the same. Common Position 2001/154/CFSP was a response to the UN SC Resolution dealing with bin Laden and others directly. The EU also implemented UN SC Resolution 1373 by introducing "specific measures" to combat terrorism. The "specific" was here again blacklisting of terrorists and terrorist organisations.[7] As dealt with in more detail in Torbjörn Andersson and Christina Eckes' chapters in this volume, the EU provided for (some) quality control in Article 1 para 4 by requiring "precise information or material in the relevant file which indicates that a decision has been taken by a competent authority in respect of the persons, groups and entities concerned ... based on serious and credible evidence or clues, or condemnation for [terrorist acts]". Listing thus did not require that the persons or organisations had been convicted for their actions, but something less. Starting of investigations, for instance, was sufficient. For the inclusion of persons, groups and entities that already had faced sanctions at UN level no further such requirement was set.

2. BLACKLISTING AS CRIMINAL LAW?

We may now raise the issue, is blacklisting that has followed the international and European models of sanctioning, really part of criminal law? I do not claim to give a full and definite answer to this question, but rather some thoughts around the issues. I think it is useful to compare the anti-terrorist measures with those addressing international organised crime, as these measures are in many ways parallel to each other. The biggest difference is precisely the fact that the criminal organisations have not been listed in a similar way, so that in that case you have the policing framework and the criminal law cooperation framework, but not the specific legal measure of the type referred above. Organised criminal groups are likewise not listed, but instead statistical and other information about them is being collected and published in various reports.

Terrorist blacklisting itself is as a decision outside of any criminal procedure. In that sense you could say that such a decision is administrative in nature. Only indirectly could a link be seen, as a criminal procedure could trigger also the adding of that person or entity to the list.

The characterisation of the decision to blacklist terrorists as administrative may also be problematic because the classical administrative procedures and

7 Council Common Position of 27 December 2001 on the application of specific measures to combat terrorism, OJ L 344, 28 December 2001, p. 93.

administrative decisions have dealt with quite other type of matters. Looked from the point of view of administrative law, blacklisting may look like very strongly security oriented, emergency law type of action, and thus an extension of administrative law. Another aspect which renders the decisions on listing problematic is that the instruments are actually legislative, but containing lists of individuals. Legislation typically deals with abstract matters and should not be individualised. Terrorist listing thus combines legislative and administrative instruments. The role of the individual in legislative proceedings is here much more obscure than what it is in ordinary administrative context. This again makes the entire matter highly political. It is difficult to see how one could and should secure participation rights etc. of the relevant groups. The matter is simply too extraordinary for any traditional consideration. Blacklisting legal frameworks highlight the anti-constitution of the security constitution as described by Kaarlo Tuori.[8]

My claim would be that this part of international law and European law mainly falls within the new emerging regime of security management. This is primarily administrative in nature and so it can and should be governed through administrative law and its principles, including the human and constitutional rights applicable. The connection with criminal procedure (ongoing investigations, convictions etc.) which is made a requirement of the European blacklisting system for terrorists I would see as being a guarantee (albeit a weak one) that a *pure* security approach will not be permissible. The EU blacklisting is not supposed to be based only on intelligence information: some sort *evidence* must be being collected.

The contrasting of terrorist blacklisting and other measures against terrorism with the measures against organised crime makes sense also in that respect that the two sorts of intelligence differ. Admittedly in many states the boundaries have become much more diffuse since the end of the Cold War, but anti-terrorism intelligence is still usually being dealt by the security and intelligence services, whereas organised crime is still the responsibility of the ordinary police, often that part of it dealing with national criminal intelligence.

3. BLACKLISTING, PROHIBITING: FREEDOM OF ASSOCIATION?

Blacklisting sanctions are targeting individuals and groups which share a terrorist purpose. It is worth mentioning that in Finland, when the new criminal law provisions concerning organised crime were drafted, the law of associations was regarded as relevant for the matter of defining criminal organisations. The

8 Tuori 2010. p. 25.

Act of Associations states in Section 3 that certain military-type associations are regarded as prohibited.[9] The idea is that the freedom of association does not include forming of such associations. The Constitutional Law Committee of the Finnish Parliament had, in its opinion on the bill concerning the introduction of specific terrorist offences referred, to this example because, in Finland (as in Sweden), freedom of association also applies to non-registered associations.[10] In other words, unlike the situation in many other countries, the law recognises a grouping as an association, and grants at least some of the benefits which flow from this, even before the grouping has been officially registered as an association. The Constitutional Law Committee was worried about the vagueness of the definition, and proposed specification.

However, the Law Committee, when it dealt with the same matter, did not follow that line. After the government bill had been given, the views on how an organised criminal group should be defined had developed in such a way that the analogy no longer worked. Associations could according to Finnish law be prohibited only when they have been fairly well structured, whereas one of the aims of the Palermo Convention was to lower the requirements of structuration concerning organised criminal groups.[11] The Law Committee stated that as the Constitutional Law Committee had already let the very identical definition of a terrorist group pass the preciseness test, a similar pattern should do here as well. As a result, the two legal definitions are practically identical.

In the law of associations, procedures against associations that have violated obligations of the law of associations may be either administrative or of a criminal nature. The criminal charges against individuals may be raised on the basis of illegal functioning of the association.[12]

---

9 Finnish Associations Act (503/1989) Section 3 Prohibited associations provides that "An association which due to the obedience required of members, to the division into units or groups, or to the equipping with arms is to be deemed, in full or in part, militarily organised, shall be prohibited".

10 Constitutional Law Committee 2000, 10 (PeVL 10/2000 – HE 183/1999 vp).

11 Law Committee 2002, 26 (LaVM 26/2002 vp – HE 183/1999 vp). Chapter 17 Section 1 a – Participation in the activity of a criminal organisation (142/2003) provides that "(4) A criminal organisation refers to a structured association, established over a period of time, of at least three persons acting in concert to commit the offences referred to in subsection 1". Chapter 34 Section 1 defines terrorist offences: A *terrorist group* refers to a structured group of at least three persons established over a period of time and acting in concert in order to commit offences referred to in section 1.

12 Act of Associations, Sect 62. The heavier criminal offence can be found in Chapter 13, section 4 of the Penal Code Section 4, Unlawful military operations (added by Act 578/1995) which provides that "A person who unlawfully establishes, organises or provides supplies to an association organised in a military manner and having the purpose of exerting political influence, participates in the leadership of such association, supports it financially or otherwise in a significant manner organises or provides military training in the association, shall be sentenced for unlawful military operations to a fine or to imprisonment for at most two years."

I think that here we actually have an analogy: blacklisting is a sort of recognition of a specific group as terrorist, and thus also as forbidden. The key issue is what justifies such a decision. Is it the threat to the society directly, or is it the legal procedure leading to this. The current legal and political frameworks do not allow for any real legal challenging of the underlying discretions. As noted by Eckes, "terrorists should only be identified in a legal framework that complies with the rule of law and meets a certain standard of legal protection".[13]

Today it is so evident that forming of terrorist organisations is not protected by freedom of association that the legal order in a sense ignores this middle step and proceeds immediately to the legal consequences of freezing the assets, prosecution for terrorist financing offences or other terrorist crimes etc. I think it would indeed be a strange way to argue if we would say that forming a terrorist group would be a way of exercising freedom of association and would justify our actions that way. As we normally do not treat terrorist groups as non-registered associations, the prosecutors do not request that the organisation be forbidden (at least in those states which provide for such a sanction). They simply process the charges against the individuals involved. The conviction against the individuals itself sort of automatically triggers the defining of the entity they are operating with, or in, as criminal. Blacklisting could be seen as a statement that certain groups and entities should be seen as prohibited and not protected by law. In states which provide for the prohibition of organisations deemed dangerous to the state this is indeed the case. Legal consequences follow immediately on the listing of an organisation.

In conclusion in this section I should note that, at the time of going to print, Finland introduced a bill providing for the creation of a national administrative anti-terrorist sanction system. According to the bill, the National Bureau of Investigation would decide on the freezing of assets of suspected terrorists.[14]

4. BLACKLISTING AS A GROUND FOR PROSECUTION AND CONVICTION?

We can now turn this picture also upside down. Does blacklisting mean that individuals involved in a listed group, or individuals themselves directly listed, can be convicted for terrorist offences before a court more easily than if this would not be the case?

Of course we can say first, that the listing may be in some sense relevant. If a person has been trained by Al-Qaeda, for instance, to commit terrorist attacks, I guess we all agree that we do not have to provide very detailed information about

13 Eckes 2009, p. 418.

14 Government bill 61/2012. Www.eduskunta.fi/triphome/bin/vex3000.sh?kaanna=ru&TUNNISTE =HE+61/2 012.

the fact that Al-Qaeda is a terrorist organisation. Usually it can be expected that some evidence must be presented before the court on this specific point. Perhaps some intelligence information may have to be disclosed, but probably the evidence for Al-Qaeda being a terrorist organisation would largely be in the public domain. Listing certainly is an indication that *some* evidence exists *somewhere* which speaks in favour of a group being "terrorist" in nature. But, as shown by Thomas Elholm's chapter discussing the Danish case law, in a *Rechtsstaat*, such a general indication is, and should be, by no means sufficient to prove the relevant facts before a criminal court.

The true advantage of criminal proceedings is that it is able to safeguard the interests of the accused against wrongful convictions by setting a high standard for the burden of proof, and placing the burden on the side of the prosecutor.[15] All this is very different as concerns the procedures leading to blacklisting. The individual or group in question has a much more marginal role, as such administrative procedures, especially when carried out on a transnational or international level, do not involve such types of procedural guarantees. It would be very interesting to make a comparative study of European criminal cases of conviction for terrorist offences in order to see whether blacklisting has played any role in this. Has blacklisting been brought to the agenda of the police or prosecutor, e.g. by influencing their decisions to initiate an investigation of, or a prosecution of, a person or a group? Has blacklisting been taken into account in the judgment, and if yes, in what way?

We could imagine that if a criminal charge has been brought against a blacklisted person, and this has led to a conviction, the court could even take into account the blacklisting as a *mitigating* factor, because it may have affected the life of the convicted person in many negative ways. In sentencing such circumstances could at least in principle be observed and taken into account. This would be all the more relevant if the suspect had been blacklisted on an international level.

A very interesting case would be one in which the assets of a person or of an entity have been frozen due to blacklisting for terrorist activity, but not in connection with a criminal investigation and for criminal charges. Can the police or the prosecutor request freezing and confiscation, if another regime already has dealt with the issue? If this option is excluded, then the court of course cannot decide on the freezing. And it also cannot decide on delisting, even though the criminal case ends with an acquittal. Parallel legal proceedings with different outcomes in administrative law and criminal law are not unusual. If a father, for instance, has been brought before the court on

15 This was stressed in the Swedish case concerning financing of terrorism, which dealt with collecting of funds allegedly destined for Hamas. The charges had been raised on both financing of terrorism and breaching the Swedish law of sanctions. Both instances came to the conclusion that the evidence presented was not convincing enough to reach conviction on either account. Hovrätten över Skåne och Blekinge, 2009-11-09, Mål B 685-09.

accusations of sexual crimes against his own child, and if the child welfare authorities have decided on coercive measures to protect the child (e.g. taking the child into care), then even an acquittal of the father on these charges does not automatically lead to an annulment of the administrative decisions. The two systems simply operate on different logics. The decision-makers in the administrative procedures may judge the facts differently and according to different standards of proof.

In a national setting, usually the line between criminal procedure and administrative procedure is relatively clear. However, some so-called security measures may have a mixed character, for instance the temporary withdrawal of driver's license after a case of drunk driving. It is there both to prevent the person from being a danger to traffic, and to simply punish the person. At an earlier stage, the police could order a similar measure for an interim period. Prohibitions are sanctions that can serve dual purposes.

Blacklisting which includes freezing of assets is an interesting case, because it is a security measure of the type a court can order during the course of an ordinary criminal procedure. But in the case of blacklisting the security measure is being resorted to without the usual involvement of a criminal court. It is kind of a security measure which has grown independent, one which has started a life of its own. This is a crucial feature of blacklisting sanctions. In criminal procedure, security measures always also serve the purpose of securing the criminal proceedings themselves and the possible confiscation and other enforcement orders. In criminal proceedings the security measures are *supplementary* to the proceedings themselves. If the proceedings are stopped and the case is settled, the security measures that are part of the same proceedings must also be stopped. In the case of blacklisting the story is different: the blacklisting does not terminate, unless such a mechanism has been built into the listing procedures.

It seems quite obvious that blacklisting does not have the effect that it would preclude criminal proceedings, because that would be very much contrary to the logic of the criminal law approach. The individual sanction is not tailored to be a punishment. Having said this, the individual sanction of blacklisting could, in principle, amount to a "criminal charge".[16]

So far we have discussed the relationship between individual sanctions and criminal proceedings, especially as regards prosecution concerning terrorist offences. What renders the matter more complex is that when the UN or EU individual sanctions regime requires national enforcement, this may again refer to criminalisation. The last issue to be discussed then, is, what about this case, when the prosecution directly follows from that: the duty of the state party / member state to enforce binding law.

16 See discussion in Eckes 2009, pp. 150–151.

In Finland a special Act from 1967 regulates the enforcement of sanctions when this flows from obligations as member of the UN (and later the EU). It was in fact this Act which was amended in 2002 as a result of the new UN and EU measures on individual sanctions. The amendment was needed especially in order to bring EU regulations adopted on CFSP grounds under that law and then, consequently, broaden the application of the rules on the regulatory offences respectively. The applicable law as concerning criminal law is Chapter 46 of the Finnish Penal Code, especially PC 46:1 on regulation offence. The specific sub-paragraph refers for this purpose to a Regulation, adopted on the basis of Article 60, 301 or 308 of the Treaty establishing the European Community, on the interruption or limitation of capital transfers, payments or other economic relations as regards the Common Foreign and Security Policy of the European Union (365/2002). Breaching of these regulations is punishable as a regulatory offence by fines or a custodial sentence up to two years. The offence requires intent. In minor cases, breaching is punishable by fines as a petty regulatory offence (PC 46:3). Grave breaching, in turn, is punishable by a custodial sentence from four months to four years (PC 46:2). To my knowledge, there has been no case in Finland in which this specific provision has been applied. Surely such a case would be very interesting, and it might be that at the end of the day the thresholds for a conviction on these grounds would not be so different from those as concerns terrorist financing.[17] In any case, this area of regulatory offences is the one which most clearly is directly a product of the developing sanctions regime and which is not administrative law but criminal law proper. The nexus between the sanctions regime and criminal law is, however, not quite direct. It is simply that effective enforcement has been assumed to require that the state party/member state create this link on the level of national laws.[18] As already mentioned, a bill has recently been introduced to provide for anti-terrorist sanctions in the future.

5. THE EUROPEAN CRIMINAL LAW, THEN?

At this point I would like to preliminarily conclude, that seen from the point of view of national criminal proceedings, blacklisting of terrorists and terrorist entities is not really directly a matter for the criminal law. The two regimes are parallel and coincide rather than being part of the same unity. It is maybe accidental that the development of the criminal law regime of terrorist offences

---

17 See the chapters by Thomas Elholm and Suus Hopman and Michel Uiterwaal regarding the Danish and Dutch criminal law provisions regarding implementation of EU/UN sanctions.

18 Here I can refer to the well-known ECJ formula requiring "effective, proportionate and dissuasive sanctions" for violations of EC (now EU) law, first used in C 68/88, *Commission v. Greece* [1989] ECR 2965.

has marched parallel to the erection of the international and European blacklisting sanctions regime.[19] The definition of terrorist offences on international and on European levels have perhaps, at least to some extent, secured legitimacy for the blacklisting sanctions regime, because without such a criminal law regime the international administrative security regime would look even more dubious. But this does not mean that the security regime could be built on the basis of the legitimacy of the criminal law regime. Rather, I would claim that the parallel coexistence of the two regimes shows that when very high-security agendas are involved, the influential states no longer trust the criminal law approach alone, but develop another complementing regime to provide – they hope – more efficient and preventive protection *vis-à-vis* the risks involved. In this respect I would say that the fact that UN Security Council introducing directly duties to criminalise is a very peculiar phenomenon which threatens to instrumentalise criminal law as well as being an expression of a "permanent state of exception".[20] In that sense also criminal law gets integrated into the same security regime as is the sanctions regime.

If we then look at the things at the European level, the picture is somewhat less clear. Terrorist listing has produced some of the most spectacular cases at the European courts, including the ECJ (and the CFI/General Court). At first sight these cases look like criminal cases, but on a closer look they deal with the international security regime aspect of them, not with the criminal law aspect.

I would argue that what makes the task of determining whether blacklisting is "inside" or "outside" European criminal law more complicated is that the borderlines of "European criminal law" are themselves vague and shifting. European criminal law is an umbrella under which many severe criminality/ security threats have been jointly addressed in the EU and CoE legal frameworks. Terrorism has been the threat that has maybe most influenced the introduction of European responses, having had an impact on many policies. During the period when the EU was split into "pillars" it made use of an entire "spectrum of powers" spread across all three pillars.[21] Outside the criminal law cooperation the actions have included blacklisting, control of money flows (money laundering), asylum and visa requirements. These are the areas that have developed in the shadows of the security regime, not directly linked with the emergence of the international and European criminal law regime concerning terrorism.

If we would like to develop the argument that terrorist blacklisting measures are part of European criminal law, we would have to adopt a very broad concept of European criminal law. Of course we could say that if we start from the fact

19 See, on the legal developments concerning the definitions of terrorism, Nuotio 2009, 998–1016.

20 *Cf.* Agamben 2005.

21 Husabø and Bruce 2009, p. 4.

that terrorism is a crime and that all these measures have been motivated by the aim to prevent terrorism, then in this sense they are measures of crime prevention and so part of crime policy taken in a broad sense.

We could also say that the two regimes, international and European security law/administrative law and European criminal law overlap, because the preventionist tendency has also marked very much the crime policy in the strict sense. The criminalisations introduced by a number of the framework decisions mean that people regarded as "dangerous" in some way are committing criminal offences long before any real commitment to launch a terrorist attack has taken place.[22] During the course of this reframing, the real touching points are getting weaker, and the subjective tendencies get an increased significance. This will certainly create problems for the authorities when they try to provide the courts with relevant evidence. Bearing this development in mind, the criminal lawyers, at least the Nordic ones, probably would like to see that blacklisting regime be kept at "safe distance" from criminal law, in order to minimise further erosion of the criminal law principles.

I think it is timely to notice that in a very special sense modern security oriented crime policy seems to transform the regimes in question into economic crime regime by regarding the economic aspects of it as the entry into the scene. Accordingly, the money laundering criminalisations are the "blunt instruments" in today's crime policy. In that way, much of the transformation of the regimes has already also reached the criminal law, with increased problems in safeguarding the classical virtues of legality and predictability, and with increased tendencies to place individual criminal actions into a larger frame of organised activity.

It is also well-known that in the context of EU law, ordinary disciplinary limits do not hold. European criminal law cooperation, for instance, covers both substantive criminal law and criminal procedural law. For that reason in most textbooks on European criminal law, not only criminal law is being discussed, but criminal procedure as well. As an example we could refer to the textbook by André Klip, *European Criminal Law*, which includes a brief and critical introduction to this field in a sub-chapter with the title "Sui Generis Measures: Freezing Orders, Sanctions and Boycotts", under the chapter 5 on European Criminal Procedure.[23] In Bernd Hecker's book *Europäisches Strafrecht* on the other hand, we find a much more classical structure, and very little traces about the problematique of the individual sanctions regime.[24]

We could also note that EU competences are more limited and fragmented than the national competences. As the EU always needs to give a legal basis for its actions, it is natural that two or more articles in the treaty providing for

22 See, e.g. Asp and Cameron 2010.
23 Klip 2012, pp. 265–269.
24 Hecker 2007.

different types of competence (asylum, police, competition law, criminal law etc.) are put together to justify a particular legislative proposal. As mentioned, this makes the borderlines of "European criminal law" even more difficult to draw.

The European criminal law is also a thinner concept than national criminal law, because it does not contain real directly applicable penal provisions, but it rather organises legislative and judicial cooperation and backs it up with European rules and institutions.

But even taking these observations into account, I would come to the conclusions that blacklisting itself is not part of European criminal law, but rather European administrative law, European security law, European economic law, that follows from the need to go beyond criminal law in addressing the issue of terrorism as a threat to the society.

My negative conclusion thus builds on the finding that a new type of transnational and international security law has been erected as a result to address the issue of terrorism. The recognition of this phenomenon of security law as different from traditional criminal law does not yet mean a full recognition of what it is, then, and how could and should it be "tamed".

It seems that this security law is administrative law with some criminal law characteristics, because of the intensive internal links between the two regimes. The classification that a phenomenon is part of criminal law brings certain advantages in terms of legal protection especially in the European region where the national constitutional traditions, European human rights law and the EU system of fundamental rights provide legal guarantees. It is especially against the background of such guarantees, or, as in this case, the lack of such guarantees, that the system of blacklisting with dramatic legal effects on the status of the individual being listed reveals itself as different and unpredictable.

Maybe in the final instance it does not even matter so terribly much how we decide the definitional issues as long as we are able to guarantee a high level of legal protection in all cases.

BLACKLISTING SANCTIONS AND PRINCIPLES OF CRIMINAL LAW

Petter Asp

If one is given – as I was – the task of discussing blacklisting sanctions from a criminal law perspective, the easy, expected and (at first sight) evident way out is probably to confront these sanctions with traditional criminal law principles with the view to ending up with the conclusion that the regulations that provide for blacklisting sanctions are not in conformity with basic criminal law standards and principles. For example, it could be argued that the targeted sanctions are in conflict not only with basic criminal procedural principles such as the right to be informed of the accusation, the right to be presumed innocent etc., but also with substantive criminal law principles such as the principle of legality, the principle of guilt and so on.

However, this is not what I will do. I will rather raise the question whether these targeted sanctions should – at all – be analyzed as criminal law measures and measured against criminal law principles, or whether they should rather be analyzed and measured as something completely different.

I have no definite answer to give to this question, but I am inclined to take the latter position.

What I am saying is basically that the differences between the blacklisting regime and criminal law are so great that it is not possible – or at least not very fruitful – to make direct comparisons between the systems. Such a position does not, of course, exclude the possibility that criminal law can be used as a more indirect and general standard of comparison. One can ask the rhetorical question what is the value in requiring reasonably strong legal safeguards and a fair amount of 'Rechtsstatlichkeit' within the criminal law system if we allow ourselves to take equally intrusive measures without such concerns outside this system?[1]

I will return to this at the end of this short article.

My point of departure when discussing these issues is that criminal law has sort of a Janus-faced character, i.e. it is (mainly) characterized by two different but interrelated features. Thus if one wants to distinguish criminal law from

1 Cf. Af Trampe, 1990, p. 5.

other disciplines I think that one will always end up returning to two very different characteristics:

(i) First, and on the one hand, it is of course inevitable to highlight the hard treatment and the intrusiveness of criminal law measures. Criminal law is about heavy sanctions and is often referred to as the last resort of the state. Criminal law might, in this respect, not differ that much from other branches of law if you look at the borders of the criminal law system. For example, the consequence of a fine is not necessarily more burdensome than that of a tax or a fee, but in the core areas the criminal law distinguishes itself from other areas by its brutishness. The keyword in this respect would certainly be imprisonment. If you look at criminal law as a system or as an ideal type it is clearly the most (or one of the most) intrusive measures available to the state. I will refer to this as ***the hard treatment aspect of criminal law.***

(ii) However, criminal law is not only characterized by its brutishness. When one gets down to the basic principles of criminal law one will quickly notice that criminal law is not only about hard treatment but that it is also a legal area which focuses very much on fair attribution, on establishing responsibility for a certain act and on the communication of censure. Thus, most substantive criminal law rules aim, in one way or the other, at establishing responsibility, i.e. at ensuring that the accused person can be held responsible for the act of which he is accused.[2] I will refer to this as ***the responsibility aspect of criminal law.***

The basic point of making this division is of course that sanctions may be construed in different ways and that some sanctions might resemble punishment in one way but not the other; thus if we acknowledge that we, by saying that something (a sanction) has "criminal law character", may refer to quite different aspects of a sanction or of a sanctioning regime, this will allow us to have a more nuanced discussion and debate.

If we take this Janus-faced character as a point of departure and turn to the basic principles of criminal law one could argue that some basic principles are closely connected to the hard treatment aspect of criminal law, while others are closely connected to the responsibility aspect of criminal law.

Thus, some basic principles of criminal law can be derived primarily from the burdensome character of criminal law sanctions, i.e. ***from the hard treatment aspect of criminal law.*** When a person is subject to criminal law intervention, this affects the person's life in an especially negative way and it seems quite reasonable to argue that this is, if not the only, then at least the major reason for providing certain specific criminal law safeguards which ensure that things are done in a proper way. Examples of such standards are:

2 It could actually be argued, as I have done elsewhere, that it is this interest in responsibility that provides criminal law sanctions with a censuring character, see Asp 1998, ch. 12.

(i) The Principle of Legality, which requires that the imposition of criminal law sanctions have a legal basis; this contributes both to foreseeability for the individual and makes it possible to control the use of public authority (and limits the discretion of the authorities) (Cf. Article 7 of the European Convention of Human Rights).

(ii) The right to a fair trial, which requires a fair process with reasonable safeguards for the accused party (the procedure should be balanced, the accused should have the right to be heard, to defend himself, be tried by a proper court, etc.) (Cf. Article 6 of the European Convention of Human Rights).

To summarize one could say that the especially burdensome character of criminal law justifies certain legal safeguards intended to control the use of criminal law. Basically this is also reflected in the case law of the ECHR; if one looks at the so-called Engel criteria, the severity of the sanction is one of the elements taken into account when checking whether a sanction falls under Article 6. This is not to say, however, that it is the decisive or even the most important element (the case law clearly also shows criminal law sanctions of lesser severity), but the overall severity of the criminal law system is certainly one key factor when it comes to explaining why there are special safeguards attached to it.

The other side of criminal law is the ***responsibility aspect.***

Criminal law is, to a very large extent, focused on ensuring that the person accused really is – or could be considered to be – responsible for doing the thing for which he or she is accused. And the things for which persons are accused are, typically, single and individualized acts. Thus, criminal law is special not only in that it imposes heavy sanctions, but also that it has a very strong focus on questions of responsibility, i.e. on establishing a normative connection between an individual on the one hand and a certain act (and its consequences) on the other. Thus, the basic structure is something like this:

responsibility?
Person ⟷ act incl. consequences and surrounding circumstances

Basically, one can react to wrongdoing in two different ways. Either one just uses force and simply connects undesired behaviour with a consequence, which will hopefully deter people from the behaviour in question. Treating people in this way comes pretty close to treating them like a dog or a rat in a scientific experiment. The simple message is that there is a consequence attached to a certain behaviour: "If you touch that button it will hurt."

The alternative way of dealing with wrongdoing is to treat the person as a moral agent with which one tries to communicate in a more sophisticated way. The message would be something like: you have done wrong and since you could have done otherwise we hold you responsible for doing wrong. This kind of communication makes it necessary to ensure that the person was actually responsible for "touching the button": censure presupposes, if not actual responsibility (a court might, of course, be wrong in finding someone guilty of an offence), at least that a person is being ***represented as being responsible***.

I would say that criminal law is at least trying to treat people in this second way, and that this is reflected in the fact that ***most basic substantive criminal law principles are actually concerned with establishing responsibility*** for the purpose of ensuring that a censuring response is justified and reasonable.

The most basic examples of this focus on responsibility are:

- the general requirement of a causal nexus and the related principles of (objective) attribution of consequences, and
- the general requirement of *mens rea*.

One could actually say that nearly all basic (substantive) criminal law standards aim at "connecting" the individual with his or her acts (including surrounding circumstances and consequences).

Let us start by taking a look at the principles related to the objective attribution of consequences to a person. Besides the general requirement of causality – which may be seen as a minimum requirement for responsibility for (tautologically speaking) consequences – there is under most criminal law systems some sort of doctrine which aims at establishing an "objective" connection between the individual and the consequences that the individual is being held responsible for.

For example there is, under Swedish and German criminal law, a concept of objective imputability (*objektive Zurechnung*) or "culpa as fault", which aims to connect the act of the individual and the consequences that the individual is being held responsible for.[3] Basically one can say that these doctrines require the judge to ask him- or herself:

> "whether [the perpetrator] committed the *actus reus* ... through carelessness".[4]

This requires a judgment to the effect that the actions controlled and performed by the perpetrator (e.g. to drive a car in a certain way) were careless, and that the consequences that happened as a result of his or her actions (e.g. the death of another person) can reasonably be attributed to this carelessness.

objective attribution?

person performs an act (driving) ⟵——————⟶ consequence (death)

3 See e.g. Roxin 2006, p. 343 ff. and Jareborg 1988, p. 30.

4 Jareborg 1988, p. 31.

If the consequence in question is caused in a way which cannot be attributed to an act controlled by the individual, or only attributed to an act which is controlled by the individual but which cannot be held to be careless, then he or she will not be held responsible for this consequence.

For example, if a person has driven a car with all reasonable care but nevertheless happened to cause the accident, the person will be acquitted due to the fact that her act of driving was not careless. There is a causal link between the driving and the accident, but since the driving was not careless it cannot form the basis of criminal responsibility. Similarly, a person who hopes to inherit from a relative and who gives that relative a flight ticket (with the sincere hope that the plane should crash and the relative should die) will not be convicted for murder even if the plane actually goes down: there is certainly a causal link between the act of giving a flight ticket and the death, but we would still hesitate to hold the person responsible since the act cannot reasonably be considered to be careless.

Responsibility can also be excluded if the person has performed an act that can be considered to be careless. For example, a person who drives too fast in one phase (phase 1) and then drives with all reasonable care in a second phase (phase 2) and during phase 2 happens to cause harm by pure accident, will not be held responsible for causing this harm. Even if the harm is caused ***as a result of the carelessness*** – the person would not have been in the place where the accident occurred if he or she had not been speeding – the accident is not caused ***through the carelessness***.

If these questions are not discussed under the heading of "objective attribution of consequences" they are dealt with under other headings (e.g. social adequacy and lack of adequacy of the causal nexus etc.). However, the point of all these principles are the same: to ensure that the person can reasonably be held responsible for a certain consequence of their actions.

Criminal responsibility does not only require that the act and its consequences can be "objectively attributed" to an act performed by the perpetrator, but also that the agent can be personally held responsible for the act and its consequences. Thus, there is a (more or less) general requirement of intent (here I include knowledge and recklessness) or negligence aiming at ensuring that the person did foresee, or at least could and should have foreseen, the consequences of his or her act and that, consequently, the person could be blamed for the act and the consequences following from it.

In our example with the driver who has caused the death of another person, the *mens rea* requirement ensures that the person not only has caused the death through an act that deviates from what is tolerable, but also that he or she can personally be held responsible for this (either due to the fact that she acted with some sort of required intent or due to the fact that she should have foreseen the consequences). Thus, the requirement concerns the relation between the perpetrator and his or her action (including consequences).

intent?

Perpetrator ⟵——⟶ Act including consequence (death)

The rule of excuses (one paradigmatic example is when a person is excused for having used an excessive amount of violence in self-defence) is another example of rules which shows how much weight the criminal law attaches to the idea of responsibility: even if a person has fulfilled the above-mentioned requirements (i.e. even if the act can be objectively attributed to the person and the consequences were covered by the intent of the perpetrator) the circumstances may be such that it is unfair to hold her responsible for the act.

To summarize, one can see the substantive criminal law rules as a set of rules that aims at establishing a link between the perpetrator and the act (including its consequences); visually it could be described in the following way:

criminal law

Perpetrator ⟵——⟶ Act (including consequences)

The point in making this distinction between ***the hard treatment aspect and the responsibility aspect*** of criminal law in this context is that, while it seems quite indisputable that blacklisting sanctions can be very burdensome for the individual (the blacklisting does obviously have considerable impact on the life of the persons being blacklisted), it is equally clear (if not clearer) that substantive criminal law principles that aim at establishing responsibility will be of little assistance when it comes to a system that is not at all built upon the idea of establishing responsibility for a specific act.

The blacklisting sanctions are simply another legal creature; they are not, as criminal law punishment is, imposed as a response to individualized acts, but they are rather imposed on the basis of a more general picture of the individual (based mainly on intelligence information).[5] Thus, I would argue, one cannot represent the blacklisting rules as a set of rules that aims at establishing the link between an individual and an act. It simply does not make any sense to picture the blacklisting regime as a link between a person and a specific act:

blacklisting sanctions-regime

Person ⟵——⟶ Act (including consequences)

The rules on blacklisting simply do not fulfil such a function. Thus, they must be analysed as something different from criminal law rules.

---

5 Also as regards the blacklisting regimes there should be some sort of statement of reasons indicating the reasons for putting a person on the list (see e.g. document 10826/1/07 REV 1 from the Council of the European Union paragraph 17 et seq. and Resolution 1989 (2011) from the Security Council, paragraphs 4 and 13. It seems clear, however, that we are quite far from the kind of responsibility-establishing activity which is normally performed within criminal law.

This might be a trivial conclusion, but I nevertheless think that it is important to underline, not least in these post-9/11 times where there is a clear tendency to focus on prevention and on promoting security by measures that do not really fit into the standard criminal law structures.

The blacklisting sanctioning regime is not the only example of such tendencies. Other examples are the use of preventive incarceration and the use of different types of surveillance for the purpose of intelligence (i.e. not for the purpose of investigating a crime that has been committed). What this article argues is:

- that as regards these types of measures standard criminal law models will be of little use, and
- that we – in relation to these types of measures – need to develop new models for analysis, new models for control of state power, and new standards of legal security.

This is not to say, of course, that one cannot criticise the blacklisting regime. Nor is it to say that comparison with the criminal law system is without any value. As implied at the beginning of this article, one could argue that the burdensome consequence of being blacklisted calls for reasonable safeguards and here criminal law can be used as a general standard by analogy: if the consequence of being blacklisted is approximately as burdensome as those of being punished, then the safeguards and controls should reasonably be – maybe not the same (cf. the general conclusion) – but at least at a similar level.[6] However, I do not think that we will get very far by simply transferring traditional criminal law standards to legal institutions which are, at least partly, something separate and different.

6 I guess it is fair to say that the case law on blacklisting sanctions so far has been going in this direction; see e.g. cases C-402/05 P and C-415/05 P.

EU BLACKLISTING SANCTIONS – A DANISH CRIMINAL LAW PERSPECTIVE

Thomas ELHOLM

1. INTRODUCTION

A lot of good legal research has been carried out on the EU blacklisting system. The focus has primarily been on the consequences for the blacklisted persons and the human rights deficits of the blacklisting system.

The topic of this paper is a Danish criminal Law perspective on blacklisting. So far no Danish citizens or Danish residents have been blacklisted. However, there might anyway be a number of legal consequences of blacklisting in Denmark. By looking at Danish case law concerning terrorism, I will try to outline the impact of the blacklisting system, i.e. the legal consequences of blacklisting in general.

2. LEGISLATION

Financing terrorists is criminalized according to the general provision on complicity in Section 23 of the Danish Criminal Code. However, the scope of this criminalization is broadened by Section 114 b:

> "Any person who
> 1) Directly or indirectly provides financial support to;
> 2) Directly or indirectly procures or collects means to; or
> 3) Directly or indirectly places money, other assets or financial or other similar means at the disposal of; a person, a group or an association, which commits or intends to commit acts of terrorism as included under Section 114 or Section 114 a of this Act, shall be liable to imprisonment for any term not exceeding ten years."

Thus, in order to be punishable for financing terrorists according to Section 114 b, it has to be established that the financially supported persons are actually terrorist according to the definition of terrorism in Section 114 of the Danish Criminal Code which provides that:

> "Any person who, by acting with the intent to intimidate a population to a serious degree or unlawfully coerce Danish or foreign public authorities or an international organization to carry out or omit to carry out an act or to destabilize or destroy a country's or an international organization's fundamental political, constitutional, financial or social structures, commits one or more of the following acts, when the act due to its nature or the context, in which it is committed, can inflict a country or an international organization serious damage, shall be guilty of terrorism and liable to imprisonment for any term extending to life imprisonment:
> 1) Homicide [...]
> 2) Gross violence [...]
> 3) Deprivation of liberty [...]
> 4) Impairment of the safety of traffic according to Section 184(1) [...], gross damage to property
> 5) Seizure of transportation means [...]
> 6) Gross weapon laws violation [...]
> 7) Arson [...]
> 8) [...]".

According to the *travaux préparatoires*[1] blacklisting "in itself" is not sufficient to conclude that an organization is committing terrorism within the meaning of Section 114. Also according to the *travaux préparatoires*[2] it is irrelevant for the criminal liability whether the financing of these groups has humanitarian purposes.

3. THE CASE LAW

3.1. CASE 1: SEIZURE OF DOCUMENTS (U 2007.1831 H)

An association made three documents available on its internet homepage appealing to other European associations to help collect money for FARC (Columbia) and PFLP (Palestine). The motive was challenging the Danish

---

1 Reply of 2 May 2002 to the Legal Committee of the Folketing (spørgsmål nr. 122): "As in other criminal prosecutions, the Danish court should make an independent evaluation of the evidence in the concrete case. The result of the prosecution will therefore, as in other prosecutions, be dependent on whether the prosecutor can prove the accused's guilt. The fact that an organisation is taken up on the EU's list of terrorist organisations does therefore *not in itself* mean that, in a prosecution in this country it will be regarded as proven that it is a terrorist organisation within the meaning of the provisions in question" [Italics added]. For an overview of section 114 and the travaux préparatoires see Vestergaard, 2006.

2 See bulletin from the Danish Parliament: *Folketingstidende* 2001–02, 2. samling, tillæg A, p. 1006.

legislation on terror and the EU blacklisting system. The documents were seized by the police in 2005 when the chairman of the association was charged with attempting to finance terrorist groups.[3] With reference to the EU blacklisting of FARC and PFLP – and without further exploration of the question whether FARC and PFLP are terrorist groups according to Section 114 – the City Court approved the seizure. The High Court referred to the *travaux préparatoires* according to which the definition of terrorism in Section 114 of the Criminal Code is similar to the definition of terrorism used by EU in the blacklisting procedure. Thus, the High Court approved the seizure. The decision was confirmed by Supreme Court by reference to the reasoning of the High Court.

3.2. CASE 2: THE *HAMAS* CASE (COPENHAGEN CITY COURT JUDGMENT OF 27 MARCH 2007 AND HIGH COURT JUDGMENT OF 6 FEBRUARY 2008 – UNPUBLISHED)

An association and two persons from the association were accused of financing terrorist groups by transferring money to a number of Middle East humanitarian organizations. The indictment is comprehensive and there are a number of different aspects in this case. However, I believe it is reasonable to summarize it this way: the prosecutor argued that there was a clear link between the humanitarian organizations and Hamas. The accused were acquitted at the City Court due to the lack of sufficient proof of this link. The High Court judges were divided into two groups. Three voted for conviction, considering that money from the Danish association had been transferred from the humanitarian organizations to Hamas. Three judges were of the opinion that the link/transfer had not been proven beyond reasonable doubt. Hence, all the accused were acquitted.

The issues in focus in this case were 1) whether there was a clear link between the humanitarian organizations and Hamas, and 2) (especially in High Court) whether Hamas had actually received the money transferred by the accused to the humanitarian organizations. One might expect that there would be extensive proceedings on the issue, whether Hamas could be regarded as terrorists according to Section 114 of the Danish Criminal Code. However, this was not the case. It is mentioned in the indictment and there are some sections of the trial record suggesting that this was an issue. However, it is not thoroughly dealt with and it is not part of the reasoning (i.e. of the three judges in High Court, who voted for conviction). Besides, the EU blacklisting played no explicit role in the proceedings.

---

3 Accused of attempt (Section 21 of the Criminal Code) of financing terrorists, Section 114 a, No 2 of the Criminal Code (now Section 114 b, No 2.).

3.3. CASE 3: *FIGHTERS AND LOVERS* CASE (U 2009.1453 H)

Six persons were accused of attempt of financing terrorist groups by selling T-shirts and trying to transfer the profit to FARC (Columbia) and PFLP (Palestine).[4] The intention was to buy radio equipment for FARC and printing equipment for PFLP. The sale was carried out on the internet in 2006 by the company "Fighters and Lovers" (FL). An important motive was the challenging of the Danish legislation on terrorism. There was an announcement on the FL internet homepage stating that the transfer of money to FARC/PFLP might cause legal problems. Thus one could say that the accused were aware of the fact that FARC and PFLP might be regarded as terrorist groups. The total amount of the sale of T-shirts was approximately 10.000 DKK (€ 1,400), and the profit from the sale was never successfully transferred but seized by the police.

Great effort was expended in the City Court and the High Court to find out whether FARC/PFLP were committing terrorism according to the definition of terrorism in Section 114 of the Criminal Code. A number of reports were made by political and other experts and they were called as witnesses to give extensive testimonies during trial.

All the accused were acquitted at City Court by the votes by two votes to one. The acquittal was mainly based on the fact that – according to the majority – it was not possible to assess the extent and execution of the acts committed by FARC and PFLP. Hence it was not proven beyond reasonable doubt that FARC and PFLP were terrorist organizations in the meaning of Section 114 of the Criminal Code.

At High Court (by five votes to one) two of the accused were sentenced to six months imprisonment, while the rest were sentenced to imprisonment varying from 60 days to four months (the sentences for these four persons were suspended).[5]

Much of the proceedings before High Court were directed to the question, whether FARC and PFLP are in fact involved in terrorism according to the definition of terrorism in Section 114 of the Criminal Code. A part of this aspect of the case is the question whether FARC and PFLP are freedom fighters, fighting illegitimate governments. Numerous experts were asked to write reports about this issue and called to give extensive testimony in court.

In the reasoning of the court it is said that PFLP and FARC have killed civilians in a number of cases during the years. On the basis of an overall or comprehensive assessment of the case ("*samlet vurdering*") the majority of judges finds that PFLP and FARC have carried out terrorism according to the definition in Section 114 of the Danish criminal code. These judges were not of the opinion

4 Section 114 a, No 2 of the Criminal Code (now moved to Section 114 b, No 2).

5 I.e. the execution of the sentence is deferred on the condition that the convicted will not commit any offences during the probation period.

that violations of fundamental human rights by Israel and Columbia could legitimize killing of civilians by FARC and PFLP. Neither did the judges find that the declaration made by the EU during the adoption of the Framework Decision on Terrorism – in which the EU says that the definition of terrorism does not include freedom fighters – could legitimize the severe attacks on civilians by FARC and PFLP.

Furthermore, the majority finds that the accused were aware of the fact that PFLP and FARC were carrying out acts of terrorism according to Section 114. This is clear from the testimony of the accused and from the (above-mentioned) announcement on the homepage of FL.

One dissenting judge at High Court did not find that FARC and PFLP were terrorist organizations but instead characterized these as freedom fighters.

The judgment was appealed to the Supreme Court. The Supreme Court is not capable of reviewing the evidence in cases like this, but the accused claimed that Section 114 of the Criminal Code had been applied wrongly, because the killing of civilians did not "in itself" amount to terrorism according to Section 114. They argued that the court has to make an overall or comprehensive assessment, taking the special circumstances of the fight for freedom into account.

The Supreme Court confirmed the conviction in the High Court thereby rejecting the argument of the accused. Supreme Court states that they have to rely on the evidence placed before the High Court, including the fact that FARC and PFLP were killing civilians. The Supreme Court found that even though Israel and Columbia were violating democratic and human rights principles, the acts committed by FARC and PFLP against civilians were of a very serious nature and should therefore be regarded as terrorism. The fact that the accused did not regard PFLP and FARC as terrorist organizations was not decisive for the *mens rea* of the accused.

However, the Supreme Court changed the sentencing.[6] The two convicted persons who had been sentenced to six months imprisonment had the sentences suspended due to doubt about the scope of Section 114 b.[7] It might seems strange that Supreme Court refers to Section 114 b and not to Section 114. One might say that it is the scope of 114 and the definition of terrorism which is unclear. At least this seems to have been the core issue of the reasoning at Supreme Court. It is supported by the fact that in the official abstract of the publication of the judgment, reference is made to "Section 114" on this point and not Section 114 b.

---

6 It also changed the sentencing of one of the other convicted persons, reducing the suspended sentence from four months imprisonment to 60 days.

7 In Danish: "*den nærmere rækkevidde af §114 b har givet anledning til tvivl*".

3.4. CASE 4: THE INTERNET APPEAL CASE (COPENHAGEN CITY COURT, 15 MARCH 2010)

A Danish activist group, Rebellion, formed in 2004 with the aim of challenging the recently adopted anti-terrorism legislation. The chairman (the so-called "spokesman") of this association was accused of participation in financing terrorist organisations.[8] According to the prosecutor he had been involved in the collection and transfer of 50,000 DKK to both FARC and PFLP – all made in the name of the association. This was the first part of the indictment.

According to the second part of the indictment the chairman was accused of attempting to finance terrorists by uploading documents on the internet homepage of the association. On the home page the association appealed to other European organizations to collect money for PFLP and FARC.

In this case the police had previously seized the uploaded documents (see case 1 above). One core problem of the case was the question whether money had been transferred at all (the first part of the indictment) another problem was whether the chairman was attempting terrorist financing. He claimed during the trial that the uploading of the appeal to other European organizations was a media stunt attempting to create debate about laws on terrorism, but with no intention of actually financing groups like FARC and PFLP (the second part of the indictment).

The reasoning of the court is more comprehensive than in most Danish criminal cases. The court starts by saying that the High Court found FARC and PFLP involved in terrorist acts according to Section 114 of the Danish Criminal Code and Supreme Court did not deny this decision.

Secondly, according to the City Court, the accused has not provided new information which could challenge the status of PFLP and FARC according to Section 114 of the Criminal Code.

Thirdly, the accused knew about (or found it most likely) that PFLP and FARC were performing activities covered by Section 114 of the Criminal Code.

Fourthly, concerning the first part of the indictment (transfer of money to FARC and PFLP) the court finds that money has been collected (or at least there has been an attempt to collect money[9]) with the intention of transferring the money to PFLP and FARC. However, the court did not find it proved beyond reasonable doubt that money had been transferred. Thus, the accused was convicted of attempt. Furthermore, the accused was convicted of "participation" (according to Section 23 of the Criminal Code), because the collection of the money had been carried out via the activities of the association, where the accused was spokesman.[10]

---

8 For a more detailed resume, see Sullivan and Hayes 2011, p. 54 et seq.

9 This was the opinion of one dissenting judge.

10 Section 23 provides (in relevant part) "the penalty in respect of an offence shall apply to any person who has contributed to the execution of the wrongful act by instigation, advice or

Concerning the second part of the indictment (attempt to collect money for PFLP and FARC by appealing to other organizations on the internet) two judges find that – because the intention was to challenge the Danish legislation on terrorism – the accused did intend to finance – "at least" – groups listed in the blacklists.[11]

The prosecutor mentions in his charge that the accused has not contested the fact that he knew about the blacklisting of the two organizations. What this means for the criminal liability in the case is unclear. However, the referral to the blacklisting by the two judges seems to indicate that this has some influence on the *mens rea*.

One of the judges did not find it proven beyond reasonable doubt that the aim of the appeal on the internet was to collect money for PFLP or FARC (as mentioned, the accused had said it was only a media stunt).

The accused was sentence to six months imprisonment. However, with reference to the judgment by Supreme Court in Fighters and Lovers case – and the fact the scope of Section 114b was doubtful at the time where the acts were committed – the sentence was suspended.

3.5. CASE 5: 2011 CASE (COPENHAGEN CITY COURT, 16 JUNE 2011 – UNPUBLISHED)

An association and its chairman were both accused of financing terrorist groups on two occasions; the first one in 2005, when 1,000 DKr was transferred to another Danish association collecting money for FARC and PFLP.[12] The second occasion was in 2010/2011, when 17,690 DKr was transferred directly to PFLP.[13] The association was founded after the Second World War in order to help freedom fighters all around the world. The motive for the acts was to challenge the Danish legislation on terrorism and on the second occasion the money was collected even after the High Court judgment in the *Fighters and Lovers* case mentioned above. The association forwarded a number of letters to the Danish Minister of Justice explaining to the minister that money was going to be transferred to PFLP and FARC and why.

action. The punishment may be reduced for any person who has only intended to give assistance of minor importance, or to strengthen an intent already resolved and if the offence has not been completed or an intended assistance has failed" (trans, Høyer, Spencer, Greve 1991).

11 It is stated in the judgment: "the whole idea was to start a debate on the terrorism legislation, which is why it necessarily involved organisations which were at least taken up on the terrorist organisations list" (*Hele tanken var ifølge tiltalte at skabe debat om terrorlovgivningen, hvorfor der nødvendigvis måtte være tale om organisationer, som i det mindste måtte være opført på terrorlisten.*).

12 Section 114a, No. 1 + 2 of the Criminal Code.

13 Section 114b, No. 1 + 2 (since 2005, the former Section 114 a is moved to Section 114b of the Criminal Code).

The City Court found both the accused guilty of attempt.[14] The chairman was sentenced to six months imprisonment, four of which were suspended (one dissenting judge of three voting for suspending the whole sentence – "*ingen straffastsættelse*").[15] The association was sentenced to 20 day fines of 500 DKK each.[16] The court refers to the Supreme Court judgment in the Fighters and Lovers case, saying that the 2005 incident took place at the same time. Thus PFLP is to be regarded as a terrorist organisation at that time.

As for the 2010/2011 incident the City Court mentions that the prosecutor has not proven the "status" of PFLP. The prosecutor has only referred to the fact that PFLP in January 2011 is still blacklisted by EU. The City Court does not find that the blacklisting alone is enough to characterize PFLP as a terrorist group according to Section 114. Thus, the court does not say that PFLP is a terrorist organization in 2011.

However, the court (by two votes to one) convicts the accused anyway for *attempt* to finance terrorist groups. The reasoning of the court seems to be that the accused was aware that the PFLP was to be seen as a terrorist organization (especially after the judgment in the *Fighters and Lovers* case). Hence, whether PFLP *is* in fact a terror organization is irrelevant, because the accused wanted to finance a terrorist organization.[17]

3.6. CONCLUSIONS REGARDING THE CASE LAW

The fact that a person or group is blacklisted by EU seems to be a sufficient ground for applying some coercive measures. However, it does not suffice to convict for terrorist financing (section 114 b). This seems to be the result from

14 Convicted of attempt, because it was not proved that the money had been transferred.

15 Reasoning of the sentencing was very short stating simply that some of acts were committed before Supreme Court decision in the Fighters and Lovers case and the accused previously never was punished.

16 One of the three judges dissented on the sentencing issue, voting for a suspended sentence for the natural person and 1 day fine of 10 DKK for the legal person. The two judges voting for 20 day fines of 500 DKK referred to the act committed ("*overtrædelsens karakter*") and the fact that the annual fees held by the association amounted to 34,000 DKK.

17 I must admit that the reasoning seems a bit strange, and my interpretation could be wrong. The court states: "The court finds that the reference to the EU terrorist list does not alone prove that the PFLP, at the time the offence was committed, falls under section 114. Two judges find that [the accused] has had intent to breach the sections mentioned in the indictment also after the judgment of the Supreme Court in the T-shirt case when he did not justify his continued collection of money for and support of [the organisation] on the basis that he believed that the PFLP had changed its status" (Retten finder det ikke alene ved en henvisning til EU's terrorliste bevist, at PFLP i gerningsperioden var omfattet af straffelovens §114. 2 dommere finder, at [den tiltalte person] har haft forsæt til at overtræde de i tiltalen nævnte bestemmelser, også efter Højesterets dom i T-shirt sagen, da han ikke som begrundelse for at fortsætte indsamlingen og støtten har forklaret, at han havde en opfattelse af, at PFLP havde ændret status.").

the case law and thus the case law corresponds to the *travaux préparatoires* of the Danish legislation on terrorism (where it is said that blacklisting in itself does not suffice for the conviction of somebody for terrorist financing).[18]

Because the blacklisting in itself is not enough to convict, it is necessary for the courts to have – sometimes very – comprehensive testimonies from experts as to the fact whether persons or groups might be considered terrorists. This is certainly true in the Fighters and Lovers case. The fact that this question was not extensively dealt with in the Hamas case must be due to a mistake.[19]

If there already has been this kind of proof concerning the relevant person/group at a previous court proceeding, the court in a subsequent case can – of course – base their decision on these findings. However, after a number of years the courts will have to make a new evaluation. This seems to be the conclusion from the 2011 case.

4. DISCUSSION

As mentioned above blacklisting is sufficient for taking coercive measures but not for convicting somebody for terrorist financing.

4.1. THE PROSECUTORIAL LEVEL

In the *travaux préparatoires* there is a passage stating that blacklisting "in itself" is enough to charge and possibly prosecute the person financing the blacklisted organization. It says in the *travaux préparatoires* that the prosecutor will have to assess whether acts connected to blacklisted persons or organizations should lead to charge/prosecution.[20] On one hand this might be regarded as problematic: prosecution is being brought on a basis and on criteria which do not correlate with the criteria for conviction (blacklisting is sufficient for prosecution, but not for conviction).

---

18 See Greve et al. 2008, p. 39 et seq.

19 Luckily, the mistake had no consequences for the accused. They were acquitted. But the dissenting judges – voting for conviction – should have addressed this question.

20 "Even if the immediate consequence that an organisation is taken up on the EU list is today limited to the legal effects which follow from the Common position and the regulation, the cumulative effect, after the introduction of L 35 [bringing in the present wording of section 114], is that the Danish police must determine, in accordance with the Code of Judicial Procedure, whether there is a basis to initiate an investigation of [people and entities] related to the organisation in question" ("Selv om den umiddelbare konsekvens af, at en organisation optages på EU-listerne i dag er begrænset til de retsvirkninger, der følger af den fælles holdning og forordningen, så vil dette sammenfald efter vedtagelsen af L 35 [indførelsen af straffelovens nugældende §114], som gennemføre rammeafgørelsen, bevirke, at dansk politi må vurdere, om der inden for rammerne af retsplejeloven er anledning til at indlede efterforskning her i landet af forhold, der knytter sig til den pågældende organisation.").

On the other hand one might regard this as everyday work of a prosecutor: In order to use coercive measures there has to be some degree of suspicion of a certain criminal act. This suspicion might lead to prosecution later on. Similar with blacklisting: Providing money for blacklisted persons indicates a certain suspicion. Thus, there is a sufficient basis for using coercive measures and – possibly – for prosecution.

4.2. THE JUDICIAL LEVEL

It is clear from the case law mentioned above that blacklisting is in general not referred to in the *reasoning* of the courts – apart from the reference by the City Court in the 2011 case to the *travaux préparatoires* according to which blacklisting alone is enough to characterize a group as terrorist. In, for example, the Fighters and Lovers case it did not seem to play any role, either in the reasoning of the City Court (by the one dissenting/convicting judge) or by the majority of the judges at High Court or by the Supreme Court. The conviction is instead based on the – very extensive – testimony by the experts.

Furthermore, the prosecutor does not emphasize the blacklisting in his procedure and the defence lawyer does not question the inconsistency between different national blacklists. If, for example, a state maintaining a list of terrorist organizations has *not* blacklisted FARC, how does that influence the Danish judgment and the burden of proof on the Danish prosecutor?

Thus, blacklisting is "in itself" not enough to link someone to terrorism according to Section 114. Furthermore, it does not seem to play an important role in the criminal proceedings.

However, would it be naive to believe that the blacklisting does not play *any* role? We might have to make a distinction between the objective criteria (*actus reus*) and the subjective criteria (*mens rea*).

Concerning *actus reus*: The *travaux préparatoires* seem to suggest that blacklisting do play *some* role, cf. the wording "not in itself". Furthermore, Section 114 of the Danish Criminal Code is implementing the EU Framework decision on terrorism, so the understanding of the word "terrorism" in EU law and Danish law has to be related. Additionally, it must be fair to assume that the blacklisting influences the perception of the judges. And from the case law mentioned above, we know at least that the accused were asked about the blacklisting (see *Fighters and Lovers* case and also the *2011* case).

On one hand the status of blacklists as "not in itself decisive" forces the courts to have extensive testimony and reports on the acts of foreign organizations and governments. On the other hand "not in itself decisive" means that blacklisting has some (not clarified) legal value. And blacklisting most probably has a psychological influence on judges.

The comprehensive analysis by the courts as to whether FARC and PFLP are terrorist according to Section 114, is *de facto* (directly or indirectly) an evaluation of the *political decision* to blacklist FARC/PFLP. Is that reasonable and appropriate? Does this "evaluation" influence the decision of the judge (one might say, the judges are under a political pressure to label these organizations terrorists?).

I do not find sufficiently grounds for a conclusion on these matters from the case law mentioned. But it is interesting to see that the Danish system provides for a thorough review in court of the label "terrorist" according to the blacklisting. Unfortunately, this is not a right for the blacklisted organizations but exclusively for those who support them.

Separated from blacklisting problems in a narrow sense, but still related to the topic, is the question whether definitions of terrorism are suitable for legal analysis and decisions by courts. The comprehensive evidence in Fighters and Lovers with reports and testimony by numerous of experts – explaining why FARC/PFLP are (or are not) freedom fighters, fighting a legitimate or illegitimate state, killing civilians or having only military aims, threatening populations, etc. – raises the question if it makes any sense to have a court in Denmark deciding whether a group of people in a foreign country are terrorists according to Danish law. On the other hand one might argue that this is exactly what courts do all the time: evaluate whether the criteria for criminal liability are fulfilled.

Concerning *mens rea*: Does the blacklisting of some organizations influence the *mens rea* of persons financing these organizations? In the Fighters and Lovers case the accused were aware of the fact that the organizations might be regarded as terrorist organizations. The same goes for some of the other cases (the *2011* case and the *Internet appeal* case).

FARC and PFLP are both listed on the EU terrorist list, and it is clear from the judicial record in the Fighters and Lovers case that the accused were asked about this fact during the trial. They admitted that they knew about the blacklisting. On the other hand what if FARC and PFLP are not blacklisted on all terrorist lists?[21] Does it influence the *mens rea* of the accused – that an organization is blacklisted on some, but not on other terrorist lists? In the Fighters and Lovers case the accused did not themselves regard the organizations as terrorist, but in the judgment the High Court refers to the testimony given by the accused and the announcement on the homepage of Fighters and Lovers (stating that buying a T-shirt might cause legal problems). Does this mean that the High Court has taken the fact that the accused knew about the blacklisting, into account? It is hardly possible to say.

21 It is, of course, no surprise that they are absent from the UN terrorist blacklist because this list is solely of individuals and groups associated with the Taliban and Al-Qaeda.

In the 2011 case the blacklisting seems even to play an decisive role for the *mens rea*. Two judges find that – because the intention of the accused was to challenge the Danish legislation on terrorism – they did intend to finance ("at least") groups listed on the blacklists.

What does this mean? It is difficult to give a clear answer to the question. Maybe it is fair to say that blacklisting plays some role, because it is part of the questioning of the accused, but it is probably not decisive for the question of *mens rea* because it is not (explicitly) part of the reasoning of the court – at least not in most of the cases. Furthermore, the prosecutor does not seem to emphasize the blacklisting in her/his argumentation for *mens rea* and the defence lawyer does not mention the fact that FARC and PFLP are listed on some, but not all lists.

I have the feeling that – as quite often concerning the application of the law on terrorism – we are faced with a gap between the law and our more abstract or general sense of justice.

PROCEDURAL SAFEGUARDS FOR BLACKLISTING SANCTIONS – A COMPARISON WITH THE EU FRAMEWORK DECISION ON ORDERS FREEZING PROPERTY OR EVIDENCE

Malin Thunberg Schunke

1. INTRODUCTION

The fight against international terrorism has led to measures within the European Union in several different areas. Apart from the blacklisting sanctions general improvements in the legal instruments regarding transnational criminal investigations and judicial cooperation have been adopted. The measure of "freezing" has thereby been created in "parallel systems". The subject of this article is a comparison between the procedural safeguards and legal remedies for the freezing of assets used within the criminal law model with the blacklisting regime. The EU blacklisting sanctions system based on UN resolution 1373 (hereafter "*autonomous sanctions system*")[1] and UN resolution 1267 (hereafter "*UN-based sanctions system*")[2] will be compared with the Framework Decision from year 2003 on the Execution in the European Union of Orders Freezing Property or Evidence (hereafter the "FD on Freezing Orders").[3] I will mainly focus on some basic legal safeguards related to two central stages of the procedure; the decision to freeze assets and the right to challenge a freezing order.

2. THE FD ON FREEZING ORDERS

The FD on Freezing Orders is based on the principle of mutual recognition and execution of decisions within the EU and is applicable to freezing orders both for

1 Security Council Resolution 1373 of 28 September 2001.
2 Security Council Resolution 1267 of 15 October 1999.
3 Council Framework Decision 2003/577/JHA of 22 July 2003, OJ L 196, 2.8.2003, p. 45–55.

the purposes of securing evidence and for a subsequent confiscation.[4] It is generally applicable, meaning that it applies in proceedings concerning all types of offences. A freezing order is issued by a judicial authority in one state and is sent directly to a judicial authority in another state, where it must be executed promptly (if possible, it must be decided and communicated within 24 hours).[5]

After the execution of the order, the property in question remains frozen, until a subsequent request for assistance is made. If the freezing order concerns evidence, a request for international legal assistance is made. If the purpose is confiscation, a request for the enforcement of a confiscation order has to follow.[6] This construction of the Framework Decision setting out two different sets of proceedings may be the reason for the very limited use so far of the instrument among the practitioners in the EU. In the area of confiscation however, a Framework Decision on the Application of the Principle of Mutual Recognition to Confiscation Orders has been adopted, which obliges a Member State to execute foreign confiscation orders issued by a court competent in criminal matters.[7] The use of the system of mutual recognition also to the subsequent requests simplifies the handling of the freezing orders, and may lead to a more frequent use of the FD on Freezing Orders in the future.[8]

3. THE TERM "FREEZING"

The term "freezing" is used both in the criminal law model and in the blacklisting sanctions regime. At first sight there are also some similarities. In both systems the factual effects of the measure may at the first stage be identical; property or assets are being frozen, which means that there is a restriction of the owners' use of the property. Another similarity is that in order to permit the

4 Article 3(1) of the FD on Freezing Orders.

5 Articles 4(1) and 5 of the FD on Freezing Orders.

6 See Articles 6(1) and 10 of the FD on Freezing Orders.

7 Council Framework Decision 2006/783/JHA of 6 October 2006, OJ L 328, 24.11.2006, p. 59–78 and Amending Act hereto; Council Framework Decision 2009/299/JHA of 26 February 2009, OJ L 81, 27.3.2009, p. 24–36.

8 Another instrument which would – in a similar way – facilitate by avoiding the need for a further request for legal assistance is Council Framework Decision 2008/978/JHA of 18 December 2008 on the European Evidence Warrant for the Purpose of Obtaining Objects, Documents and Data for Use in Proceedings in Criminal Matters, OJ L 350, 30.12.2008, p. 72–92. The date for national implementation of this framework decision was 19 January 2011, but there is already a proposal for replacing the system of European evidence warrants with a European Investigation Order (EIO). See Council Document 9145/10, 29.4.2010, Initiative taken by the Kingdom of Belgium, the Republic of Bulgaria, the Republic of Estonia, the Kingdom of Spain, the Republic of Austria, the republic of Slovenia and the Kingdom of Sweden with a view of adopting a Directive of the European Parliament and of the Council regarding the European Investigation Order in Criminal Matters. Agreement has been met on a general approach. See Council Doc. 18918/11, 22.12.2012.

measure to be effective, the affected persons have in neither of the systems any right to be informed before the freezing-measure has been put in place. However, the use of the identical term is rather misleading, as the legal consequences for affected parties and the claimed aims of the methods differ radically.

The introduction of freezing orders within the mutual recognition system aimed at providing the judicial authorities with a measure quickly to secure property which is easily movable.[9] This was especially important, since the traditional system of letters rogatory with requests for seizure were considered to be too slow. Freezing is here thus a question of a *temporary criminal procedural safety-measure*, where property or assets are seized pending the collection of further evidence, investigation and criminal proceedings. The use of freezing of assets in the context of the blacklisting sanctions regime is different. According to the UN Sanctions Committee, the purpose of asset freezing is to deny the listed individuals or entities the means to support terrorism, and is to be seen as a temporary precautionary measure with a *preventive* aim.[10]

The mutual relationship of these systems may also be discussed. Are they meant to complement and be used parallel to each other, or is one of the systems subordinate? This is a question which national judicial authorities might have to consider when investigating offences related to the financing of terrorism. Freezing of assets on the basis of blacklisting procedures is, however, often held to be an *alternative* to criminal proceedings. The Financial Action Task Force for example states that "the measures serve as a preventive or disruptive tool when criminal action is either not possible or not practical".[11] This is supported by the fact that decisions not to initiate criminal proceedings or acquittals for terrorist-offences by national courts in parallel criminal proceedings have often had no effect for the blacklisting-decisions.[12] I will later come back to the question of whether it is suitable to have such administrative alternatives to the criminal law model.

---

9 See Section (2) in the Preamble to the FD on Freezing Orders.

10 See UN Security Council Sanctions Committee, Assets Freeze: Explanation of Terms para. 2, available at www.un.org/sc/Committees/1267/pdf/EoT%20assets%20freeze%20-%20English.pdf *(accessed 18 January 2012)* and further, on the definition of asset freezing, van den Broek, Hazelhorst & de Zanger 2010, pp. 20 and 26–27.

11 Financial Action Task Force, Guidance Document, International Best Practices: Freezing of Terrorist Assets, 23 June 2009, para. 11, p. 5, available at www.fatf-gafi.org/dataoecd/30/43/34242709.pdf (accessed on 18 January 2012).

12 Compare for example the standpoint of the European Commission expressed in para. 60 of Case T-85/09, *Yassin Abdullah Kadi v. European Commission,* Judgment of the General Court [2010] ECR II-05177. See further Thomas Elhoms chapter, this volume, on the effect of blacklisting decisions for the Danish courts in criminal cases.

4. PROCEDURAL SAFEGUARDS AND LEGAL REMEDIES

4.1. THE DECISION TO FREEZE ASSETS

Starting with the FD on Freezing Orders, the decision to freeze assets is initially taken by a judicial authority in the issuing state.[13] The Framework Decision uses the term "freezing order" as a comprehensive term, and the final question on the definition is left to national law in the Member States which use the set of national coercive measures available to them.[14] The substantive and procedural requirements for taking such a measure is in the first place decided by the legislation in the issuing state, which means that the criteria regarding the level of evidence needed or the proscribed penalty scale for the offence in question may differ. Common to all criminal law systems in the EU and confirmed in the FD on Freezing Orders is, however, the application of the proportionality principle, which demands a reasonable relationship between measure and aim.[15]

The executing state must recognize and execute a freezing order without any further formality, and must not reconsider the substantive reasons.[16] There is, however, some non-mandatory limited grounds for non-recognition. If the executing State has implemented them, there is e.g. a possibility to refuse to recognize a freezing order in cases of violations of immunity or privileges or in cases of ne bis in idem.[17] However, in the case of certain serious offences identified in a list – the offence of "terrorism" is interesting here – there is no possibility to demand double criminality.[18]

An individual is thus protected at this stage through the national substantive and procedural requirement for the coercive measure in an issuing State, and through the few grounds for non-recognition of a freezing order in the executing State. Article 1 of the FD on Freezing Orders further underlines the obligation to respect fundamental rights in Article 6 of the Treaty on the European Union (TEU).

The decision to freeze assets under the autonomous sanctions system is governed by Common Position 2001/931/CFSP and Regulation No. 2580/2001.[19] When it comes to the measure of freezing, these instruments are exclusively

13 Articles 2(a) and 4(1) of the FD on Freezing Orders.

14 Compare Article 2(c)-(e) of the FD on Freezing Orders.

15 See Section (4) in the Preamble of the FD on Freezing Orders.

16 Article 5(1) of the FD on Freezing Orders.

17 Article 7 of the FD on Freezing Orders.

18 Article 3(2) of the FD on Freezing Orders.

19 Council Common Position of 27 December 2001, OJ L 344, 28.12.2001, p. 93–96 and Council Regulation of 27 December 2001, OJ L 344, 28.12.2001, p. 70–73.

applicable to EU external terrorists.[20] The decision to designate persons, groups or entities on the autonomous blacklist takes place both at the national level and the Community level. In the first stage a competent national authority takes a freezing-decision. Such an authority is a judicial authority – or where judicial authorities have no competence in such an area – an equivalent authority. According to Article 1(4) of the Common position such a decision may concern the instigation of investigations or prosecution for terrorist acts or attempts to perpetrate, participate in or to facilitate such an act. The decision is to be based on "serious and credible evidence or clues, or condemnation for such deeds". In the *Sison* case of 2009, the Court of First Instance clarified that such a decision must primarily aim at the imposition of preventive or punitive measures by reason of that person's involvement in terrorism and that a decision solely concerned with the legality of a refusal of an asylum application could not serve as a valid basis.[21]

As discussed in more detail in Christina Eckes' chapter in this volume, in the second stage a decision on listing is taken by the Council by consensus. Hereby it is to be verified on the basis of information or material in the relevant file that the criteria in the Common position has been met. In one of the *PMOI* line of cases in 2006, the Court of First Instance emphasized that significant for the autonomous system is that the identification of the persons to be listed and the adopting of the specific sanction involve the exercise of the Community's own powers entailing a discretionary assessment. The Council is hereby bound to observe the right to a fair hearing. This means for example that after the listing-decision the Council is obliged to notify a listed person and provide a statement of reasons, which must be sufficiently detailed to allow those listed to understand the reasons and to allow the Courts of the European Union to exercise their power of review. If there is new evidence supporting the maintenance of a party on the list; the parties must be notified and heard before any subsequent decision on listing is being made.[22]

A decision to include a person on the list in the UN-based sanctions system is taken after nomination by states by consensus of the members of the Sanctions Committee. According to the guidelines of this Committee the criteria should be "supporting evidence of association with Al Qaida", but a criminal charge or conviction is not necessary. The states must provide a "detailed statement of case" when submitting names, but there is no obligation to disclose supporting confidential evidence.[23]

---

20 Regarding EU internal terrorists, compare Article 4 in the Council Common Position of 27 December 2001, OJ L 344, 28.12.2001, p. 93–96.

21 Case T-341/07, *Sison v. Council of the European Union*, Judgment of the Court of First Instance, 30 September 2009 [2009] ECR II-3625.

22 See further Case T-228/02, *Organisation des Modjahedines du people d'Iran v. Council of the European Union*, Judgment of the Court of First Instance, 12 December 2006 [2006] ECR II-4665.

23 See further Section 6(d) and (h) in the Guidelines of the Committee for the Conduct of Its Work of 30 November 2011, available under www.un.org/sc/committees/1267/pdf/1267_guidelines.pdf (accessed on 18 January 2012).

As discussed in more detail in Torbjörn Andersson's chapter in this volume, the EU states have implemented this sanctions-regime through Regulation No. 881/2002 and Common Position 2002/402/CFSP.[24] In the *Kadi* decision in 2008 the ECJ ruled that a lack of information to the individuals about the grounds for the listing and the evidence against them had the consequence of denying them a right to be heard and preventing them from obtaining a full review of the lawfulness of the freezing-measure.[25] As a consequence of the ruling, the blacklisting-procedure in the EU was amended through *Regulation No. 1286/2009* so that after the initial decision to freeze assets, the statement of reasons is sent to the listed person with an invitation to give opinions. Before the final decision to designate a person on the list, the Commission must take account of such views.[26]

4.2. THE RIGHT TO CHALLENGE A FREEZING ORDER

In the criminal law model Article 11 of the FD on Freezing Orders obliges the Member States to provide national provisions to ensure that any interested party have legal remedies against a freezing order. Such action shall be brought before a court in the issuing or executing state in accordance with national law. However, the substantive reasons for issuing the freezing order can only be challenged in the issuing state. There is further an obligation to *facilitate* the right to judicial review, in particular by providing adequate information and by ensuring that any time limit for bringing an action is acceptable.

The main remedies in order to challenge decisions available to persons in the blacklisting sanctions regime – whether autonomous or UN-based – consist firstly of the possibility to make a request for de-listing.[27] Secondly, there is the possibility of actions for annulment of the community decisions or instruments before the Community judiciary.[28] Thirdly the validity and interpretation of a regulation may be brought before the community courts in the form of a request for preliminary ruling from national courts.[29] Fourthly there may be a possibility

---

24 Council Regulation of 27 May 2002, *OJ* L 139, 29.5.2002, p. 9–22 and Council Common Position of 27 May 2002, OJ L 139, 29.5.2002, pp. 4–5.

25 Joined cases C-402/05 P and C-415/05 P, *Yassin Abdullah Kadi, Al Barakaat International Foundation v. Council of the European Union and Commission of the European Communities*, Judgment of the Court of Justice of the European Communities, 3 September 2008 [2008] ECR I-6351.

26 See Art. 7a in the Council Regulation of 22 December 2009, OJ L 346, 23.12.2009, pp. 42–46.

27 For a general overview of the possibilities of challenging EU blacklisting sanctions, see for example Sullivan & Hayes 2010, Cameron 2003, pp. 243–248 and Rosas 2011.

28 According to Article 275 TFEU the EU courts have jurisdiction to rule on actions on annulment concerning CFSP-decisions providing for restrictive measures against natural or legal persons. Action for annulment of regulations may be brought according to Article 263 TFEU.

29 See Article 267 TFEU.

regarding certain decisions from national authorities to appeal at the national level. Actions for damages have not yet played a major role in the case law in this field, but the possibility exists.[30]

Regarding delisting-requests the Council is within the autonomous sanctions system required to review the names on the list at regular intervals, and at least every six months to ensure that there are grounds to keep them on the list. A listed party may also at any time submit a request for de-listing.[31] Some procedural reforms have taken place in the UN-based sanctions system – the latest in 2011 – to improve due process rights.[32] Accordingly, a party may at any time submit an application for being de-listed. This is to be handled by an Ombudsperson which makes a recommendation for a decision. The de-listing decision is, however, still made by the Sanctions Committee alone.

Regarding the right to a judicial review, a listing decision is first taken by a national authority in the autonomous sanctions system. This means that there may be certain procedural rights in the national context. When it comes to the right of judicial review of freezing-decisions by the Council, judgments have confirmed that the review by the Community judiciary extends to the question of whether the criteria for a freezing decision in the Common Position and the EU Regulation are fulfilled. This means an assessment of the facts and circumstances, and to the evidence on which that assessment is based. Further it has been ruled that the Council cannot base its decisions on information in the file, if it is not communicated to the Community judicature.[33]

In the UN-based sanctions system the *Kadi* decisions have been crucial for the right to judicial review.[34] In the latest judgment of 2010 the General Court for example has ruled that as long as the European Commission finds itself bound by the findings of the Sanctions Committee, the rights of the individuals are only observed in the most formal and superficial sense.[35] Unless a system is developed within the UN to provide affected parties with their full procedural rights, the Community judiciary must ensure a full review of the lawfulness of

---

30 See Articles 268 and 340 TFEU. Following the judgment in the *Sison* case of 30 September 2009, where a listing-decision was annulled (*see above Section 4.1*), an application for compensation for damage resulting from the illegal freezing of the funds was made by Mr. Sison. This claim for damages was however dismissed by the General Court, which argued that the infringement, although clearly established, was not sufficiently serious to incur the non-contractual liability of the Community to Mr. Sison. See further Case T-341/07, *Sison v. Council of the European Union*, Judgment of the General Court, 23 November 2011, nyr.

31 Article 1(6) Council Common Position 2001/931/CFSP, above footnote 19.

32 Compare for example Resolutions 1730 and 1735 (2006), 1822 (2008), 1904 (2009) and 1989 (2011).

33 See for example case T-284/08, *People's Mojahedin Organization of Iran v. Council of the European Union*, Judgment of the Court of First Instance, 4 December 2008 [2008] ECR II-3487 and Case T-47/03, *Sison v. Council of the European Union* [2007] ECR II-73.

34 The *Kadi* cases have been extensively discussed in doctrine; see for example de Búrca 2010, Azarov & Ebert 2009, Vestergaard 2011 and Sullivan & Hayes 2010, especially pp. 57–61.

35 Para. 171 in Case T-85/09, above footnote 12.

the regulation. It has been confirmed that such a review must extend to a substantive assessment of the listing-decision, which in many cases must mean access – at least to the court – of underlying material including classified evidence.[36]

4.3. THE DURATION OF A FREEZING MEASURE

There are of course several other important procedural safeguards, for example limits to the duration of a freezing measure. According to the FD on Freezing Orders, the property shall remain frozen in the executing state until that state has responded definitively to a subsequent request for legal assistance or confiscation.[37] There is no time limit as such on the duration of the order, which is to be seen as a shortcoming especially in view of the slow handling of international requests for assistance. However, states may have provisions in their national law to limit the measure, for example the Swedish legislation obligates the court in different ways to control the duration of a freezing order.[38] In addition Article 6 ECHR demands that a criminal trial takes place within reasonable time. In the blacklisting sanctions regime, neither of the two systems provides rules for any time limits of freezing measures. There are only the rules on periodic review and requests for de-listing.[39] In spite of its characterization as a temporary measure, these measures may thus go on forever.

5. CONCLUSIONS

The only reasonable conclusion after having studied the blacklisting sanctions system is that it should be abolished altogether. Firstly, the type of authority to make blacklisting decisions and the vague criteria for placing someone on the list are problematic.[40] For example in the autonomous system the basis for a listing decision may in some states be a decision from a security police authority to start investigations in a very early stage on the basis of intelligence material.

Secondly, any procedural rights in this area do not have much substance as long as there are no enforceable rights regarding access to the full information

36 See further Joined Cases C-402/05 P and C-415/05 P, above footnote 25 and Case T-85/09, above footnote 12. Compare Sullivan & Hayes 2010, pp. 107–111.

37 Article 6(1) of the FD on Freezing Orders.

38 Compare Article 6(2) of the FD on Freezing Orders and Chapter 3 Section 17 of the Act (2005:500) on Recognition and Execution of European Union Freezing Decisions. See further on the Swedish act in Thunberg Schunke 2011, pp. 155–156 and 161.

39 See above Section 4.2.

40 Compare para. 49–79 in Case T-284/08, above footnote 33, where the Court of First Instance criticized the re-listing of PMOI on the basis of a decision to investigate persons connected to PMOI made several years earlier by a French anti-terrorist prosecutor's office.

justifying a decision. Even if the EU judiciary has confirmed that there should in principle be a full judicial review of the legality of freezing sanctions, the question is still to what extent such a "full review" is possible. One problem concerns the access to classified material. Neither the *Kadi* case nor the *PMOI* cases elaborate in any detail on whether the applicant and/or his lawyer must be provided with all confidential information or whether such information must only be provided to the court.[41] Even though it has been concluded in the *PMOI* cases that a listing cannot be based on secret information which is not disclosed to a Court, these cases were quite special since the court was even lacking basic information to review what national authority and what national decision the listings were based on.[42] As discussed in more detail in Christina Eckes' chapter, it remains to be seen how far the courts can and will go in this area.

Freezing of assets may, in my opinion, be accepted as a temporary procedural measure if it is followed by an independent and impartial judicial review. If restrictive measures are based on or connected to any accusations of criminal offences, then the standard of evidence and the procedure provided for in the criminal law system should be used. A strange feature of the autonomous system is that the underlying offence for a listing-decision is often under national law qualified as criminal; the measures at EU level are however classified as administrative.[43] It is obvious that blacklisting is for law-enforcement agencies an easier alternative to act against the financing of terrorism. However, within the EU today there are several possibilities for close and fast transnational cooperation for investigating measures as well as for the freezing and confiscation of assets.[44] Within the national criminal law model there is also experience of handling and protecting intelligence information, for example, by the use of *in camera proceedings*. Since the substantive reasons for a freezing order are not to be considered by an executing State, there is also a possibility to "protect" classified evidence within transnational proceedings.

The advantages of the FD on Freezing Orders when it comes to due process rights are obvious in comparison with the poor possibilities available to a blacklisted person. At the same time it must be underlined that by no means does the FD on Freezing Orders provide a perfect system. The problems of challenging a freezing order in an issuing state from abroad can be significant. In the absence of common procedural standards or transnational enforceable EU rights on legal assistance, legal aid or the right to an interpreter, the

41 Cortright & de Wet 2010, p. 7.

42 See further para. 155–158 and para. 166–173 in Case T-228/02, above footnote 22 and para. 68 and 73–76 in Case T-284/08, above footnote 33.

43 Van den Broek, Hazelhorst & de Zanger 2010, p. 26.

44 Many instruments to promote effective law-enforcement activities have been adopted in the last years. For example improvements within the intelligence exchange arrangements, setting up of joint investigation teams, the Framework Decision on the European Evidence Warrant and the proposal for a EIO, compare above footnote 8.

individual faces the problems of legal proceedings in a different procedural system and in a foreign language. The development of cross-border defence rights within the EU has – in spite of certain new initiatives in the last years – moved remarkably slowly. Additionally, in the area of confiscation there is a trend – both nationally and internationally – to extend the powers to confiscate property, i.e. to confiscate property without a connection to a criminal offence or to adopt rules on a reversal of the burden of proof.[45] This means that freezing orders and confiscation also in the area of criminal proceedings partly become preventive features. There is no space here to go into detail, but there is clearly room for improvement as regards the due process rights also in the criminal law model of freezing as developed so far with the EU.

---

45 See for example Council Framework Decision 2005/212/JHA of 24 February 2005 on Confiscation of Crime-Related Proceeds, Instrumentalities and Property, OJ L 68, 15.3.2005, pp. 49–51.

SANCTIONS AGAINST TERRORISM AND THEIR IMPACT ON FREEDOM OF EXPRESSION

Thomas Bull

"[...] the fitting remedy for evil counsels is good ones"[1]

1. INTRODUCTION

This volume is partly about the difficult balance between freedom and security that haunts every society in times of crisis. The "added value" of an analysis from the constitutional perspective of freedom of expression is mainly that it so clearly sets basic values of democratic societies at (potential) odds with each other. Democracy is a system of decision-making that creates peaceful ways of handling conflicts. The promise of peace and security is one of the main reasons for accepting the democratic system of government – a sometimes bad system, but the best we know.

One of the core values of that system is the protection of anyone's right to express their view in order to influence others. Without such a protected area for the wise, unique, stupid or misled opinions of people, we would not be able to have a democratic system. At the same time, this freedom poses a threat as it can be used to undermine the very foundations of the democratic system, a fact that different political and legal cultures in the democratic world have tackled in their own ways. In some systems, the rights can never be used to overthrow the constitutional system itself (Germany, ECHR), while in others the faith in the "market-place of ideas" is greater and restrictions even on incitement to crime are viewed with suspicion (US).

Now we are closing in on the concrete theme of this contribution. Some of the actions taken against the threat of terror acts have had an impact on the protection of freedom of expression. This is most clearly shown by such laws that criminalize "glorification of terrorism" or the like, but also laws that make the

1 Cited from Justice Brandeis' concurring opinion in *Whitney v. California*, 274 U.S. 357 (1927) p. 375.

connection between financing and terrorism, such as blacklisting of terrorist organizations, have a potential for coming into conflict with free speech and the related right of freedom of association.[2]

I will treat these difficulties under three themes: the impact on free speech doctrine, the impact on institutional competences and the impact on the media as a whole.

2. CRIMINALIZATION AS A CONSTITUTIONAL PROBLEM FOR FREE SPEECH PER SE

Let us begin with stating the obvious: prohibiting speech that encourages, incites or supports acts of violence can be seen as perfectly uncomplicated from a constitutional perspective. At different times and in different countries, such speech has not even been recognized as having *anything* to do with the constitutionally protected freedom of speech, as that right is about spreading political ideas, scientific knowledge and cultural experiences. Violence has nothing to do with free speech, has been the approach. Such a sharp division between speech that is protected and speech that is not (such as "fighting words") has, however, been difficult to uphold both theoretically and in practice. "Kill the king!" can be an incitement to murder, a call for political change or a rock n' roll-song. Meaning is contextual and this insight has had consequences for the constitutional analysis on how the protection of freedom of speech affects the efforts to criminalize certain types of expressions.

The constitutional problem is rather straightforward; how to reconcile the legitimate concerns with speech that encourages violence with the fundamental idea of a society built on a pluralism of ideas, thoughts and values – a democracy. If we take a look around, two rather different solutions to this question stand out.[3] In the U.S. the position is, since the famous *Brandenburg* case in the 1960s, that speech with violent content can only be prosecuted or otherwise restricted on the basis of its content if there is a "clear and present" danger of violence in immediate connection with the speech itself.[4] More hypothetical or speculative reasons for restricting the speech such as the risks of future violence are not accepted in the jurisprudence of the Supreme Court of the U.S., which takes a very strict view of any attempt to regulate the content of speech in general, while

2 There is, of course, a vast literature on this subject and this contribution will only touch upon some of the issues that the war on terrorism raises from the perspective of free speech. For some examples, see Boyne 2009, Freedman 2010–2011, Stone 2009, Parker 2009, Lebowitz 2010–2011, Chemerinsky 2011, Morrison 2010–2011, Banisar 2010, Letsas, Keller and Sigron 2010, Tanenbaum 2006, Margulies 2012, Maiman 2011 and Barak-Erez and Scharia 2011.

3 See Barak-Erez and Scharia 2011 at p. 5.

4 *Brandenburg v Ohio* 395 U.S. 444 (1969).

being more lenient on regulation that is perceived as content neutral.[5] In other words, the US approach can be said to be one of categories, and if an expression falls within a protected category, it will be almost absolutely protected, other interests notwithstanding.

The approach taken in many, if not all, European states is quite different. Here, regulations often target the content of speech, perhaps best illustrated by the various provisions on hate-speech that European countries have adopted.[6] The conflict with freedom of speech is not handled by isolating speech from regulative ambition; instead a balancing of interests is used in the formula of proportionality, a well-known legal concept in European law and in national administrative and constitutional law of the States of Europe.[7] The formula includes identifying the interests, assessing the need for regulation and whether the purpose of the regulation/decision at hand could be achieved by less intrusive means as well as whether a fair balance of interests has been struck. It is, in essence, a case by case approach to the conflict of freedom of speech with other values in society, such as the protection of lives and security.

The case-law of the European Court of Human Rights (ECtHR) is instructive in how this formula works in practice. In *Vejdeland and Others v Sweden*[8], the application of a hate-speech prohibition on homophobic pamphlets distributed in a school was found to be in accordance with the conventions' Article 10. However, no less than five out of seven judges wrote separate opinions on the specific reasons for finding no violation, stressing the educational environment as the critical issue to accept the Swedish courts weighing of interests. In *Kiliç and Eren v Turkey*[9], the Turkish courts application of a statute criminalizing the praising of criminal actions on a number of slogans used in support of a Kurdish leader was held disproportional. The Court stressed, in a very summary judgment, that no actual advocacy of violence occurred and that no clear and imminent danger of disorder was present. The use of criminal law in that case was thus not "necessary in a democratic society" as the proportionality test of the European Convention on Human Rights is phrased in the convention.[10] It is noteworthy that in the Swedish case, no advocacy of violence or actual disorder

5 See *Texas v. Johnson* 491 U.S. 397, 412 (1991) and *City of Ladue v. Gilleo* 512 U.S. 43, 59 (1994) for examples. For a critical discussion on the concept of content-based and content neutral regulation, see Wright, 2006. Some exceptions have been accepted, such a prohibition of child pornography.

6 See Barendt 2005 at p. 170 et seq. See also EU Council framework decision 2008/913/JHA on combating certain forms of racism and xenophobia by means of criminal law.

7 See Cohen Elia and Porat 2010 for an overview of the origins of the test of proportionality.

8 No. 1813/07, 9 February 2012.

9 No. 43807/07, 29 November 2011. See also the similar *Gül and Others v Turkey*, No. 4870/02, 8 June 2010.

10 It is noteworthy that the difference in approach between the US and most European countries not necessarily leads to a difference in results. The two cases from ECtHR mentioned above would in all likelihood have been decided the same way in the US, see *Bethel School District No. 403 v Fraser* 478 U.S. 675 (1986), but with a different methodology.

occurred, making the school environment and the theme of the expression the distinguishing items. In my reading, it is the former that decides the case.

For the purposes of this contribution, the most interesting thing to note about these different approaches is their connection to the historical experience of the countries concerned. In the U.S., socialism and communism was framed in terms of a threat to society as a whole from (at least) the 1920s and onward for almost 50 years. Drastic intrusions in the rights of free speech and free association were accepted due to the graveness of the perceived threat, with a reasoning that is not far from the principle of proportionality used in Europe today.[11] This experience finally pushed the Supreme Court of the U.S. into adopting a much stricter and inflexible approach to restriction on free speech based on the perceived dangers of the expressions – the Brandenburg-test of "clear and present danger". American experience has thus shown that the formula of proportionality is a double-edged sword. With an interest like defending the future of democratic society in one side of the scales of justice, it becomes hard for free speech to come out on top.

A legislator (and a public) that is really fearful will tend to ignore niceties such as free speech. The balancing approach cannot easily withstand that, as it puts the courts in the position of either having to defer to the judgment of the political branches[12] or to act in an area where legal criteria are almost absent and the institutional competence of courts is low. To choose the first of these alternatives will be very tempting (and perhaps even wise from a constitutional perspective), and this is exactly what the American experience shows us. The stricter Brandenburg test binds the court (and the legislator) in a way that free speech (and other constitutional rights) cannot be the objects of compromise and thus frees the court from the temptation of deferring to the other branches of government.

In Europe, at least in Western Europe, the experience of fascist regimes in general, and Nazism in particular, has contributed to an attitude that is much more understanding of restrictions on free speech on the basis of content. The reasoning is that in order to prevent that kind of development from happening again, some ideas and words must and can be stopped. The human catastrophe of the Holocaust is evidence enough for many for the need of such a control of the use of free speech. Rights should not be used in order to undermine the very system that protects those rights, as is expressed i.e. in the German constitution Articles 19 and 20 and in ECHR Article 17. Prohibition of hate-speech and other expressions with a potential for long-term damage to society is thus constitutionally accepted in most countries of Europe, perhaps most aptly illustrated by the various criminalisations of denying the Holocaust that can be found in, e.g. Germany and France. In a political climate no so inclined to take

---

11 See *Whitney v. California* 274 U.S. 357 (1927) and *Dennis v. U.S.* 341 U.S. 494 (1951).

12 National security being one of the areas where you could expect the courts to be reluctant to exchange the governments views with their own.

excessive measures against perceived threats as the US was during the Cold War and arguably still is today this approach has worked well enough from the perspective of free speech.

The reasons for the relative success, or at least, acceptability, of the balancing approach of course vary, but one single factor is, it is submitted, of greatest importance; the lack of any real conflict of values until recently. The interest of right or left-wing political extremism has not had anyone defending it in a credible way, and the balancing of free speech against respect for others, decency and similar values has been easy.[13] This is beginning to change. Terrorism has put political and religious extremism in the center of political attention and this conflict is not peripheral as it reflects the growing multi-cultural nature of our societies. "Western" values are under (a perceived) pressure from this new pluralism and, additionally, there is a very real tension in European democracies, based on issues of ethnical discrimination, religious freedom and practical access to all of the goods of the welfare-state. In this context, measures against the terrorist threat can easily be perceived as ethnocentric, discriminatory and exclusionary and opposed by both the groups so affected as well as by other groups that are more generally worried about the way society develops in the shadow of terrorism. Suddenly we have a counter-force and the balancing of constitutional rights and security is not so self-evident anymore.[14] It might be that the protection of freedom of speech in the European legal order(s) stands before a tougher challenge than it has faced ever before.

This can also be illustrated by the case law of the ECtHR, which have had the opportunity to balance freedom of speech against interests of national security, respect for others etc. on several times. The case *Zana* from 1997 concerned a former mayor of a big Turkish city, interviewed in jail on his views on recent terrorist acts by the PKK. According to the newspaper he said:

> "I support the PKK national liberation movement; on the other hand, I am not in favour of massacres. Anyone can make mistakes, and the PKK kill women and children by mistake ..."[15]

13 The left-wing extremism of Baader-Meinhof etc. did get a lot of attention, but few acknowledged it as a wider social movement with potential for political success, even if the context of the Cold war made the threat of communism a credible one at times. Most Western Europeans states seem to have responded to the left-wing extremism of the 1970s and 1980s not by criminal sanctions for expressing the ideas of revolution etc., but by extensive surveillance and registration of potential "threats" to the democratic system of government. Such surveillance can, of course, in itself be a threat to free speech. See for example, *Segerstedt-Wiberg and Others v. Sweden*, No. 62332/00, 6 June 2006.

14 A parallel is the development of information technology, that has spurred increasing legislative responses in order to protect personal integrity and intellectual property in a way that also might be perceived as a threat to constitutional rights such as free speech and freedom of information, see the CJEU decision C-360/10 *SABAM v. Netlog*, 16 February 2012 (nyr).

15 Zana v. Turkey, No. 69/1996/688/880, 25 November 1997, para 12.

He was punished according to the same material criminalization as mentioned above for defending criminal acts and endangering public order. The Grand Chamber of the ECtHR, by a rather slim majority of 12–8 found no violation of Article 10 of the convention. The majority's reasons was that the statement itself was ambiguous –supporting PKK while denouncing massacres at a time where PKK had committed bombings of civilians – and that it was done in what already was an "explosive situation" in Turkey. Furthermore, the national authorities' margin of appreciation in matters of national security was stressed as well as the fact that the punishment of two months in prison was quite lenient. All together, the majority did not find the restriction disproportionate.[16]

Another illustration is the more recent case Leroy v. France.[17] It concerned a cartoonist that on 11 September 2001 made a drawing of the attack on the twin towers of the World Trade Centre in New York with the accompanying text: "We have all dreamt of it ... Hamas did it." The drawing was published in a newspaper on 13 September. French authorities prosecuted the editor and the illustrator for condoning terrorism and they were convicted and punished with a fine. In the Court of Appeal the reasoning was that "by making a direct allusion to the massive attacks on Manhattan, by attributing these attacks to a well-known terrorist organisation and by idealising this lethal project through the use of the verb 'to dream', [thus] unequivocally praising an act of death, the cartoonist justifies the use of terrorism, identifies himself through his use of the first person plural ("We") with this method of destruction, which is presented as the culmination of a dream and, finally, indirectly encourages the potential reader to evaluate positively the successful commission of a criminal act."

Arguing before the ECtHR, the cartoonist complained that the French courts had ignored the real intention of his drawing, which was to communicate his anti-Americanism through a satirical image and illustrate the decline of American imperialism. The ECtHR noted that the tragic events of 11 September 2001 had given rise to global chaos, and that the issues raised on that occasion were subject to discussion as a matter of public interest. However, it did not think that the drawing was limited to criticism of American imperialism. Instead, it supported and glorified violence against America. According to the ECtHR, the text accompanying the drawing expressed moral support for the presumed perpetrators of the attacks of 11 September 2001 and thus approval of the violence, simultaneously diminishing the dignity of the victims. Furthermore, the court stressed that the date of publication increased the applicant's responsibility, whether considered from an artistic or a journalistic perspective. Lastly, the court referred to the impact of such a message in a politically sensitive

---

16 The dissenting judges, among other things, stressed that the Government had less intrusive means at disposal to protect security and public order, that the statements was taken out of context and, even if regarded as quoted, was such shocking and disturbing ideas that the freedom of speech protects.

17 No. 36109/03, 2 October 2008.

region like the Basque Country. It held that the drawing's publication had provoked a certain public reaction, capable of stirring up violence and demonstrating a plausible impact on public order in the region. In conclusion, there had not been a violation of Article 10 of the convention.

Here is not the place to discuss these cases in detail, even though they do deserve a closer analysis. From our perspective it can be enough to say that taken together, these cases do not bode well for the European method of balancing the interests when freedom of speech collides with terrorism.[18] They show that under pressure of dramatic contemporary events European courts are subject to the same temptations as the American courts were during the period mentioned above. My conclusion is that the use of the principle of proportionality in such circumstances can make the whole balancing act unbalanced.[19] This has potentially severe consequences for freedom of speech as a constitutional value; it leads to a chilling effect of expressions in an area of immense importance today, it leads to problems with foreseeability and it risks making speech by or in support of organizations such as ANC and PLO criminal for reasons that are not immediately easy to rationalize from a freedom of speech point of view.[20]

Now, even though the picture painted above is somewhat gloomy as to the possibilities of balancing free speech with the threat of terrorism with the European approach, all is not so dark. We can also see a development in the way of expressing the limits of regulation in tension with the freedom of speech that resembles the US approach. In some of the cases on Article 10, the ECtHR has used a language that resembles the "clear and present danger" of the Brandenburg test. In above mentioned case of *Kiliç and Eren* the Court stated:

> "The Court observes that, in the circumstances of the present case, by shouting these slogans, the applicants did not advocate violence, injury or harm to any person. Furthermore, neither in the domestic court decisions nor in the observations of the Government is there any indication that there was a clear and imminent danger which required the interference faced by the applicants (Gül and Others, cited above, §42)."[21]

18 See also Boyne 2009, p. 480 et seq., who draws the same conclusion but more based on the European approach to human dignity as a constitutional base-value and Donohue 2005, p. 339. Compare with Barak-Erez and Scharia 2011, who draw the opposite conclusion on the basis of more or less the same material and who find that "content-based prohibitions can be enforced in a way that assigns significant weight to the protection of speech", p. 28.

19 There are, of course, counter-examples, such as the British case mentioned below (note 29).

20 Parker 2007 mentions some of these consequences at 752 et seq. as well as the fact that (up to 2007 when she was writing) the offence of glorification of terrorism created by the UK Terrorist Act 2006 had only been used sparingly. The continued limited use of this offence was confirmed by brief statements in the official reviews of the legislation, SSHD 2011, p. 32 and Andersson 2011 and Carlisle 2010, p. 53 f. For freedom of expression concerns, see also Article 19, 2006.

21 Above note 9 at para. 29.

This use of "clear and imminent danger" has the potential of being a stricter test than a "pure" test of proportionality and thus holds a promise for a development more sensitive to the need for a wide breathing-space for free speech, even in troubled times.[22]

3. CRIMINALIZATION AS A PRACTICAL ISSUE OF INSTITUTIONAL COMPETENCE

At the core of the problem discussed above is an even greater problem – can we trust governments and parliaments in times of crises? It is the political branches of government that takes action due to the threat of terrorism. The factual basis for such action is often, at least partly, secret. This is how the issue of trust comes into play. It gets even more complicated when you involve courts and other judicial actors in the process. Courts are by tradition – and common sense – reluctant to put their own judgment in place of the decisions of the other branches of government, as those institutions are generally better placed to decide on complex matters of social and economic nature. Military actions and national security are also included in this area traditional of "wide discretion". But is such an attitude defensible in the situation when very basic human rights are on the line? From a constitutional point of view, the issue is one of institutional competence – what institution is better at solving the issues at hand and how should that affect other institutions' behaviour vis-à-vis the one best placed to decide?[23]

Two recent cases, both consequences of blacklisting decisions, can illustrate the difficulties and pitfalls of these issues in the context of freedom of speech. The first example is the famous and debated decision by the US Supreme Court in Holder v. Humanitarian Law Project.[24] The case concerned the offence of "knowingly providing material support or resources to a foreign terrorist organization."[25] In supplementary regulations the meaning of "material support" was clarified as to include, among other things, training and expert advice. The Humanitarian Law Project (HPL) was giving advice on the use of international law to two organizations that had been designated as terrorist organizations, namely the Kurdish PKK and the Tamil LTTE. The case concerned the constitutionality of the criminal provisions in regard to the

22 See also Stone 2009 at 955 and OSCE/CoE 2006, p. 23.

23 The idea of institutional competence in a constitutional context is old and related to a number of issues on separation of powers, judicial review and protection of constitutional rights. The "political question"-doctrine of US constitutional law is one example of a way to try to find a balance between what a court is suited to do and what it is not so well equipped for. The literature on institutional competence is vast, see e.g. Cross 1999–2000.

24 561 US _ (2010).

25 18 U. S. C. §2339B(a)(1).

procedural guarantees in the Fifth Amendment (unconstitutionally vague?) and the protection of free speech in the First Amendment (permissible limitation of free speech?).

The majority of the Court (6–3) found the provisions constitutional, and in respect to the challenge on basis of free speech, it found that the limitation was narrowly tailored and well-founded in the factual findings of the Congress and the Government on the relationship between support of the non-violent parts of a terrorist organization's activities and its more violent actions. In this part, the court more or less accepted the view of the government wholeheartedly and it is this that interests me here. The majority opinion just shows a great deference to the other institutions and the issue is if this is problematic.

First of all, the majority do find that the legislation in question is content based, as the criminal responsibility is dependent upon what the HLP wants to speak about with the terrorist organizations. It must therefore be scrutinized under a more rigorous standard then the government thought appropriate.[26] In the following reasoning the majority never really states exactly what standard it is following. Instead, a lengthy part of the opinion is devoted to the evidence on how teaching and talking to terrorist about international law may advance their terrorist ambitions. It is emphasized that such organizations do not have a clear separation between social, political, and terrorist operations or between money raised for wholly different purposes. The very association with terrorist organizations is difficult to separate from support of the organizations, the court implies with a quote from Congress.[27]

Furthermore, the court relies heavily on the Governments view that all contributions to foreign terrorist organizations – even those for seemingly benign purposes – further those groups' terrorist activities. The court finds that this evaluation of fact, like that of Congress, is entitled to deference. The reason for this is the sensitive national security and foreign relations interests at stake. Respect for the Government's factual conclusions is, according to the court, appropriate in the light of the courts' lack of expertise with respect to national security and foreign affairs, that counter-terrorism measures occur in an area where information is difficult to obtain, and where the impact of certain conduct can be difficult to assess. The court even holds that it can even be dangerous to demand "hard proof" of the allegations that prosecutors and other authorities' make towards conduct that is connected to terrorism, as judgments in this field often cannot be based on concrete evidence, but rather on "informed judgment". The court concludes:

> "Given the sensitive interests in national security and foreign affairs at stake, the political branches have adequately substantiated their determination that prohibiting

---

26 561 U.S. ___ (2010) p. 22.

27 "[...] organizations that engage in terrorist activity are so tainted by their criminal conduct that *any contribution to such an organization* facilitates that conduct.", Holder, p. 24.

> material support in the form of training, expert advice, personnel, and services to foreign terrorist groups serves the Government's interest in preventing terrorism, even if those providing the support mean to promote only the groups' nonviolent ends."[28]

So, we can see a court faced with the complex reality of terrorism that chooses to defer to the institutional competence of the political branches of the state. It is interesting to compare the approach of the American court with that of the British House of Lords in 2004, when faced with the – admittedly more dramatic – question of indefinite detentions of "terrorists" according to British law at the time.[29] There the court found it prudent to defer to the political branch's decision that the national security was at risk, but not to the decision that detention of certain persons without trial was necessary in order to combat the terrorist threat.[30] That case also shows the dangers inherent in dealing with issues such as terrorism in the court-room. Half a year later, terrorist bombings took place in London. Even if all the courts misgivings about the legislation's discriminatory effects turned out to be true, as the terrorists were not foreigners, but British citizens, it not impossible that the public's impression was one of a court "soft on terrorism", and partly to blame for the following tragedy. I read the majority opinion of the US Supreme Court decision as very conscious of that risk.

Let us now turn to a case from Sweden, decided by a Court of Appeal in 2009, on criminal responsibility for financial support to terrorist organizations.[31] A man had through work in a foundation called Al-Aqsa Grain gathered money and sent it to organizations on the West-bank and Gaza in the Middle-east. The foundation is part of a wider net-work of charity organizations – Union of Good – but decides independently on where its contributions go. The prosecutor considered that these organizations were part of a network around Hamas, an organization on the EU (and US) lists of terrorist organizations. Under the Sanctions Act (*sanktionslagen*, SFS 1996, 95), it is an offence to provide financial support to an entity on a UN or EU sanctions list. The Swedish court held that the central issue at hand was how close the connections were between Hamas and the organizations belonging to the Union of Good.

The prosecution submitted a large amount of evidence on the connections between the organizations involved as well as on the accused's sympathy for Hamas in general. It consisted of letters, tapped phone calls, expert witness statements, TV interviews and academic studies of terrorist organizations. More

---

28 Holder, p. 31. The minority has a totally different approach, see Justice Breyer's dissent p. 8 et seq., in which they question the majority's interpretation of Congress intent and the factual basis for the government's approach to finding a connection between talking to terrorists and aiding them.

29 *A (FC) and others (FC) (Appellants) v. Secretary of State for the Home Department (Respondent)* [2004] UKHL 56.

30 See opinion of Lord Bingham, p. 28 et seq.

31 *Hovrätten över Skåne och Blekinge*, case B 685–09, decided 9 November 2009.

or less all of this evidence was indirect and circumstantial, but there was a lot of experts' opinions on how different organizations active in the Middle east were inter-related in a complex way and how it was difficult to make a clear distinction between those that dabbled in terrorism and those that did not.

The Court of Appeal did not find this mass of evidence conclusive. Some of the evidence consisted of documents from Israeli authorities and the court started out by stating that, as Hamas and Israel at the time of the proceedings were in a war-like conflict, such documents had only a low value as evidence. Furthermore, the large amount of reports from the mass-media, books and the Internet on connections between organizations such as Union of Good and Hamas was, according to the court, impossible to evaluate and had therefore very low value as evidence. More specific information based on military/security intelligence from Israel and the USA was found to be old and of dubious origin and thus not of very high evidential value. The rest of the evidence consisted of various photos, letters and other written documents that had very little to do with the specific person involved in the case before the court and the organization Al Aqsa Grain and its Swedish part. The Court of Appeal found, as had the district court, that the connection between the support of Al Aqsa Grain and its activities was not proved to include support of Hamas and thus no criminal responsibility for support of terrorism could come in question.

This case and the *Holder* case naturally do not deal with identical fact-situations. In the *Holder* case, the support was going directly to the listed organization. Nonetheless, the Swedish case shows that a strict evidentiary evaluation of material that "paints a picture" without giving specific and concrete facts on how terrorists have benefitted from certain behaviour, like giving money for charity or teaching conflict resolution techniques, can be made. Moreover, such an approach might be preferable to a deferential attitude towards material that the prosecution submits. The alternative to a sceptical approach like that of the Swedish courts seems to be acceptance that the only type of legal safeguards that need apply are those applying inside the prosecutors' office. Even allowing for the – Swedish – prosecutor's relatively high degree of professionalism, and her/his duty of objectivity, this is obviously not enough for a legal system built on the rule of law.

However, a more far-reaching conclusion can perhaps be drawn as well. As the idea of proportionality has its downside, the idea of institutional competence – alluringly attractive for anyone wanting a middle of the road solution to judicial review as an institution – has a very clear downside. As we have seen, the idea of institutional competence implies that courts are not suited to do the complex weighing of interests in cases of national security, something the executive and legislative branches are better equipped to do. This can lead to a very deferential approach to cases involving terrorism, something that in end is detrimental to other important legal and political values such as protection of rights and respect for the independence of the judiciary.[32]

A way out from the dilemma posed by such a result is to stress not the institutional competence, but rather the institutional role of courts. In fact, courts are seldom better than other decision-makers (parties) when it comes to knowledge of the realities of the world. And it is not even clear that they are better at law than other actors on the legal arena such as lawyers, professors and prosecutors. It is as the passive receivers of the other actors' arguments and actions and as final arbiters of the conflicts brought before the bench that they have a particular role. The courts are the institution you have to persuade that the law is on your side. Seen from that perspective, deference due to competence can be exactly the opposite of what we expect from courts, namely to judge on issues they have imperfect knowledge on, to the best of their abilities and with acknowledgement of the basic legal principles of the legal system.[33] A high regard for institutional competence – that can be a valid argument in discussions on the scope and intensity of judicial review in general – is in the context of terrorism and the protection of individual rights, such as free speech, dangerously close to an abdication of the traditional role of courts in the *Rechtstaat.*

4. CRIMINALIZATION AS A PROBLEM FOR THE MEDIA AND ITS CONSTITUTIONAL ROLE

The media is often described as the watch-dog of the political and legal system in a country. Legal protection of free speech is in practice often about the speech that comes through mass-media institutions like newspapers, TV and the internet (the media). Journalists, writers and the engaged public use the media for information, debate and critique, reaching a wide public. We expect the media to fill this role, a role that is even more important in times of (perpetual) crisis like the "war on terror", as such circumstances can easily foster the view that openness, debate and critique are an obstacle to "victory" in this "war". Secrecy, unity and purposefulness are perceived as the way to combat global terrorism and such concepts are often contrary to the ideals of a well-functioning media.

---

32 Whether courts in countries that have more extensive experience with the terrorist threat have in fact taken a deferential stance towards the prosecution is somewhat of a debated issue. Maiman 2011 is of the view that on the whole, the courts in the U.S. and the UK have not abdicated in favour of executive authorities (p. 18). Harris argues that there is a more complex picture of how the British House of Lords (now the Supreme Court) have responded to terrorism in the context of human rights (p. 33).

33 Something that seems to work reasonably well, see Cavanagh /Sarat 1979–1980 and Hershkoff 2000–2001.

The new trends in the laws on crimes and sanctions related to terrorism that are discussed in this volume are part of this way of combating the threats to a free society. However, they have profound effects on the media and its role in several respects. Criminalization of things like material support of or incitement to terrorism can easily bring contacts with journalistic sources within the criminalized area. Reporters may, for example want to report on radical individuals or groups in society that have connections to terrorism. This can be done for a number of reasons that have nothing to do with actual support of terrorism as such. At the same time the sanctions or crimes involved treats *anyone* that has *any* contact with *anything or anyone* that is even distantly related to terrorism as someone supporting terrorism.[34] This is of course a huge problem for media that wants to fulfil its role as watch-dog of the political sphere.

Let us take a closer look at two more specific problems, namely how the extensive use of secrecy is affecting journalistic sources and how the regulatory framework of "the war on terror" is affecting the capacity of media to make legal and political developments understandable to a wider public.

That government need to classify certain information may not in itself be a problem for the media's constitutional role. The problem is rather how such classifications can become a routine that is not actually warranted by the material as such and the obvious fact that any use of secrecy makes it more difficult for reporters to access material. In the context of journalist's sources, this is of more profound importance, as the legal protection of sources is weakened or ignored in cases of leaks on classified material in most systems of free speech.[35] It is quite clear that "the war on terror" has brought new fuel to the debate on the balance between secrecy and openness in times of stress and turmoil.[36] Wikileaks' huge disclosure of government secrets in 2010 is the peak of this battle of interests.[37]

The use of legislation on state secrets has increased substantially in the last ten year period. A trade mark of such legislation is that it often is broad in scope and gives wide discretion in the application of rules on disclosure. Legal

34 This is of course illustrated by the *Holder* case above. Two Swedish journalists came to realise this a bit belatedly in a case in late 2011 concerning their alleged attempt to investigate the Swedish company Lundin Oil and its operations in Ethiopia. They were convicted by an Ethiopian court of collaboration with terrorists as they had been guided illegally over the border into Ethiopia by a group of what the government considered to be terrorists, and apprehended together with them, and any such connection was enough to make the journalists "terrorists" as well.

35 The connection is also made by Stone 2011–2012.

36 See Stone 2009, p. 956 et seq. for the example when *New York Times* in 2006 published information on Presidents Bush's secret directive authorizing the NSA to engage in warrantless electronic surveillance. Numerous examples from the European context are given in Banisar 2009, p. 45 et seq. and 58 et seq.

37 See Benkler 2011 and Barron 2011. It is interesting to note that there is still a controversy of exactly what Wikileaks did.

challenges to decisions not to disclose have difficulties to succeed, as once again the issue of deference to the position of the executive branches of government becomes a real problem.[38] Of course, this leads to less available information to the media and, as a consequence, less information to the public. The implications for democratic governance are obvious.[39] But, as already indicated, the problem is wider, as a wide classification of governmental information as secret puts criminal law in action when leaks occur. Public officials who inform reporters are doing so under the threat of criminal charges and this will naturally lead to a chilling effect on journalistic sources. On top of that, journalists and editors may face legal consequences if they go public with the secrets disclosed by leaks. Even if such legal actions against reporters, editors or their sources, often end in acquittals or convictions for more minor crimes, the signals they send are evident; dealing with secret information means a lot of trouble![40] Criminal proceedings may not even be the worst of any leakers' concern, as the loss of work, social exclusion and public "fame" can be more damaging to the individual than the criminal system.

As for the more specific issue of the legal protection of journalistic sources, most countries would not protect someone who leaked classified information in the area of national security – on the contrary. And in most countries, reporters could be forced to expose their source under criminal liability, thus giving them the choice of following the law or their professional ethics. Experience show that this puts journalists in a very difficult position indeed, choosing between facing many years of imprisonment and abandoning their ideals.[41] The effects of this difficulty is enhanced by the risk that law-enforcing authorities can use the threat of terrorism as an argument for disclosure of sources in cases where there is in fact very weak suspicions of any terrorist activity. In this way, there is a real risk of "over-spill" into journalistic contacts that should be protected, but where this is obvious only after the damage has been done.

As for the other problem, it is perhaps even more threating to the role of the media, even if it is more of a structural problem. The anti-terrorist legislation is often very complicated, even for experienced lawyers with expertise in the field of criminal law.[42] The legislation is often not found in the ordinary (for civil law

---

38 Banisar 2009, p. 45 et seq. and Donohue 2005, p. 312 et seq.

39 James Madison said: "A popular Government, without popular information, or the means of acquiring it, is but a Prologue to a Farce or a Tragedy; or, perhaps both." As quoted by Stone 2011–2012, p. 82.

40 Benkler 2011 describes all the trouble disclosure of official secrets can get someone in, when private actors, in order to protect their public image, under pressure from politicians and/or for contractual reasons, stop dealing with the whistler-blower, as Wikileaks have experienced to the full.

41 See Banisar 2007 and McNamara 2009. For the U.S., the leading case on journalists testifying before courts on their source is *Branzburg v. Hayes* 408 U.S. 665 (1972). See also Anderson 2009, Neinas 2009 and Laptosky 2010.

42 See McNamara 2009, p. 36 et seq.

states, codified) criminal law. It does not always follow the usual systematic approach of criminal law and it is prone to be changed, adjusted and expanded much more frequently than ordinary criminal law, by procedures that are less transparent and often very fast as compared to other legislative changes. All in all, the complexity of this field of law – so central to human rights and the core values of the democratic system – makes it very difficult for the media to fulfil its role as the watch-dog of the public power and educator/informer of the public. If you do not understand the legislation it is difficult to know what to look for and where to look for it.

Even if you do understand it, it is a challenge to make it comprehensible to a wider audience in a critical discourse, as the technicalities can also function as wall against outside scrutiny. Any mistake in how the rules or procedures are described can (and often will) be used by the authorities to discredit the reporting as unfounded, tendentious or, at least, based on old information. When the object of scrutiny is fast moving, ever-changing and oblique, critical journalism has small chances of reporting on anything before it is too late to affect public opinion in any useful way. The watch-dog cannot stop anything anymore.

If this is true, and I do think it is to an extent that gives rise to anxiety, the impact of anti-terrorist legislation on the media and its traditional role in our democratic societies is more far-reaching than is obvious at first glance. Taken together with modern governments sometimes aggressive use of media – using well-rehearsed press- conferences, imbedded journalists and the like as tools in getting their view out to the public – there is cause for renewed reflection on the media's constitutional role. Perhaps traditional media cannot function as a watch-dog anymore? One can argue, in the age of the internet, that this might not be such a big problem, when anyone can be journalist and report on anything on the internet. But then again, can professional journalism and its commitment to facts and objectivity really be replaced by everyone writing for everyone without loss? If our understanding of the world is built upon the information we get, surely it must matter how that information is gathered and presented? This is especially so if building common understandings is a vital part of belonging to a political community. The decline of traditional media that we seem to see might be something to fear from this point of view.

5. CONCLUSION

It is evident that blacklisting and other regimes of sanctions introduced on national and international level to combat terrorism have had a profound impact on the scope and intensity of protection of freedom of expression in our democratic societies. Some things cannot be said anymore without risking prosecution or other sanctions. Thus they cannot be heard either, not thought about, discussed and accepted or rejected.[43] Fear is the mechanism behind these regimes and fear is seldom a good bedfellow to liberty, the overarching ideal of the liberal democracies of the western world. Men feared witches and burned women in the 16th and 17th centuries.[44] The governments of today fear terrorists and, at least in the case of the former US government, reacted by torturing young men. The restrictions on free speech and on the ways and means to communicate ideas and views are in this perspective something to be feared itself.

43 For a theoretical approach that would be line with this way of reasoning, see Shiffrin 2011.

44 Cited from Justice Brandies concurring opinion in *Whitney v. California* 274 U.S. 357 (1927), p. 376.

DECISION-MAKING IN THE DARK? AUTONOMOUS EU SANCTIONS AND NATIONAL CLASSIFICATION

Christina ECKES*

1. INTRODUCTION

In the past decade, the European Union has taken an active role in counter-terrorism. It has adopted a broad range of measures, including a comprehensive European Union Counter-Terrorist Strategy as well as a common definition of what is a 'terrorist offence'.[1] Amongst the EU's counter-terrorist policies, sanctions (asset freezing) remains the cornerstone. The EU runs two different regimes of counter-terrorist sanctions: autonomous EU sanctions[2] and EU sanctions implementing UN lists of terrorist suspects.[3] The latter became very well known in EU law circles through the abundant discussion of the case of *Kadi*.[4] The former have attracted less attention but have very similar effects on the human rights of those sanctioned. The core problem under both regimes remains that the high level of secrecy makes fair procedures impossible. The inability or unwillingness of the Council and ultimately of the Member States to share the relevant information even with the EU judiciary – let alone with those

---

* I would like to thank Vigjilenca Abazi for her insightful comments and Margot de Vries for her research assistance.

1 Council Doc. 14469/4/05 of 30 November 2005, see also the important role that terrorism plays in the general security strategy: 'A Secure Europe in a Better World', European Security Strategy, Brussels, 12 December 2003; Council Framework Decision of 13 June 2002 on combating terrorism (OJ L 164, 13.7.2002, p. 3), amended by Council Framework Decision 2008/919/JHA of 28 November 2008 (OJ L 330, 9.12.2008, p. 21–23).

2 Common Position 2001/931/CFSP (OJ L 344, 28.12.2001, p. 93); Council Regulation (EC) No 2580/2001 (OJ L 344, 28.12.2001, p. 70).

3 The UN list of terrorist suspects, originally containing those 'associated with Al-Qaeda' and those 'associated with the Taliban', is now separated into two different regimes (UN Security Council Resolutions 1988 and 1989 (2011)).

4 Case T-85/09 *Kadi II* [2010] ECR 00000; Joined Cases C-402/05 P and C-415/05 P Kadi I [2008] ECR I-6351; Case T-315/01 *Kadi v Council and Commission* [2005] ECR II-3649; see also the pending appeal at: Case C-584/10 P *Commission v Kadi* (Application OJ C 72, 5.3.2011, p. 9); Case C-593/10 P *Council v Kadi* (Application OJ C 72, 5.3.2011, p. 9); Case C-595/10 P *UK v Kadi* (Application OJ C 72, 5.3.2011, p. 10).

sanctioned – remains the main reason why the EU courts cannot offer judicial review of the merits.

This chapter focuses on the problems resulting from the current treatment of sensitive information under the composite procedure leading to the adoption of autonomous EU counter-terrorist sanctions. It considers changes that could make it possible to offer substantive judicial review while ensuring the confidentiality of certain information. The reason for the choice to focus on autonomous sanctions rather than sanctions implementing UN lists of terrorist suspects is that the EU and its Member States *should have* full control over the listing procedure and *should have* all the relevant information, while in the case of sanctions giving effect to UN lists the information appears simply not accessible, either for the EU or its Member States. Hence, even though both types of sanctions are adopted in a similar secretive manner and even though both types of sanctions are equally invasive when it comes to human rights, under the autonomous listing procedure the EU should have the means and the relevant information to adopt counter-terrorist sanctions lawfully – *if* that is possible. This chapter focuses on the problems resulting from the current treatment of sensitive information under the composite procedure leading to the adoption of autonomous EU counter-terrorist sanctions. It explores how substantive judicial review could be offered while ensuring the confidentiality of certain information.

The chapter is structured as follows. *Section Two* introduces the autonomous listing procedure and examines the treatment of sensitive information under this procedure. The Council's inability or unwillingness to share information with the EU judiciary and with those sanctioned is the main reason for the procedural flaws that have led time and again to the annulment of autonomous EU sanctions. The core question that arises from the discussion and that connects Section Two with the following Section Three is whether the Council is or should be obliged to share with the EU Courts all the relevant information that constitutes the basis of the listing decision. *Section Three* turns to the Council's attempt to justify the refusal to share information with a reference to classification under national law. It discusses *inter alia* the 'originator controls' principle. Sharing information is a basic requirement for cooperation between the EU and its Member States. If Member States are unable to exclude further dissemination of information that they make available to the EU institution, this might negatively affect their willingness to share that information. *Section Four* examines potential procedural mechanisms that might allow the Court of Justice to consider sensitive information, on which the listing decision is based while at the same time ensuring the applicant's rights to a fair trial. The very last section brings together the *conclusions*.

2. ADOPTING AUTONOMOUS EU SANCTIONS IN SECRET?

2.1. INFORMATION FLOW UNDER THE ADOPTION PROCEDURE

Under the autonomous EU regime of counter-terrorist sanctions suspects are listed pursuant to a composite procedure set out in Common Position 931/2001/CFSP.[5] The composite listing procedure takes place in two phases. First at the national level, a 'competent national authority' takes a 'decision' within the meaning of Article 1(4) of Common Position 2001/931/CFSP. The 'competent national authority' should in principle be a *judicial* authority but often is not.[6] The 'decision' must entail that the individual is a terrorist suspect. Second, the Council decides to sanction an individual or organisation on the basis of the 'precise information or material in the relevant file', which indicates that a decision has been taken at the national level.[7] The sanction is then imposed on those listed in a directly applicable regulation (Council Regulation 2580/2001[8]) implementing Common Position 931/2001/CFSP.

Lists of terrorist suspects are prepared and maintained in a permanent CP 931 Working Party.[9] A competent national authority proposes a specific name to the other members of the CP 931 Working Party. After this proposal, the representatives have two weeks to consult other governmental officials. Pursuant to its mandate, the permanent CP 931 Working Party is in charge of (i) examining and evaluating information with a view to listing; (ii) assessing whether the information meets 'the criteria in Common Position 2001/931/CFSP and in the Council's statement agreed when the Common Position was adopted'; (iii) preparing the regular review; and (iv) making recommendations for listings and de-listings.[10] Any listing is finally agreed in a unanimous decision of the Council, usually, if there are no objections, in written procedure (A-point).[11]

The procedure, as it is set out in Common Position 2001/931 and in the working methods of the CP 931 Working Party, appears to require that Member States share

5 Article 1(4) of Council Common Position 931/2001/CFSP (n 2 above). The most recent list was adopted in: Council Decision 2011/872/CFSP (OJ L 343, 22.12.2011, p. 54).

6 Eckes and Mendes 2011, pp. 651–670.

7 See Case T-49/07 *Sofiane Fahas v Council of the European Union* [2010] ECR 00000, para. 81.

8 Council Regulation (EC) No 2580/2001 (n 2 above). The most recent implementation measure under Regulation 2580/2001 is: Council Implementing regulation (EU) No 1375/2011 (OJ L 343, 22.12.2011, p. 10).

9 Council Document 10826/07 on the fight against the financing of terrorism – implementation of Common Position 2001/931/CFSP, of 21 June 2007, Annex II. Until the establishment of the permanent working party in 2007, the listings were prepared in an ad hoc forum.

10 See the Working Party's mandate: Council Document 10826/07 (n. 9 above), Annex I, p. 4.

11 The Ministry of Foreign Affairs: Finland and Terrorism: http://formin.finland.fi/doc/eng/policies/repterro.htm.

the relevant information with the Council and the permanent CP 931 Working Party. 'Relevant information' refers to the facts and the national law that in the view of the competent national authority justifies a listing at the EU level. However, the specific level of scrutiny that the Council and its CP 931 Working Party exercise over the listing proposed by a Member States remains ambiguous. Many details of the adoption procedures of autonomous EU sanctions, including the precise listing requirements remain blurry. This is partially due to the formulation of Common Position 2001/931 and partially due to the fact that national judicial systems differ considerably and deal very differently with terrorist suspects.

So far, the Court of Justice has not ruled directly on the legality of the autonomous sanctions procedure. Its involvement has been limited to preliminary references[12] and appeals[13] on very particular issues. In *France v PMOI*, Advocate-General Sharpston discussed the listing requirements. It would further contribute to legal clarity and would therefore be desirable if the Court specified and interpreted the conditions for a listing at the EU level. Unfortunately and contrary to the explicit suggestion of Advocate-General Sharpston,[14] the Court of Justice limited in *France v PMOI* its observations to this very point and did not seize the opportunity to also rule on the interpretation of the listing requirements set out in Article 1(4) and (6) of Common Position 2001/931 and Article 2(3) of Regulation 2580/2001. However, further cases against autonomous EU sanctions are pending in Luxembourg, which might require the Court of Justice to interpret the different requirements of the listing procedure. An appeal by the Netherlands is pending against the decision of the General Court in the case of *Al Aqsa*.[15] The General Court had held that an order of a national court hearing the application for interim measures could no longer serve as the basis for a listing after the 2003 Netherlands regulation on sanctions for the suppression of terrorism[16] was repealed. Al Aqsa brought a second appeal against the same ruling,[17] challenging whether 'the Sanctieregeling', in

---

12 Relevance under national criminal law of EU listings adopted pursuant to flawed procedure: See Case C-550/09 *Generalbundesanwalt beim Bundesgerichtshof v E and F* [2010] ECR I-6213; refugee status: Joined Cases C-57/09 and C-101/09 *Bundesrepublik Deutschland v B and D* [2010] ECR 00000.

13 Access to information: Case C-266/05 P *Sison v Council* [2007] ECR I-1233; issues of representation: Case C-229/05 P *PKK and KNK v Council* [2007] ECR I-439; jurisdiction: Case C-355/04 P *Segi and Others v Council* [2007] ECR I-1657.

14 AG Sharpston, Opinion in C-27/09 P *France v OMPI/PMOI* [2011] ECR 00000, paras. 118–120.

15 Case C-550/10 P *Al-Aqsa v. Council* (OJ C 46, 12.2.2011, p. 3) appeal brought on 24 November 2010 by the Netherlands against the judgment delivered by the General Court on 9 September 2010 in Case T-348/07 *Al-Aqsa v Council*.

16 Regeling van 3 april 2003, nr. DJZ/BR/219–03 houdende beperkende maatregelen tegen de Stichting Al Aqsa met het oog op de strijd tegen het terrorisme (Sanctieregeling terrorisme 2003), *Staatscourant* 7 april 2003, nr. 68, p. 11.

17 Case C-539/10 P *Al-Aqsa v. Council* (OJ C 46, 12.2.2011, p. 2) appeal brought on 22 November 2010 by Stichting Al-Aqsa against the judgment delivered by the General Court on 9 September 2010 in Case T-348/07 *Al-Aqsa v Council*.

conjunction with the order of the court hearing the application for interim measures, can be regarded as a decision of a competent national authority meeting the definition contained in Article 1(4)' Common Position 2001/931. Further, the latter appeal challenged the General Court's interpretation of 'knowledge' within the meaning of Article 1(3)(k) Common Position 2001/931, and Article 1(4) Regulation 2580/2001.[18] Rulings in these cases will at least incrementally shed more light on the precise listing requirements.

Article 2(3) of Regulation 2580/2001 stipulates that the Council shall 'establish, review and amend the list of persons, groups and entities'. For the grounds and procedures for listing Article 2(3) of Regulation 2580/2001 refers to Article 1(4), (5) and (6) of Common Position 2001/931/CFSP. According to the General Court, '[T]he Council enjoys *broad discretion* with regard to the matters to be taken into consideration for the purpose of adopting or of maintaining in force a measure freezing funds'[19] in particular 'the assessment of the considerations of appropriateness on which such decisions are based'.[20] Indeed, the CP 931 Working Party has pursuant to its working methods the mandate to ensure that 'the information provided meets the criteria in Articles 1(3) and 1(4)' of Common Position 2001/931/CFSP.[21] Article 1(3) defines the meaning of 'terrorist act' and 'terrorist group'. Article 1(4) stipulates that listings are based on 'precise information or material in the relevant file which indicates that a decision has been taken by a competent [usually judicial] authority in respect of the persons, groups and entities concerned (...).' Furthermore, the working methods provide for the possibility 'to invite a representative from EUROPOL or the Situation Centre to attend the meeting of the [CP 931] Working Party to make a presentation of background information in order to facilitate discussion on a particular subject.'[22] The wording of the working methods reveals that the CP 931 Working Party does indeed discuss the substance of the information that supports the proposal. Moreover, the working methods stipulate that the CP 931 Working Party 'will check *in particular* whether the proposal complies with the fundamental principles and the rule of law' when the proposal was submitted by a third country

---

18 Article 1(3)(k) Common Position 2001/931: 'For the purposes of this Common Position, 'terrorist act' shall mean one of the following intentional acts, [...] committed with the aim of: [...] (iii) seriously destabilising or destroying the fundamental political, constitutional, economic or social structures of a country or an international organisation: [...] (k) participating in the activities of a terrorist group, including by supplying information or material resources, or by funding its activities in any way, with knowledge of the fact that such participation will contribute to the criminal activities of the group.

19 Case T-49/07 *Sofiane Fahas* (n 7 above), para. 57, referring also to Case T-228/02 *People's Mojahedin Organization of Iran v Council* (OMPI/PMOI I) [2006] ECR II-4665, para. 159, and Case T-341/07 *Jose Maria Sison v Council* [2009] ECR II-3625, paras. 65 and 66.

20 See Case T-49/07 *Sofiane Fahas* (n 7 above), para. 83.

21 Council Document 10826/07, see (n 9 above), Annex II, para. 2.

22 Council document 10826/07 (n 9 above), Annex II, paras. 13–14.

(a state that is not a Member State of the EU).[23] 'In particular' implies that the CP 931 Working Party will also check the proposals of Member States.

At the same time, the General Court has explicitly held that the Council could not examine whether the decision of the national authority is well-founded[24] because this would undermine the principle of sincere cooperation.[25] In the light of the wording of Common Position 2001/931 referring to 'judicial authorities' this argument might appear to have merit in order to safeguard the separation of powers. However, Advocate-General Sharpston argued in *France v PMOI* that a decision of a 'judicial authority' must be interpreted to mean not only 'a finding of guilt by a court' but also 'include the investigating and prosecuting authorities of the Member State(s)'.[26] Indeed, judging from the case law this appears to be common practice. In a number of EU states, the prosecutor is indeed in law and fact a part of the judiciary, and so the principle of separation of powers does not stand in the way of a substantive assessment. On the contrary, the additional adverse effects that a listing in an autonomous EU list of terrorist suspects imposes on individuals[27] warrant that the Council checks that the requirements for a listing are met at the EU level. This must include the fact that the relevant information provided sufficiently supports the assessment that the person is a terrorist suspect.

Both the General Court[28] and the Court of Justice[29] have ruled that there is a distinction between the *initial* listing decision and *subsequent* listing decisions. The verification by the Council of a decision by a national authority for the adoption of the initial decision to freeze funds is an essential precondition. After the initial sanctioning decision, the Council must ensure at least every six months that there are sufficient grounds for keeping an organisation on the list.[30] The General Court ruled in *Sofiane Fahas* that verification of the consequences of the national decision is 'imperative in the context of the adoption of a subsequent decision to freeze funds.'[31] At the same time, the Council remains obliged 'to defer as far as possible to the assessment conducted by the competent national authority, at least where it is a judicial authority [...].[32] In the *Al Aqsa* case, the General Court ruled that when at national level police or

23 Council document 10826/07 (n 9 above), Annex II, para. 4 (emphasis added).

24 Case T-256/07 *People's Mojahedin Organization of Iran v Council (OMPI/PMOI II)* [2008] ECR II-3019, para. 147, this section concerned the listing in Council Decision 2007/445/EC (OJ 2007 L 169, 28.6.2007, p. 58).

25 Case T-256/07 *OMPI/PMOI II* (n 24 above), para. 133; Case T-228/02 *OMPI/PMOI I* (n 18 above), para. 122.

26 AG Sharpston, Opinion in C-27/09 P *France v OMPI/PMOI* (n 14 above), para. 133.

27 See below Section 4 on the adverse effects.

28 Eckes and Mendes, 2011, pp. 651–670.

29 Case C-27/09 P *France v People's Mojahedin Organization of Iran (OMPI/PMOI)*[2011] ECR 00000, para. 63.

30 See Case T-49/07 *Sofiane Fahas* (n 7 above), para. 81. See also Article 1(4) and (5) of Council Regulation (EC) No 2580/2001 (n 2 above), p. 70.

31 See Case T-49/07 *Sofiane Fahas* (n 7 above), para. 81.

32 See Case T-49/07 *Sofiane Fahas* (n 7 above), para. 86. See also para. 69.

security enquiries are closed without giving rise to any judicial consequences, the Council is bound to take that into account.[33] In the *Sison* case, the Court also explicitly stated that 'a decision to prosecute may end in the abandoning of the prosecution or in acquittal in the criminal proceedings. It would be unacceptable for the Council not to take account of such matters, which form part of the body of information having to be taken into account in order to assess the situation (...). To decide otherwise would be tantamount to giving the Council and the Member States the excessive power to freeze a person's funds indefinitely, beyond review by any court and whatever the result of any judicial proceedings taken.'[34] This indicates scrutiny of the further development of the substantive allegations and not only the existence of a proposal as such.

However, irrespective of the level of actual scrutiny at the EU level the Council needs to possess the relevant information simply because in the event of a legal challenge both the General Court[35] and the Court of Justice[36] require the Council to submit the relevant information to the EU judiciary. Neither court accepts the legality of listing decisions based on information that cannot be shared with the judiciary. With the large number of judicial challenges pending,[37] the CP 931 Working Party will have to verify that the Council is in the position to submit the relevant information to the Court.

2.2. FAILURE TO DISCLOSE RELEVANT INFORMATION

The General Court has repeatedly annulled sanctions decisions of the Council.[38] The core problem is the Council's failure to disclose the relevant information to the judiciary and to those sanctioned.

Most recently, the failure to disclose relevant information was demonstrated in the appeal case of *France v PMOI*.[39] The PMOI was subject of a subsequent listing, after a national quasi-judicial body had annulled the reason for the initial listing. The EU Courts distinguish between the initial (first) listing of a person and

---

33 See Case T-348/07 *Al Aqsa v Council* [2010] ECR 00000, para. 168.

34 Case T-341/07 *Jose Maria Sison* (n 19 above), para. 116.

35 Case T-284/08 *People's Mojahedin Organization of Iran v Council (OMPI/PMOI III)* [2008] ECR II-3487, para. 71–73.

36 Case C-27/09 P *France v OMPI/PMOI* (n 29 above).

37 More than 40 cases are pending against different EU sanctions (including country regimes), see in particular: Case C-130/10, *Parliament v Council, joined by the Commission, the Czech Republic, Sweden, and France as interveners* (order of 10 August 2010); C-584/10 P *Commission v Kadi* (n 4 above); C-593/10 P *Council v Kadi* (n 4 above); C-595/10 P *United Kingdom v Kadi* (n 4 above).

38 T-228/02 *OMPI/PMOI I* (n 19 above); Case T-256/07 *OMPI/PMOI II* (n 24 above); appeal pending: Case C-576/08 P *People's Mojahedin Organization of Iran* (OJ C 55, 7.3.2009, p. 15–16); Case T-284/08 *OMPI/PMOI III* (n 34 above); Case T-47/03 *Jose Maria Sison v Council and Commission* [2007] ECR II-73 (summ.pub.).

39 Case C-27/09 P *France v OMPI/PMOI* (n 29 above).

subsequent (following) listings. In the case of the former the reason for the listing and the relevant information may be communicated at the same time as the actual sanctioning decision. The General Court justified this with considerations of effectiveness: the effect of the surprise is necessary when the assets are frozen for the first time.[40] In the subsequent listings, those already listed must be provided with the information beforehand for it to be legally valid. In *France v PMOI*, the new information on which the subsequent listing was based was not communicated to the applicant before the listing or even at the time of the legal challenge. Only reluctantly was part of the relevant information communicated to the Court. On 26 September 2008, the General Court had ordered the Council to provide the relevant information that had led to the subsequent EU listing of PMOI.[41] The Council responded in two stages. On 10 October 2008, the Council first provided eight documents. Seven were not confidential and were also shared with PMOI. One document was confidential. It was not provided to PMOI.[42] The Council further informed the Court 'that it was unable to produce, at that stage, certain further documents setting out the proposed new basis for listing PMOI and explaining the reasons for its proposal, since these were *classified as confidential by the French Republic and could not be made available* at the time the response was submitted.'[43] On 6 November 2008, the Council then provided three further documents: two in full and a third in part.

Most interesting with regard to this communication between the Court and the Council is the fact that the Council delayed or refused submission to the Court of documents that were classified by France as confidential for that reason only. It did not make an assessment of the need of confidentiality itself. In this regard, the General Court made clear that 'the Council's contention that it is bound by the French authorities' claim for confidentiality [...] does not explain why the production of the relevant information or material in the file to the Court would violate the principle of confidentiality, whereas their production to the members of the Council, and thus to the governments of the 26 other Member States, did not.'[44] This is in line with the General Court's basic position that 'the Council is not entitled to base its funds-freezing decision on information or material in the file communicated by a Member State, if the said Member State is not willing to authorise its communication to the Community judicature whose task is to review the lawfulness of that decision.'[45]

All documents were considered by the General Court as insufficient to support the Council's contention.[46] The obstacle to informing the EU institutions

40 Case C-27/09 P *France v OMPI/PMOI* (n 29 above), para. 62.
41 Case C-27/09 P *France v OMPI/PMOI* (n 29 above), para. 40.
42 Case C-27/09 P *France v OMPI/PMOI* (n 29 above), para. 41.
43 Case C-27/09 P *France v OMPI/PMOI* (n 29 above), para. 42.
44 Case T-284/08 *OMPI/PMOI III* (n 35 above), para. 72.
45 Case T-284/08 *OMPI/PMOI III* (n 35 above), para. 73.
46 Case T-284/08 *OMPI/PMOI III* (n 35 above).

of all the evidence lay in French national law. Further evidence relating to the judicial inquiry 'must, under French law, remain confidential during the course of the inquiry.'[47] As a consequence, the Council did not receive all the evidence either. The Council was not informed of the identity of the alleged members of PMOI who were under investigation in France. Nor was the Council informed about the future steps of the inquiry.[48] The General Court specifically related the lack of information to the refusal of the Council and the French authorities to provide part of the third document mentioned above.[49] This stands in contrast with the Council's assertion that it did not possess any information beyond what was supplied in the statement of reasons.[50] It remains unclear whether the part of the third document would have been sufficient to support the listing.

3. CAN SECRECY REMAIN A NATIONAL CHOICE?

3.1. IMPLICATIONS OF NATIONAL CLASSIFICATION

In the case of *France v PMOI*,[51] the Council's justification for not submitting part of the relevant information to the EU judiciary was that France had classified this information as confidential under national law. Hence, the Council possessed the information but felt that its hands were tied by national classification rules. National declassification laws prevented France from declassifying the documents in time for the Council to provide the information to the General Court.

The Court of Justice did not specifically address this point, but Advocate-General Sharpston did. She was not very sympathetic towards the Council's reference to national classification as justification for the refusal to share the relevant information with the EU judiciary:

> 'As regards the Council's contention that it is bound by the French authorities' claim for confidentiality, this does not explain why the production of the relevant information or material in the file to the Court would violate the principle of confidentiality, whereas their production to the members of the Council, and thus to the governments of the 26 other Member States, did not.'[52]

---

47 See para. 11 of the Council's first response to the court order of 26 September 2008, at para. 58 of AG Sharpston, Opinion in C-27/09 P *France v OMPI/PMOI* (n 14 above).

48 *Ibid.*

49 Case T-284/08 *OMPI/PMOI III* (n 35 above), para. 76.

50 Para. 11 of the Council's first response to the court order of 26 September 2008, at para. 58 of AG Sharpston, Opinion in C-27/09 P *France v OMPI/PMOI* (n 14 above).

51 Ibid.

52 AG Sharpston, Opinion in C-27/09 P *France v OMPI/PMOI* (n 14 above), para. 72.

As shown below in section 3.2, the Council's position clashes with the principle of openness[53] and right of access to documents,[54] as they are given expression in Regulation 1049/2001 (the so-called transparency regulation),[55] and also causes problems as regards the applicant's right of access to justice and fair trial. As mentioned, the ostensible reason for the Council's position was that it was 'unable to comply with the [General] Court's Order in relation to [the classified] documents as it does not have the authorisation to provide them to the Court, even on a confidential basis.[56] Under French law, evidence must remain confidential during the course of a judicial inquiry. The Council had 'not been informed of the specific identity of the persons under investigation' but only that they 'are alleged members of the applicant'.[57] Nor was the Council informed about the future steps of the inquiry'.[58]

Member States may have a legitimate interest in keeping confidential (part of) the relevant information that supports that someone is terrorist suspect. If Member States could not trust in the confidential treatment of information that might threaten their national interests they might very well become less cooperative in sharing this information. The consequences for the accuracy of autonomous EU sanctions might be very negative. In the adoption procedure that culminates in EU counter-terrorist sanctions (as well as potentially in other composite procedures, where national and EU authorities cooperate) the relevance of national classification at the EU level is crucial to the applicant's right to fair trial. What does the national classification of documents mean for the EU level? Can the EU authorities share information that has been classified as confidential under national law with the Court? Or even with the applicant?

3.2. ORCON, AUTHORSHIP RULE, OR?

The core problem of the adoption procedure of autonomous EU sanctions is the use of secret information. This raises the question of who decides which information is secret. Does the rule of originator control (ORCON) apply?[59] The concept of originator control is well entrenched in the handling and sharing of sensitive information. In March 2011, the Council adopted the decision on the

53 Article 15(1) TFEU.

54 Article 42 of the Charter of Fundamental Rights.

55 Regulation 1049/2001 of the European Parliament and of the Council of 30 May 2001 regarding public access to European Parliament, Council and Commission documents (OJ L 145, 31.5.2001, p. 43).

56 AG Sharpston, Opinion in C-27/09 P *France v OMPI/PMOI* (n 14 above), para. 6.

57 AG Sharpston, Opinion in C-27/09 P *France v OMPI/PMOI* (n 14 above), para. 12.

58 AG Sharpston, Opinion in C-27/09 P *France v OMPI/PMOI* (n 14 above).

59 More comprehensively on secrecy and its implications: Curtin, 2011.

security rules for protecting EU classified information.[60] It applies the ORCON rule to all EU classified information (EUCI).[61] Additionally in July 2011, the Member States meeting within the Council (but not acting as the Council) adopted an agreement on 'the protection of classified information exchanged in the interests of the European Union', in which the Member States agreed to apply the ORCON rule.[62] Under the ORCON rule, the party that provides information retains (nearly) complete control over the dissemination of that information by the EU body that receives it. This is highly relevant in the case of autonomous EU sanctions, since as we have seen above, all relevant information that leads to a listing at the EU level originates from national authorities. ORCON also means that if the information has been classified under national procedures, it cannot be reclassified or declassified by the EU, unless the originator consents. Further, information provided by a Member State cannot be passed on to any other institution or body without the consent of that Member State. If ORCON applied the national control over shared information would be nearly absolute. Particularly, if there is no requirement for the designating Member State to justify on the merits (!) its choice to classify or refuse to declassify or consent to the release of information which it has provided to the Council. If a simple reference to national rules on classification sufficed, the Council would be prevented from making an independent judgment about the wisdom of releasing the relevant information that has informed the listing decision, only because it has been classified by a Member State.

Before the introduction of the ORCON rule, the EU institutions applied the so-called "authorship rule" which followed essentially the same rules as ORCON.[63] The authorship rule 'meant that, where the author of a document held by an institution was a natural or legal person, a Member State, another [Union] institution or body, or any other national or international organisation, the request for access to the document had to be made directly to the author of the document.'[64] The terminology changed with the Council decision on the security of EUCI.

In both the Council decision of March 2011 and the agreement of July 2011 between the Member States the claim is made that existing transparency rules are respected. The Decision for instance states that it is 'taken without prejudice to the existing practices in Member States with regard to informing their national Parliaments'.[65] The agreement sets out that '[n]othing in this [a]greement shall

60 Council Decision of 31 March 2011 on the security rules for protecting EU classified information (OJ L 141, 27.5.2011, p. 17).

61 See Article 3(2) on downgrading or declassifying of EUCI; see Article 12(4) on exchange of EUCI with third states or international organisations.

62 Agreement between the Member States of the European Union, meeting within the Council, regarding the protection of classified information exchanged in the interests of the European Union (OJ C 202, 8.7.2011, p. 5), see in particular Article 4.

63 See e.g. for the Commission: Commission Decision of 8 February 1994 on public access to Commission documents (OJ L 46, 8.2.1994, p. 58).

64 Case C-64/05 P *Sweden v Commission* [2007] ECR I-11389, para. 56.

65 Council decision (n 60 above), recital 10.

cause prejudice to the national laws and regulations of the [Member States] regarding public access to documents […]'.[66] Neither the decision nor the agreement specifically mentions the EU Courts or court proceedings.

The legal regime on classified information should be contrasted with the transparency regulation, which aims to give the fullest possible effect to the right of public access to documents held by an institution, including not only documents drawn up by an institution but also documents received from third parties, including the Member States (expressly stated in Article 3(b)). Article 4(4) of the latter extends access to documents originating with third parties. It sets out: 'As regards third-party documents, the institution shall consult the third party with a view to assessing whether an exception in paragraph 1 or 2 is applicable, unless it is clear that the document shall or shall not be disclosed.' The latter should be read as a reference to classified information. Yet, it applies to 'third parties' and hence not to Member States. Article 4(5) of Regulation 1049/2001 stipulates: 'A Member State may request the institution not to disclose a document originating from that Member State without its prior agreement.' Neither paragraph 4 nor 5 unambiguously express an ORCON principle. Paragraph 5 seems to be slightly more nuanced in that they make clear that the Member State needs to *request* the institutions to treat the document confidential and that this is not an automatic consequence of the fact that it originates from a Member State. This raises the question how nationally classified information should be treated. Under Article 4(4) (applicable to third parties) it might fall under the 'unless' exception. Under Article 4(5) national classification might constitute an automatic 'request'. However, while paragraph 4 speaks of an obligation to *consult* the originator before taking a decision to release information (the final decision lies with the EU institutions), paragraph 5 requires agreement. Hence, under Article 4(5) the institutions are not free to share information without the agreement of the Member States. However, the Court of Justice interpreted Article 4(5) of Regulation 1049/2001 *not* to give Member States 'a general and unconditional right of veto, so that it can oppose, in an entirely discretionary manner and without having to give reasons for its decision, the disclosure of any document held by a [Union] institution simply because it originates from that Member State, is not compatible with the objectives […]' of the Regulation.[67] The Court made clear that Member States' power to oppose disclosure is limited by the exceptions set out in Article 4(1) to (3) of Regulation 1049/2001. This does not, at least not directly, answer the question of who should be in charge of taking the final decision whether or not a document can be released. However, it places the decision firmly within the EU law context and does not grant a general exception for information classified under national law.

---

66 Agreement (n 62 above), Article 3(2).

67 Case C-64/05 P *Sweden v Commission* (n 64 above), para. 58.

In the *IFAW* ruling in January 2011,[68] the General Court applied and specified the Court of Justice's earlier ruling. It clarified the conditions under which it is possible for the Commission to refuse access to documents originating from Member States.[69] It made clear that first, it is for the EU institutions to decide whether a document can be shared and not for the Member States (the EU institution is responsible that one of the Article 4 exceptions applies). Second, the Court emphasised that the EU judicature will carry out a *full review* of the grounds for opposition invoked by the Member States. At the same time, the exceptions can require an assessment of the interests of the Member States (as distinguished from the interest of the Union). In particular, Article 4(1)(a) of Regulation 1049/2001 refers to the '[...] the protection of the public interest as regards public security, defence and military matters, international relations [...] *of a Member State*'. Member States do have broad discretion in determining their interest within the meaning of this exception under EU law. However, any decision to conceal information based on any of the exceptions in Article 4 falls within the jurisdiction and control of the Court of Justice. This implies of course disclosure to the Court.

More specifically with regard to the sanctioning procedure we should turn to the CP 931 Working Party. It forms part of the Council. Its working methods declare with regard to confidentiality that:

> '– meetings will be held in a secured environment so as to enable discussion up to SECRET UE, and will be held as and when necessary;
> – adequate steps will be taken to ensure the confidentiality of the proceedings of the CP 931 [Working Party];
> – the date of the meeting, agenda and organisational details will be classified CONFIDENTIEL UE;
> – the Council Secretariat will hold any documents relevant for the listing or de-listing of persons, groups or entities. Such documents will, if appropriate, bear an EU or national classification marking. The rules on public access to Council documents apply.'[70]

The reference to the Council's rules on public access to documents confirms that the rules applicable to the Council, including Regulation 1049/2001 directly apply to the information held by the Working Party. This requires that the decision to refuse or allow access to sensitive documents is justified within the legal framework of EU law. Neither the Council nor the Member States can simply invoke *national* rules of classification as justification to refuse access.

---

68 T-362/08 *IFAW Internationaler Tierschutz-Fonds v Commission* [2011] ECR 00000.

69 *Ibid*, paras. 73–88.

70 Council Document 10826/07(n 9 above), Annex I. The EU works with four levels of classification: très secret UE/EU top secret; secret UE/EU secret; confidential UE/EU confidential; restraint UE/EU restricted.

Classifying rules under national law before submitting them to the WP cannot be a way to circumvent rules of access to information. These are of course for the public not for the Court. Yet, what applies within the framework of public access to information under Regulation 1049/2001, applies *a fortiori* to the information that is shared with the EU judiciary. Again the Court has full jurisdiction, which is only possible if it is given access to the concealed information.

3.3. HOW MUCH SECRECY IS NEEDED?

In principle, Member States are under an obligation to cooperate and provide relevant information supporting listing under the sanctions regime set up by Common Position 2001/931 and Regulation 2580/2001.[71] They are equally obliged to keep the Council and each other informed about developments in the cases of those that are already listed by the EU. However for the adoption of autonomous sanctions the Council depends on the willingness of the competent national authority to submit its decision and the relevant information. Assuming that autonomous EU sanctions do make a contribution to reducing the threat of terrorism, which admittedly cannot be taken for granted, then a failure to provide the Council with the necessary information to make listings diminishes the EU's capacity to take action in order to keep the EU safe. Excluding the sensitive information will further in many cases make it impossible for the Council to make an informed decision or to protect the measures from attack in Court.

At the same time, some secrecy might have to be guaranteed to the Member State to ensure cooperation. A comparison with Europol, where the applicable rules specifically address the balance between access and secrecy could be useful. Europol is a well-established EU agency whose core task is receiving, examining and providing (often sensitive) information. It can only carry out its task if Member States are willing to provide it with information. Europol has a legal framework that specifically determines how sensitive information that it receives from Member States should be handled.[72] In principle the choice of classification of any information that a Member State provides to Europol lies with that Member State.[73] However, the assessment should take place pursuant to the rules of EU law.[74] This does not exclude re-classification by Europol, but it

71 See Article 4 Common Position 2001/931/CFSP (n 2 above) and Article 8 Council Regulation (EC) No 2580/2001 (n 2 above).

72 Council Decision 2009/968/JHA of 30 November 2009 adopting the rules on the confidentiality of Europol information (OJ L 332, 17.12.2009, p. 17), see in particular Articles 10 and 11.

73 Council Decision 2009/968/JHA (n 72 above), Article 11(1).

74 Council Decision 2009/968/JHA (n 72 above), Article 11(1) and (2) in combination with Article 10.

requires Europol to 'inform the Member State concerned and seek to agree on an appropriate classification level. Europol shall not specify, change, add or remove a classification level without such agreement.'[75] Hence, Member States' appear to possess a 'veto right' as regards the information that they share with Europol but they have to argue their case (if necessary before court) on the basis of EU law.

Giving the Member States a 'veto right' on the information they provide goes far, considering that all Member States are represented in the Council and that cooperation in the EU is based on an assumed high level of trust and confidence. An adaptation of the rules for access to information that were discussed in the previous section might be more appropriate. Under these rules the EU institutions take responsibility for the correct application of the exceptions under Article 4 of the transparency regulation. One option could be to require the Council or its CP 931 Working Party to determine the classification of the relevant information, after they have collected all the information relevant to any one particular listing and given it their own interpretation. This assessment would have to take place within the EU law framework and give particular attention to the interest that the providing Member State claims to have in classifying the document. This would also ensure that the appropriate level of classification to protect the interests of the EU and its individual Member States is applied after all the information is compiled and assessed in the light of the question of the person's ability to contribute terrorist activities. The necessary classification might change as a result of new assessments or of a more extensive contextualisation. This would place the responsibility with the EU institutions and bodies. It would result in greater coherency, break the link with national classification, and allows to consider the adverse effects of EU sanctions. At the same time, it offers the possibility to ensure confidentiality where needed.

Finally, the EU institutions would have to take responsibility for the classification in court and, as a result, share the relevant information with the EU Courts. The following section will consider what procedural mechanisms could be employed to ensure a fair trial and confidentiality to the extent strictly necessary.

4. SECRET INFORMATION IN COURTS: LESSONS THAT COULD BE TAKEN FROM NATIONAL LAW

The main reason for annulment of autonomous EU sanctions is the infringement of the procedural and judicial right of those sanctioned resulting from the Council's failure to share the relevant information with the EU Courts. The EU

[75] Council Decision 2009/968/JHA (n 72 above), Article 11(3).

Courts have unambiguously ruled that the Council cannot impose sanctions without sharing the relevant information that has led to the sanctions decision. If we accept that part of the relevant information is indeed sensitive and that dissemination could harm the interests of the EU and its Member States, the EU Courts will need to be able to ensure confidentiality.

Counter-terrorist sanctions exemplify the problem that the EU judiciary does not have a procedural framework on how to deal with sensitive information. The Statutes of the Court of Justice do not provide for mechanisms to offer judicial review of the merits while protecting confidentiality.[76] The Court of Justice's Rules of Procedure generally state that '[t]he Judge-Rapporteur and the Advocate General may request the parties to submit within a specified period all such information relating to the facts, and all such documents or other particulars, as they may consider relevant. The information and/or documents provided shall be communicated to the other parties.'[77] The rules only address the specific point of limiting the access of *interveners* to 'secret or confidential documents'.[78]

The obvious places to look for inspiration are national legal systems. Particularly in the UK, discussion has recently focussed on the treatment of sensitive information in courts.[79] One option, currently under discussion in the UK for civil procedures, could be closed material procedures.[80] However, particularly in the light of the critical evaluations of how closed hearings with secret evidence have been used in court proceedings challenging 'preventive' security measures,[81] it is in order to start with the clarification that the following examination aims to evaluate and assess the implications of the closed material procedures without presupposing that such measures are automatically necessary in legal challenges against sanctions.[82] The assumption is rather that while secret evidence might be inappropriate in certain contexts (*e.g.*, excessively long duration of sanctions) it might be unavoidable if we want to have an independent judicial control of the hidden sanctioning practices of the Council. The principle of openness must continue to inform the decision of whether any

---

76 Protocol (No 3) on the Statute of the Court of Justice of the European Union, (OJ C 83, 30.3.2010, p. 21).

77 Consolidated Version of the Rules of Procedure of the Court of Justice (OJ C 177, 2.7.2010, p. 1), Article 54a.

78 Consolidated Version of Rules of Procedure of the Court of Justice (n 76 above), Article 93(3).

79 See two recent cases of the UK Supreme Court, *Al Rawi v the Security Service* [2011] UKSC 34 and *Tariq v Home Office* [2011] UKSC 3. See also: UK Government, Justice and Security, Green Paper, October 2011, available at www.official-documents.gov.uk/document/cm81/8194/8194.pdf.

80 UK Government Green Paper (n 79 above); consider also the existing procedures in the Special Immigration Appeals Commission.

81 Van Harten 2009. Specifically on the use of Australia's National Security Information (Criminal and Civil Proceedings) Act 2004, see: Mark Rix 2011. On the United States' Classified Information Procedures Act (CIPA), see Melanie Reid 2011.

82 The argument that discussing the details of the closed materials procedure presupposes the acceptance of the need for secrecy was eloquently made by Murphy 2011.

particular part of evidence cannot be provided to the applicant. This is necessary because 'no procedural adaptation can entirely remove the inherent weaknesses arising from secrecy.'[83]

As a consequence, national procedural mechanisms should not be blindly copied but must be carefully examined as to their consequences on fair trial. Closed material procedure can be divided into two stages. A key procedural component is the use of special advocates with high security clearance, who are given access to sensitive information that will not be disclosed to those whom these advocates represent (in line with the terminology of the EU Courts this would be the applicant). At the first stage, the decision must be made whether the material is indeed confidential and cannot be revealed to the applicant. The claim of necessary confidentiality must be made by the public authority and assessed by the Court. The Court must hence be placed in the position to judge whether a closed material procedure is necessary. This obviously implies that the Court must see the confidential material in order to make the necessity assessment. Already at this stage the involvement of the special advocate is of essence in order to represent and argue the case not only from the particular interests of the applicant but also more generally for openness and transparency. This allows drawing a line between the impartial court and the interests of the applicant. The Court should make the assessment with the additional insights of the special advocate's argument. At the second stage, the case is argued on the merits. Here, the special advocate represents the applicant and can access all relevant information, including the confidential part that is not provided to the applicant. In this procedure it is necessary for the special advocate to communicate with the applicant not only before but also after he or she has reviewed the confidential material. This would require the special advocate to make an assessment about how much of the confidential information (and in what detail) he or she can discuss with the applicant. This might appear to place too much responsibility on the special advocate. However, first of all, strict rules should apply at the first stage that ensure that only the absolute minimum of sensitive information stays secret in the first place. This information can also be revealed to the special advocate with explicit instructions concerning what could be discussed with the applicant. Second, we should not think of special advocates as ordinary lawyers. They should be highly screened and trained individuals that are employed by and responsible to public authority (the EU) for contesting the 'prosecution' and arguing for the side of the applicant. They should not be dependent on the applicant. Finally, the Court of Justice would possibly have to render part of its ruling in secret. The latter entails further difficulties concerning the transparency of judicial dialogue, the accountability of the judiciary, and the ability of future parties to argue their case. In any event, a summary of the reasons and the ruling must be available both to the applicant and to the general

83 Van Harten 2009, p. 27.

public.[84] The Court of Justice has an inquisitorial role also in ordinary proceedings. This should be emphasized in closed evidence procedures. Beyond this it would be desirable that judges are given training on how to handle sensitive information, evaluate disclosure decisions, and give closed judgment.

In order to make use of a closed material procedure at the EU level, it would be indispensable to establish a sophisticated legal framework that reasons on the basis of a general presumption that all information is open and accessible and sets out minimum rules on communication with the applicant, support of the special advocate, and minimum openness requirements. If these standards cannot be met public action against any 'terrorist suspect' must be excluded. Any exception from the general presumption of openness would have to be specifically justified and compatible with EU law. The difficulties arising from a closed material procedure would have to be studied in detail and rules to anticipate any illegitimate restrictions would have to be put in place. The legal framework would have to ensure as a minimum that the standards required by the ECHR as interpreted by the ECtHR are met despite the fact that (part of the) relevant information is not shared with the applicant. Interesting in this context is the ruling of the ECtHR in the case of *A and Others v UK*.[85] Although *A and Others* concerned preventive detention and therefore dealt with the special provision of Article 5(4) ECHR,[86] the case is a recent illustrative example of the requirements that the ECtHR imposes on the use of confidential information in court proceedings. The Court referred to its own case law concerning the right to a fair trial and explained that it was significant that the trial judge had 'full knowledge of the issues in the trial' and can 'carr[y] out the balancing exercise and that steps had been taken to ensure that the defence were kept informed and permitted to make submissions and participate in the decision-making process as far as was possible without disclosing the material which the prosecution sought to keep secret'.[87] The Court explained that competing public interest can restrict the rights of the defendant; yet if the defendant 'has had no opportunity to examine or to have examined [...] the rights of the defence would be restricted to an extent incompatible with the guarantees provided by Article 6' ECHR.[88] The Strasbourg Court, while it had referred to special advocates in earlier rulings, endorsed in *A and Others* for the first time 'the possibility of using special advocates to counterbalance procedural unfairness caused by lack of full

84 See on the summary: UK Government Green Paper (n 79 above), p. 69.

85 ECtHR, *A and Others v UK* (Application no. 3455/05), [2009] ECHR 301; see also earlier: ECtHR, *Chahal v UK* (1997) 23 *EHRR* 413.

86 ECtHR, *A and Others* is a sequel of: *House of Lords, A (FC) and others*; *X (FC) and others v Secretary of State for the Home Department (Belmarsh detainees* case), judgment of 16 December 2004 [2004] *UKHL* 56, [2005] 2 AC 68, [2005] 2 *WLR* 87, [2005] *HRLR* 1. Article 5(4) ECHR is *lex specialis* to Article 13 ECHR and requires less stringent procedural safeguards as Article 6 ECHR.

87 ECtHR, *A and Others v UK* (n 86 above), para. 206.

88 ECtHR, *A and Others v UK* (n 86 above), para. 207.

disclosure [...].'[89] It came to the conclusion that in the cases of five of the applicants[90] Article 5(4) ECHR had not been violated because 'the special advocate could provide an important, additional safeguard though questioning the State's witnesses on the need for secrecy and through making submissions to the judge regarding the case for additional disclosure.'[91] '[T]he special advocate could perform an important role in counterbalancing the lack of full disclosure and the lack of a full, open, adversarial hearing by testing the evidence and putting arguments on behalf of the detainee during the closed hearings.'[92] The ECtHR found a violation of Article 5(4) ECHR in the case of four applicants because they did not have contact with the special advocate after she had seen the confidential material and because the open allegations (that the applicants had seen) were too general in nature to allow them to provide the special advocate with information to effectively challenge the charges.[93]

Autonomous EU counter-terrorist sanctions differ from preventative detention. However, open-ended asset freezes that last for more than a decade impose so far-reaching human rights restrictions that their 'preventative' or 'administrative' nature is widely questioned.[94] Yet so far neither the Court of Justice nor the ECtHR has settled whether they should be considered to be of a criminal nature. Even though the criminal nature of autonomous EU sanctions is not uncontroversial it is desirable that the legal framework provides for procedural safeguards that meet the required level of Article 6 ECHR for proceedings determining a criminal charge. Not only would this place the EU on the safe side in the event of a future determination that indeed counter-terrorist sanctions are a criminal charge. It would also contribute to the trust and confidence of EU citizens in the Union's commitment to the rule of law. It is worth recalling: In the UK, special advocates originate in immigration proceedings.[95] More recently, they have been used in counter-terrorist procedures.[96] The UK Government in its Justice and Security Green Paper discusses the transfer to criminal law.[97] They have not actually been used in criminal procedures.

---

89 ECtHR, *A and Others v UK* (n 86 above), para. 209–224.

90 ECtHR, *A and Others v UK* (n 86 above), para. 222.

91 ECtHR, *A and Others v UK* (n 86 above), para. 219.

92 ECtHR, *A and Others v UK* (n 86 above), para. 220.

93 ECtHR, *A and Others v UK* (n 86 above), paras. 223–224.

94 See on sanctions giving effect to UN lists: Case T-85/09 *Kadi II* (n 4 above); Report to the General Assembly of the United Nations of 2 September 2009, entitled 'Report on the protection of human rights and fundamental freedoms while countering terrorism', document A/HRC/12/22, point 42.

95 Special Immigration Appeals Commission Act 1997, 1997 Chapter 68, 17 December 1997, available at www.unhcr.org/refworld/docid/3de739304.html [accessed 22 February 2012].

96 Before the Proscribed Organisation Appeals Commission.

97 UK Government Green Paper (n 79 above).

5. CONCLUSIONS

The effective sharing of information between the EU and its Member States is crucial to the quality of the decisions under the autonomous EU sanctions procedure where the Council lists a person as a terrorist based on the decision of a competent national authority. The Council cannot simply rubberstamp a national decision that someone is a terrorist without independently assessing the situation. This can be supported by three observations. First, the national decision is taken in a completely different procedure that culminates in a different outcome (e.g. conviction for a crime under national law as opposed to the freezing of assets). Second, the Council exercises discretion when it takes the listing decision. Discretion implies assessment. Hence, the Council cannot exercise discretion without having a basis for assessment. Third, the Council's decision to list someone as terrorist and freeze that person's assets might be reviewed in court. Indeed, a large number of legal actions against different types of sanctions, including autonomous counter-terrorist sanctions are pending. In the event of a judicial challenge, the Court will not accept to be kept out of the loop. National classification as confidential will not be enough to refuse informing the Court.[98]

Finally, there is a public dimension that should not be underestimated in the EU context. EU citizens must be able to have confidence that the EU institutions and bodies do not act outside of the law but that they are subject to independent judicial scrutiny. The EU must not only be a Union of law but also be able to rely on the trust and confidence of its citizens that this is the case. It is risky for the EU project to enter into contentious areas of restrictive policy-making, such as counter-terrorism and the prevention of crime, if this public confidence is not ensured.[99] The EU is in this regard in a special place. It does not possess either the same 'natural' legitimacy to impose human rights restrictions or the same enforcement mechanisms as a state. Indeed, the Union's case to argue that it is a Union of law is more difficult and should be made with great care – to the extent that it should seek to avoid even the appearance of arbitrariness.

Setting up a legal framework that enables the Council to list individuals based on confidential information without infringing the applicant's procedural rights does not appear impossible – even in the light of the far-reaching human rights restrictions imposed by counter-terrorist sanctions. A closed materials procedure would require a clear set of rules for the disclosure process, including rules on the participation of a trained special advocate not only in the main proceedings but also in the disclosure process, rules on the communication between the special advocate and the applicant (in particular after the former

98 This justification came up in Case C-27/09 P *France v OMPI/PMOI* (n 14 above). However, the Court of Justice did not mention the issue in its appeal decision.

99 *Cf.* Nuotio 2006.

has seen the closed material), and rules on giving – if necessary – even a partially closed judgment. The disclosure rules would have to start from the basic assumption that all material is open to the applicant and that any exception to this assumption must be justified to the EU Courts within the framework of EU law.

Arguing the case for closed material procedures at the EU level is a difficult one. It accepts the necessity of an exceptional need for secrecy under the autonomous sanctions procedure. However, the need for a careful case-by-case assessment of whether some of the relevant information cannot be revealed to the applicant can be argued. There should be an option to *consider* closed material procedures. In an area as sensitive as counter-terrorism this might be the only way to ensure Member State's willingness to share information, particularly if they are not permitted simply to exclude any access at all by classifying the information before providing it to the Council – and they should not be. Only if comprehensive information is provided to the Council can the quality of sanctions decisions be ensured. The same is true for the Court. Only if the Court of Justice is in the position to consider comprehensively all relevant information is it in the position to render a well-founded decision. The issue of whether those sanctioned can be allowed to access all relevant information is a separate matter and should be considered separately. As a general rule, individuals who are subject to public decisions that (may) have adverse effects on their legal position have the right to be heard during the administrative procedure and the right to challenge such decision in court. For the exercise of both rights access to the relevant information that has led to the decision of the public authority is of the essence. Only if the affected person is confronted with the allegations can he or she effectively rebut these allegations. Only then is the applicant able actively to participate in the judicial proceedings rather than being made subject to the proceedings. A careful and differentiated approach to a strictly limited need for secrecy might make a greater contribution to individual rights than a blunt claim for total transparency – particularly in the complex interaction between EU institutions and Member States in the autonomous sanctions procedure.

PROSCRIPTION OF ORGANISATIONS IN UK COUNTER-TERRORISM LAW

Sofia Marques da Silva and Cian C. Murphy*

1. INTRODUCTION: A PARODY OF LAW

In Rome, under the dictatorship of Sulla, a *lex de proscriptione* was published along with a *tabula proscriptionis* – a law and list that designated the enemies of the public. Such persons' property could be seized, they could be killed with impunity, and their family name was forever stained. Cicero, who was himself killed under proscription, spoke in favour of such a person in the speech *Pro Roscio Amerino*. 'My duty' the great orator began, 'does not require me to be acquainted with the exact basis of legality on which my opponents justify their treatment of my client. I only say that nothing in their *lex* – whatever its title – that has reached my ears, justifies them at all'. Cicero was, it has been argued, referring to the 'lex' as a 'parody of law'.[1]

In the UK today the power to proscribe an organisation sits amongst a wide range of domestic, EU and international powers to subject individuals and organisations to financial and other restrictions such as targeted asset-freezing sanctions.[2] It remains a potent, if 'at best a fairly blunt instrument' in the regulation of politics.[3] It offers the potential to severely restrict the rights of speech, association and assembly in respect of any group against which the power is used. Proscription is a readily available tool for the Government in combating terrorism and its use is often dependent on intelligence that cannot be, or at least is not, released to the proscribed group. Deproscription is difficult to achieve with the administrative process tilted against the proscribed organisation and the availability of judicial review restricted by the cost involved

* We are grateful to the participants of the conference in Uppsala for their comments on an earlier version of this paper and to Iain Cameron in particular for his editorial work.

1 Donkin 1991, p. xiii.

2 For a useful overview of the different systems of targeted sanctions and financial restrictions operating in the UK see the official report by Anderson 2011. For a brief historical summary of proscription in UK counter-terrorism law see Horne 2011.

3 See the official report by Lord Carlile of Berriew, 2010, para 73.

in bringing an action. The power is therefore a difficult one that blurs the lines between political and legal action drawing 'a political maze that it is unfair to ask the police to enter'.[4] The threat of contemporary political violence in the UK (outside of Northern Ireland) tends not to involve easily identifiable groups such as uniformed militia (below section 3). Thus, it may be that proscription does not serve sufficient strategic purposes to merit the costs it entails for political freedom.

This paper seeks, through an analysis of the law and legal practice, to critique the operation of the system of proscription. It relies on a range of primary sources, including government materials that have made their way into the public sphere, as well as a triumvirate of literatures that each contribute to our understanding of the proscription system. These literatures, which are cautiously categorised as literatures of law, criminology, and security studies, each offer a part of the picture. It is only through a critical synthesis of these literatures that the debate as a whole can be brought forward.

Although proscription is a long-established tool of counter-terrorism it is (perhaps surprisingly) somewhat neglected by the legal literature. The definitive analysis of legal doctrine in UK counter-terrorism is Walker's *Terrorism and the Law*.[5] Walker's analysis is entirely necessary insofar as it provides a comprehensive account of the proscription power. However, the breadth of the subject has an inevitable effect on the extent to which Walker can examine the political and societal context in which the power operates. Though doctrine may be an essential starting point the gap between legislative power and the operation of the law in this field makes a contextual assessment an essential rather than an elective methodological approach.

Although there is no sustained socio-legal critique of the power of proscription in the existing literature there have been several strong interventions in the debate from the field of critical criminology. Thus, the recent work of Pantazis and Pemberton, which deploys Hillyard's *Suspect Community* thesis, is relevant to the debate, as is the ongoing work of Sentas in relation to the effects of proscription on diaspora communities.[6] Just as this paper aims to better inform the debate on legal doctrine through a more contextual analysis of the law so too does it seek to anchor the more sociological accounts found in critical criminology. These critiques, though compelling, often situate the power to proscribe within a broad policy milieu and render it difficult to isolate which aspects of the legal power and related processes are most troublesome.

---

4 Ewing and Gearty 1990, p. 217.
5 Walker 2011. For a critique of Walker see Murphy 2012.
6 Hillyard 1993, Pantazis and Pemberton 2009, Sentas 2010a and Sentas 2010b.

The final field of scholarship upon which the analysis draws can be called security studies, war studies, terrorology, or some other cognate term. The authors make no claim to expertise in this field and acknowledge that, much like critical criminology, the field itself is contested.[7] The literature is nonetheless useful both because of the insights it offers into the logic of counter-terrorism and because of the manner in which it can, of itself, be used to debunk the claims to effectiveness made on behalf of the power of proscription. After all – it is a core requirement of the principle of legality that any legal powers be fit for the purpose.[8]

The touchstone throughout this account is the idea of constitutional governance. It is not the purpose of this article, and nor is there the space in it, to articulate a full account of constitutional governance. One could drown in the barrels of ink spilt by the post-September 11 scholarship on whether the legislative or judicial branches offer better safeguards against the executive, whether such checks should be embedded within public law or instead be extra-legal or extra-constitutional, and indeed whether any such checks should exist at all.[9] This paper assumes that such checks should exist and argues that in the complex politico-legal constitution of the United Kingdom both Parliament and the courts have an essential role to play.

2. THE LOGIC OF PROSCRIPTION

The logic behind the use of proscription in the UK is contestable but well-entrenched. The Jellicoe Report of 1983 was a review of the operation of the Prevention of Terrorism (Temporary Provisions) Act 1976.[10] The Report offered three arguments in favour of a system of proscription: first, that it encapsulates the 'public aversion' to groups which use violence for politics, second, that it prevents public displays which may provoke outrage and disorder, and third, that it prevents the funding of such organisations. In 1983 a Home Office Minister claimed that proscription prevented the Irish Republican Army from being able to 'flaunt' itself in public.[11] Today, there is something of a consensus amongst both the government and successive Independent Reviewers on the stated purposes of proscription. These are: to deter proscribed organisations from coming to the UK; to disrupt the ability of such organisations to operate; to support foreign governments in disrupting activity and to denounce the claims

7 See Breen Smyth et al. 2008. For a response see Horgan and Boyle 2008.
8 Murphy 2010.
9 De Londras and Davis 2010.
10 See the official reports by Lord Jellicoe 1983, and Lord Lloyd of Berwick and P. Wilkinson 1996, pp. 29–30.
11 See discussion in Ewing and Gearty 1990, pp. 215–217.

of proscribed organisations to legitimacy.[12] Walker, in recent evidence to Parliament, summarises the long-standing view of UK Governments that proscription has a deterrent effect, provides a useful tool to address 'some of the lower-level support for terrorist organisations', and, most pertinently, is a 'powerful signal of the rejection by the Government – and indeed by society as a whole of organisations' claim to legitimacy'.[13] There is a clear mixture of goals here as this list includes both the symbolic and the strategic. The question as to whether proscription actually achieves these goals is an open one.

There has been some discussion in recent years of extending the system to capture a wider ranger of 'extremists' such as the Islamist group Hizb ut-Tahrir. The coalition Government's programme declared an intention to proscribe 'any group that has recently espoused or incited violence or hatred ... subject to the advice of the police and security and intelligence agencies'.[14] However, following a review of counter-terrorism powers, the pursuit of a broadened power of proscription has been abandoned. The review, carried out in 2010 with the oversight of former Director of Public Prosecutions, Lord Ken MacDonald, highlighted practical difficulties that would arise if the system were to be used to proscribe racial, religious, or other hate speech.[15] The Independent Reviewer of Terrorism Legislation, David Anderson QC, has also warned against changing the system of proscription to catch extremist group Hizb ut-Tahrir.[16] There is also reluctance within government. The Deputy Prime Minister has claimed that proscription must 'always be a last resort, never a knee-jerk reflex'. Thus, while he supported the Government decision to proscribe the Pakistani Taliban he also supported the decision 'against increasing the government's powers to proscribe'. This is, he claimed, part of a system of 'smart engagement'.[17] Thus, proscription has broad support across the UK political system – although the boundaries of its use remain open to discussion.

The reluctance to extend the system may in part be due to a 'residual taboo against banning indigenous groups'.[18] That taboo may be losing force – as the use of proscription to target Islam4UK and Muslims Against Crusades demonstrates.[19] The targeting of these organisations is notable because they are

12 See the official reports by Lord Carlile of Berriew 2010 and Anderson 2011, paras 4.16–4.19.
13 Home Affairs Committee 2012, Ev w14: 20.
14 HM Government 2010, p 24.
15 See the official report, MacDonald 2011, pp. 7–8.
16 'Watchdog recommends Tory U-turn on banning Hizb ut-Tahrir', *The Guardian* 19 July 2011.
17 N. Clegg, 'An Open, Confident Society', 3 March 2011, available at www.newstatesman.com /2011/03/open-liberal-violent.
18 Gearty 2007, p. 159.
19 These groups were deemed, in January 2010 and November 2011 respectively, to be aliases of al-Ghurabaa and the Saved Sect (organisations which are designated for their glorification of terrorism). See further the discussion below.

not necessarily violent, but are extremist – and are caught because they 'glorify' rather than seek to commit acts of terrorism. It is likely to be the even more difficult task of drawing limits on the idea of 'extremism' as compared to 'terrorism' that has stayed the hand of successive Governments.

Proscription, as the experience of the above groups demonstrates, has a significant effect on political freedom. It is not the only tool by which the Government can 'sanction' groups suspected of political violence. In recent years the development of smart sanctions to target groups that may cause a threat to international peace and security has attracted much criticism. Thus the United Kingdom has had to take steps to implement UN Security Council resolution 1267 (as amended) imposing sanctions against Al-Qaeda and UN Security Council resolution 1373 which requires sanctions against those identified as 'terrorists' by national authorities. The implementation of both systems in UK law has a somewhat complicated legal history. Today, the Terrorist Asset-Freezing etc. Act 2010 serves to implement the UK's resolution 1373 obligations. For the sanctions against Al-Qaeda the UK now relies on EU law to give effect to the UK system.[20] Proscription is also a form of sanctions list but the restrictions on those on the proscription list are even more significant that those that the UN and EU impose when freezing assets. Proscription is not just about asset freezing but ensures that any type of support for a proscribed organisation is made illegal. The existence of multiple systems results in different standards and procedures being applied to different groups – depending on which system it is being targeted by and what process applies. Thus, before examining the impact of the proscription system it is necessary to consider the process by which designation occurs.

3. THE PROCESS OF DESIGNATION

The process of designation of an organisation for proscription is set out in section 3(4) Terrorism Act 2000. Although the Secretary of State for the Home Department takes the decision, the process leading up to proscription involves the police and intelligence agencies, and the decision to proscribe is approved by Parliament and can be subject to review in the courts. Listing decisions are made based on intelligence provided by security services. It is impossible to assess the reliability of the information provided to the Home Secretary as it contains both open and closed evidence (and the latter is not disclosed). However, as the system of proscription is heavily reliant on these services it is worth noting that their effective operation has come into question in recent years.[21]

20 See Anderson 2011.

21 For a discussion of the need for appropriate legal safeguards in light of intelligence failures see Roach 2009, pp. 164–167. In the UK context see Kavanagh 2011 and Leigh 2009.

A decision to proscribe an organisation requires the Home Secretary to satisfy herself that two parts of a test are met. The first part of the test requires a 'belief' that the organisation is 'concerned in terrorism'. This clumsy term is held to mean that the organisation commits, participates in, promotes, encourages, glorifies, or is otherwise 'concerned in terrorism'. Some aspects of this test are elaborated on by the legislation, such as what is meant by 'glorification', added to the law by the Terrorism Act 2006. Nonetheless the legislation does not define how an organisation can be 'otherwise' concerned in terrorism. The list of behaviour that can trigger the first part of the test is thus non-exhaustive and therefore indefinitely broad. 'Terrorism' for the purposes of proscription is defined by section 1 of the Terrorism Act 2000 (as amended). The definition is a rather broad one.[22] The courts have played a role in restricting the definition of what it means to be 'concerned in terrorism'. In *Lord Alton of Liverpool* the Court of Appeal established that a listed organisation must be concerned in terrorism in the present day. Previous activities are not sufficient to justify listing on an ongoing basis if those activities have ceased. And, most importantly, potential future activities are not enough to sustain proscription.[23]

Nevertheless, this initial part of the test is likely to be met by a broad range of organisations – and yet only a selection of those organisations are actually proscribed. It is the second part of the test that determines which organisations are included on the list. If the organisation is 'concerned in terrorism' the Home Secretary must consider five discretionary factors to determine whether or not to use the power to proscribe. These factors are the nature and scale of the organisation's activities; the specific threat that it poses to the United Kingdom; the specific threat that it poses to British nationals overseas; the extent of the organisation's presence in the United Kingdom; and the need to support other members of the international community in the global fight against terrorism.[24] The key point here is discretion. There is broad scope for the Home Secretary to use the power for a wide range of goals. These goals, as has been seen, are both symbolic and strategic. The determination as to whether or not to proscribe a group can be seen to turn on political rather than legal considerations.

The initial check on the Home Secretary's power is Parliament, which must consent to proscription orders. The parliamentary consent process uses the

---

22 See in general Walker 2011, para 1.107–1.154.

23 *Lord Alton of Liverpool & Others v SSHD* Appeal PC/02/2007 Open Determination 30 November 2007, paras 122–28.

24 These criteria were laid down in 2001 and are included in Explanatory Memoranda to proscription orders. See, for example, Explanatory Memorandum to the Terrorism Act 2000 (Proscribed Organisations) (Amendment Order) 2011. The Independent Reviewer of Terrorism Legislation has recently proposed tightening these discretionary factors. See Anderson, 2012 (para 4.64).

affirmative procedure for orders listing organisations and the negative procedure for orders relating to aliases of proscribed organisations already proscribed. Thus, Parliament votes on proscription by affirming the whole list of proscribed organisations. It cannot resolve against listing one organisation without resolving against listing all organisations. Often Parliament has little or no information about the organisations in question as the evidence used to justify the listing is not divulged.[25] The effectiveness of Parliamentary review of the initial decision to designate is therefore minimal. It has never refused its consent to a proscription order.

Once Parliament has approved proscription of an organisation a range of offences are triggered in relation to that organisation. It is an offence to belong to such an organisation,[26] to support, or invite support for such an organisation,[27] or to wear or carry a uniform or article of a proscribed organisation.[28] These offences were first created to target Irish Republican and other groups in Northern Ireland and some appear archaic in modern counter-terrorism where groups or organisations do not necessarily wear uniforms or obvious articles of association. There are therefore good reasons to be sceptical as to whether proscription can have a positive impact in today's efforts to combat political violence.

4. THE IMPACT OF THE PROSCRIPTION SYSTEM

There are, at present, 62 organisations listed in the Schedule to the Terrorism Act 2000. These comprise 14 groups in Northern Ireland and 48 groups of an international nature.[29] The impact of the proscription system on those it targets is difficult to discern. For example, Peter Neumann, a strategic studies expert, notes that 'one should not expect too much in terms of a tangible impact when you are dealing with an organisation that does not have much of a structure, does not have money in bank accounts, does not rent offices in the first place'.[30] The absence of a tangible impact may suggest that in some cases at least proscription is a purely symbolic gesture – and yet its effects can be profound. Impact can be considered in four respects: first, in terms of facilitating the

---

25 See the discussion in the House of Commons of the Terrorism Act 2000 (Proscribed Organisations) (Amendment) Order 2006: House of Commons, *Hansard*, 20 July 2006 col 490–509.

26 S 11 Terrorism Act 2000.

27 S 12 Terrorism Act 2000.

28 S 13 Terrorism Act 2000 For a discussion of these offences in practice see Walker 2011, paras 8.39–8.48.

29 The list, as of 6 July 2012, can be found at www.homeoffice.gov.uk/publications/counter-terrorism/proscribed-terror-groups/proscribed-groups (last accessed 20 August 2012).

30 Home Affairs Committee 2012, Ev 70.

prosecution of those suspected of terrorism; second, in deterring and disrupting attacks on the United Kingdom; third, in furthering Government diplomatic goals; and fourth, in broader societal terms.

4.1. PROSECUTION OF SUSPECTS

Given the many critiques of post-September 11 counter-terrorism that focus on the absence of prosecutions the system of proscription might be considered a welcome departure from this trend.[31] The Independent Reviewer notes that proscription offences 'are among the most commonly charged offences under the terrorism legislation'.[32] Between 2001 and 2010 seventeen convictions were secured from thirty-one British cases in which proscription offences were the principal offence charged. In Northern Ireland, in the same period, four out of five charges were for membership of a proscribed organisation.[33] Anderson therefore notes that the system 'produces real, if modest, gains in terms of convictions and has the ability to disrupt harmful organisations and to change their behaviour'.[34] His predecessor as Independent Reviewer came to a similar conclusion – stating that 'prosecution for membership ... is a useful way of dealing with lower level activity, and with early signs of involvement in terrorism'.[35]

The system of proscription therefore provides a means by which prosecutions for terrorist offences may be obtained. However, despite the prosecutions it facilitates, Lord Carlile has admitted that proscription 'provides little in terms of protection of the public from terrorists'.[36] Indeed, an analysis of the 133 individuals who were convicted of Islamist-related terrorism offences in the UK between 1999 and 2010 concluded that two-thirds of the offenders had no direct link to any organisations currently proscribed in the UK.[37] Thus, while proscription may facilitate prosecutions and convictions, it is reasonable to ask to what end? If proscription-related convictions do not help to protect the public, and the majority of terrorist convictions are for other offences, then the basis for the proscription convictions must be found in another policy goal.

---

31 See, in general, Roach 2011.
32 See the official report, Anderson 2011, para 4.15.
33 *Ibid.*
34 *Ibid.*, para 4.18.
35 See the official report Carlile 2010, para 62.
36 *Ibid.*
37 Simcox, Stuart and Ahmed 2011.

4.2. DETERRENCE AND DISRUPTION

It may well be that the purpose of prosecutions arising from proscription is not to punish those who have caused harm – but to deter them (and others) from causing harm and to disrupt groups of persons who seek to carry out violent acts. This may be relevant in both the domestic context and in the international context. Thus, one argument in favour of maintaining the proscription of the 'Irish Republican Army' is that the designation denies a name of significant historic importance to any new group that may form.[38] Although this argument is persuasive it must be remembered that organisations bearing the name 'Irish Republican Army' have persisted since the Irish war of independence and their proscription, in both Ireland and the UK, appears to have had little effect on their longevity. In addition, there may be equal force to the argument that the decision to continue proscription maintains the mystique of the 'IRA' as the vanguard of Irish republicanism fighting against a repressive, occupying, British state. Those that seek justification for violent resistance to British presence in Ireland will always believe that the Union flag outside Stormont Castle is sufficient cause.[39] However, this does not mean that proscription remains necessary. It might well be a step in the 'normalisation' of the government of Northern Ireland for non-violent republican groups to be delisted and for only those groups that refuse to enter into a cease-fire to remain subject to proscription.[40]

The usefulness of proscription in deterring and disrupting political violence is even harder to ascertain outside of the Northern Ireland context. The proscription of Islam4UK in 2010 to prevent a march in Wootton Bassett (the town into which the caskets of British soldiers killed in action in Iraq arrived) may be understood as either a convenient use of the power to avoid a protest or an entirely sensible proscription that was marred by poor timing.[41] The link between Islam4UK and the already-proscribed al-Ghurabaa and the Saved Sect was declared by the Government and summarised by the Independent Reviewer:

> Al-Muhajiroun, Islam4UK and three other appellations were ordered in January 2010 to be treated as alternative names for al-Ghurabaa and the Saved Sect, each of which had been proscribed in 2006. Al-Muhajiroun was founded in the United Kingdom in

---

38 See the official report, Anderson 2011, para 4.36.

39 Frenett and Smith 2012.

40 These organisations, which are 'specified' under the Northern Ireland (Sentences) Act, are those 'whose members are not eligible for early release from prison because the organisations are concerned in terrorism connected with the affairs of Northern Ireland and have not entered into a ceasefire'. This consideration was raised by the Independent Reviewer of Terrorism Legislation in his 2011 report: Anderson 2011.

41 Raymond 2010.

1996 by Omar Bakri Mohammed. It was disbanded in 2004, Al Ghurabaa and the Saved Sect being successor organisations.[42]

In November 2011, to prevent yet another controversial protest, Muslims Against Crusades was proscribed.[43] The group was deemed to be another alias of the already-listed organisations. The successive proscription of different aliases of this group poses questions of constitutional governance.[44] Two highly controversial protests were banned through the use of proscription. However, these groups were involved in glorification of terrorism rather than in terrorism itself. This raises the question as to the effect that proscription has in preventing an extremist organisation from becoming a *violent* extremist organisation, and in preventing violence inspired by extremists. There is a school of thought that holds that the existence of proscription prevents 'radicalisation' in this sense.[45] Jamie Bartlett of Demos states that though he is 'not in favour of proscription', 'having the Sword of Damocles constantly hanging over groups like Hizb ut-Tahrir has been quite helpful in forcing them to moderate in many respects'.[46]

The effect of the mere threat of proscription is an indication of the 'chilling effect' that the system can have on both freedom of expression and freedom of association. Although such an effect may have its merits it is an indication of a tendency towards 'militant democracy' – 'the idea that democracies are justified in denying freedoms associated with democracy to those who reject democracy'.[47] Despite the Deputy Prime Minister's call for 'smart engagement' it is easy to characterise the proscription of extremist organisations as a clumsy swing of the cudgel of state power. This tendency has restrictive effects when it involves national politics but can be rather problematic in international context.

4.3. PROSCRIPTION AND INTERNATIONAL DIPLOMACY

One of the persistent criticisms of proscription is that the system is little more than a tool of diplomacy. A majority of the organisations are based overseas and many, if not most, do not pose any apparent threat to UK security. The Home Secretary may take action to proscribe a group in furtherance of 'the need to

---

42 See the official report by Anderson 2011, para 4.10.

43 'Muslims Against Crusades to be banned from midnight', *The Guardian* 11 November 2011.

44 Section 22 of the Terrorism Act 2006 amended the Terrorism Act 2000 to provide the Secretary of State with the power to designate by order an alias of an already-proscribed organisation.

45 The concept of 'radicalisation' is recognized as being problematic despite the development of significant efforts to 'counter radicalisation'. See Sedgwick 2010. See also Kundnani 2009.

46 Home Affairs Committee 2012, Ev 66.

47 See Roach 2004, pp. 171, 177–80; Roach 2011, p. 257. For an early use of the phrase see Loewenstein 1937.

support other members of the international community in the global fight against terrorism'. There is therefore a link between this tool, a relic of domestic problems in Northern Ireland, and the 'war on terror'. Indeed, in the post-September 11 environment the dictates of the 'hegemonic' UN Security Council effectively requires states to implement some form of blacklisting of terrorist groups. This can, of course, vary from an asset-freezing system to a full system of proscription.[48] However, the relevant UN Security Council resolution, 1373, has been described as 'out-sourcing' the definition of terrorism. Thus, the designation terrorist is no longer the subject of public or political debate but is defined in law.[49] There is therefore scope for domestic policy to have transnational effect. If the Sri Lankan government decides that the LTTE are 'terrorists' then the determination may lead to proscription in the UK – as indeed it did.

One understanding of the post-September 11 spread of counter-terrorism law is that it seeks to re-establish 'the supremacy of the nation state'. Muller argues that there has been an effort to discredit 'any liberation or resistance movement who prey in aid of the principle of democracy or self-determination in their purported fight against oppressive states'.[50] This goes beyond militant democracy as all governments, not just democratic ones, are protected by the definition of terrorism and the proscription power predicted upon that definition. States that have a vested interest in opposing self-determination movements find common cause with those who seek to combat threats that – though real – are far from existential.[51] Proscription of organisations on foreign policy grounds contributes to this affirmation of state power. Sentas goes as far as to argue that proscription 'forecloses opportunities for peaceful settlement of conflict, it also legitimates and facilitates state terrors, ethnic cleansing and genocide of other states'.[52] She argues that there is therefore a link between proscription and the escalation of military conflict. These rather strong claims are the subject of ongoing research and require further evidence to be sustained. Nonetheless, before the People's Mujahedin Organisation of Iran was delisted by the Proscribed Organisations Appeals Commission, although it asserted it was 'involved in a legitimate struggle [with] no choice but to resort to armed resistance', the Home Secretary stated that he 'does not, accept, however, any right to resort to acts of terrorism, whatever the motivation…'.[53] Thus, the organisation was proscribed notwithstanding the legitimacy of its struggle or the fact that it did not pose a threat to the UK.

48 Alvarez 2003.
49 Muller 2008, p. 115.
50 Muller 2008, p. 120.
51 Muller 2008, p. 119.
52 Sentas 2010a, p. 16.
53 See Muller 2008, p. 123.

This decision might be acceptable if all groups 'concerned in terrorism' were proscribed – it would be draconian but it would at least be a consistent application of the law. However, as highlighted above, the test for proscription allows the Home Secretary much discretion – and not every group that is 'concerned in terrorism' is subject to the proscription system. The choice of proscription targets demonstrates the regions in which the UK seeks to maintain influence. The most-represented state in the list is Pakistan – with between nine and eleven groups based in that territory.[54] After Pakistan and the surrounding region the next most-represented territory is Palestine (four groups) with Turkey (three groups) also well-represented. Thereafter the list is more disparate, with organisations in North Africa, the Middle East and South-East Asia included. No groups in South America are proscribed, although some, such as FARC, would surely meet both the 'concerned in terrorism' criteria and several of the discretionary factors. These choices are thus ones of foreign policy and gives rise to criticism that proscription is used in accordance with political priorities rather the interests of national security or in compliance with the requirements of constitutional governance. This causes problems for the ethical conduct of foreign policy but also for the broader societal impact of these choices.

4.4. SOCIETAL IMPACT

For many critics of UK counter-terrorism powers it is not the technical flaws in the legislation, but rather the societal impact, that is of greatest concern. There is strong condemnation of the system of proscription within the critical literature because of its broader impact in both political and societal terms. Thus, for Sentas, it is 'a state violence which seeks to [sever] migrants' legitimate links with their country of origin by expressly criminalising diverse forms of transnational affiliation and support'.[55] The examples Sentas cites – the LTTE in Sri Lanka and the PKK in Turkey – demonstrate the manner in which proscription implicates the UK by helping to delegitimise certain groups pursuing ethno-nationalist or secessionist causes. Because the definition of terrorism does not distinguish between legitimate and illegitimate political violence it raises the problem of the relationship between terrorism and self-determination. There are states where democratic means for the expression of claims of self-determination (or simply dissent) have been closed off. In such circumstances violent politics may be the only option left to bring about constitutional change. But this is not recognised by either international or domestic law in post-September 11 counter-terrorism. The proscription system, in tandem with other global counter-

---

54 Nine groups are based in Pakistan, with a further group based in India/Kashmir and a final group operating between Iran, Afghanistan and Pakistan (Baluchistan).

55 Sentas 2010a.

terrorism measures, can therefore be seen as causing 'a dangerous political and human rights lacuna' in international law.[56]

This poses three related questions. The first question is one of foreign policy – is it in the interest of the UK Government to support the Sri Lankan and Turkish states in suppressing violent insurrection by ethno-nationalist groups (bearing in mind that asymmetrical warfare often involves action of questionable legitimacy on both sides)? Even if the answer to this first question is affirmative there remains the distinct question of whether the criminal law in the UK should be deployed to this end. It is one matter for the government, as a matter of foreign policy, to decide to support the Sri Lankan government against the LTTE. However, it is a much more significant step to then enshrine that support in the criminal law of the state and thus restrict the choice of the citizens of Britain (as well as the Tamil diaspora) to decide to support or denounce the LTTE. The *LTTE* case is now moot but in the context of the ongoing conflict in Palestine the decision to proscribe Hamas could have real implications for public debate on a perennial topic of international affairs. The third question, raised by the 'suspect community' thesis, is the extent to which the targeting of groups that engage in political violence delegitimises the cause those groups pursue and criminalises not violence, but the expression of a particular political view and indeed an entire community.

In his critique of UK counter-terrorism, *Suspect Community*, Paddy Hillyard argued that the use of proscription – and other counter-terrorism powers – amounted to the official construction of the Irish as a 'suspect community'. Hillyard's critique has itself been the subject of criticism within the academy on methodological grounds. Greer alleges that Hillyard is guilty of over-generalisation from individual experiences and of failing to define what 'community', in his thesis, means.[57] Despite these reservations about the 'suspect community' thesis it has been updated and applied to the British Muslim population.[58] Pantazis and Pemberton claim that the Terrorism Act 2000 has allowed the designation of British Muslims as a new 'suspect community'.[59] In his criticism of the recent application of the 'suspect community' thesis to the Muslim population of Britain, Greer argues that the legislation 'unquestionably criminalizes those associated with banned

56 Muller 2008, p. 130. International law, of course, permits and even protects the right to self-determination (see Brownlie 2008, p. 553). However, the post-September 11 restriction on the lawfulness of violence for political ends renders most struggles for self-determination rather difficult. Where a state is willing to use force to maintain control of a territory then waging a *lawful* struggle of secession or revolution may now be impossible.

57 Greer 1994, pp. 510–511.

58 Pantazis and Pemberton 2009. See further Peirce 2008.

59 Pantazis and Pemberton 2009, p. 652.

organizations, since this is, after all, the whole point of proscription'. However he claims that Pantazis and Pemberton 'provide no evidence whatever to support the claim that banning an organization also brings under official suspicion those not associated with it'. Therefore, he concludes, it is not clear 'how wide the official suspicion stretches'.[60] Despite the force of Greer's critique the suspect community thesis has been used as the basis of a recent, highly critical, empirical study – albeit one that does not address proscription powers in particular.[61]

The effects of the proscription system are therefore rather wide. They are legal in character but are political (domestic & international) and social in effect. There is a chilling effect on certain political movements and ideologies. However, it is questionable as to whether or not this effect, which is both a direct and indirect result of listings and prosecutions, actually improves public safety and national security. This tool of militant democracy may drive dissent underground where seductive narratives of rebellion become more persuasive in the absence of challenge in the public sphere.[62] Given the likely public revulsion in response to the sort of demonstrations planned by Islam4UK and Muslims Against Crusades proscription may be the less effective means of combating their message. Rather, proscription may suit the narrative of state repression that such organisations seek to develop while doing little to further national security.

A comparison of the list of proscribed organisations with national, European, and global asset-freezing sanctions systems makes for interesting reading. The list of proscribed organisations in UK law includes a number of organisations that do not feature in the UN, US, Canadian or Australian lists. This may indicate that the groups have been included because of national, rather than global, counter-terrorism priorities. Furthermore, a majority of organisations that are the subject of proscription in the UK but not elsewhere do not feature in HM Treasury's consolidated list of organisations and entities subject to asset-freezing sanctions. Thus, when it comes to dealing with organisations that are national priorities, it appears that the state's preference is to proscribe rather than to impose an asset-freeze.

5. SYSTEMS OF REVIEW AND DELISTING

If the system for listing makes it rather straightforward for the Home Secretary to designate an organisation, and the effects can be profound, then it is vital that there are effective systems of review in place. However it is far easier to achieve

60 Greer 2010. See further the reply: Pantazis and Pemberton 2011.
61 Hickman et al. 2012.
62 For the classic case in this respect see Mill 1859.

proscription than deproscription. Gearty puts it succinctly: 'once banned it would take almost eccentric courage on the part of a mainstream political leader to take the risks inherent in making a de-proscription order.'[63] This has been borne out in practice. The Home Office received 11 applications for delisting between 2001 and 2010 but all were refused by the Home Secretary. The only organisation to secure delisting, the People's Mujahedin Organisation of Iran, did so by challenging the Home Secretary's refusal before the Proscribed Organisations Appeal Commission. There are therefore two stages to the review system – administrative review within Government and judicial review by the Proscribed Organisations Appeal Commission (POAC) and the Court of Appeal.

5.1. ADMINISTRATIVE REVIEW

In 2006, Baroness Scotland, then Minister of State in the Home Office and later Attorney General, offered the House of Lords the assurance that if 'an organisation no longer met the criteria for proscription, then it would be considered for deproscription'.[64] This review is, it has been confirmed, a legal obligation. POAC has held that both the language of the Terrorism Act 2000 and the 'nature of the powers with which it is concerned' place the Home Secretary under a legal duty regularly to review the necessity of any organisation's inclusion on the list. There are two administrative groups within Government with responsibility for reviewing proscription decisions: the Proscription Review & Recommendation Group and the Proscription Working Group. Little information on either group is available in the public sphere. However, the Independent Reviewer summarises their operation as follows:

> Proscription issues are considered by the Proscription Review and Recommendation Group [PPRG] and the Proscription Working Group [PWG]. Both are chaired by OSCT. The PPRG is attended principally by representatives from the Home Office, Foreign Office and [the Joint Terrorism Analysis Centre]. In its meetings … it reviews the status of the proscribed groups, on the basis of a review produced by JTAC, ensuring that each group is reviewed at least once in each year. It also ensures that the necessary evidence exists for the proscription of new groups to be considered. The PWG is a more senior group, attended in addition by representatives from police, the security and intelligence agencies, Cabinet Office and a range of Government departments. It pays particular attention to any "difficult cases" identified by the PPRG and makes recommendations to the Home Secretary on which groups should be proscribed or deproscribed.[65]

---

63 Gearty 2007, p. 158.
64 House of Lords, *Hansard*, 24 July 2006, col 1618–1619.
65 See the official report by Anderson 2011, para 4.6.

The usefulness of regular administrative review within Government should not be understated. Anderson notes the Home Secretary is given 'thorough advice, with clear reference to the legal criteria, and has sight of all the supporting documentation'. She is also advised on how to respond to the applicant. However, he notes 'the ineffectiveness of annual administrative reviews, conscientious though they may be, to achieve deproscription in the face of what may often be a considerable political incentive to maintain proscription'.[66]

Although it would be a fallacy to equate a failure by the administrative review process to delist any organisation with the conclusion that such a process is incapable of affording a fair review, the correlation is striking. In principle, justice in a common law legal system is based on the idea that adversarial proceedings are most likely to get to the truth of a matter. Though there are two groups within the Government tasked with reviewing the designations, there is no-one within either group subject to a duty to advocate delisting and there is no incentive for any member of the review group to propose delisting. As Walker puts it in relation to the Proscription Working Group:

> without any transparency in its constitution, including published criteria, membership, and timetable, and without any fairness in its process, including notice to those potentially affected and an invitation to make representation and to divulge the continuing grounds for proscription, [one] ought to be highly sceptical that this administrative system is effective or fair.[67]

Thus, despite the legal duty of the Home Secretary to consider regularly deproscription, the system that assists her in fulfilling that duty is designed with a view to ensuring the effective operation of proscription rather than to ensuring due process for those subject to it.

5.2. PROSCRIBED ORGANISATIONS APPEAL COMMISSION & JUDICIAL REVIEW

POAC was established by section 5 of the Terrorism Act 2000 as the forum for review of the Home Secretary's decisions on deproscription.[68] It is modelled on the Special Immigration Appeals Commission and so is chaired by a High Court judge and hears challenges on grounds of fact and law. The Commission can operate in both open and closed sessions with special advocates representing the

66 *Ibid.*, para 4.33.
67 Home Affairs Committee 2012, Ev w14: 20.
68 An attempt to directly apply for judicial review was refused in *Kurdistan Workers' Party & Ors, R (on the application of) v Secretary of State for the Home Department* [2002] EWHC 644 (Admin).

interests of the proscribed group in the latter sessions. POAC may issue open and closed judgments and is subject to appeal to the Court of Appeal on points of law.

The only case to be brought before POAC to date was *Lord Alton of Liverpool* – a challenge brought by 35 parliamentarians concerning the listing of the People's Mujahedin Organisation of Iran. The case examined a number of aspects of the proscription system including the appropriate standard of judicial review. The Home Secretary had called for deference on the part of the judiciary – claiming that the *Wednesbury* standard of review should be used.[69] POAC rejected this argument and conducted a review of the question as to whether the organisation was 'concerned in terrorism' using the standard of 'intense scrutiny'. Thus, it held that the Home Secretary must have reasonable grounds for belief that there is involvement in terrorism. It held that most of the material before it that was relevant to the test of 'concerned in terrorism' was 'essentially factual and is of a type that courts are familiar with assessing.'[70] POAC concluded that the People's Mujahedin Organisation of Iran had not been 'concerned in terrorism' for several years and as such ordered that it be delisted. Indeed, it declared that it would have arrived at the same conclusion even if it had used the (more deferential) *Wednesbury* standard of review. The Court of Appeal supported the Commission's conclusions.[71]

5.3. PROBLEMS WITH DEPROSCRIPTION

Despite the robust approach of both POAC and the Court of Appeal in *Lord Alton of Liverpool* there remain problems with reliance on this system of review. The first significant problem with the deproscription process is the cost involved in bringing an action. Although a group may itself request a review of the decision to designate it, taking the challenge further is likely to involve retaining legal services. This cost has, it seems, deterred at least some potential applicants from pursuing their case.[72] This issue of cost is exacerbated by the fact that any attempt to raise money to fund the legal action may be an offence under the

69 The *Wednesbury* test for judicial review is a rather deferential one. It entails that the judiciary will only intervene where the action by the executive is 'so unreasonable that no reasonable authority could ever have come to it'. See *Associated Provincial Picture Houses Ltd v Wednesbury Corporation* [1947] EWCA Civ 1. This may be contrasted with the much more rigorous scrutiny that now exists in UK human rights law. See, in general, Endicott 2011.

70 *Lord Alton of Liverpool & Others v Secretary of State for the Home Department* Appeal PC/02/2007 Open Determination 30 November 2007, paras 116–119.

71 *Secretary of State for the Home Department v Lord Alton of Liverpool & Others* [2008] EWCA Civ 443.

72 Anderson, 2011, para 4.32: the International Sikh Youth Foundation described POAC proceedings as 'slow, secretive and costly'.

Terrorism Act 2000 or may otherwise be unlawful (for example by breaching asset-freezing sanctions directed against the organisation).[73]

The second problem concerns the system of closed material proceedings using secret evidence.[74] POAC may hold closed proceedings to consider evidence that the Home Secretary is unwilling to disclose to the applicants. A 'special advocate' who is privy to the secret evidence but cannot share it with the person on whose behalf they are acting represents the applicant. This system has been the subject of significant criticism for failing to uphold due process. POAC requires the Home Secretary to 'disclose all relevant material' including 'exculpatory material'. This system was held to be satisfactory in *Lord Alton of Liverpool* but is deeply problematic from the point of view of due process.

A further concern relates to the scope for the state to take retaliatory action against any individual who seeks to challenge a particular designation.[75] Although there is no evidence of such action by the state the potential for such action may be enough to deter applicants. It is worth recalling that the group that brought the sole case to reach POAC were parliamentarians – a group that is not legally, politically or socially vulnerable. Not all organisations subject to proscription are so fortunate in their advocates.

6. PROSCRIPTION & THE POST-SEPTEMBER 11 LANDSCAPE

The key trope in post-September 11 counter-terrorism has been the shift towards a pre-emptive form of governance that privileges executive power over constitutional governance. Proscription is an unusual tool in the British state's counter-terrorism toolbox. It is an example of the politicisation of the law (and also the juridification of politics).[76] The system is a tool of militant democracy but as it pre-dates the September 11 attacks it might not fit with the post-September 11 paradigm. Aside from the rise of executive power the two characteristics of a pre-emptive measure are that its targets are chosen based on unproven suspicion rather than evidence and that its intervention aims to indefinitely incapacitate rather than punish. Proscription must be considered in both respects to determine its pre-emptive potential.

---

73 *Ibid.*, para 4.31.

74 See, in general, Murphy 2011.

75 Walker 2011, para 8.33.

76 On the boundaries between the legal and the political see the introduction in Stone et al. 2012.

In terms of the targets of the system, the definition of terrorism in UK law is sufficiently broad to enable proscription of organisations 'concerned in terrorism' to be pre-emptive. It is pre-emptive in the sense that it can be used to target a range of political action – regardless of its legitimacy or proximity to causing harm. Emails uncovered by the *New Statesman* showing the behind-the-scenes operation of the system are far from edifying for the New Labour government.[77] The correspondence sheds light on a debate within the Home and Foreign Offices on whether Hamas, Hizbullah, Hizb ut-Tahrir and Al Muhajiroun could and should be added to the proscription list. There are several noteworthy points: reluctance on the part of the intelligence services to change their assessment to suit policy changes, a concern that legal challenges would be upheld, but also an observation that such challenges would 'help identify' those involved in the organisations. Although there is pre-emptive potential the correspondence suggests a clumsy, rather than a cunning, state apparatus.

The case of the People's Mujahedin Organisation of Iran demonstrates that the judiciary will, however, examine whether or not the organisation does indeed meet the test of 'concerned in terrorism'. The attempts by the Government to secure judicial deference or to have the judiciary accept the group's potential for violence as grounds for proscription were unsuccessful. The judiciary's interpretation and application of the law therefore mitigates against a determination that proscription is pre-emptive. In this respect the judiciary have taken a more muscular approach than their US counter-parts who have been entirely accepting of the pre-emptive justification for the US system of proscription.[78] However, the practical difficulties in challenging the decision to proscribe means that pre-emptive enforcement of the law is possible. Thus, in terms of the targets of the action proscription can be said to have pre-emptive potential that is exacerbated by the operation of the law in practice.

The second aspect of pre-emption, a change in the type of action, has more ambiguous implications for an examination of proscription. A decision on proscription is implemented through law but has effects that are as much political as they are legal. Proscription therefore blurs the line between the legal and the political in an attempt to restrict the participation of certain organisations in public discourse. In terms of the organisation itself the effect of proscription is incapacitation. For example, after the recent listing of Muslims Against Crusades, the group disbanded. This incapacitation is brought about through criminal justice or at least the threat of criminal justice. The effect on the organisation's members is just as profound. What was acceptable action one day (the support of an organisation) becomes a criminal offence the next. And

77 'Losing the plot', *New Statesman* 30 January 2006.
78 *Holder v. Humanitarian Law Project*, 561 U.S. ____ (2010).

while proscription uses criminal justice it predicates the involvement of the criminal justice system on the operation of an administrative system of justice that is tilted against those targeted.

The problems with the targets of proscription and the effect on those targeted both stem in part from the 'executive-friendly' nature of the system. It is pre-emptive, in large part, because of the imbalance in powers between the Government, Parliament and the courts in relation to the system. Proscription could therefore be much improved with better safeguards. However, in his final report as Independent Reviewer, Lord Carlile commented that reform of the proscription system 'has not enjoyed a high priority in Ministerial thinking or activity'.[79]

7. REFORM OF SYSTEMS OF REVIEW

It is possible to envisage discrete reforms of the current system that would improve its operation while still providing a counter-terrorism tool for government. A true liberal critique would argue that the whole system of proscription is unacceptable, that the 'militant democracy' is a counter-productive fallacy and that the system should be abandoned. Such a critique may well be valid but given the longevity of proscription in British law the system is unlikely to be repealed.[80] The key question then is which institution is in the best position to check the Government's decision to deploy the proscription power. The answer is likely to be both the courts and Parliament – albeit in different ways.

The courts have in their favour their independence, their experience in conducting detailed reviews of complex factual situations, and their ability to elaborate and apply legal standards. The courts are thus in the best position to determine whether or not an organisation is 'concerned in terrorism'. In addition to their competence, leaving such a determination to the courts is an acknowledgement of the severe effect a proscription order can have on the rights that give effect to political freedom. The willingness of the courts to review counter-terrorism action has improved since the rather deferential judgment in *Rehman*.[81] Today, the courts are more willing to examine ministerial decision-making in the field of national security – as both *Belmarsh* and *Ahmed*

79 See the official report by Carlile 2010, para 64.

80 For a similar caveat see Lynch et al. 2009, p 3: 'the authors do not deny the strength of the objections that have been raised as to both the conceptual and practical aspects of the Australian proscription regime'.

81 *SSHD v Rehman* [2001] UKHL 47.

demonstrate.[82] In *Lord Alton of Liverpool* the Proscribed Organisations Appeal Commission, and the Court of Appeal, demonstrated 'judicial assertiveness over proscription without precedent'.[83] However, POAC itself acknowledged that while on factual assessments (the 'concerned in terrorism' test) it would be robust on matters of policy it would be more deferential to the Government. The courts therefore may not be the best institution to assess compliance with the five 'discretionary factors' that the Home Secretary uses as the second part of the proscription test.

Parliament's role in the process of proscription could be strengthened in this respect. At present, Parliament's scrutiny is little more than a formality. The Houses are required to either accept or reject the entire list of proscribed organisations as a whole. It is impossible to take a decision on particular organisations and so Parliament has always assented to the proscription orders laid before it. In an early debate on a proscription order Jeremy Corbyn MP lamented that:

> Debate is being limited to an hour and half, late at night, with a catch-all 21 different organisations that the Order proposes to ban. We have been given no opportunity to discuss those organisations in any detail, or to engage in any other form of parliamentary scrutiny of the legislation ... The Home Secretary should also tell us ... where the list came from. I am very well aware that the Indian government, the Turkish government, the Sri Lankan government, the Iranian government and undoubtedly many other governments have been constantly pressing the British government to close down political activity in this country by their opponents.[84]

The all-or-nothing power of scrutiny is not the only hurdle faced by Parliament. A further problem is its lack of access to confidential information by Parliament means that it is likely to be deferential towards the Home Secretary. As Parliament is the only institution that provides a prior check on the Government's power, it should be afforded effective powers of scrutiny. In Australia, for example, the Parliamentary Joint Committee on Intelligence and Security (PJCIS) provides scrutiny of proscription. However, the system has been criticised for its 'arbitrary and over-politicised decisions'. The Australian experience therefore points to the difficulty in determining the appropriate institution to review proscription.[85]

---

82 *A v SSHD* [2004] UKHL 56, *Her Majesty's Treasury v Mohammed Jabar Ahmed & Others* [2010] UKSC 1. For a critical discussion of the evolving standard of review see Tomkins 2010.
83 Walker 2011, para 8.38.
84 House of Commons, *Hansard*, 13 March 2001, col 964.
85 Lynch et al. 2009, p. 12. See further Hocking 2003.

There remains a strong argument for the creation of a Parliamentary Committee with access to the secret evidence upon which proscription is based. The Committee could then make a recommendation to Parliament for a decision, on a case-by-case basis, whether an organisation should be proscribed. This system would ensure that secret evidence remains confidential while increasing the influence of Parliament in the decision making process.[86] The Independent Reviewer has suggested a further improvement. Anderson has recommended a sunset clause for the listing of each organisation subject to proscription. A sunset clause would require Parliament to reaffirm its support for the continuing listing of each organisation and thus ensure that the Home Secretary continues to justify proscription. However, in responding to this recommendation the Home Secretary simply stated that the Government is 'considering all options'. The prospects for reform therefore appear doubtful.[87]

8. CONCLUSION: BEYOND THE PARODY OF PRE-EMPTION

Although proscription is indeed a blunt tool it suits the toolbox of a militant democracy.[88] Such a tool may have made sense when faced with paramilitary groups such as the IRA which, at times, represented a real and significant challenge to the state's effective territorial control. In 'Free Derry', for example, neither the Royal Ulster Constabulary nor the British Army could exercise effective control between 1969 and 1972. The threat to British control of parts of Northern Ireland was very much a real one. It is merely unhelpful hyperbole to suggest that the same threat exists today. Indeed the form of organisation against which proscription is said to be useful – those 'that have some sort of formal organisation, that have bank accounts, that have offices' – do not fit the images of the post-September 11 public enemies of the either a disparate network of terrorists or a self-radicalising lone wolf. Today's threats do not come in uniform and their bank accounts are targeted by financial surveillance and asset-freezes rather than mere criminalisation.[89]

---

86 The use of an Independent Reviewer of Terrorism Legislation is a commendable innovation but the Reviewer does not comment on individual decisions and in his current form could not fulfil such a role. Indeed, the benefit of the Independent Reviewer is that he sits outside all three organs of government and can review the operation of the system as a whole. If the Reviewer were to be afforded a role in reviewing individual cases this independence would be lost as he would become part of the system itself.

87 Though note that this point has recently been given an airing by the Independent Reviewer for Terrorism Legislation. See Anderson 2012 (para 4.52).

88 Roach 2011, p. 257.

89 Walker refers to an 'endemic weakness' in proscription as a means to target Islamist groups which have many names and aliases and thus do not invoke the same historical significance as the 'Irish Republic Army' does (para 8.71).

Proscription also fits with the post-September 11 paradigm – but it need not do so. The parody of law in contemporary proscription is to be found in the absence of effective review of listing decisions and the restricted system of review of delisting decisions. Even if these aspects were improved proscription would remain the subversion of law for political ends. The system is potent and can effectively incapacitate domestic organisations that 'glorify' terrorism and overseas revolutionaries. Of course, the conclusion that proscription is political is neither original nor controversial – all law that seeks to afford special powers to the state because of the political motivation of suspects necessarily involves the legal system in politics.

In the recent case of *Maryam Rajavi* the High Court conducted judicial review of the Home Secretary's decision to refuse entry to the UK to Maryam Rajavi, a dissident Iranian politician invited to address Parliament. The High Court concluded, reluctantly, that the Home Secretary's decision was lawful. Stanley Burnton LJ declared in closing that the Home Secretary 'is accountable for her decisions legally and politically ... she has shown that her decisions are lawful. Her political accountability, for the wisdom or otherwise of her decisions, is to Parliament'.[90] It is this joint review, by Parliament and the courts, that is necessary to examine decision of the Government which involve not only law, but also politics-as-law. The delisting of the People's Mujahedin Organisation of Iran may have been brought about by judicial review but there was also a concerted political campaign involved. If a system of proscription is to be retained it must be reformed to ensure that organisations do not need the heirs of Cicero to ensure they are heard.

---

90 *Lord Carlile of Berriew CBE QC and Others and Maryam Rajavi v Secretary of State for the Home Department* [2012] EWHC 617 (Admin). The case is not unrelated to the substantive discussion here as Rajavi has been involved in the activities of the People's Mujahedin Organisation of Iran.

THE IMPLEMENTATION OF EU TERRORISM BLACKLISTING SANCTIONS IN THE DUTCH NATIONAL LEGAL SYSTEM

Suus HOPMAN and Michel UITERWAAL*

1. INTRODUCTION

On 21 October 2011 five Tamil activists were convicted by the Hague District Court and were given prison sentences of between two and six years, for activities supporting the LTTE from the Netherlands. The fact that the LTTE had been blacklisted in the EU system was central to the case. The activists were acquitted of taking part in a terrorist organisation, but convicted of continuing the activities of an organisation that had been blacklisted by the EU as a terrorist organisation. How was the EU legislation translated into Dutch law and what led to this – at first glance – paradoxical verdict? In this paper we will explore the Dutch implementation of the EU terrorism blacklisting sanctions and then discuss this criminal test case in more detail.

The EU sanctions regime required implementation into the Dutch system. This implementation was effectuated in both administrative and criminal law. Both these areas of law overlap but will be discussed separately.

2. SANCTIONS IN ADMINISTRATIVE LAW

2.1. SANCTIONS ACT 1977

The history of the implementation of international sanctions in Dutch law dates back to the 1930s.[1] The Sanctions Act (*Sanctiewet*) that is currently in force dates

* Until recently, both authors were active as attorneys at Böhler Advocaten in Amsterdam. Both authors participated in several procedures concerning blacklisting in their capacity as attorneys. They would like to thank (former) colleagues Marieke van Eik and Tamara Buruma for their contributions to this article. Translations are our own unless otherwise noted.

1 Coomans 1995, Soons 2004, pp. 341–380. Alfred Soons has given a detailed description of the development of the implementation of international sanctions in Dutch law since the 1930s.

back to 1977 and is a successor of the 1935 Sanctions Act and the 1935 Prohibitions of Exports Act (*Uitvoerverbodenwet*). The 1977 Act was drafted to provide a basis for not only UN sanctions, but also EC and national sanctions. As the influence of the EC increased, the role of national legislation diminished but remained essential for (amongst other things) the penalization of offences. In the beginning of the 21st century the 1977 law was amended in several respects in order to be more effective with regard to the anti-terrorism measures that are the subject of this book.

2.2. NEW SYSTEM, OLD STYLE

The Dutch asset-freezing regime is statutorily based in the Sanctions Act 1977, which was substantially amended in 2002 to include the possibility of sanctions against groups and individuals involved in (international) terrorism.

Older international sanctions had been directed towards states (or regions) but the new blacklisting system required the freezing of assets of groups and individuals.

The Sanctions Act had already been altered significantly in 2000, precisely to make the implementation of just international obligations under this law quicker and easier. This was mostly a procedural change, which increased the importance of the role of the Minister for Foreign Affairs when implementing international legislation.[2] In 2002 the Sanctions Act was altered again[3] to refer explicitly to the fighting of terrorism, besides the earlier objectives of keeping or restoring of international peace and security and the furthering of the international legal order. The earlier limitations of the law to certain states or regions were now struck.[4]

The relevant section of the Sanctions Acts 1977 then read:

> Part 2. Administration of international sanctions
> Article 2
> 1. By Order in Council, rules may be adopted with regard to the subjects referred to in articles 3 and 4, in order to comply with treaties, decisions or recommendations of organs of international organisations, or with international understandings, related

2 Wet van 13 april 2000 tot wijziging van de Sanctiewet 1977 en van de In- en uitvoerwet tot vereenvoudiging van de implementatie van internationale verplichtingen, *Stb* 2000, 196.

3 Wet van 16 mei 2002 tot wijziging van de Sanctiewet 1977 met het oog op de implementatie van internationale verplichtingen gericht op de bestrijding van terrorisme en uitbreiding van het toezicht op de naleving van financiële sanctiemaatregelen, *Stb* 2002, 270.

4 Soons 2004 and Wijmenga 2002.

to the keeping or restoring of international peace and security, or to the furthering of the international legal order, or to the fighting of terrorism.
2. If the rules to be adopted relate only to the performance of obligations under treaties or binding decisions of international organisations, they may be adopted by Our Minister.
Article 3
1. The rules referred to in article 2 may apply to the movement of goods and services, financial transactions, shipping, aviation, road transport, post and telecommunication, and all that is required in order to comply with the treaties, decisions, and recommendations, or the international understandings, referred to in article 2.
(...)

Thus, in 2002 the implementation of the EU blacklistings required a Ministerial Order by the Minister for Foreign Affairs (when necessary in cooperation with another Minister) for each new individual or every new group that the Dutch government deemed necessary to be placed under the asset freezing regime. Such a Ministerial Order is referred to as Sanctions Regulation (*Sanctieregeling*). Contrary to what Article 2(2) of the Sanctions Act might suggest, there is no absolute need for an international decision freezing the assets of an individual or group before a national Dutch freezing decision can be taken. A decision by the Ministers in Council (*Ministerraad*), formalised by an Sanctions Regulation is sufficient.

The first two relevant Sanctions Regulations, that are named Sanctions Regulation Terrorism 2002 and 2002-II respectively (Sanctieregeling Terrorisme 2002 and 2002-II) refer to Council Regulation (EC) No 2580/2001 and Council Common Position of 27 December 2001 nr. 2002/931/CFSP respectively, and the individuals and organisations marked with an asterisk in the annex to the Common Position.

The relevant section of Sanctions Regulation Terrorism 2002 reads:

Article 1

1. It is forbidden to act contrary to Articles 2(1) and 2(2), 3 and 4 of Regulation (EC) No 2580/2001 of the European Union of 27 December 2001 on specific restrictive measures directed against certain persons and entities with a view to combating terrorism (OJ L 344) (hereinafter Regulation No 2580/2001).

And of Sanctions Regulation Terrorism 2002-II:

Article 1

1. The Articles 1, 2(1) and 2(2), 3, paragraph 4(1)(1) and 4(1)(2) and 5(1), of Regulation No 2580/2001 shall apply mutatis mutandis to persons, groups and entities with an asterisk that are identified in the Annex to Common Position of

> the Council of the European Union of 27 December 2001 No 2002/931/CFSP on the application of specific measures to combat terrorism (OJ EC L 344) (hereinafter CP 2002/931/CFSP).
> (...)
>
> Article 2
>
> To the extent that they have been declared by Article 1 [of this Regulation] to be analogously applicable, violation of Articles 2(1) and 2(2) and 3 and 4, first paragraph under the first and second indent, as regards the individuals, groups and entities meant by Article 1, first paragraph, is prohibited

The later Sanctions Regulations 2002-III, 2003, 2006 and 2007 specifically mention persons and organisations that are blacklisted for the Netherlands.[5] Apart from the 2002-III Regulation, which relates to the Communist Party of the Philippines[6] these listings were directed at people or groups suspected of involvement with Islam-related terrorism. Most of these listings were intended as a temporary measure and have been removed again after the entities were blacklisted on the European level.

The Sanctions Act provides also for the supervision of financial sanctions by financial institutions (Articles 10 and further) and for exemptions and dispensations (article 9). The latter can be granted by the Minister for Foreign Affairs. Several dispensations have been issued in different cases, but information about these dispensations is generally not disclosed to the public, so it is not possible to provide an overview in this article.

Because of the general nature of a Ministerial Order under Dutch law there are no individual administrative recourses available against such a decision.[7]In the Netherlands it is, however, possible to start a civil tort action against the Dutch State and then to start expedited proceedings (*kort geding*) in a civil court. This instrument was mentioned in the legislative history as a way for individuals to challenge an asset-freezing and it has in fact been used for that purpose.

---

5 Sanctieregeling terrorisme 2002-III, 13 August 2002, no. DJZ/BR/749-02, Sanctieregeling terrorisme 2003, 3 april 2003, no. DJZ/BR/219-03, Sanctieregeling terrorisme 2006, 3 April 2006, no. DJZ/BR/0287-06, Sanctieregeling terrorisme 2007, 21 February 2007, no. DJZ/BR/0185-07.

6 Related to the Netherlands because of the residence of Mr. Sison, well known from several international procedures against his blacklisting, in the city of Utrecht.

7 A Ministerial Order is a form of national legislation used for example to have a tailor-made implementation of laws. It is of a general nature (binding a generic group of people) as opposed to an administrative decision of non-general nature (*Beschikking*), *see* General Administrative Law Act (*Algemene wet bestuursrecht*) in Article 1:3.

The case of *Al-Aqsa* is a good example of such a procedure, in that it shows both the possibilities and limitations of this particular system. (The national expedited proceedings are furthermore of interest because the Dutch government later came to rely upon them in the proceedings at the Court of First Instance.)

2.3. AL-AQSA

The case is worth noting because it gives an example of some obstacles that have been removed since then and also because of the way the Dutch national procedure worked out in the European proceedings.

In April 2003 Al-Aqsa was placed under the sanctions regime of the Sanctions Law 1977. In the explanatory memorandum, the Government explicitly mentioned that the decision was made 'pending listing of Al-Aqsa on the European asset-freezing list'. The listing was made as a result of Dutch Secret Service information stating that Al-Aqsa had provided funds to an organisation, which had in its turn funded organisations that had links with Hamas.[8]

Al-Aqsa sued the Dutch State in expedited proceedings before the civil court of The Hague. In an interim order on 13 May 2003,[9] the court noted that the sanctions were based on Secret Service information that was only given to Al-Aqsa in a broadly summarised form. The court found the information too vague to judge whether or not the listing had a good justification based on the facts. Al-Aqsa had argued that it had never given any funds to terrorist activities or organisations.[10]

With the consent of Al-Aqsa the court took the quite unusual step of examining the underlying Secret Service information while Al-Aqsa, as a party, was not allowed to examine the information.

It should be noted that the Dutch Code of Civil Procedure (*Wetboek van Burgerlijke Rechtsvordering*) does not provide the express possibility of the judge examining documents that were not available to one of the parties to the proceedings. However, in expedited proceedings certain rules of civil procedure may not apply but while Article 6 ECHR applies to expedite proceedings as well,

8 It should be noted that in 2003 Hamas was considered by the European Council to be divided in a terrorist and a non-terrorist wing, the latter therefore not being subject to EU sanctions.

9 Rechtbank 's-Gravenhage 13–5–2003, KG 03/514, *LJN* AF8506.

10 Important parts of the interim order in English translation can be found in para. 123 of the *Al-Aqsa* judgement of the General Court, Case T-348/07 *Stichting Al Aqsa v. Council* [2010] ECR II-4575.

the adversarial principle cannot be dispensed with.[11] The examination of the Secret Service Information should probably be viewed in this light.

In doing so the court itself noted that this seemingly infringed the adversarial principle, one of the fundamental principles of civil proceedings. The court reasoned that public policy considerations, which it deemed applicable in this case, could raise an exception to the adversarial principle. Furthermore, as the court also noted, the General Administrative Law Act (*Algemene wet bestuursrecht*) in Article 8:29 provides that courts may examine documents without the applicant being given that opportunity if the applicant agrees to this. This article is frequently used. As we will describe below, the current legal asset-freezing regime is the subject of administrative proceedings, so that this Article 8:29 is directly applicable. The consent of Al-Aqsa was quite relevant in that respect.

In its final judgement on 3 June 2003[12] the court considered that on the basis of the Secret Service information it had seen, there were adequate grounds to support the finding that funds raised by Al-Aqsa had been used for the benefit of organisations associated with the Palestinian Islamist movement Hamas, and may also support the finding that some of those organisations (associated with Hamas) are making funds available for the purposes of committing or facilitating the terrorist activities of Hamas.

The court therefore denied the order sought by Al-Aqsa to stop the Dutch State from continuing to freeze its assets. By then, Al-Aqsa had already been placed under the EU sanctions regime. The national sanctions regime against Al-Aqsa was then repealed on 3 August 2003.[13]

2.4. NEW SYSTEM, NEW STYLE

On 23 December 2007 the Terrorism Sanctions Regulation 2007-II (*Sanctieregeling Terrorisme 2007-II*) entered into force.[14] There were no relevant substantial changes but the procedural remedies against a national listing of a person or organisation under the Dutch national sanctions regime became different from that moment onwards.

Previously, the only remedy available against a listing was a civil tort action (whether in expedited proceedings or not) against the Dutch State. It was

11 Tjong Tjin Tai, T.F.E. 2010.

12 Rechtbank 's-Gravenhage 3-6-2003, KG 03/514, *LJN* AF9389.

13 See the discussion of the Joined Cases C 539/10 P and C 550/10 P, *Stichting Al-Aqsa v. Council*, 15 November 2012, nyr, in the introductory chapter.

14 DJZ/BR/1222-07.

obvious already from the civil judgement of the The Hague court in the *Al-Aqsa* case described before that an administrative proceeding would fit much better to the nature of such a Ministerial decision. This was acknowledged in the explanatory note to the Terrorism Sanctions Order 2007-II. From then on, persons or organisations who fall under the Dutch anti-terrorism asset-freezing system will not be mentioned directly in the Sanctions Regulation anymore but in a separate decision of the Minister of Foreign Affairs.

There are currently two organisations and four individuals listed based on their alleged links with Islam-related terrorism and two organisations and six individuals for alleged links to the internationally listed LTTE, that will be discussed in more detail later on.[15]

The person or organisation that is blacklisted under Dutch law shall have the possibility to lodge administrative proceedings against such a decision in accordance with the General Administrative Law Act.

Such proceedings start with an administrative objection directed to the Minister of Foreign Affairs, who will decide on the applicant's complaints. In the case of a negative decision on this objection, the applicant can lodge an appeal with the administrative section of the District Court. Another appeal of the outcome of that decision is possible with the Council of State, which rules in highest resort on administrative matters.

2.5. MORE RECENT CASES

On 20 July 2011 the national freezing order with regard to the Dutch branch of the IHH foundation (Stichting Internationale Humanitaire Hulporganisatie Nederland) was suspended following proceedings before the administrative section of the District Court of Amsterdam in an oral order.[16] The court reasoned that the Minister of Foreign Affairs had based the initial listing on the

15 Www.rijksoverheid.nl/documenten-en-publicaties/rapporten/2012/01/13/personen-en-organisaties-met-bevroren-tegoeden-15-01-2012.html (consulted on 22 January 2012) Besluit 11 January 2012, no. DJZ/BR/0016-2012 (*Stcrt* 2012, 916), 26 April 2011, no. DVB/TN-053/11 (*Stcrt* 2011, 7634), 18 April 2011, no. DVB/TN/054-2011 (*Stcrt* 2011, 7209), 15 March 2011, no. DVB/TN-240/10 (*Stcrt* 2011, 5018), 15 March 2011, no. DVB/TN-239/10 (*Stcrt* 2011, 5019), 8 June 2010, no. DJZ/BR/0403-2010 (*Stcrt* 2011, 9224), 8 June 2010, no. DJZ/BR/0401-2010 (*Stcrt* 2011, 9227), 8 June 2010, no. DJZ/BR/0400-2010 (*Stcrt* 2011, 9229), 8 June 2010, no. DJZ/BR/0398-2010 (*Stcrt* 2011, 9233), 8 June 2010, no. DJZ/BR/0402-2010 (*Stcrt* 2011, 9234), 8 June 2010, no. DJZ/BR/0399-2010 (*Stcrt* 2011, 9235), 21 February 2007, no. DJZ/BR/0185-07 (*Stcrt* 2007, 239), 21 February 2007, no. DJZ/BR/0185-07 (*Stcrt* 2007, 239) and (*Stcrt* 2007, 248).

16 Rechtbank Amsterdam 21-7-2011, AWB 11/3132 BESLU, *LJN* BR2619.

fact that IHH supported Hamas via its German parent organisation. However, on the day of the court hearing, IHH provided the court with a German *Bundesverwaltungsgericht* judgment that held, in short, that IHH Germany was allowed to continue its operations provided it would not transfer money to the Gaza strip of the West bank. The Amsterdam Court then considered the fact that the German Minister of the Interior is checking that the terms of this order are being complied with. The Amsterdam Court considered that no funds transferred by IHH Holland to IHH Germany would end up sponsoring terrorism. The Court therefore suspended the freezing decision until a decision in administrative appeal would be taken.

After having reconsidered the arguments of both parties in administrative appeal the Minister of Foreign Affairs again decided to freeze IHH's assets in October 2011. On 15 November 2011, the Amsterdam District Court also suspended this new freezing decision with very similar reasoning as in the decision mentioned before.[17] The Court added that the Minister of Foreign Affairs had conceded at the court hearing that there were no indications that indeed IHH would still transfer money to Hamas in any way.

Several Tamil individuals blacklisted under the Terrorism Sanctions Regulation 2007 II have lodged appeals against blacklisting decisions concerning them.

In a decision of the District Court Zwolle-Lelystad one of these appeals was considered unfounded.[18] The Court rejected the arguments of the applicant that the UN resolution 1373 did not oblige the Netherlands to list him and that consequently there was no sufficient legal basis in national law for listing him. The court further considered that a secret service memorandum concerning the applicant and a criminal case started against him formed sufficient basis to consider the applicant to be amongst those designated by UN Resolution 1373. Finally, the court reasoned that the burden was on the applicant to adduce evidence to the fact that the measure of complete freezing of assets was disproportionate and not in accordance with the ECHR (as opposed to the State having to prove the proportionality of the listing infringement on the applicant's right to personal life and property). An appeal against this decision is still pending.

17 Rechtbank Amsterdam 15-11-2011, AWB 11/5163 WET, unpublished.
18 Rechtbank Zwolle-Lelystad 20-12-2011, AWB 11/, *LJN* BV2139.

3. CRIMINAL LAW

3.1. GENERALLY

The other component of the Dutch national regime that implements EU blacklisting sanctions is the criminal law. There are different ways in which support for a blacklisted organisation can lead to a prosecution under Dutch law, which can lead to divergent results once prosecution takes place.

Prosecution for support of such an organisation might typically concern people that are not blacklisted, or active participants, in the relevant organisations. These people lack the procedural rights that blacklisted individuals or groups have to resist their listing. The only way for them to challenge the listing of the entity they support is therefore in criminal court. The different modes of criminalisation leave them a different margin of argumentation before the court.

3.2. CRIMINAL TERRORIST ORGANISATIONS

In response to the Framework Decision of 13 June 2002 on combating terrorism (2002/475/JHA) there was a package of new anti-terrorist legislation implemented in the Netherlands.[19] One of the measures was criminalising terrorist organisations under the new Article 140a of the Dutch Criminal Code (*Wetboek van Strafrecht*).[20]

The concept of a criminal organisation had been tried and tested in Dutch criminal law. The article in the Criminal Code that dealt with participation in a criminal organisation, Article 140 of the Criminal Code was at that point approximately a century old. This article had been applied in different contexts and case-law had been developed. The Dutch legislator chose to base the new article closely on the older one and as such avoid the problems with interpretation that new legislation might provoke.

The old Article 140 of the Criminal Code read:

> 1. Participation in an organisation that has as its object the commission of serious offences is punishable by a term of imprisonment of not more than six years or a fine of the fifth category.
> (...)

19 Husabø 2009, p. 200.
20 Kamerstukken II 2001/2002, 28463 No. 2.

3. With respect to the founders, leaders or directors the term of imprisonment may be increased by one third.
4. Participation as described in the first paragraph is understood to mean the giving of financial or other material support to and/or the raising of funds or recruiting of persons for the benefit of the organisation referred to in that paragraph.

A debate ensued on the issue of the consequences under criminal law for participation in the organisations on the EU blacklist.[21] Such criminalisation, based merely on the blacklisting, was at first excluded by the Government because of limitations in the procedure for listing, mainly the lack of judicial review available.[22] Certain members of parliament argued for the aforementioned criminalisation, but the minister of justice, Donner, as the relevant member of the government defended their refusal to amend the proposed legislation with references to legal certainty.

"The organisations placed on the EU lists are being designated as terrorist organisations by law without a judge making a decision on the possible involvement of these organisations in terrorist activities on the basis of available information. The institution of such an offense would therefore mean that a person may be penalized for having participated in an organisation of which it is not (yet) legally established that it has the intention to commit criminal acts."[23]

"Mr Eerdmans has also proposed an amendment to Article 140a to insert the EU's list of criminal organisations. Again, this list is compiled based on intelligence information. There is no requirement regarding these organisations to demonstrate whether they have indeed committed terrorist activities."[24]

"Citizens often do not even know that these organisations are included in the list, also because this list can be constantly adjusted. This would enter a provision in the criminal code with flexible content, so I insist on the approach chosen by the government, that the public prosecution should have extended possibilities to be able to have those organisations be dissolved under civil law. The government does not want to arrange this directly through criminal law."[25]

"A basic principle in our criminal law is that it should be very clear what criminal behaviour is. We cannot just refer to a list of the European Union. It is the responsibility of the government to ban organisations."[26]

21 Kamerstukken II 2002/2003, 28600 No. 15.
22 Kamerstukken II 2002/2003, 28666 No. 1.
23 Kamerstukken II, 2002–2003, 28 666, no. 1, p. 5.
24 Kamerstukken II, 2003–2004, 28 463, no. 33, p. 2361.
25 Kamerstukken II, 2003–2004, 28 463, p. 2361.
26 Kamerstukken II, 2003–2004, 28 463, p. 2345.

To ensure proper implementation the proposed Article 140a of the Criminal Code was altered so that financial support for terrorist organisations was also explicitly criminalised.[27] The new Article 140a Criminal Code[28] provides

1. Participation in an organisation that has as its object the commission of terrorist crimes is punishable with a term of imprisonment of not more than fifteen years or a fine of the fifth category.
2. Founders, leaders or directors are punishable with life imprisonment or a term of imprisonment of not more than twenty years or a fine of the fifth category.
3. Article 140, paragraph four, applies by analogy.

Article 83 of the Criminal Code implements the EU Framework Decision on Terrorism in specifying what is to be considered a 'terrorist crime', by referring to a number of common crimes when they are committed with a 'terrorist objective' and a number of crimes that include that form of intent.

The terrorist objective is set out in Article 83a of the Criminal Code, which also follows the Framework Decision.[29]

3.3. CONTINUED ACTIVITIES OF A PROSCRIBED ORGANISATION

In 2006, however, a new proposal on the criminalisation of participation in blacklisted organisations was accepted by parliament. This change is remarkable, considering the earlier aversion towards such a criminalisation and the fact that such a direct criminalisation is not required by EU legislation.

Before the 2006 legislation the blacklisting of an organisation did not automatically lead to a prohibition of the organisation under Dutch law. The effects of the blacklisting were strictly financial and limited in character. As Bulterman has pointed out, the organisation itself could continue to exist – without funds – and would not be punishable for requesting financial donations, even if anyone that would indeed donate upon such a request could be prosecuted.[30]

---

27 Kamerstukken II 2002/2003, 28463, no. 7.

28 Wet van 24 juni 2004 tot wijziging en aanvulling van het Wetboek van Strafrecht en enige andere wetten in verband met terroristische misdrijven (Wet terroristische misdrijven) *Stb.* 2004, 290, Adopted by parliament on 24 June 2004, in force 10 August 2004.

29 Article 83a provides that "A terrorist objective is understood to mean the objective to cause serious fear in part of the population in a country and/or to unlawfully force a government or international organisation to do something, not to do something, or to tolerate certain actions and/or to seriously disrupt or destroy the fundamental political, constitutional, economic or social structures of a country or an international organisation".

30 Bulterman 2006.

There was, however, already a procedure available to achieve just that effect. This procedure had been referred to in the parliamentary debate on the issue as an alternative to the automatic prohibition of the blacklisted organisations. Under Article 2:20 of the Dutch Civil Code (*Burgerlijk Wetboek*) the Dutch public prosecutor could request a civil judge to prohibit the organisation if its activity or goal would be contrary to public order. Such a prohibition would result in the criminalisation of the continuation of the organisation under the aforementioned Article 140 Criminal Code.

The Dutch public prosecutor has only in one case started such a proceedings for the prohibition of a blacklisted organisation, the (originally UN-)listed Stichting Al Haramain Humanitarian Aid. Both the District Court and the Appeals Court of Amsterdam refused to prohibit the organisation, because they did not find the claim of the prosecution that the organisation would support terrorism to be substantiated. The UN listing was not regarded as a sufficient reason for a prohibition. The Appeal Court furthermore found that the prohibition and dismantling of the organisation, as a definitive measure, seems to be at odds with the (alleged) temporary nature of assets freezing.[31]

Shortly after the decision of the Amsterdam Appeals Court the procedure under Article 2:20 Civil Code was made redundant[32] by legislation that provided for the automatic prohibition of all blacklisted organisations.[33] The criminalisation was achieved not under the new Article 140a Criminal Code on terrorist organisations but by altering the old Article 140 Criminal Code on criminal organisations in combination with a separate law, the Corporations (Conflict of Laws) Act (*Wet conflictenrecht corporaties*), which declares all UN and EU blacklisted organisations to be illegal under Dutch law.[34]

Article 140 of the Criminal Code was changed on 1 February 2007 from:

> "2. Participation in the continued activities of a legal person that has been proscribed in a final judgment and consequently has been dissolved is punishable by a term of imprisonment of not more than one year or a fine of the third category" to

---

31 Rechtbank Amsterdam 31-3-2005, HA RK 04-948, *JOR* 2005/118 and Gerechtshof Amsterdam 5-1-2006, 987/05, *JOR* 2006/200.

32 This is why we have chosen not to describe the procedure in detail.

33 This form of prohibition is in effect almost similar to the system that was already available under civil law, but does not lead to automatic dissolution and liquidation of the organisation because of the possible temporary character of the freezing measures.

34 Wet van 20 november 2006, houdende goedkeuring van het op 24 april 1986 te Straatsburg totstandgekomen Europees Verdrag inzake de erkenning van de rechtspersoonlijkheid van internationale niet-gouvernementele organisaties, alsmede invoering van enige regels met betrekking tot in een terrorismelijst vermelde organisaties en andere organisaties waarvan het doel of de werkzaamheid in strijd is met de openbare orde, *Stb.* 2006, 600.

> "2. Participation in the continued activities of a legal person that has been proscribed in a final judgment or is proscribed by law or with respect to which an irrevocable declaratory judgment has been pronounced within the meaning of article 5a paragraph one of the Conflict of Laws Corporation Act is punishable by a term of imprisonment of not more than one year or a fine of the third category."

Article 5b of the Corporations Act provides the legal basis for proscription of non-Dutch organisations, namely "A corporation that is not a Dutch legal entity and is included in the list referred to in Article 2(3), Regulation No 2580/2001 or in Annex I of Regulation (EC) No 881/2002 of 27 May 2002 (OJ L 139) or is listed and identified with an asterisk in the Annex to CP No 2001/931 is legally prohibited and not authorized to perform legal acts."

From 1 January 2012 this article has been replaced by the more comprehensive Article 123 Book 10 of the Civil Code.[35]

The Dutch blacklisted organisations are covered by Article 20 Book 2 of the Civil Code:

> "3. An entity named in the list referred to in Article 2(3) of Regulation (EC) No 2580/2001 in Annex I to Regulation (EC) No 881/2002 of the Council of 27 May 2002 (OJ L 139) or is listed and identified with an asterisk in the Annex to CP No 2001/931 is prohibited by law and not authorized to perform legal acts."

It is interesting to note that even the 'internally' placed organisations, marked with an asterisk in CP No. 2001/931, have been included in this measure. This was a conscious choice of the legislator.[36] These 'Europeans' are not within the

35 "A corporation that is not a Dutch legal entity and is included in the list referred to in Article 2 paragraph 3 of Regulation (EC) No 2580/2001 of the European Union of 27 December 2001 (OJ L 344) on specific restrictive measures against certain persons and entities with a view to combating terrorism, or in Annex 1 of Regulation (EC) No 881/2002 of the European Union of 27 May 2002 (OJ L 139) imposing certain specific restrictive measures against certain persons and entities associated with Usama bin Laden, the Al-Qau'ída network and the Taliban, and repealing Regulation (EC) No 467/2001 imposing a ban on export of certain goods and services to Afghanistan, strengthening the flight ban and extending the freeze of funds and other financial resources in respect of the Taliban in Afghanistan, or is listed and identified with an asterisk in the Annex to Common Position No 2001/931 of the Council of the European Union of 27 December 2001 (OJ L 344) on the application of specific measures to combat terrorism, is prohibited by law and are not authorized to perform legal acts." Article 140 of the Criminal Code has been adjusted slightly from the same date, changing article 5a paragraph one of the Conflict of Laws Corporation Act to Article 122 paragraph one of book 10 of the Civil Code, but since the blacklisted organisations are proscribed by law, that alteration is not immediately relevant to our subject.

36 Kamerstukken II, 2004–2005, 28 764, no. 6.

EU system included in the freezing of assets, but have even less possibilities to challenge their listing before a court.[37]

The following reasoning was given for this new legislation:

> "The arrangement complements the system of penalties resulting from European regulations with regard to the freezing of assets. These regulations are limited to the freezing of assets. The proposed system is necessary to shut down all operations that are not limited to property and assets. This may for example involve the banning of recruiting, appointing new directors (to be able to state that they have ceased hostilities) and the establishment of a new organisation (so that the game can start all over again). Experience shows that it is generally not that well understood when an organisation whose financial assets have been frozen because they are or have been included in a terrorism-list, in other matters still can act and even organize rallies."[38]

The Council of State (*Raad van State*), the judicial institution that scrutinizes and comments on future Dutch legislation during the legislative process inquired about the change of heart with regard to the criminalisation. It referred to the fact that the government previously had resisted amendments with a similar character, in essence because of the need for judicial control. The government referred to a policy adjustment and claimed to have objected to earlier amendments based on mere technical reasons. It did not discuss the issue of judicial control.[39] When questioned again on this issue by a member of the Socialist Party the minister acknowledged that judicial review is very limited, especially for the 'internal' organisations, but referred to the possibility to start an interim procedure before the Civil Court and referred to the previously discussed *Al-Aqsa* case.[40] Several amendments to provide for judicial control (in a national court) were proposed but failed.[41]

This new approach has been widely criticised in the Netherlands, because it is a very blunt measure, which leaves practically no room for judicial control. It is clearly a restriction of the freedom of association set out in Article 11 ECHR. While there may be a large measure of agreement amongst commentators that terrorist acts can be attributed to all the organisations on the present EU lists, this does not mean that there is agreement that everything these organisations do is "terrorism". The automatic blacklisting allows for no input from the Dutch parliament. There is little scope for the Dutch courts to consider whether the decision to list was proportionate. Even allowing for a margin of appreciation

---

37 De Hert 2009, Tappeiner 2005.
38 Handelingen II, 28 764, no. 6, p. 3.
39 Kamerstukken II, 2004–2005, 28 764, no. 7.
40 Kamerstukken II, 2004–2005, 28 764, no. 8.
41 Kamerstukken II, 2004–2005, 28 764, nos. 10, 12, 13, 15.

test, we are doubtful if this legislation is compatible with general principles of EU law and the ECHR.[42]

The main issue however seems to be that the Netherlands chooses to apply a much more severe measure than is required by the European rules it seems to base the legislation on. In framework decision 2002/475/JHA Article 8(d) there is a mere suggestion of 'a judicial winding-up order' for legal persons, which is a long way from the automatic prohibition the Dutch government has chosen to impose. The Dutch stance is all the more remarkable because the Netherlands, unlike for example Spain or the UK, does not have a long history of being gravely threatened by national or international terrorism.

3.4. OFFENCE AGAINST THE SANCTIONS ACT 1977

The third and last form of criminalisation is the most traditional approach.

Before the implementation of the Framework Decision there had been a long tradition of Economic Sanctions in Dutch legislation.[43] As described with regard to the administrative part of the implementation, the predecessors of the 1977 Sanctions Act has been used for implementation since the 1930s.

The 1977 Sanctions Act, however, does not itself provide for penalization. It is one of many laws that depend on the Economic Offences Act of 1950 (*Wet op de economische delicten*) for criminalization of its provisions. The 'economic offences' that are included in the Economic Offences Act are taken very seriously under Dutch law and the prosecution is provided with certain extended powers with regard to these offences. The Economic Offences Act provides for two different types of the offence, the intentional type (Articles 1, 1°, 2, and 6(1) Economic Offences Act) with a maximum penalty of 6 years imprisonment or a fine of max. €78,000 (before 1 January 2012 €67,000) and with the absence of criminal intent 1 year imprisonment and a fine of €19,500 (before 1 January 2012 €16,750). There are also possibilities to impose community service, the prohibition to exercise a certain profession, to impound certain items and several ways for the authorities to take control of a convicted legal person (Articles 7 and 8 Economic Offences Act). Criminal prosecution with regard to violations of the Sanctions Act has taken place in the context of the Southern Rhodesia and Yugoslavia conflicts.[44]

---

42 *Cf.* Eskes 2006.

43 Soons 2004 provides a thorough overview over the implementation of UN sanctions in the national Dutch legal order, pp. 344–345.

44 Soons 2004, p. 361.

Furthermore, the criminalisation based on the Sanctions Act is based on the aforementioned Article 1(1) Terrorism Sanctions Regulation 2002 or 2002-II in combination with Article 2(1) and (2) and Article 3 of EC Regulation 2580/2001.

It is interesting to notice that this construction does, in a more limited way, also cause a direct criminalisation of contributions to a blacklisted organisation. It seems to leave no greater room to the judge in a criminal trial to evaluate the question of whether the organisation has justly been labelled as terrorist. It has, however, caused much less of a debate in the Netherlands. Maybe because it is a more literal translation of the EU rules in that it is limited to the freezing of assets, and does not criminalize the organisation as such. It could be argued that it therefore poses less serious problems with the ECHR.

3.5. TAMIL COURT CASE

In October 2011 the District Court of The Hague concluded a criminal trial that involved all three of the aforementioned approaches.[45] This is the first criminal trial in which the new criminal system has been put to the test, which is the reason why this case will be discussed in some detail in this article.

To be able to understand the reasoning of the Court it is important to understand that the Netherlands has a relatively monist legal system and is as such quite open to the international legal order. International law is part of the national legal order, and in some cases (directly applicable treaty provisions and decisions of international organisations) is prioritized over conflicting norms of national law, even legislation by parliament and the Dutch Constitution (*Grondwet voor het Koninkrijk der Nederlanden*) based on Articles 93 and 94 of the Constitution. Because the Constitution prohibits judicial review against the Constitution itself of parliamentary legislation by the Courts under Article 120, the review, by all Courts, of the compatibility of Dutch legislation with international law is common and widespread.

The somewhat paradoxical outcome of the case currently discussed was that the suspects were not convicted of taking part in a terrorist criminal organisation, but were indeed convicted on the counts that were more directly based on the

---

45 Rechtbank 's-Gravenhage 21-10-2011, 09/748802-09, *LJN* BU9716, Rechtbank 's-Gravenhage 21-10-2011, 09/748801-09, *LJN* BU7200; both published with an English translation on www.rechtspraak.nl.

listing of the same organisation on the EU list of terrorist organisations.[46] They all received prison sentences varying in length between 6 and 2 years.

The relevant organisation was the 'Liberation Tigers of Tamil Eelam' or LTTE, which has been blacklisted on the EU level since 28 June 2007.[47]

A large-scale criminal investigation in the Netherlands was started officially in 2009, based on information from the General Intelligence and Security Service (*Algemene Inlichtingen- en Veiligheidsdienst*, the Dutch internal and external secret service) from 2008 and involved arrests, questioning and searches and seizures among a significant part of the Tamil community in the Netherlands. A group of 5 suspects was detained for a longer period and chosen to be part of the first trial at the district court of The Hague, the case that is under review here. They were selected based on their alleged seniority within the organisation. So far none of the other suspects have been formally charged.

The defence argued for adjournment of the case. One of the reasons was the procedure at the General Court that had been lodged parallel to the criminal prosecution. The Hague District Court ruled that even if that procedure would be successful that decision would not have retroactive force. It considered the previous listings, which covered the period in the charges, to have obtained legal effect. The defence also requested a preliminary question to the European Court of Justice, with regard to the applicability of counter-terrorism measures in the context of armed conflict. The District Court asserts that it will be able to answer that question directly and does not deem a preliminary question to be necessary.[48]

The prosecution built a case that was based on activities in both Sri Lanka and the Netherlands. The defendants are considered to be members of the international LTTE through a Dutch subsection of that organisation. The international element of the case was thus significant.

The charge of a membership of a terrorist organisation (1A) was related solely to the international LTTE and focused on acts committed in Sri Lanka within the conflict with the national military forces (manslaughter, bombing, arson etc.). There was a subsidiary charge of membership of a criminal organisation (1B), containing the aforementioned acts (in case the objective of the organisation to commit terrorist offences could not been proven with regard to those) and the

46 Not all the remaining charges were, however, solely based on the blacklisting, there were also elements that were based on the Dutch legislation on gambling (with a fund-raising lottery) and coercion.

47 Council decision 2007/445/EC, later followed by 2007/868/EC, 2008/583/EC and 2009/62/EC.

48 A decision that seems questionable at least based on the decision in EU CJEU 29 June 2010, case C-550/09 (*Generalbundesanwalt beim Bundesgerichtshof v. E en F*).

acts in Sri Lanka that could not be brought under a terrorist charge (recruitment for armed combat, conscripting or enlisting children under 15 into armed forces or groups and the imprisonment or severe deprivation of physical liberty of civilians in an attack on the civilian population).

A second charge of membership of a criminal organisation covered the activities of the national Dutch organisation. In this charge the focus was on both the making of propaganda for the international LTTE and the provision of funds for the same organisation. In collecting these funds, Dutch legislation on gambling (with a fundraising lottery) and coercion and extortion was considered to have been violated.[49] But the collecting of funds was also prosecuted under this count based solely on the listing of the LTTE by the EU, together with the Sanctions Act. This charge is similar in nature to the last charge that will be discussed, but here it is used separately to build the criminal organisation charge.

The third charge is the participation in the continued activities of a proscribed organisation, as discussed above, in this case the LTTE, based on the Corporations Act.

The fourth charge is the aforementioned offence against the Sanctions Act, in fact the funding of an organisation that has been listed by the EU, here as a separate charge.

Some of the suspects were also faced with a fifth and sixth charge: incitement against the authorities and dissemination of matter containing incitement against the authorities. The defendants were acquitted on both these counts. Since these offences are not related to the EU blacklisting they will not be discussed in this article any further.

The District Court of The Hague has only convicted the suspects on the last three common counts, in which the EU listing plays a decisive role (only in the second count are there unrelated acts). These convictions are relatively short and straight forward as the Court does not discuss or evaluate the listing of the LTTE and considers the criminality of the acts to follow straight from the EU listing. Some minor attention is given to the question whether the defendants had been aware of the EU listing.

The District Court then evaluates the evidence for the raising of funds by the defendants on behalf of the LTTE and other activities for the organisation. When it finds that evidence sufficient, it comes to a clear-cut conviction.

49 The element of extortion led to a partial acquittal.

The District Court seems to weigh the blacklisting of the LTTE as an incriminating circumstance at the sentencing stage.

> "The defendant was aware that the LTTE had been included in the European terrorism list and that their activities were proscribed. This has not prevented the defendant from continuing in his function within the LTTE. Thus the defendant very knowingly ignored both European regulations and national legislation. These regulations are of great international significance as its purpose is joint enforcement or the restoration of international peace and security or the promotion of the international legal order or combatting terrorism. By offending against these regulations for a prolonged period of time the defendant contributed substantially, just because of his indispensable role, to (the advancing) destabilisation and danger in Sri Lanka."

The reasoning of the District Court is, especially when compared to the first charge, very limited. The arguments of the defence with regard to the fact that the LTTE is taking part in a non-international armed conflict are not considered in the context of these counts, although they are of significance to the Court in the decision on the first count. The District Court does not consider the arguments of the defence with regard to the validity and legitimacy of the EU blacklisting. The District Court also fails to discuss several arguments of the defence with regard to the ECHR.[50] The defence argued that Articles 11, 13, 7 and 6 of the ECHR would be violated by a conviction based on participation that has been blacklisted without any form of judicial review.[51]

---

50 Because of the monist nature of the Dutch legal order, a criminal court should consider whether the national criminal law infringes the ECHR. If applying it would do so, the court would then be obliged to declare the fact not punishable (*ontslag van rechtsvervolging*). This is not a theoretical issue. When judging cases that are related to the freedom of speech for example, it is quite common for a court to take the text and court practice of the ECHR into account when determining the scope Dutch criminal law could have.

51 The defence focuses on Article 11 ECHR and, apart from the more general question whether this form of legislation can be considered 'necessary in a democratic society', refers to the recent *Sanoma* judgement of the ECHR. This judgement concerned the element 'prescribed by law' common to several articles of the ECHR. This infers not only that the measure has a basis in domestic law but also requires the domestic law to live up to certain quality standards, amongst which 'first and foremost' 'review by a judge or other independent and impartial decision-making body'. *Sanoma Uitgevers v. Netherlands*, No. 38224/03, 14 September 2010 at paras 83 and 90. The *Sanoma* case involved Article 10 ECHR but the Hague Court of Appeal seems to consider the principle generally applicable, and has used it in a case concerning a breach of article 8 ECHR, that was upheld by the Dutch Supreme Court. Gerechtshof 's-Gravenhage 8-11-2010, 200.076.673/01, *LJN* BO3682, Hoge Raad 28-10-2011, no. 10/05147, *LJN* BQ9880 The defence claims that the lack of such a review in the case of blacklisting, results in a violation of the ECHR when a conviction takes place. Unfortunately the Court did not consider this express argument, which is in itself a breach of Dutch criminal procedure.

With regard to the first count, the Court partially bars the prosecution and partially acquits the defendants.

The Court considers the main issue with regard to the first part of the first count to be the exception in item 11 of the preamble to the framework decree of the Council of 13 June 2002 on combating terrorism (2002/475/JBZ):

> "This framework decree is not applicable to acts by armed forces during armed conflict as defined in and subject to international humanitarian law, nor is it applicable to acts undertaken by the armed forces of a state in the discharge of their official duties in as far as they are subject to other provisions of international law."

The first question with regard to the first charge is then whether the conflict that the LTTE is part of should be qualified as an armed conflict. Since the conflict is internal in nature that would have to be a non-international armed conflict. The District Court finds, based on the legislative history of the Dutch International Crimes Act (*Wet internationale misdrijven*) that it has to analyse the actual situation and make an assessment, using reference points in Protocol II and the Statute of the International Criminal Court, whether the situation is a non-international armed conflict.[52]

> "From the above it is clear that armed or other acts committed by groups within the context of for instance (organised) crime are not easily qualified as non-international armed conflict, although this depends on the aims of these groups. Legitimate hostilities committed by liberation fighters within a context of the right to self-government, however, can of course give rise to such a qualification."[53]

Statements by international or regional organisations are no more than an important indication of how the international community views the conflict, and do not relieve the judge of making an assessment himself.[54] Thus when the District Court proceeds to assess the nature of the conflict between the armed forces of the Sinhalese government and the armed forces of the LTTE it states that it is not bound to what the Council has decided in this matter and comes to the conclusion that there is indeed a relevant non-international armed conflict, with the following reasoning:

> "The armed forces of the LTTE were comparable to those of the government. Combat did not bear the marks of internal disorder and tension, like riots, isolated and sporadically occurring acts of violence and other acts of a similar nature that are not considered as armed conflicts. So this was an armed conflict."

52 TK 28337, no. 3, p. 12.
53 *Ibidem* p. 13.
54 *Ibidem* p. 5.

The District Court thus finds that common Article 3 of the Geneva Conventions of 12 August 1949 as well as the Additional Protocol II of 8 June 1977 are applicable to the conflict and the combat engaged in.[55]

With regard to the first count (1A) the District Court thus comes to the conclusion that "Considering that count 1.A. concerns charges which are all related to the non-international armed conflict there can be no question of participation in an organisation, the object of which was to commit terrorist crimes. Although it is possible that incidentally certain violent actions carried out by members of the LTTE bear all the marks of a terrorist crime, and at the same time are not or insufficiently related to armed conflict (such actions have not been established on the basis of the case file), so that such actions may constitute terrorist crimes, but such incidental actions do not entail that the LTTE should be considered a terrorist organisation for that reason alone. If this were otherwise then the rights conferred by the Geneva Conventions and Protocol II could be withheld from persons wrongfully." This leads to an acquittal on this count.

With regard to the second part of the first count (1B), of which the elements, with some minor exceptions, were crimes against humanity, war crimes within the meaning of the ICA and offences under ordinary law, committed in Sri Lanka during the armed conflict the District Court investigates whether there is a bar to prosecution under Article 6 of Protocol II, stating that prosecution and punishment of criminal offences related to armed conflict can only take place on the basis of individual penal responsibility.

The District Court investigates whether the Netherlands really accepted this impediment to national prosecution and comes to a positive conclusion. It then turns to the dilemma of how the Dutch offense of participation in a criminal organisation should be related to 'individual penal responsibility':

> "The prosecution rightly argued that membership of a criminal organisation is an individual responsibility, with which prosecution under article 6 paragraph 2 of Protocol II is, literally, not incompatible. Sanctioning prosecution on the grounds of Article 140 CC concerning an organisation which has the object to commit offences (so strictly on the basis of the individual decision to become or remain a member of such an organisation) which offences are related to a non-international armed conflict, without any further individual responsibility for committing these offences being required, would, however, constitute circumvention and therefore an

55 Sri Lanka did not ratify Protocol II but is bound nonetheless because its provisions have become international customary law. The LTTE made a statement on 24 February 1988 at the headquarters of the United Nations and the International Red Cross that it accepted the Geneva Conventions and the additional Protocols.

infringement of the aforesaid impediment to prosecution in article 6 of Protocol II. Such an infringement is unacceptable."

The District Court then considers whether, based on the Dutch International Crimes Act or the Rome Statute of the International Criminal Court in conjunction with legal precedents of international tribunals, crimes within a non-international armed conflict could be prosecuted in spite of the absence of individual penal responsibility, but comes to a negative conclusion.[56]

The District Court thus dismisses the entire first count, awarding the defendants protection under international humanitarian law because the offenses are a part of a non-international armed conflict. The District Court does not award the same protection however, with regard to the counts that are more directly based on the EU blacklistings. The difference between the first count on one side and the third and fourth (and in a very minor way also the second) counts is made explicit in the verdict:

> "For the assessment of the charge under 1.A and 1.B therefore the nature of the conflict between the armed forces of the Singhalese government and the armed forces of the LTTE is important; in principle this needs to be determined independently by a Netherlands court. In this respect, a Netherlands court is not bound to what the Council has decided in this matter.
> The court finds it important to observe at this point already that this is not true for the charges under 3. and 4. because they concern Netherlands law, where the prohibitory provision has been made directly dependent on what the Council decides."

The Court does not explain in more detail why it does not consider item 11 of the preamble to the framework decree of the Council of 13 June 2002 on combating terrorism (2002/475/JBZ) to have any relevance in relation to the 3rd and 4th charge. An argument for conform interpretation, as the Court uses in the first part of the first count, could certainly be made.

But even if the interpretation of the Court is legally correct, there is the question whether the Dutch legislation is satisfactory. This case shows clearly that the Dutch Court does not see any room for the evaluation of the blacklisting, not even for procedural errors that the defence is claiming have been made. These people did not individually have access to any Court to challenge the very blacklisting of the organisation they wish to support. They can challenge only their own blacklisting in the national administrative procedure. This is because an individual supporting an organisation blacklisted by the EU can of course not

56 With regard to the minor exceptions mentioned earlier the District Court comes to an acquittal because it finds no legal and conclusive proof.

challenge the listing of that group. When, however the individual is listed in a national procedure for having supported the group that had been listed on a European level, the group's listing is not part of the national procedure. The LTTE has now finally decided to challenge their listing at the General Court, but the individuals in this case could not have started the same procedure and that procedure cannot alter their conviction either, according to the District Court. The suspects in this case do not seem to have any access to a judge to challenge the listing of the organisation they wish to support. The criticism that was directed at the Dutch legislation during the legislative process seems to be at least partially vindicated by the decisions of the Hague District Court of 21 October 2011.

Both the suspects and the prosecution have appealed the decision. The first hearing before the Hague Court of Appeal has already taken place on 16 January 2012.

4. CONCLUSION

The Netherlands has provided for a very broad implementation of the EU blacklisting system in the national legal order. The implementation under administrative law was changed in 2007 so that there is more room for judicial control in the national legal order. The case law under the new system is, however, very limited and it remains to be seen what shape judicial control might take. With regard to criminal law the Dutch government seems to have chosen forms of implementation that exceed the international obligations under the EU legislation, especially with regard to the 'internally' blacklisted entities. This broad form of implementation may lead to a lack of judicial control and infringements on other fundamental rights, mainly the right expressed in Article 11 ECHR when the legislation is being applied. The recent conviction of five Tamil activists by the District Court of The Hague could be an occasion for a renewed discussion on the Dutch implementation.

BIBLIOGRAPHY

BOOKS AND ARTICLES

af Trampe, A., *Gärningens samhällsfarlighet.* Studier i polsk straffrätt, Iustus, 1990.

Agamben, G., *State of Exception* (trans. Attell K.), University of Chicago Press, 2005.

Allen, S. H., Political Institutions and Constrained Response to Economic Sanctions, 4 *Foreign Policy Association* 255 (2008).

Almqvist, J., Human Rights Critique of European Judicial Review: counter-terrorism sanctions, 57 *ICLQ* 303–331 (2008).

Alvarez, J. E., Hegemonic International Law Revisited, 97 *American Journal of International Law* 873–888 (2003).

Andersson, T., Cameron, I., Nordback K., EU Blacklisting: the renaissance of imperial power, but on a global scale, 14 *European Business Law Review* 111–141 (2003).

Andersson, T., Harmonization and Mutual Recognition: How to Handle Mutual Distrust in M. Andenas, B. Hess P. Oberhammer (eds), *Enforcement Agency Practice in Europe*, BIICL, 2005.

Anthony, I., Sanctions Applied by the European Union and the United Nations, in *SIPRI Yearbook 2002 Armaments, Disarmament and International Security*, OUP, 2002.

Arnove, A. (ed.), *Iraq Under Siege: the deadly impact of sanctions and war*, Pluto, 2003.

Asp, P., Cameron, I., Terrorism and Legal Security – a Swedish and European perspective, *De Lege Årsbook* 2009, Iustus, 2010.

Asp, P., *EG:s sanktionsrätt. Ett straffrättsligt perspektiv*, Iustus, 1998.

Azarov, V., Ebert, F.C, All Done and Dusted? Reflections on the EU Standard of Judicial Protection against UN Blacklisting after the ECJ's Kadi Decision, 5 *HanseLR* 99–114 (2009)

Baldwin, D.A., *Economic Statecraft*, Princeton UP, 1985.

Baldwin, D.A., Pape, R.A., Evaluating Economic Sanctions, 23 *IS* 189–198 (1998).

Bartels, L., *Human Rights Conditionality in the EU's International Agreements, Studies in European Law Series*, OUP, 2005.

Bartels, L., The WTO Legality of the EU's GSP+ arrangements, 10 *Journal of International Economic Law* 869–886 (2007)

Bergström, M. EU Anti-Money Laundering Regulation: Multilevel Cooperation of Public and Private Actors, in Eckes, C., and Konstadinides, T. (eds.), *Crime within the Area of Freedom, Security and Justice: A European Public Order*, CUP, 2011.

Bergström, M., Svedberg Helgesson, K., Mörth, U., A New Role for For-profit Actors? The Case of Anti-Money Laundering and Risk Management, 49 *Journal of Common Market Studies* 1043–1064 (2011).

Bianchi, A., Assessing the Effectiveness of the UN Security Council's Anti-terrorism Measures: the quest for legitimacy and cohesion, 17 *EJIL* 881–919 (2007).

Biersteker, T., Eckert, S. (eds.), *Countering the Financing of Terrorism*, Routledge, 2008.

Boucht, J., Civil Assset Forfeiture and the Presumption of Innocence – particularly in the light of Art. 6 ECHR, in Rui, J.P. and Sieber U. (eds), *Non-Conviction Based Confiscation in the EU – Human rights, harmonisation, effective implementation and international cooperation*, OUP, 2013.

Braithwaite, J. and Drahos, P., *Global Business Regulation*, CUP, 2000.

Breen Smyth, M., Gunning, J., Jackson, R., Kassimeris G. and Robinson, P., Critical Terrorism Studies – An Introduction, 1 *Critical Studies on Terrorism* 1–4 (2008).

Brownlie, I., *Principles of Public International Law*, 7th ed., OUP, 2008.

Brzoska, M., Putting More Teeth in UN Arms Embargoes, in Cortright, D. and Lopez, G. A. (eds.), *Smart Sanctions: targeting economic statecraft*, Rowman & Littlefield, 2002.

Bulterman, M, Oh, baby, baby, it's a wild world. Over terrorismefinanciering, financiële sancties en rechtsbescherming, 8 *NJCM-bulletin* 1069–1084 (2006).

Bures, O., EU Counterterrorism Policy: a paper tiger? 18 *Terrorism and political violence*, 57–78 (2006).

Cameron, I., Blacklisting and Financial Sanctions against Suspected Terrorists, in Leigh, I., Born H. and Wills, A., *International Intelligence Cooperation and Accountability*, Routledge, 2010

Cameron, I., European Union Anti-Terrorist Blacklisting, 3 *Human Rights Law Review* 225–256 (2003) (Cameron 2003b).

Cameron, I., Targeted Sanctions, Legal Safeguards and the ECHR, 72 *NJIL* 159–214 (Cameron 2003a).

Cameron, I., Thunberg Schunke, M., Påle-Bartes, K., Wong, C. and Asp, P., *International Criminal Law from a Swedish Perspective*, Intersentia, 2011.

Charron, A., *UN Sanctions and Conflict: responding to peace and security threats*, Routledge, 2011.

Chesterman, S., Pouligny, B., Are Sanctions Meant to Work? The politics of creating and implementing sanctions through the United Nations, 9 *Global Governance* 503–518 (2003).

Collins, A., (ed.), *Contemporary Security Studies*, 2nd ed., OUP, 2010.

Conte, A., *Handbook on Human Rights Compliance while Countering Terrorism*, Center on Global Counterterrorism Cooperation, 2008.

Conte, A., *Human Rights in the Prevention and Punishment of Terrorism: Commonwealth Approaches*, Springer, 2010.

Coomans, A.P.M., Grünfeld, F., Hartogh, K.J., Jansen, J.F.R., Doorwerking en effecten van sanctiemaatregelen van de Verenigde Naties, 7/8 *Sociaal-economische wetgeving* 501–513 (1995).

Cortright, D., Lopez, G., Are Sanctions Just? The problematic case of Iraq, 52 *Journal of International Affairs* 735–755 (1999).

Cortright, D., Lopez, G., Gerber, L., *Sanctions and the Search for Security: challenges to UN action*, Lynne Rienner, 2002 (Cortright 2002a).

Cortright, D., Lopez, G., *Smart Sanctions: targeting economic statecraft*, Rowman and Littlefield, 2002 (Cortright 2002b).

Cortright, D., Lopez, G., with Wagler, J., Conroy, R.W. and Dashti-Gibson, J., *The Sanctions Decade: assessing UN strategies in the 1990s*, Lynne Rienner Publishers, 2000.

Cosgrove, E. Examining Targeted Sanctions: Are Travel Bans Effective?, in Wallensteen, Staibano (eds.), *International Sanctions: Between Words and Wars in the Global System*, New York: Frank Cass, 2005.

Craven, M., Humanitarianism and the Quest for Smarter Sanctions, 13 *EJIL* 43–61 (2002).

Crawford, N.C., Klotz, A., How Sanctions Work: a framework for analysis, in Crawford, N.C. and Klotz, A. (eds.), *How Sanctions Work: lessons from South Africa*, St. Martin's Press, 1999.

Curtin, D., Top Secret Europe, inauguration speech, 20 October 2011, available at www.jur.uva.nl/acelg-news/news.cfm/79CDFCB7-D34E-43C5-82E327BAC76BF3F4.

Dashti-Gibson, J., Davis, P., Radcliff, B., On the Determinants of the Success of Economic Sanctions: an empirical analysis, 41 *American Journal of Political Science* 608–618 (1997).

de Búrca G., The EU, the European Court of Justice and the International Legal Order after Kadi, 51 *Harvard International Law Journal* 1–49 (2010).

De Goede, M., The Politics of Preemption and the War on Terror in Europe, 14 *European Journal of International Relations* 161–185 (2008).

De Hert, P.J.A. and Weis, K.A.P.G., Terrorismelijsten en de paradox van de rechtsbescherming, 9 *Sociaal-economische wetgeving* 336–342 (2009).

De Londras, F., and Davis, F., Controlling the Executive in Times of Terrorism: Competing Perspectives on Effective Oversight Mechanisms, 30 *Oxford Journal of Legal Studies* 19–47 (2010).

de Vries, A., EU Sanctions against Yugoslavia (1998-2000), in Cortright, D. and Lopez, G. (eds.), *Smart Sanctions: targeting economic statecraft*, Rowman & Littlefield, 2002.

de Wet, E., *The Chapter VII Powers of the United Nations Security Council*, Hart, 2004.

della Cananea, G., Global Security and Procedural Due Process of Law between the United Nations and the European Union 15 *Col. J of Eur. Law* 511–530 (2009).

Dewulf, S., Pacuée, D., Protecting Human Rights in the War on Terror: challenging the sanctions regime originating from Resolution 1267, 24 *Netherlands Quarterly of Human Rights* 607–640 (2006).

Donkin. E. (ed.), *Cicero: Pro Roscio Amerino*, Duckworth Publishing, 1991.

Doxey, M. P., *United Nations Sanctions: Current Policy Issues*, Centre for Foreign Policy Studies, Dalhousie University, 1999.

Drezner, D. W., *The Sanctions Paradox: Economic Statecraft and International Relations*, CUP, 1999.

Eckes, C., and Mendes, J., The Right to be Heard in Composite Administrative Procedures: Lost in between Protection?, 36 *European Law Review* 651–670 (2011).

Eckes, C., *EU Counter-Terrorist Policies and Fundamental Rights: The Case of Individual Sanctions*, OUP, 2009.

Eckes, C., EU Counter-Terrorist Sanctions against Individuals: Problems and Perils, 17 *European Foreign Affairs Review*, 113–132 (2012).

Eckes, C., Protecting Supremacy from External Influences: A Precondition for a European Constitutional Legal Order? 18 *European Law Journal* 230–250 (2012).

Eckes, C., The Legal Framework of the European Union's Counter Terrorism Policies, in Eckes, C., and Konstadinides, T. (eds.), *Crime within the Area of Freedom, Security and Justice: A European Public Order*, CUP, 2011.

Edwards, A., and Gill, P., (eds.), *Transnational Organised Crime: Perspectives on Global Security*, Routledge, 2003.

Eeckhout, P., Community Terrorism Listings, Fundamental Rights, and UN Security Council Resolutions: in search of the right fit, 3 *European Constitutional Law Review* 183–206 (2007).

Elsuwege, P. van, EU external action after the collapse of the pillar structure: in search of a new balance between delimitation and consistency, 47 *Common Market Law Review* 971–986 (2010)

Emmers, R., Securitization, in Collins, A. (ed.), *Contemporary Security Studies*, 2nd ed., OUP, 2010.

Eriksson, M., *Targeting Peace: Understanding UN and EU Targeted Sanctions*, Ashgate, 2011.

Eskes, J.A.O., Het recht van vereniging op de schopstoel?, 36 *Nederlands Juristenblad* 2062–2065 (2006).

Ewing, K.D. and Gearty C.A., *Freedom Under Thatcher*, OUP, 1990.

Farral, J. and Rubestein, K. (eds.), *Sanctions, Accountability and Governance in a Globalised World. Connecting International Law with Public Law*, CUP, 2009.

Farrall, J. M., *United Nations Sanctions and the Rule of Law*, CUP, 2007.

Fitzgerald, P. L., Smarter "Smart" Sanctions, 26 *Penn State International Law Review* 37–56 (2007).

Fitzgerald, P., "If Property Rights Were Treated Like Human Rights, They Could Never Get Away with This": Blacklisting and due process in U.S. economic sanctions programs, 51 *Hastings Law Journal* (1999)

Flynn, E. J., The Security Council's Counter-Terrorism Committee and Human Rights, 7 *Human Rights Law Review* 371–384 (2007).

Foot, R., The United Nations, Counter Terrorism, and Human Rights: Institutional Adaptation and Embedded Ideas, 29 *Human Rights Quarterly* 489–514 (2007).

Foucault, M., *Madness and Civilization: A History of Insanity in the Age of Reason*, Pantheon Books, 1965.

Franck, T., Chesterman, S., Malone, D., *Law & Practice of the United Nations: documents and commentary*, OUP, 2007.

Frenett, R. and Smith M.L.R., *IRA 2.0: Continuing the Long War – Analysing The Factors Behind Anti-GFA Violence Terrorism and Political Violence* (2012) forthcoming.

Galli, F. and Weyembergh, A., *EU counter-terrorism offences: What impact on national legislation and case-law?* Editions de L'université de Bruxelles, 2012.

Galtung, J., On the Effects of International Economic Sanctions: with examples from the case of Rhodesia, 19 *World Politics* 378–416 (1967).

Gargantini, G., European Cooperation in Counter-Terrorism and the Case of Individual Sanctions, 3 *Perspectives on Federalism* 155–179 (2011).

Gearty C., *Civil Liberties*, OUP 2007.

Geiss, R., Humanitarian Safeguards in Economic Sanctions Regimes: a call for automatic suspension clauses, periodic monitoring, and follow-up assessment of long-term effects, 18 *Harvard Human Rights Journal* 167–200 (2005).

Ginsborg L. and Scheinin, M., You Can't Always Get What You Want: The Kadi II Conundrum and the Security Council 1267 Terrorist Sanctions Regime, *Essex Human Rights Review*, Special issue September 2011, www.ehrr.org.

Giraldo, J., and Trinkunas, H., Transnational Crime, in Collins, A. (ed.), *Contemporary Security Studies*, 2nd ed., OUP, 2010.

Giumelli, F., *Coercing, Constraining and Signalling: explaining and understanding UN and EU sanctions after the cold war*, ECPR Press, 2011.

Gottemoeller, R., The Evolution of Sanctions in Practice and Theory, 49 *Survival* 99–110 (2007).

Gowlland-Debbas, V., *United Nations Sanctions and International Law*, Graduate Institute of International Studies, Kluwer Law International, 2001.

Greer, S., Anti-Terrorist Laws and the United Kingdom's "Suspect Muslim Community". A Reply to Pantazis and Pemberton, 50 *British Journal of Criminology* 1171–1190 (2010).

Greer, S., Review of Hillyard, P., Suspect Community: People's Experience of the Prevention of Terrorism Acts in Britain, 34 *British Journal of Criminology* 510–11 (1994).

Gregory, F., The EU's Response to 9/11: a case study of institutional roles and policy processes with special reference to issues of accountability and human rights, 17 *Terrorism and Political Violence* 105–123 (2005).

Greve, V., Jensen, A., Jensen, P., Nielsen, G., *Kommenteret Straffelov*, Speciel Del, 9. udgave, Jurist og Økonomforbundets Forlag, 2008

Hall, P.A., Aligning Ontology and Methodology in Comparative Politics, in Mahoney, J. and Rueshemeyer, D. (eds.), *Comparative Historical Analysis in the Social Sciences*, CUP, 2003.

Harlow, C., Rawlings, R., National Administrative Procedures in a European Perspective: Pathways to a Slow Convergence, 2 *Italian Journal of Public Law* 215–258 (2010).

Harten, G. van, Weaknesses of adjudication in the face of secret evidence, 13(1) *International Journal of Evidence & Proof* 1–27 (2009).

Hawkins, D., Lloyd, J., Questioning Comprehensive Sanctions: the birth of a norm, 2 *Journal of Human Rights* 441–454 (2003).

Hazelzet, H., *Carrots or Sticks? EU and US reactions to human rights violations*, European University Institute: Department of Social and Political Science, 2001.

Hecker, B, *Europäisches Strafrecht*. Zweite Auflage. Springer, Berlin 2007.

Herlin-Karnell, E., The EU's Anti Money Laundering Agenda: Built on Risks? in Eckes, C., and Konstadinides, T. (eds.), *Crime within the Area of Freedom, Security and Justice: A European Public Order*, CUP, 2011.

Hickman, M.J., Thomas, L., Nickels H.C. and Silvestri, S. Social cohesion and the notion of "suspect communities": a study of the experiences and impacts of being "suspect" for Irish communities and Muslim communities in Britain, 5 *Critical Studies on Terrorism* 89–106 (2012).

Hillyard, P., *Suspect Community: People's Experience of the Prevention of Terrorism Acts in Britain*, Pluto Press, 1993.

Hocking, J., Counter-Terrorism and the Criminalisation of Politics: Australia's new Security Powers of Detention, Proscription and Control, 49 *Australian Journal of Politics and History* 355–71 (2003).

Hood, C., Rothstein, H. and Baldwin, R., *The Government of Risk: Understanding Risk Regulation Regimes*, OUP, 2001.

Horgan, J. and Boyle, M.J., A Case Against Critical Terrorism Studies, 1 *Critical Studies on Terrorism* 51–64 (2008).

Hovi, J., Huseby, R., Sprinz, D.F., When Do (Imposed) Economic Sanctions Work?, 57 *World Politics* 479–499 (2005).

Høyer, G., Spencer, M., Greve, V., *The Danish Criminal Code*, Kriminalistik Institutets Stencilserie, nr. 39, 1991

Hufbauer, G.C., Schott, J.J., assisted by Elliott, K., *Economic Sanctions Reconsidered: history and current policy*, MIT Press, 1985.

Hufbauer, G.C., Schott, J.J., Elliott, K., *Economic Sanctions Reconsidered: history and current policy*, 2nd ed, MIT Press, 1990.

Hufbauer, G.C., Schott, J.J., Elliott, K., Oegg, B., *Economic Sanctions Reconsidered*, 3rd ed., Peterson Institute for International Economics, 2007.

Hurd, I., *After Anarchy: legitimacy and power in the United Nations Security Council*, Princeton UP, 2007.

Husabø, E.J., and Bruce, I., *Fighting terrorism through multilevel criminal legislation: Security Council Resolution 1373, the EU framework decision on combating terrorism and their implementation in Nordic, Dutch and German criminal law*, Martinus Nijhoff, 2009

Jareborg, N., *Essays in Criminal Law*, Uppsala, 1988.

Jentleson, B.W., Economic Sanctions and Post-Cold War Conflicts: challenges for theory and policy, in Stern, P.C. and Druckman, D. (eds.), *International Conflict Resolution after the Cold War*, National Academies Press, 2000.

Jimeno-Bulnes, M., After September 11th: the fight against terrorism in national and European law. Substantive and procedural reforms: some examples, 10 *ELJ* 235 (2004).

Kaempfer, W., Lowenberg, A., International Sanctions, 17 *JEP* 233 (2003).

Katzenstein, P., *The Culture of National Security: Norms and Identity in World Politics*, Columbia UP, 1996.

Kavanagh A., Constitutionalism, Counterterrorism, and the Courts: Changes in the British Constitutional Landscape, 9 *International Journal of Constitutional Law* 172–199 (2011).

Kersten, A., 'Financing of Terrorism – A Predicate Offence to Money Laundering?', in M. Pieth (ed.), *Financing Terrorism*, Kluwer Academic Publishers 2002.

King, G., Keohane, R., Verba, S., *Designing Social Inquiry: scientific inference in qualitative research*, Princeton UP, 1994.

Klip, A., *European Criminal Law*, 2nd ed., Intersentia, 2012.

Knight, A., Improving the Effectiveness of UN Arms Embargoes, in Price, R. and Zacher M. (eds.), *The United Nations and Global Security*, Palgrave, 2004.

Kratochwil, F., Looking Back from Somewhere: reflections on what remains "critical" in critical theory, 33 *Review of International Studies* 25–45 (2007).

Kratochwil, F., Ruggie, J. G., International Organization: a state of the art on an art of the state, 40 *International Organization* 753–775 (1986).

Kratochwil, F., *Rules, Norms, and Decisions: on the conditions of practical and legal reasoning in international relations and domestic affairs*, CUP, 1989.

Kundnani, A., *Spooked! How Not to Prevent Violent Extremism, Institute for Race Relations*, London, 2009.

Lavranos, N., Judicial Review of UN Sanctions by the Court of First Instance, 11 *European Foreign Affairs Review* 471–490 (2006).

Lavranos, N., UN Sanctions and Judicial Review, 76 *NJIL* 1–17 (2007).

Lehto, M., *International Responsibility for Terrorist Acts. A Shift Towards More Indirect Forms of Responsibility*, Acta Universitatis Lapponiensis 139, 2008.

Leigh, I., Changing the rules of the game: some necessary legal reforms to United Kingdom intelligence, 35 *Review of International Studies* 943–955 (2009).

Levi, M., Combating the Financing of Terrorism: A History and Assessment of the Control of 'Threat Finance', 50 *Brit. J. Criminol.* 650–669 (2010).

Loewenstein, K., Militant Democracy and Fundamental Rights, XXXI *American Political Science Review* 417–432 (1937).

Lynch, A., McGarrity, N. and Williams, G., The Proscription of Terrorist Organisations in Australia, 37 *Federal Law Review* 1–40 (2009).

Meliá, M.C., The Wrongfulness of Crimes of Unlawful Association, 11 *New Criminal Law Review* 563–589 (2008).

Mill, J.S., *On Liberty*, J.W. Parker and Son, 1859.

Mitsilegas, V., Countering the Chameleon Threat of Dirty Money: "Hard" and "Soft" Law in the Emergence of a Global Regime against Money Laundering and Terrorist Finance", in Edwards, A., and P. Gill (eds.), *Transnational Organised Crime: Perspectives on Global Security*, Routledge, 2003.

Mitsilegas, V., *Money Laundering Counter-Measures in the European Union: A New Paradigm of Security Governance versus Fundamental Legal Principles*, Kluwer Law International, 2003.

Muller, M., Terrorism, Proscription, and the Right to Resist in the Age of Conflict, 20 *Denning Law Journal* 111–131 (2008).

Murphy C.C., The Principle of Legality in Criminal Law under the ECHR, *European Human Rights Law Review* 192–207 (2010).

Murphy, C.C., *EU Counter-Terrorism Law: Pre-Emption and the Rule of Law*, Hart Publishing, 2012.

Murphy, C.C., *Counter-Terrorism and the Culture of Legality: The Case of Special Advocates*, available: http://papers.ssrn.com/sol3/papers.cfm?abstract_id=2009902 (2011).

Murphy. C., Terrorism and the Law, 1(2) *State Crime* (2012) forthcoming.

Nuotio, K, Terrorism as a Catalyst for the Emergence, Harmonization and reform of Criminal Law, 4 *Journal of International Criminal Justice* 998–1016 (2006).

O'Neill, M., *The Evolving EU Counter-Terrorism Legal Framework*, Routledge, 2012.

Pantazis C. and Pemberton S., Restating the case for the 'suspect community: A reply to Greer, 51 *British Journal of Criminology* 1054–1062 (2011).

Pantazis, C. and Pemberton, S., From the "Old" to the "New" Suspect Community: Examining the Impacts of Recent UK Counter-Terrorist Legislation, 49 *British Journal of Criminology* 646–66 (2009).

Pape, R., Why Economic Sanctions Do Not Work, 22 *IS* 90–136 (1997).

Pape, R., Why Economic Sanctions Still Do No Work, 23 *IS* 66–77 (1998).

Peirce, G., Was it like this for the Irish? 30(7) *London Review of Books* 3–8 (2008).

Pieth, M. (ed.), *Financing Terrorism*, Kluwer Academic Publishers, 2002.

Porretto, G., The European Union, Counter-Terrorism Sanctions against Individuals and Human Rights, in Gani, M. and Matthew, P. (eds.), *Fresh Perspectives on the "War on Terror"*, ANU EPress, 2008.

Portela, C., *European Union Sanctions and Foreign Policy: when and why do they work?*, Routledge, 2010.

Portela, C., *The Efficacy of Sanctions of the European Union: when and why do they work?*, European University Institute, 2008.

Power, M., *Organized Uncertainty: Designing a World of Risk Management*, OUP, 2007.

Power, M., *The Risk Management of Everything*, Demos, 2004,

Rackow, P., Stegmiller, I., EC Regulations: targeted sanctions, 71 *Journal of Criminal Law* 25–28 (2007).

Raymond, C. Z., *Al Muhajiroun and Islam4UK: The Group Behind the Ban*, ICSR, London 2010.

Reid, M., Secrets Behind Secrets: Disclosure of Classified Information Before and During Trial and Why CIPA Should Be Revamped, 35 *Seton Hall Legislative Journal* (2011) 272–300.

Rix, M., Counter-terrorism and information: The NSI Act, fair trials, and open, accountable government, 25(2) *Journal of Media & Cultural Studies* 285–297 (2011).

Roach, K., Anti-Terrorism and Militant Democracy: Some Western and Eastern Responses, in Sajo, A. and Rutt Bentch L., *Militant Democracy*, Eleven Publishing, 2004

Roach, K., Judicial Review of Anti Terrorism Legislation: The Post-9/11 Experience and Normative Experiences for Judicial Review, 3 *Indian Journal of Constitutional Law* 138 (2009).

Roach, K., *The 9/11 Effect: Comparative Counter-Terrorism*, CUP, 2011.

Roe, P., Societal Security, in Collins, A., (ed.) *Contemporary Security Studies*, 2nd ed., OUP, 2010.

Rosand, E., Millar, A., Ipe, J., *Human Rights and the Implementation of the UN Global Counter-Terrorism Strategy, Center on Global Counter-Terrorism Cooperation*, 2008.

Rosand, E., The Security Council's Efforts to Monitor the Implementation of Al Qaeda/ Taliban Sanctions, 98 *EJIL* 745–763 (2004).

Roxin, C., *Strafrecht. Allgemeiner Teil.* Band I, 4th ed., CH Beck, 2006.

Ruggie, J., *Constructing the World Polity: essays on international institutionalization*, Routledge, 1998.

Scheinin, M., Is the ECJ ruling in Kadi incompatible with international law? 28 *Yearbook of European Law*, 2010.

Searle, J., *Speech Acts*, CUP, 1969.

Searle, J., The *Construction of Social Reality*, Allen Lane, 1995.

Sedgwick, M., The Concept of Radicalisation as a Source of Confusion, 22 *Terrorism and Political Violence* 479–494 (2010).

Sentas, V., Terrorist Organisation Offences and the LTTE: R v Vinayagamoorthy, 22 *Current Issues in Criminal Justice* 159–169 (2010) (Sentas 2010b).

Sentas, V., The Violence of Terrorist Organisation Bans, 82 *Criminal Justice Matters* 16–17 (2010) (Sentas 2010a).

Shagabutdinova, E., Berejikian, J., Deploying Sanctions while Protecting Human Rights: are humanitarian "smart" sanctions effective?, 6 *Journal of Human Rights* 59–74 (2007).

Sideek, M., *European Community Law on the Free Movement of Capital and the EMU*, Norstedts, 1999.

Sideek, M., Legal Instruments to Combat Money Laundering in the EU Financial Market, 6 *Journal of Money Laundering Control* 66–79 (2002).

Simcox, R., Stuart H. and Ahmed, H., *Islamist Terrorism: the British Connections*, 2nd ed., Centre for Social Cohesion, London, 2011.

Simma, B. (ed), *The Charter of the United Nations: A Commentary*, 3rd ed., OUP, 2011.

Soons, A.H.A., The Netherlands, in V. Gowlland-Debbas (ed.), *National Implementation of UN Sanctions*, Brill, 2004.

Stenhammar, F., *Riktade FN sanktioner och Rule of Law i Folkrätten*. Dissertation on Targeted UN Sanctions and the Rule of Law, Jure, 2008.

Stiles, K., Thayne, A., International Law on Terrorism at the United Nations, 41 *Cooperation and Conflict* 153–176 (2006).

Stone, M., Wall, I. and Douzinas, C., "Introduction: Law, Politics and the Political" in Stone, Wall and Douzinas (eds.), *New Critical Legal Thinking: Law and the Political*, Birkbeck Law Press, 2012.

Strandow, D., *Sanctions and Civil War Targeted Measures for Conflict Resolution*, Uppsala University, Department of Peace and Conflict Research, 2006.

Sullivan G., Hayes, B., *Blacklisted: Targeted sanctions, preemptive security and fundamental rights*, ECCHR, 2011

Sutterlin, J., *The United Nations and the Maintenance of International Security*, 2nd ed., Praeger, 2003.

Tappeiner, I., The fight against terrorism. The lists and the gaps, 1 *Utrecht Law Review* 97–125 (2005)

Tjong Tjin Tai, T.F.E., [annotation of] Art. 254 Rv, aant. 14, in *GS Burgerlijke Rechtsvordering*, Kluwer, 2010.

Tomkins, A., National Security, Counter-Terrorism and the Intensity of Review: A Changed Landscape? 126 *Law Quarterly Review* 543–567 (2010).

Tostensen, A., Bull, B., Are Smart Sanctions Feasible?, 54 *World Politics* 373–403 (2002).

Touri, K., The Many Constitutions of Europe, in Tuori K. and Sankari S. (eds.), *The Many Constitutions of Europe*, Ashgate, 2010.

van den Broek, M., Hazelhorst, M. & de Zanger, W., Asset Freezing: Smart Sanction or Criminal Charge?, 27 *Merkourios Utrecht Journal of International and European law* 18–27 (2010).

Vestergaard, J., Strafferetlig lovgivning om bekæmpelse af terrorisme, *Tidsskrift for Kriminalret*, 2–13 (2006).

Vestergaard, J., Terror Financing – Asset Freezing, Human Rights and the European Legal Order, 2 *New Journal of European Criminal Law* 175–200 (2011).

Vines, A., Can UN Arms Embargoes in Africa Be Effective?, 83 *International Affairs* 1107–1121 (2007).

Vonnegut, K., *Palm Sunday*, Delacorte Press, 1981

Wakefield, J., Changes in liability of EU institutions: Bergaderm, FIAMM and Schneider 12 *ERA-Forum* 625–639 (2012)

Walker, C., *Terrorism and the Law*, OUP 2011.

Walker, R.B.J., *Inside/Outside: International Relations as Political Theory*, CUP, 1993.

Wallensteen, P., Characteristics of Economic Sanctions, 5 *Journal of Peace Research* 248–267 (1968).

Wallensteen, P., Staibano, C. (eds.), *International Sanctions: between words and wars in the global system*, Frank Cass, 2005.
Wendt, A., *Social Theory of International Politics,* CUP, 1999.
Wetzling T, *Containing Secret Power in Europe? A study on oversight and accountability,* unpub. thesis, Geneva Graduate Institute of International Studies, 2006.
Wijmenga, B.N., Internationale sanctieregimes en de gewijzigde Sanctiewet 1977, 2 *Sociaal-economische wetgeving* 43–51 (2002).
Winer, J.M., Globalization, Terrorist Finance, and Global Conflict – Time for a White List? in Pieth M. (ed), *Financing Terrorism*, Kluwer Academic Publishers, 2002.
Wood, M., United Nations, Security Council, *Max Planck Encyclopedia of Public International Law*, OUP, 2011.

REPORTS

UK OFFICIAL PUBLICATIONS

Lord Jellicoe (1983), Review of Operation of the Prevention of Terrorism (Temporary Provisions) Act 1976, Cmnd 8803
Lord Lloyd of Berwick & P Wilkinson Inquiry into Legislation against Terrorism 1996 vol 1
Home Affairs Committee Roots of Violent Radicalisation HC1446 (London TSO 2012)
HM Government, The Coalition: Our Programme for Government (London Cabinet Office 2010) p 24.
Lord MacDonald of River Glaven QC, Review of Counter-Terrorism and Security Powers Cm 8003 (London TSO 2011
D Anderson QC First Report on the Operation of the Terrorist Asset-Freezing etc Act 2010 (TSO London 2011).
D Anderson QC The Terrorism Acts in 2011 (TSO London 2012).
Alexander Horne, The Terrorist Act 2000: Proscribed Organisations, SN/HA/00815 (House of Commons Library, 2011).
Lord Carlille of Berriew QC Report on the Operation in 2009 of the Terrorism Act 2000 and of Part 1 of the Terrorism Act 2006 (2010 London TSO)
Explanatory Memorandum to the Terrorism Act 2000 (Proscribed Organisations) (Amendment Order) 2011.

UK PARLIAMENTARY DEBATES AND PAPERS

House of Commons Hansard 20 July 2006 col 490–509 (House of Commons of the Terrorism Act 2000 (Proscribed Organisations) (Amendment) Order 2006)
House of Lords, Hansard, 24 July 2006, col 1618–1619.
House of Common, Hansard, 13 March 2001, col 964.
House of Lords, Impact of Economic Sanctions: Evidence. Memorandum and Witness Testimony by Mikael Eriksson, European University Institute. The Impact of

Economic Sanctions. Evidence provided to the House of Lords Select Committee on Economic Affairs, 2nd Report of Session 2006–07 The Impact of Economic Sanctions, pp. 142–147. House of Lords Paper 96-II (London, May 2007).

House of Lords European Union Committee, Money Laundering and the financing of terrorism: Volume II: Evidence, 19th Report of Session 2008–09, (22 July 2009), HL Paper 132-II.

OTHER REPORTS AND CONFERENCE PAPERS

Allam, M. and D. Gadzinowski, Combating the Financing of Terrorism: EU Policies, Polity and Politics, EIPASCOPE 2009/2.

Archik, K., U.S.-EU Cooperation against Terrorism, Congressional Research Service Report for Congress, 2 May 2011.

Biersteker, T., Eckert, S., Strengthening Targeted Sanctions through Fair and Clear Procedures. Report commissioned by the governments of Germany, Switzerland, and Sweden, Watson Institute for International Studies, Brown University, 2006.

Brzoska, M. (ed), Design and Implementation of Arms Embargoes and Travel and Aviation Related Sanctions: Results of the Bonn-Berlin Process, Bonn International Center for Conversion, 2001, www.watsoninstitute.org/tfs/CD/booklet_sanctions.pdf

Cameron, I., Targeted Sanctions and Legal Safeguards: Report to the Swedish Foreign Ministry, Uppsala University, Faculty of Law, October 2002, www2.statsvet.uu.se/Portals/5/SIFIR/Dok/sanctions.pdf

Cameron, I., Respecting Human Rights and Fundamental Freedoms and EU/UN sanctions: state of play. A report commissioned by the European Parliament. Policy Department External Policies. Directorate-General for External Policies of the Union (2008).

Cameron, I., The European Convention of European Rights, Due Process and United Nations Security Council Counter-Terrorism Sanctions, Council of Europe, 2006.

Cameron, I., The Security Concept in the TEU and TFEU, unpublished manuscript, Conference on EU Common Foreign and Security Policy, Faculty of Law, University of Uppsala, February 2011.

Carish, E., Loraine, R.-M., Global Threats and the Role of United Nations Sanctions, Report, International Policy Analysis, Friedrich Ebert Stiftung, 2011.

Chesterman, S., The UN Security Council and the Rule of Law: the role of the Security Council in strengthening a rules-based international system. Final Report and Recommendations from the Austrian Initiative, 2004–2008. Institute for International Law and Justice New York University School of Law and Federal Ministry for European and International Affairs (2008).

Emerson, B., Second Annual Report of the Special Rapporteur on the promotion and protection of human rights and fundamental freedoms while countering terrorism 26 September 2012, A/67/396

Eriksson, M., In Search of a Due Process: listing and delisting practices of the European Union, Department of Peace and Conflict Research, Uppsala University (2009).

Eriksson, M., Supporting Democracy in Africa: African Union's use of targeted sanctions to deal with unconstitutional changes of government. FOI Report no. FOI-R – 3000--SE, FOI (2010).

Fassbender, B., Targeted Sanctions and Due Process. The responsibility of the UN Security Council to ensure that fair and clear procedures are made available to individuals and entities targeted with sanctions under Chapter VII of the UN Charter. Study commissioned by the United Nations Office of Legal Affairs – Office of the Legal Counsel, March, Office of the Legal Counsel, United Nations, (2006).

Financial Action Task Force, Guidance Document, International Best Practices: Freezing of Terrorist Assets, 23 June 2009, available under www.fatf-gafi.org/dataoecd/30/43/34242709.pdf (accessed on 18 January 2012).

Financial Action Task Force on Money Laundering, Terrorism Financing, 2008.

Fruchart, D., Holtom, P., Wallensteen, P., Wezeman, S., Strandow, D., United Nations Arms Embargoes: their impact on arms flows and target behaviour, Stockholm International Peace Research Institute and the Department of Peace and Conflict Research, Uppsala University, 2007.

Lopez, G., Millar, A., Ipe, J., Cortright, D., Marbarger, A., Lawall, K., Standards and Best Practices for Improving States' Implementation of United Nations Counter-terrorism Mandates. Report prepared for the Netherlands' Ministry of Foreign Affairs (2006).

Luck, E., Choosing Words Carefully: arms embargoes and the UN Security Council. Paper of the First Expert Seminar on Smart Sanctions, the Next Step: Arms Embargoes and Travel Sanctions (Bonn, 1999).

Mark Yeandle, M., Mainelli, M., Berendt, A, Healy, B., Anti-money Laundering Requirements: Costs, Benefits and Perceptions, City Research Series, no 6, June 2005 www.zyen.com/PDF/AMLR_FULL.pdf.

Marty, D., United Nations Security Council and European Union Blacklists. Report by the Council of Europe, Committee on Legal Affairs and Human Rights. Doc. 11454, (2007).

Millar, A., Rosand, E., Building Global Alliances in the Fight against Terrorism. Report Commissioned by the Better World Campaign of the UN Foundation. Center on Global Counter-Terrorism Cooperation (2006).

Murphy, C., Counter-Terrorism and the Culture of Legality: The Case of Special Advocates, Presentation at IACL Terrorism Research Group Workshop, 'Secrecy, National Security, and Vindication of Constitutional Law', Milan, 1–2 December 2011.

Rydell, R., Monitoring United Nations Arms Embargoes. Paper, first Expert Seminar on Smart Sanctions, the Next Step: Arms Embargoes and Travel Sanctions (Bonn, 1999).

Sandler, T. Collective Action: Theory and Applications, Ann Arbor, University of Michigan Press, 1992.

Wallensteen, P., A Century of Economic Sanctions: a field revisited. Uppsala Peace Research Papers, no. 1, Department of Peace and Conflict Research, Uppsala University (2000).

Wallensteen, P., Eriksson, M., Staibano, C., Routes to Democracy in Burma/Myanmar: the Uppsala Pilot Study on Dialogue and International Strategies. Report presented to the Swedish Foreign Ministry, Uppsala University, 2004.

Wallensteen, P., Eriksson, M., Staibano, C., The 2004 Roundtable on UN Sanctions against Iraq: lessons learned, Uppsala University Department of Peace and Conflict Research Uppsala, 2005.

OTHER PUBLICATIONS AND WEBSITES

Watchdog recommends Tory U-turn on banning Hizb ut-Tahrir' The Guardian 19 July 2011.
N Clegg, 'An Open, Confident Society' 3 March 2011 available at www.newstatesman.com /2011/03/open-liberal-violent.
Muslims Against Crusades to be banned from midnight' *The Guardian* 11 November 2011.
Losing the plot, New Statesman 30 January 2006.
Stockholm Process on the Implementation of Targeted Sanctions (aka. *Special Program on the Implementation of Targeted Sanctions*). Located at www.smartsanctions.sem.
The Interlaken Process. Located at www.seco.admin.ch/themen/00513/00620/00639/index.html?lang=en.
The Bonn-Berlin Process. Located at: www.bicc.de/

TREATIES

UN CONVENTIONS

United Nations Convention against Illicit Traffic in Narcotic Drugs and Psychotropic Substances, 19 December 1988.
United Nationals International Convention for the Suppression of the Financing of Terrorism, 9 December 1999.
United Nations Convention against Transnational Organized Crime, 15 November 2000.

COUNCIL OF EUROPE

Council of Europe Convention on Laundering, Search, Seizure and Confiscation of the Proceeds from Crime and on the Financing of Terrorism, 16 May 2005 (Warsaw convention)
Council of Europe Convention on Laundering, Search, Seizure and Confiscation of the Proceeds from Crime, 8 November 1990 (Strasbourg Convention)

LEGISLATION

THE NETHERLANDS

Regeling van 3 april 2003, nr. DJZ/BR/219–03 houdende beperkende maatregelen tegen de Stichting Al Aqsa met het oog op de strijd tegen het terrorisme (Sanctieregeling terrorisme 2003), *Staatscourant* 7 april 2003, nr. 68.
Wet van 13 april 2000 tot wijziging van de Sanctiewet 1977 en van de In- en uitvoerwet tot vereenvoudiging van de implementatie van internationale verplichtingen, *Stb* 2000, 196

Wet van 16 mei 2002 tot wijziging van de Sanctiewet 1977 met het oog op de implementatie van internationale verplichtingen gericht op de bestrijding van terrorisme en uitbreiding van het toezicht op de naleving van financiële sanctiemaatregelen, *Stb* 2002, 270

Wet van 24 juni 2004 tot wijziging en aanvulling van het Wetboek van Strafrecht en enige andere wetten in verband met terroristische misdrijven (Wet terroristische misdrijven) *Stb.* 2004, 290

Wet van 20 november 2006, houdende goedkeuring van het op 24 april 1986 te Straatsburg totstandgekomen Europees Verdrag inzake de erkenning van de rechtspersoonlijkheid van internationale niet-gouvernementele organisaties, alsmede invoering van enige regels met betrekking tot in een terrorismelijst vermelde organisaties en andere organisaties waarvan het doel of de werkzaamheid in strijd is met de openbare orde, *Stb.* 2006, 600

Sanctieregeling Terrorisme 2002 (DJZ/BR/0489-02), 2002-II (DJZ/BR/0618-02) and 2007-II (DJZ/BR/1222-07) for general rules

Sanctieregeling Terrorisme 2002-III (DJZ/BR/749-02), 2003 (DJZ/BR/219-03), 2006 (DJZ/BR/0287-06) and 2007 (DJZ/BR/0185-07) for individual placements

EU

REGULATIONS AND DIRECTIVES

Council Directive 91/308/EEC of 10 June 1991 on prevention of the use of the financial system for the purpose of money laundering, OJ 1991, L 166/77.

Directive 2001/97/EC of the European Parliament and of the Council of 4 December 2001 amending Council Directive 91/308/EEC on prevention of the use of the financial system for the purpose of money laundering, OJ 2001, L 344/76.

Council Regulation (EC) No. 2580/2001 of 27 December 2001 on Specific Restrictive Measures Directed against Certain Persons and Entities with a View to Combating Terrorism, OJ L 344, 28.12.2001, p. 70–73,

Council Regulation (EC) No. 881/2002 of 27 May 2002 imposing Certain Specific Restrictive Measures Directed against certain Persons and Entities associated with Usama bin Laden, the Al-Qaida Network and the Taliban and repealing Council Regulation (EC) No. 467/2001 Prohibiting the Export of Certain Goods and Services to Afghanistan, Strengthening the Flight Ban and Extending the Freeze of Funds and other Financial Resources in Respect of the Taliban of Afghanistan, OJ L 139, 29.5.2002, p. 9–11

Regulation (EC) 1889/2005 of the European Parliament and of the Council of 26 October 2005 on controls of cash entering or leaving the Community, OJ 2005 L 309/9.

Directive 2005/60/EC of the European Parliament and of the Council of 26 October 2005 on the prevention of the use of the financial system for the purpose of money laundering and terrorist financing, OJ 2005, L 309/15.

Directive 2007/64/EC of the European Parliament and of the Council of 13 November 2007 on Payment Services (PSD) in the internal market, OJ 2007, L 319/1.

Regulation (EC) 1781/2006 of the European Parliament and of the Council of 15 November 2006 on information on the payer accompanying transfers of funds, OJ 2006, L 345/1.

Council Regulation (EU) No. 1286/2009 of 22 December 2009 amending Regulation (EC) No. 881/2002 imposing Certain Specific Measures Directed against certain Persons and Entities associated with Usama bin Laden, the Al-Qaida Network and the Taliban, OJ L 346, 23.12.2009, p. 42–46.

Council Regulation (EU) 1286/2009 of 22 December 2009 amending Regulation (EC) 881/2002 imposing certain specific restrictive measures directed against certain persons and entities associated with Usama bin Laden, the Al-Qaida network and the Taliban, OJ 2009, L 346/42.

DECISIONS AND FRAMEWORK DECISIONS

Council Decision 2000/642/JHA of 17 October 2000 concerning arrangements for cooperation between financial intelligence units of the Member States in respect of exchanging information, OJ 2000, L/271/4.

Council Framework Decision 2001/500/JHA of 26 June 2001 on money laundering, the identification, tracing, freezing, seizing and confiscation of instrumentalities and the proceeds of crime, OJ 2001 L 182/1.

Council Framework Decision 2002/475/JHA of 13 June 2002 on Combating Terrorism, OJ 2002, L 164/3.

Council Framework Decision 2003/577/JHA of 22 July 2003, on the Execution in the European Union of Orders Freezing Property or Evidence, OJ L 196, 2.8.2003, p. 45–55.

Council Framework Decision 2005/212/JHA of 24 February 2005 on Confiscation of Crime-Related Proceeds, Instrumentalities and Property, OJ L 68, 15.3.2005, p. 49–51.

Council Framework Decision 2006/783/JHA of 6 October 2006 on the Application of the Principle of Mutual Recognition to Confiscation Orders, OJ L 328, 24.11.2006, p. 59–78 and Amending Act hereto; Council Framework Decision 2009/299/JHA of 26 February 2009 amending Framework Decisions 2002/584/JHA, 2005/214/JHA, 2006/783/JHA, 2008/909/JHA and 2008/947/JHA, thereby Enhancing the Procedural Rights of Persons and Fostering the Application of the Principle of Mutual Recognition to Decisions Rendered in the Absence of the Person Concerned at the Trial, OJ L 81, 27.3.2009, p. 24–36.

Council Framework Decision 2008/978/JHA of 18 December 2008 on the European Evidence Warrant for the Purpose of Obtaining Objects, Documents and Data for Use in Proceedings in Criminal Matters, OJ L 350, 30.12.2008, p. 72–92.

COMMON POSITIONS

Council Common Position of 27 December 2001 on the Application of Specific Measures to Combat Terrorism, OJ L 344, 28.12.2001, p. 93–96.

Council Common Position 2001/931/CFSP of 27 December 2001 on the application of specific measures to combat terrorism, OJ 2001, L 344/93.

Council Common Position of 27 May 2002 concerning Restrictive Measures against Usama bin Laden, Members of the Al-Qaida Organisation and the Taliban and other Individuals, Groups, Undertakings and Entities Associated with them and Repealing Common Positions 96/746/CFSP, 199/727/CFSP, 2001/154/CFSP and 2001/771/CFSP, OJ L 139, 29.5.2002, p. 4–5.

Council Common Position 2009/67/CFSP of 26 January 2009 updating Common Position 2001/931/CFSP on the application of specific measures to combat terrorism and repealing Common Position 2008/586/CFSP, OJ 2009, L 23/37.

EU AGREEMENTS

Agreement between the European Union and the United States of America on the processing and transfer of Financial Messaging Data from the European Union to the United States for the purposes of the Terrorist Finance Tracking Program, OJ 2010, L 195/5.

COUNCIL DOCUMENTS

Council Document 9145/10, 29.4.2010, Initiative taken by the Kingdom of Belgium, the Republic of Bulgaria, the Republic of Estonia, the Kingdom of Spain, the Republic of Austria, the Republic of Slovenia and the Kingdom of Sweden with a view of adopting a Directive of the European Parliament and of the Council regarding the European Investigation Order in Criminal Matters.

Council of the European Union, Council document 18918/1, 21.12.2011, Initiative of the Kingdom of Belgium et al. for a Directive of the European Parliament and of the Council regarding the EIO: Text agreed as general approach.

Council of the European Union, EU Action Plan on Combating Terrorism, last updated on 9 December 2011.

Council of the European Union, EU Action Plan on Combating Terrorism, 15 November 2010.

Council of the European Union, the European Union Counter-Terrorism Strategy, 30 November 2005.

Council of the European Union Discussion paper, EU Counter-Terrorism Strategy – Discussion Paper, 23 May 2012.

Council of the European Union, Revised Strategy on Terrorist Financing, 17 July 2008.

COMMISSION DOCUMENTS

Communication from the Commission to the Council and the European Parliament on the Prevention of and the fight against Terrorism financing through measures to

improve the exchange of information, to strengthen transparency and enhance the traceability of financial transactions, COM (2004) 700 final.
Green Paper, Strengthening mutual trust in the European judicial area – A Green Paper on the application of EU criminal justice legislation in the field of detention, Brussels 14.6.2011 COM(2011).

UNITED NATIONS RESOLUTIONS AND DOCUMENTS

SECURITY COUNCIL RESOLUTIONS

Security Council Resolution 1267 (1999). On the situation in Afghanistan.
Security Council Resolution 1373 (2001). Threats to international peace and security caused by terrorist acts.
Security Council Resolution 1390 (2002). The situation in Afghanistan.
Security Council Resolution 1566 Threats to international peace and security caused by terrorist acts.
Security Council Resolution 1730 (2006).
Security Council Resolution 1735 (2006).
Security Council Resolution 1822 (2008).
Security Council Resolution 1904 (2009).
Security Council Resolution 1989 (2011).

OTHER UNITED NATIONS DOCUMENTS

UN S/1995/300. Letter dated 13 April 1995 from the Permanent Representatives of China, France, the Russian Federation, the United Kingdom of Great Britain and Northern Ireland and the United States of America to the United Nations Addressed to the President of the Security Council. Letter dated 13 April (1995).
UN SG/SM/7360, Press Release. Secretary-General Reviews Lessons Learned during "Sanctions Decade" in Remarks to International Peace Academy Seminar 2000-04-17 (2000).
UN Security Council Sanctions Committee, Assets Freeze: Explanation of Terms para. 2, available under www.un.org/sc/committees/1267/pdf/EoT%20assets%20freeze%20-%20English.pdf (accessed 18 January 2012).
Security Council Sanctions Committee, Guidelines of the Committee for the Conduct of Its Work, 30 November 2011, available under www.un.org/sc/committees/1267/pdf/1267_guidelines.pdf (accessed on 18 January 2012).
Statement by Martin Scheinin to UNGA 3rd Committee, 26 October 2010, www.ohchr.org/Documents/Issues/Terrorism/statement_GA26.10.10.pdf.

INDEX

W

www.ingramcontent.com/pod-product-compliance
Ingram Content Group UK Ltd.
Pitfield, Milton Keynes, MK11 3LW, UK
UKHW051926100926
8556IPUK00022B/1401

9 781780 681412